FAST & FUN FOOD

For People on the Go!

"Cooking for the Love of Life"
Series ©

FAST & FUN FOOD

For People on the Go!

LOW TO ZERO FAT

GOURMET NATURAL

VEGETARIAN

ALTERNATIVES

By Karen Claffey

FAST & FUN FOOD *For People on the Go!*

Copyright © 1995 by Karen Claffey

Cover design by Karen Claffey, Jaqui Spreekmeester and Shari Blaukopf
Cover photo by Photo Oskura (Setting: LeguMylene, Marché de l'Ouest, Dollard des Ormeaux, Quebec)
Caricature drawings by Karen Claffey

Canadian Cataloguing in Publication Data

Claffey, Karen 1959-
    Fast & fun food for people on the go! : low to zero
fat, gourmet, natural, vegetarian alternatives

(Cooking for the love of life series)
Includes index.
ISBN 0-9680173-0-4

    1. Vegetarian cookery. 2. Low-fat diet—Recipes.
I. Title. II. Title: Fast and fun food for people on the
go! III. Series.

TX837.C59 1996   641.5'636   C96-900323-4

Published by KAREN'S KITCHEN®, Montreal, Quebec
Printed in Canada
10 9 8 7 6 5 4 3 2 1

Disclaimer and Limits of Liability

DEDICATION

To all you Superwomen and Supermen of our times
who are trying to integrate career, fitness, fun and
healthy eating into dynamic paced lives.

SPECIAL THANKS

To my beautiful mother, Sylvia Hamilton, for her unconditional love, support and faith in my goals and dreams. I could not have done this without your help; testing recipes, final editing and proofreading, grocery shopping and cooking for us while I was glued to the computer for months without coming up for air, and always being there in the best of spirits.

I am indebted to Michio and Aveline Kushi who no less than saved my life through their teachings and guidance.

In December 1984 I began my journey in the land of the living in harmony with nature. Wendy and Edward Esko's Macrobiotic Cooking for Everyone became my bible-cookbook that was instrumental in my healing process. It is with great honor and deep gratitude that I acknowledge, over eleven years later, Edward Esko, who wrote the Foreword, and his wife Wendy. They are highly respected International Macrobiotic Teachers and Authors who are lighting the way for all of us on the road to health and planetary transformation.

Alex Jack, accomplished Macrobiotic Author and Editor of One Peaceful World, the Kushi Institute Newsletter, has kindly permitted the use of his book Let Food Be Thy Medicine as information source for the HEALTH AND HEALING INFORMATION HIGHWAY—H.H.I.H.

Jane Quincannon and Lino Stanchich, esteemed International Macrobiotic Teachers and Authors as well as Licensed Nutritionists have been a genuine boost of blessings and praise.

Del Foxton, a dynamo and wonderful person, rallied to the rescue by typing a large part of Chapters 8 and 9, the GLOSSARY and the H.H.I.H.

Lynda Swidzinski contributed highly valued expertise in natural foods cooking and friendly and supportive constructive comments, and also proofread the final text.

Josée Baillargeon gave her love and time with suggestions towards ensuring a user-friendly cookbook, including testing many of the recipes.

Cindy Gamble offered her culinary talents and tested recipes, sharing them with her non-vegetarian family and getting valuable feedback. Her husband, Stephan saved us in the final hour when it looked as though our obstacles were insurmountable.

Tosh Kagemori of Koyo Foods, Cecile Michaud of Sobaya Noodles, Ives Potvin of Ives Veggie Cuisine and Carl Karush of Maine Coast Sea Vegetables helped make this possible with their conscientious and token financial support.

Jaqui Spreekmeester and Shari Blaukopf, talented graphic artists, put their magical finishing touches on the cover design. Jaqui went so far beyond the call of duty that I now call her Saint Jaqui.

Alain Leduc and the staff at Gagné Printing were always attentive and a great pleasure to work with.

Martine Picard is a human angel who compiled information for part of the H.H.I.H.

Marcy Claman, author of the successful Bed & Breakfast cookbook, Rise & Dine, and her accountant/computer genius/dear husband Lenny benefited me with their first hand experience, and provided a wealth of guidance.

Christina and Robert Pirello, publishers of MacroChef in Philadelphia have been very supportive and encouraging.

Martha Demarais gave vital, uplifting advice and took great interest in the achievement of this endeavor in its beginning stages.

Kathleen Thoma, Publisher of the Seraphim Journal offered help in getting the word out, and practicable advice.

Laura Lea Golding gave her time, talent and creativity in word-processing part of the book.

Dear friends and colleagues expressed their enthusiasm and encouragement and participated in Project Feedback.

Always in my prayers of gratitude are steadfast students and faithful fans, too numerous to mention, you know who you are. You have taught and inspired me through your experiences, stories and questions to delve deeper and reach higher beyond my noblest expectations.

This book would not be what it is without all the direct and indirect help of so many wonderful people. The story behind the story is an unbelievable tale of happenings, that somehow, were all blessings in disguise. We have an inside joke. It's the behind the scenes title I gave the book that, at the time, more accurately described the process. Instead of FAST & FUN *For People on the Go!*, for months it was definitely SLOW & TORTUROUS *For Workaholics with Insomnia!* We hope you enjoy it as much as we *didn't* creating it. *HA!* But seriously, we hope that everything we put into it helps you get more out of it.

Thank-you for the blessings, love and friendship we have given, received and shared.

TABLE OF CONTENTS

CHAPTER 2 continued...

CHAPTER 5 - VEGGIE VENTURES

CHAPTER 5 continued...

FOREWORD

People often have the impression that eating well means sacrificing the pleasures of life. In this book, Karen Claffey shows how healthy eating can be delicious and fun. There's no doubt that a grain, bean and vegetable based diet is better for health. Study after study has revealed that we can lower our risk of heart disease, cancer, diabetes and other chronic illnesses by eating according to the guidelines set forth in this book.

Karen's cooking appeals to the palate while fulfilling the dietary guidelines of health organizations around the world. She is a busy active person - gives regular cooking classes at Karen's Kitchen, is the star of her own cooking show on Montreal's CF Cable TV, practices a regimen of aerobics, bicycling, meditation, power walking, roller blading, weight training and yoga, gives dietary and lifestyle counseling and shiatsu massage, and still finds time to create such wonderful new recipes. Her approach to fast, fun food comes from her own daily experience of cooking and enjoying healthy eating in the dynamic paced modern world. She is a role model for millions of other men and women today.

Karen studied macrobiotic healing at the Kushi Institute in Massachusetts and, while there, she organized macrobiotic educational programs throughout the United States. She worked and studied with Wendy Esko (author *of Macrobiotic Cooking for Everyone* and several other best selling natural foods cookbooks), and was the Head Chef at the KI, designing recipes and menus for up to 80 people per day. Upon graduating from the Institute, Karen returned to her native Canada where she became Head Chef and Manager of Ecos Cafés in Toronto where she cooked for up to 400 patrons on a daily basis. She was then flown out to Santa Monica, CA to consult, train and create menus for Real Food Daily, a popular macrobiotic restaurant frequented by Hollywood movie stars. Audrone Kairys, President of Audra Travel in Toronto invited Karen on an Alaskan Cruise aboard the Norwegian MS Windward. Karen consulted the Chefs for Audrone's group of travelers who requested a macrobiotic diet. Karen has also guided individuals and families facing chronic illness toward a healing natural diet and lifestyle through her cooking and advice.

Alternative Medicine and Holistic Health Care have become an international trend. During a recent trip to Belgium, I was surprised to discover that more than half the population are using alternative healing methods. Surveys show that one third of North Americans regularly consult alternative practitioners. At the forefront of this international trend is the movement toward healthy natural eating.

FAST & FUN FOOD, *For People on the Go!* brings healthy natural eating to the mainstream. I have tasted many of these recipes and can say that they are truly healthful, delicious and fun.

Edward Esko
International Macrobiotic Teacher and Author
Becket, MA. USA
August 1995

INTRODUCTION

There's no getting around the fact that we **"HAVE NO TIME!"** And we won't pretend that shopping for, preparing and cooking food requires no added work load. It's easy to "grab a bite on the way" or "pick something up while I'm there" or "order in from...". But while saving time, we are sacrificing a great deal by eating in the fast lane.

Imagine you are in your car eating a meal you bought from a drive-through fast food outlet. A burger perhaps or chicken (for our example's sake, nevertheless, it is some kind of butchered dead animal flesh and other parts ground up that we don't want to know about) with a slice of bio-engineered tomato, chemically sprayed lettuce, sauce make of petroleum products and food coloring, on a bun of bleached processed preservative laden wheat, fiber (tree by-products), dehydrated dairy by-products and hydrogenated tropical oils. **Yumm!** How do you feel and how will this food affect you **mentally, physically, emotionally, spiritually?** (See Cholesterol, and Saturated Fat in the GLOSSARY).

Now contemplate eating a meal in your kitchen at home made from natural food— grown organically, washed and chopped with love by your hands, cooked and seasoned to your taste. Maybe you fancy a savory Hearty Minestrone with white beans and pasta. Then how about gorgeous, rich, yet low fat Pumpkin Seed Pesto with Parsley Garlic Ribbons and colorful, spicy Tri-Color Antipasto in Italian Dressing. All delicious, healthy and **promoting a peaceful, harmonious body, mind and spirit**. How do you feel and how will this food affect you and your life?

Granted we don't always have the luxury of a relaxed meal at home and often need to eat on the run. All the more reason you need a nutritious meal that is prepared in your kitchen oasis which you can transport wherever you go. This calming, nourishing, revitalizing food will sustain you in the hectic rush of the day.

Did you know that vegetarians are better lovers? Michio Kushi's, The Gentle Art of Making Love outlines how diet makes it happen. According to James Redfield in the Celestine Prophecy, vegans are **more insightful and spiritually attuned**. We also **live longer**. Guess which diet makes for **superior athletes**. (See Food and Endurance in the HEALTH & HEALING INFORMATION HIGHWAY—H.H.I.H.). Food that is full of vitality, nutrition and harmony promoting qualities inevitably produces an **optimal, stress-free state of health**. Our food is broken down into amino acids and various components that are utilized by our body to regenerate and rebuild billions upon billions of cells. The quality of our blood is determined by the quality of our food. Our food becomes us and we become equal to our food. You can't build a Rolls Royce out of Hyundai parts.

Eating well is fundamental to our well being.

Sure exercise is important and so is positive thinking. Yet our performance, strength and endurance is provided by the fuel we put into our bodies. Our emotions and ability to cope with stress is greatly the cause and effect of our daily food and beverage choices. We often place a greater emphasis on everything else in our life and neglect the food aspect. We find plenty of time to lovingly and meticulously wash and buff our cars, motorcycles or bicycles. We fit shopping for clothes, entertainment, music, toys and other objects of desire into our agenda without a second thought. Put the same enthusiasm and sense of adventure into selecting your food as you do everything else. Contemplate and plan your meals as you would other joyful aspects of your life. Share it with your family and friends.

Still with me? Wonderful! If you have never experienced eating **natural foods** (see GLOSSARY) like brown rice, beans, tofu and organically grown vegetables you are in for a treat. This is **REAL** food—not devitalized, adulterated, disguised and insulted technological simulations. Also, these foods enhance the growth and prosperity of our environment, Mother Nature. Animal husbandry undermines the health of humans and the life of our planet. (For information on the effects of an animal based diet on our health and the environment please see the video or best selling book Diet for a New America by John Robbins and his second book, May All be Fed, Diet for a New World.)

You may think that fitting this healthy food shopping and preparing into an over loaded schedule is easier said than done. Once you develop healthy habits and get into a routine with the **TIME SAVING STRATEGY** it becomes second nature.

Planning ahead eliminates the dilemma of "What am I going to eat?", or "There's nothing to eat!". This is always followed by the quick fix response to satisfy your hunger due to the fact that you've waited until 11:55 AM to think about lunch, or 6:45 PM to consider your options for dinner. Creatively using STAPLES in various ways, and making sure they are always on hand, ensures that we receive a wholesome balanced diet, and guarantees that our meals are delicious, fun and interesting.

TIME SAVING STRATEGY

- Set aside time slots (e.g., one hour per day and /or a few hours on your "day off") to devote to your labor of love, nourishing yourself and your family. Establish a routine of healthy habits.

- Make large amounts of meal staples; beans, grains, pasta and seitan to be used in various quick recipes to create variety. See **STAPLES** for lists of foods to stock and easy cooking instructions.

- Have non-perishable ingredients stocked in your cupboards and frozen items available at all times. See **PANTRY PERENNIALS** for lists of groceries.

- Have basic essential vegetables always on hand and arrange your refrigerator in an organized manner, so you know exactly where everything is and what needs to be replenished. See the **FRIDGE MAP** for directions.

EATING ON THE RUN

- When you know that your schedule for the following days will require eating-on-the-run, plan ahead. Package leftovers; grains, pasta, beans and vegetables, into portable meals. With a little imagination you can have greatly satisfying meals.

HANDY-HELPER-BOX

- To really get a meal on the table in record time, again, plan ahead. The HANDY-HELPER-BOX tells you how many days cooked grains or pasta store refrigerated, and about preparing vegetables in advance. All there is to do when you come home is chop and boil, sauté, steam or stir-fry some vegetables, add your cooked grains or pasta, season to taste and voila. Bon appetit!

Groceries	• **Groceries & fresh vegetables you need in each recipe.** **Seasonings, herbs & spices.**
Do Ahead	• **Steps to dramatically reduce your meal preparation time.** **Fridge & freezer storage times.**
Hot Tips	• **Fat & calorie cutting techniques.** **Quick & simple cooking options.** **Ideas to create variety.**
Meal Balance*	• **How the recipe fits into a balanced meal.** **Serving suggestions & combinations.**

*For detailed guidelines of a balanced diet see **Ideal Proportions** in the H.H.I.H. These are the leading Health Authorities' recommendations of daily foods for health and well being and abundant energy to keep you ON THE GO!

MENU MAGICIAN has two sample weekly menus. The first is **FAST**, integrating the TIME SAVING STRATEGY. It shows how to creatively use STAPLES in various recipes throughout the week. Simply by substituting ingredients, you can transform your menus to always be new and interesting. The second menu is **FUN**, giving examples of a wide variety of family favorites and gourmet international meals. The menus include full meals from soup to dessert. These are ideas of how to combine recipes from different cuisines. In real life, we may not have time for full course meals every day, and we generally don't eat desserts every day either, or at least shouldn't.

Quality is very important, but variety is the spice of life. Color, freshness, taste, texture and visual appeal, should all be considered when planning meals.

CUTTING TO THE CHASE has simple instructions on storing, washing, and cutting vegetables for variety and artistry.

TRICKS OF THE TRADE has chef's secrets and preparation techniques to enhance the taste and your enjoyment of the food.

Now for one last issue. FAT. The current obsession. The recipes are all **LOW to ZERO FAT**. Once we begin to eat a balanced, grain-based diet with legumes and vegetables and reduce or omit animal products from our diet, fat no longer becomes a problem. Unless you go heavy on the nuts, seeds, oils, and sweets you will probably have more trouble being too thin than too fat. And that's that!

We use the highest quality natural ingredients in these **FAST & FUN** recipes. You'll be happy to know they contain absolutely no animal products, poultry, eggs or dairy, and no sugar or honey. They are favorites among friends and students at our cooking school and highly requested by our clients of our catering/take-out service. These dishes have been **lined up for** and **raved about** by patrons of Ecos Cafés in Toronto and Real Food Daily in Santa Monica, CA where I was head chef-manager. Viewer response to our television cooking series, **KAREN'S KITCHEN**, based on this book has been very enthusiastic and appreciative. We hope you love them too!

Now lets get the show on road!

QUANTITY VS. QUALITY

Fast Food Restaurants produce as fast as possible, the largest volume of food, with the most taste, at the lowest cost. Quantity, not quality.

Homemade food "to go" ensures convenience, great taste and the security of knowing that your daily meal requirements are taken care of. What is more important, your nutritional needs are fulfilled with the highest quality natural ingredients.

CHAPTER 1

GOURMET TO GO

*Pack 'n Portable, Party & Picnic
Super Sandwiches*

SEITAN SOUVLAKI

Prep Time: 10   **Cook Time: 20**   **Serves: 4**

Groceries

Seitan, Oregano, Rosemary, Tamari, Whole Wheat Pita Bread, Lettuce, Tomato, Cucumber, Paprika.

Do Ahead

Marinate the seitan for 1 hour, and up to 5 days, refrigerated in a covered dish. Seitan Souvlaki keeps well for 1 week refrigerated in a sealed container, or frozen for 3 months. Tofu Tzatziki can be made up to 5 days in advance.

Hot Tips

Crush the dried rosemary so that the twigs are not too large. Use fresh oregano and rosemary if possible, 2-3 tablespoons instead of the 1 tablespoon of dried.

Meal Balance

Pita bread and seitan are wheat/grain products, Tofu Tzatziki is a soybean product, and the vegetables complete this delicious portable meal. For an authentic Greek meal, serve with the Greek Salad with Tofeta.

Athens is the place to experience Souvlaki. Every street corner has a food stall offering yet another variation of the traditional recipe, except the Greek vendors aren't using seitan. This is one of our most fast and popular dishes.

4 cups of Seitan*, pressed** and 1" cubed
3 tablespoons Olive Oil
3 tablespoons Tamari***
1 tablespoon Oregano
1 tablespoon Rosemary
4 Whole Wheat Pocket-Style Pita Bread
Fresh Lettuce, shredded
Chopped Cucumber and Tomato
Tofu Tzatziki, see recipe on page 168
Paprika

1. Preheat your oven to 350°F, and oil an 11" by 17" baking tray. Toss the cubed seitan with the oil, tamari and herbs to coat.
2. Spread seitan cubes onto the tray, and try not to overlap them so they all brown evenly. Bake for approximately 20 minutes, or until browned and caramelized on the edges.
3. Slice pita pockets into two half moons, and stuff with the seitan and vegetables. Add a dollop of the Tofu Tzatziki and finish with a dusting of Paprika.

Variation:
Souvlaki Kebabs
Place the seasoned seitan cubes (Step 1) on a skewer, with 1" diced onion, red and green pepper and whole mushroom caps placed in between. Bake as above, or grill on the barbecue, basting with the seasonings.

* See SPEEDY HOMEMADE SEITAN
** See Seitan in TRICKS OF THE TRADE
*** See GLOSSARY

NORI ROLLS with MARINATED TOFU & VEGETABLES

Prep Time: 20

Cook Time: 2   **Makes: 4**

Groceries

Nori, Cooked Rice, Tofu, Carrot, Cucumber, Ginger, Tamari, Mustard, Umeboshi Paste.

Do Ahead

Rice may be cooked 5 days in advance and stored refrigerated in a sealed container. Tofu can be marinated for up to 5 days, sealed and refrigerated. The vegetables may be marinated up to 2 days in advance. The Nori Rolls stay fresh for 2-3 days refrigerated, wrapped in plastic, and encased in the sushi mat for protection.

Hot Tips

Nori Rolls made with freshly cooked rice, should cool to room temperature before wrapping in plastic or the nori sheet will become soggy from the steam inside the plastic. When you make the rolls from pre-cooked and stored rice, simply steam the rice for 1-2 minutes if it has become too hard and dry to work with.

Meal Balance

You can put all kinds of exciting fillings in here. Rice supplies an ample grain serving, and all the fillings complete this portable meal.

Also known as Nori Maki in Sushi Bars, this is a highlight and conversation piece at parties, and an attention-getter at traffic lights.

2 tablespoons grated fresh Ginger
3 tablespoons each Tamari* + Rice Vinegar*
¼ lb. Tofu*, pressed**, sliced into ¼" logs
1 - 7" long Carrot, sliced into 4 logs***
1 - 7" long Cucumber, sliced into 4 logs***
4 Toasted Nori Sheets*
±6 cups Freshly Cooked Warm Rice****
4 teaspoons Mustard*, Natural Stone Ground
4 teaspoons Umeboshi Paste*

1. Combine the ginger, tamari and vinegar in a shallow flat dish with the tofu. Fill a pot with a ¼ cup of water. Place a steamer basket inside and steam the carrot logs for 3-4 minutes, until tender crisp.
2. Add the remaining cooking water to the marinade. Marinate the carrot and cucumber logs with the tofu. Cover and set aside for 1 hour, or refrigerate overnight. Turn them occasionally to coat all sides in the juices.
3. See Nori Maki in TRICKS OF THE TRADE for simple rolling instructions. In each roll, spread 1 teaspoon each of the mustard and umeboshi paste, along with ¼ of the tofu, the vegetables, and the marinade.
4. a) Keep the rolls whole and wrap in plastic "to-go".
b) Slice each roll into 8 sections, and serve as the main part of your meal, or as hors d'oeuvres for buffet style dining.

* See GLOSSARY
** See TRICKS OF THE TRADE
*** See CUTTING TO THE CHASE
**** See BROWN RICE in STAPLES

SOMEN NORI MAKI
WITH TEMPEH TERIYAKI

Prep Time: 20

Cook Time: 20   **Makes: 4**

Groceries

Somen Noodles, Nori, Tempeh, Garlic, Ginger, Maple Syrup, Toasted Sesame Oil, Tamari, Sake, Lettuce, Red Cabbage, Tamari, Rice Vinegar.

Do Ahead

Thaw frozen tempeh for 1 hour and pat with a towel to dry excess moisture before using. Marinate your tempeh for 1 hour, and up to 4 days refrigerated in a sealed container. Once cooked, the tempeh will keep for 10 days to 2 weeks refrigerated in a sealed container, freezing changes the texture but is possible for 2-3 months.

Hot Tips

The Toasted Sesame Oil will add a little fat but is suggested for a meatier, richer flavor. Use Sake or Mirin instead of the water for Japanese authenticity and flavor.

Meal Balance

The heartiness of the complete soy protein of the tempeh is extremely versatile and adds savory substance to many recipes; grains, pasta, salads, soups and stews. Seitan or tofu can be substituted for tempeh for variety.

The noodles make a light and refreshing change from rice or grains as a filling, the tempeh is hearty and rich, balanced with crisp romaine lettuce.

2 tablespoons grated fresh ginger**
1 large Garlic Clove, minced
3 tablespoons Tamari*
1 tablespoon Maple Syrup*
1 tablespoon of Sake***, Mirin*** or Water
1 teaspoon Toasted Sesame Oil*
½ of a 12 oz. package Tempeh* sliced lengthwise into 6 logs 1/3" thick
4 Toasted Nori Sheets**
Somen Noodles cooked in 4 bundles**
±3 cups of finely sliced Romaine Lettuce,
±1 cup of very finely sliced Red Cabbage
±¼ cup Rice Vinegar* or to taste

1. Combine the ginger, garlic, tamari, syrup, sake and oil in a flat baking dish (large enough to for the length of the logs, but small enough so the marinade is as deep as possible to cover the tempeh). Marinate the tempeh for 1 hour or more.
2. Preheat oven to 375°F. Bake the tempeh for 20 minutes, uncovered until golden brown and the liquid is caramelized.
3. See Nori Maki in TRICKS OF THE TRADE for simple rolling instructions. Spread ¼ of the lettuce over the center line of the noodles, topped with ¼ of the red cabbage. Sprinkle 1-2 teaspoons of vinegar over the vegetables and lay the tempeh logs on top. You may need to use 2, and cut 1 of the logs to fit exactly across the length of the nori sheet.
4. Slice each roll into 8 sections to serve on a plate, or wrap them whole, in plastic "to-go".

* See GLOSSARY
** See Noodles in TRICKS OF THE TRADE
*** Rice wine (Mirin is available in natural food stores).

RED LENTIL PATÉ IN PITA

Prep Time: 15   **Cook Time: 25**   **Serves: 4**

Groceries

Red Lentils, Whole Wheat Pita Bread, Onion, Garlic, Miso, Basil, Oregano, Thyme, Toasted Bread Crumbs, Salad Ingredients.

Do Ahead

Lentils can be precooked and stored refrigerated in a sealed container for 3 days before completing the recipe. The paté will keep in a sealed container for 1 week refrigerated (made with fresh cooked lentils) or 3 months frozen.

Hot Tips

Sautéing the vegetables in oil adds flavor and richness. You can omit the oil to cut fat, and to save time, you can simply boil the vegetables in with the lentils. Toasted bread crumbs add substance—the paté is lighter and softer without them. Make extra lentils for the Lentil Dahl with Vegetables and Basmati.

Meal Balance

Whole wheat chappati rolled up with lentils and vegetables provide a balanced meal that is easy to eat on the go. Enjoy the paté with fresh whole grain bread, or as a side dish to your grains or pasta. Include a soup or stew and some steamed or sautéed vegetables for a full course meal.

You can also make this pate with brown or green lentils, or other varieties of beans. Serve as a dip for chips and tortillas, or spread it on crackers and rice cakes.

1 cup Red Lentils
1 tablespoon Olive Oil
1 Medium Onion, diced
1 large Garlic clove, minced
1 teaspoons Basil
½ teaspoon each of Oregano and Thyme
1-2 tablespoons Miso*
½ teaspoon Sea Salt or to taste
¼ teaspoon Pepper or to taste
Cayenne Pepper to taste
¼ cup Toasted Bread Crumbs**(optional)
Whole Wheat Pita Bread, Pocket Style
Fresh Lettuce, shredded, Grated Carrots, Sliced Red Cabbage, Radishes, Sprouts.

1. Sort, wash and drain your lentils. Bring to a boil in 2 cups of water over medium-high heat. Lower heat and simmer for 20 minutes.
2. Sauté the onion and garlic with the oil in a skillet over medium heat until golden.
3. Stir the sautéed vegetables into the cooked lentils with the herbs, miso, salt and pepper. Simmer for 5 minutes. Purée the mixture.
4. Mix the bread crumbs (if desired) into the puréed lentil mixture and transfer to a serving dish to cool and set for two to three hours.
5. Spread some of the paté inside one side of the pita pocket and stuff fresh vegetables along the other side. Wrap in plastic, and refrigerate for up to 2 days in advance.

* See GLOSSARY
** See Bread Crumbs - TRICKS OF THE TRADE

FUNTASTIC FAJITAS

Prep Time: 10   **Cook Time: 10**   **Serves: 6**

Groceries

Seitan, Whole Wheat Tortillas, Onion, Tomatoes, Green and Red Pepper, Tamari.

Do Ahead

The seitan and vegetable filling can be made and refrigerated in a sealed container up to 4 days in advance. Reheat before serving. The assembled Fajita, wrapped in plastic and refrigerated, will keep fresh for 2 days.

Hot Tips

Use the seitan and vegetable filling as a topping over cooked rice, pasta or other grains instead of rolled inside the tortillas. Sauté the vegetables in ¼ cup of water instead of oil to eliminate fat if desired.

Meal Balance

These make a great portable meal. A variety of fresh greens, cooked or as a salad, will balance this dish. A Sumptuous Soup or Savory Stew turns it into a hearty meal. Ideally, serve this with the California Carrot Salsa and Guacamole on the side for a light and lively Mexican meal!

The Mexican Chef at Real Food Daily in Santa Monica makes this with simple, fresh ingredients of the highest quality. You can spice it up with fresh chilies or cayenne to your taste buds' tolerance.

6 Whole Wheat Tortillas
1 tablespoon Olive Oil
2 cups Seitan*, sliced into strips
1 medium Onion, sliced ½ moons
1-2 Tomatoes diced
½ Green Pepper sliced julienne
½ Red Pepper sliced julienne
½ teaspoon Sea Salt
¼ teaspoon Pepper or to taste
2-3 tablespoons Tamari**, or sea salt to taste

1. Preheat oven to 300°F. Wrap and seal the tortillas in foil and warm them in the oven for 5-10 minutes. Meanwhile...
2. Heat the oil in a skillet over medium-high heat, and sauté the seitan for 3 minutes, until browned. Add the onion and sauté for 2 minutes, or until tender. Add the tomatoes, bell peppers, sea salt and pepper. Reduce heat and cook covered for 5 minutes.
3. Tilt the skillet and add tamari where the juices pool at the bottom. Simmer for 1 minute, and mix the vegetables with the juices. Adjust seasonings to taste.
4. Place 1/6 of the sautéed vegetables on each tortilla, roll up jelly roll fashion and place seam side down on a serving plate. Let them cool to room temperature before wrapping them for take-out.

Variation: Seitan can be substituted with either tofu or tempeh. When using tempeh, cook it for 10 minutes before adding the vegetables, for ideal digestibility and flavor.

* See SPEEDY HOMEMADE SEITAN
** See GLOSSARY

BAKED FALAFEL

Prep Time: 15　　　　　　**Cook Time: 25**　　　　**Makes: ±20 balls**

Groceries

Chickpeas, Garlic, Cumin, Paprika, Coriander, Turmeric, Cayenne, Scallions, Parsley, Chickpea Flour.

Do Ahead

The mixture can be made 3 days in advance and refrigerated in a sealed container. Once cooked, the balls or patties will keep for up to 1 week refrigerated, or 3 months frozen in a sealed container.

Hot Tips

Baking falafel gives you a drier result than the traditional deep fried recipe, but they are great once you add a sauce, as they will absorb the liquid and become moist. The deep fried are a more rich, satisfying version but are of course higher in fat and calories.

Meal Balance

These are typically served stuffed into a pita bread with some fresh salad style vegetables; shredded lettuce, sliced cucumber and tomato—turning this into a portable balanced meal. Top it with Tahini Lemon Sauce. These balls are perfect buffet-party fare, with the Tahini Lemon Sauce served on the side.

Discovering Falafel is as exciting as experiencing the historically rich sights of its origins. After you've eaten Falafel in Jerusalem, having it again will always be like a mini adventure.

3 Garlic Cloves
3 cups Chickpeas, cooked* or canned
2 teaspoons each Cumin and Coriander
2 teaspoons Sea Salt or to taste
1 teaspoon each Paprika and Turmeric
Cayenne to taste
1-1 Scallions, minced
1-2 Parsley Sprigs, minced
Chickpea or Wheat Flour as necessary

1. Preheat oven to 350°F. Mince the garlic in a food processor. Add and purée the chickpeas with some of the cooking liquid to achieve a thick paste, along with the spices and sea salt.
2. Briefly purée the scallions and parsley just to mix in with enough flour as necessary to have a stiff consistency—not too sticky, and not too dry and crumbly. Adjust seasonings to taste.
3. Shape into balls, place on a baking tray and bake uncovered for 25-30 minutes or until golden brown and no longer raw in the center.

Variations:
1. **Traditional Deep Fried** - heat vegetable oil to 375°F and deep fry balls until golden brown and crispy on the outside, 5 minutes or so. Drain on paper towels.
2. **Chickpea Patties** - shape the mixture into patties, ½" thick, 3" in diameter. Either bake for 30 minutes at 375°F, or deep fry until golden brown and crispy on the outside.

* See COOKING BEANS chart in STAPLES

KENTUCKY UN-FRIED SEITAN

Prep Time: 15   **Cook Time: 25**   **Serves: 4**

Groceries

Seitan, Tamari, Basil, Celery Salt, Curry Powder, Dried Parsley, Garlic Powder Onion Powder, Poultry Seasoning, Thyme, Flour, Bread Crumbs, Arrowroot.

Do Ahead

Marinate pressed seitan for 1 hour and up to 5 days refrigerated in a covered dish. Mix occasionally to distribute the flavor and liquid evenly. Once baked, the seitan will keep for 5-7 days refrigerated, or 3 months frozen, in a sealed container.

Hot Tips

Make the batter thick enough to coat the seitan without running off, for tastiest results. This recipe is virtually fat-free. The Kentucky Fried variation will add some fat and calories. Substitute Tempeh or Tofu (pressed), for the seitan.

Meal Balance

Serve with either the Chunky Fruit Ketchup, the Sesame, Special or Dijon Ginger Sauce, or Tofu Tzatziki. Seitan prepared in this manner is an ample grain product that is complimented by vegetables. You may also serve this as a side dish to your main grain or pasta meal.

Kids love this one. Having home-made high quality Fast Foods is much more satisfying, in so many ways. You can deep fry the battered morsels for a rich, savory treat occasionally.

2 cups Seitan*, pressed**
¼ cup water
2 tablespoons water
½ teaspoon each Basil and Celery Salt
½ teaspoon Curry Powder
½ teaspoon Dried Parsley
½ teaspoon each Garlic and Onion Powder
½ teaspoon Poultry Seasoning
½ teaspoon Thyme
½ cup Whole Wheat Pastry Flour
1 tablespoon Arrowroot***
¼ cup Bread Crumbs** or
Finely Ground Puffed Rice

1. Slice seitan into ¾" cubes and combine with the water, tamari, herbs and spices. Marinate for one hour or more.
2. Preheat your oven to 350°F. Drain the seitan, saving the marinade. Mix the flour and arrowroot with the marinade and enough water if necessary to make a thick batter. Dip the seitan and coat it with the batter, and then roll it in the bread crumbs to cover evenly.
3. Bake the coated and breaded seitan on an oiled baking tray for approximately 25 minutes, or until golden brown.

Variation: **Kentucky Fried Seitan**
Heat vegetable oil to 375°F and deep fry the battered and breaded seitan for 5 minutes or until crispy, golden brown. Drain on paper towels.

* See SPEEDY HOMEMADE SEITAN
** See TRICKS OF THE TRADE
*** See GLOSSARY

PIZZA WITH PIZZAZZ

Prep Time: 15   **Cook Time: 10**   **Serves: 6-8**

Groceries

Unbleached White Flour, Whole Wheat Pastry Flour, Baking Powder, Baking Soda, Herbs, Vegetables, A "10" Tomato Sauce (opt.), Tofu Mozzarella (opt.).

Do Ahead

The Tomato Sauce and Tofu Mozzarella keep refrigerated for 10 days, or frozen for 3 months in sealed containers. Vegetables may be washed and ready to slice a few days in advance (depending on their perishability), and stored refrigerated in sealed containers. Make the dough fresh before baking. Once baked, it keeps refrigerated for 5 days or frozen for 3 months, well wrapped.

Hot Tips

Add enough water to make a pliable dough that is not sticky, which you can roll or press into the shape of your baking pan. For all dressed variations you may want to make the crust a little thicker to support the weight of all the toppings.

Meal Balance

The whole wheat crust provides you with the grain portion of your meal and you can make your toppings as filling or as light as you like. The All Dressed with Tofu Mozzarella is a meal in itself.

Trendy Gourmet Pizzerias with old fashion wood-burning brick ovens are serving this delicious thin style crust. Home ovens also give great results.

Gourmet Thin Style Crust:
1½ cups Unbleached White Flour
1 cup Whole Wheat Pastry Flour
2 teaspoons Baking Powder
½ teaspoon each Baking Soda and Sea Salt
2 tablespoons Olive Oil

1. Preheat oven to 425°F. In a large bowl, mix the dry ingredients together. Combine the oil briefly. Add ±1 cup of water to form a pliable, and not too sticky dough.
2. Divide the dough in ½ for 2 small round pizzas, or leave the dough whole for a large round one or an 11" by 16" rectangle. Roll or press the dough onto an oiled baking tray.
3. Cover with your choice of toppings and bake for 10-15 minutes, or until the crust is golden brown around the edges.

Tomato-Herb: Spread A "10" Tomato Sauce over the dough leaving a ½" edge. Sprinkle ¼ cup (packed) chopped fresh basil, cilantro, dill, thyme, marjoram, oregano, parsley, rosemary in any combination.

Magic Mushrooms: Slice 1 cup each of sliced, fresh café, oyster, portabella and shiitake mushrooms. Thinly slice 1 cup of red onion. Toss together with 3 tablespoons of olive oil and sea salt and pepper to taste. Spread over dough and bake as above.

All Dressed: Tomato sauce is followed by your choice of sliced vegetables, olives, Dulsechovies and Tofu Mozzarella (see Index).

Variation: **Spelt Crust**
Substitute spelt flour for the wheat flour for a highly nutritious crust with a wonderful flavor and texture.

TIJUANA TOSTADAS

Prep Time: 10   **Cook Time: 30**   **Serves: 6**

Groceries

Corn Tortillas, Seitan, Beans, Crushed Dried Chili, Cumin, Oregano, Paprika, Tomato, Onion, Garlic, Lettuce, Apple Cider Vinegar, Creamy Cheesy Topping.

Do Ahead

The toasted tortillas, cooked Seitan Chorizo, and Creamy Cheesy Sauce will keep refrigerated 1 week in sealed containers. The Refried Beans can be stored for up to 4 days. All can be frozen (separately) for 3 months. Make the salad garnish fresh just before serving. The assembled Tostadas will keep for 2 days refrigerated in a sealed container, after that, the salad will no longer be fresh.

Hot Tips

To reduce fat; omit the oil in the salad topping, cook the seitan and beans in a ¼ cup of water instead of sautéing in oil. Use Pinto, Kidney or Black Beans.

Meal Balance

Corn tortillas are a whole grain product that combine with beans and vegetables to create a balanced meal. Seitan provides wheat protein, and tofu adds soy protein. Serve with the California Carrot Salsa and Guacamole with Cherry Tomatoes for an authentic Mexican meal.

In Tijuana, we watched how they make tortillas by hand, patting the dough between their palms, and cooking them on cast iron pans.

12 4" Corn Tortillas
2 cups Seitan* diced into ½" cubes
Olive Oil
1 tablespoon Tamari** or sea salt to taste
½ tablespoon each of Oregano and Cumin
½ teaspoon Paprika
½ teaspoon Crushed Dried Chili, or to taste
1 Onion, diced
2 Garlic Cloves, minced
Sea Salt and Pepper
1 Tomato, chopped
3 cups Beans***, cooked
2 cups Fresh Lettuce, shredded
2 tbsp. Apple Cider or Balsamic Vinegar
Creamy Cheesy Sauce, see page 169

1. Toast tortillas in a preheated 350°F oven for 5 minutes or until crispy and pale golden.
2. Seitan Chorizo: Toss seitan cubes with 1 tbsp. of olive oil, tamari, oregano, cumin, paprika and ¼ teaspoon of the chili. Bake on a cookie sheet 20 minutes or until browned.
3. Frijoles Refritos/Refried Beans: In a skillet, heat 1 tablespoon olive oil, sauté the onion and garlic until tender. Add the tomato and cook stirring until softened, 5 minutes. Add beans with some cooking liquid, mash them into the vegetables with 1 tsp. sea salt. Cook until thick. Adjust seasonings to taste.
4. Toss the lettuce with a drizzle of olive oil, the vinegar, and sea salt and pepper to taste.
5. On each tortilla, layer 1/6 of the Seitan Chorizo, the Refried Beans and salad, and top with a dollop of Creamy Cheesy Sauce.

* See SPEEDY HOMEMADE SEITAN
** See GLOSSARY
*** See COOKING BEANS

SUPER FAST BURGERS

Prep Time: 10   **Cook Time: 5 each**   **Makes: 8-10**

Groceries

Tempeh, Tofu, Seitan, Flour
Rolled Oats, Ketchup, Garlic,
Sunflower Butter, Miso, Thyme,
Sage, Whole Wheat Buns,
Vegetable Garnish (your choice
of; Grated Carrot, Lettuce, Sliced
Onion, Sprouts, Tomato, Pickle).

Do Ahead

Thaw tempeh 1 hour before
using. Shape the burger mixture
into patties and refrigerated in a
sealed container for 1 week, or
freeze for 3 months. The Special
Sauce takes only a moment to
whip up.

Hot Tips

Omit the sunflower butter to
reduce fat, but it adds a rich, egg-
like flavor, and a fatty-meaty
quality. Cooked grains may be
substituted for either the tempeh,
tofu or seitan. For variety and to
reduce fat choose the optional
Baking or Barbecue methods.

Meal Balance

The combination of tofu and
tempeh (complete soy protein)
and seitan (wheat protein) is very
substantial. Serve with the
Special Sauce (next page) on
whole wheat buns with plenty of
vegetables for a balanced and
happy meal!

* See GLOSSARY
** See STAPLES

*These burgers remind me of the recipe we loved as
children that mother used to make from scratch.*

2 large garlic cloves
1/3 of a 12 oz. (340 gr.) package Tempeh*
1 cup each of mashed Tofu* and Seitan**
½ cup each of Rolled Oats* and Flour
1/3 cup Ketchup*
¼ cup Sunflower Butter* or Tahini (optional)
3 tablespoons Miso*, Sea Salt or Tamari to taste
3 tablespoons Tamari*, or sea salt to taste
1½ teaspoons Thyme
½ teaspoon Sage
¼ teaspoon Pepper or to taste
Whole Wheat Buns and Vegetable Garnish

1. Mince the garlic in a food processor. Add
the rest of the ingredients, up to and including
pepper, and process until fairly smooth, with
some texture remaining. Shape into patties
3" in diameter and 1/3" thick.
2. Heat an oiled cast iron or stainless steel
skillet over medium-high heat. Fry the patties
until golden brown, 2-3 minutes on each side.
Lower the heat to medium-low after the first
side has browned, so the outside does not
burn before the inside is cooked.
3. Slice each bun in half,
and place a burger on one
half. Add special sauce, and
garnish with vegetables.

Baking Method
Lightly oil a baking tray, and
bake the patties in a preheated 375°F oven,
±20 minutes.

Barbecue Method
These patties will not crumble and fall apart
on the grill. They can be basted while grilling
with the Barbecue Sauce, with the marinade
for the Tempeh Bacon or Teriyaki, or the
Seitan Pepper Steak coating.

SPECIAL SAUCE

Prep Time: 5   **Cook Time: 0**   **Makes: ¾ cup**

Groceries

Nayonaise*, Smooth Peanut Butter, Tamari, Turmeric.

Do Ahead

This sauce keeps well in the refrigerator for at least 1 week in a sealed container, or frozen for up to 3 months.

Hot Tips

The peanut butter adds a wonderful flavor but can easily be substituted with tahini. Both will add fat and can be omitted if desired, although you will sacrifice the richer flavor.

Meal Balance

This condiment is also great on Sun Seed Rice Patties, Club Sandwich with Grilled Tofu and Tempeh Bacon, Kentucky Un-Fried Seitan and Peanutty Patties.

Enjoy the Super Fast Burgers like the song says, with "Special Sauce, lettuce, tofu-cheese, pickles, onions on a whole wheat sesame seed bun".

½ cup Nayonaise*
1-2 tablespoons Water
1 tablespoon Smooth Peanut Butter* (opt.)
1 tablespoon Tamari*
¼ teaspoon Turmeric

In a bowl, whisk together all the above ingredients until smooth. Add enough water to achieve a thick sauce-like consistency that will spread on your burgers without running off.

* See GLOSSARY

CLUB SANDWICH WITH GRILLED TOFU & TEMPEH BACON

Prep Time: 15   **Cook Time: 15**   **Makes: 4**

Groceries

Whole Grain Bread, Tofu, Tempeh, Toasted sesame Oil, Nayonaise, Mustard, Salad ingredients; Lettuce, Tomato, Sprouts and Grated Carrot.

Do Ahead

Tempeh Bacon can be made 10 days in advance, and the Grilled Tofu 5 days, refrigerated in sealed containers. Freeze the tempeh for 3 months in a sealed container. The tofu changes texture once frozen.

Hot Tips

When your bread is not "same-day-fresh" or was frozen, simply steam it in a pot fitted with a steamer basket over boiling water for 1 minute. It becomes moist as if fresh baked. You may toast it after steaming if desired.

Meal Balance

This has all the makings of a complete meal. Make a triple-layer sandwich: on one slice of bread, place the tofu and lettuce; add another slice (spread with Nayonaise and mustard); add the tempeh, tomato, grated carrots and sprouts. Three slices will increase your complex carbohydrates for more energy!

During the summer when I was fifteen years old, working as a waitress in a delicatessen, I enjoyed lunches prepared by the chef. Now we enjoy this vegan representation.

8 strips of Tempeh Bacon, recipe page188
1 pound (454 gr.) Tofu*, pressed**
1 teaspoon Toasted Sesame Oil**
1 teaspoon Corn Oil**
1-2 teaspoons Tamari*
8-12 slices Whole Grain Bread
Nayonaise*
Mustard, Natural Stone Ground*
Lettuce, Tomato, Grated Carrot, Sprouts

1. Slice tofu into 1/3" thick slabs. Heat a cast iron or stainless steel skillet over medium-high heat and add the oil. Fry tofu until browned on one side and sprinkle some tamari on top.
2. Fry the other side of the tofu until browned and sprinkle tamari on the other side.
3. To assemble the sandwich; spread one slice of bread with Nayonaise and the other slice with mustard. Add one or two slices each of the tofu and tempeh (depending on the size of your bread, and the size of your tofu slices). Garnish with lettuce, tomato, grated carrot and sprouts.

Variation: Baking and Barbecue methods are possible, see SUPER FAST BURGERS.

* See GLOSSARY
** See TRICKS OF THE TRADE

BAGELS & TOFU CREAM CHEESE
WITH MOCK-LOX

Prep Time: 5   **Cook Time: 0**   **Makes: 2**

Groceries

Bagels, Tofu Cream Cheese, Grated Carrot, Red Onion, Dulse, Lettuce, Sprouts

Do Ahead

Tofu Cream Cheese will keep refrigerated for up to 1 week in a sealed container. Freezing is possible for up to 2 months but the texture will change.

Hot Tips

If your bagel is not "same-day' fresh", simply steam it in a pot fitted with a steamer basket over boiling water for 1 minute. It will be hot and moist like it just came out of the oven. You may toast it as well if desired.

Meal Balance

Use Whole Wheat Bagels if they are available for added flavor and a more nutritious grain product. Tofu is your bean portion, full of protein, calcium and satisfaction. The vegetables complete this portable meal.

After eliminating dairy foods from one's diet, the desire for Bagels and Cream Cheese with Lox leads to experimenting with tofu as an alternative. This recipe comes close to it using top quality natural; vegan ingredients.

2 Bagels
±½ cup of Tofu Cream Cheese, page 171
Dulse*, a small handful
Grated Carrot
Fresh Lettuce (Romaine, Curly, Boston)
Slices of Red Onion
Sprouts

1. Slice each bagel in half—into 2 circles. Spread Tofu Cream Cheese onto the cut sides of the bagel halves.
2. Quickly rinse the dulse and squeeze out excess liquid (optional). Place the dulse evenly over the tofu so that it sticks and doesn't fall out of the sandwich. Sprinkle the grated carrots around the sandwich and top with lettuce, onion, and sprouts. You may serve each half separately as an open face sandwich, or close it for one large one.
3. Assemble and wrap the sandwich in plastic if you are preparing lunch one or two days in advance.

* See GLOSSARY

HUMUS ON WHOLE WHEAT

Prep Time: 20   **Cook Time: 0**   **Makes: 2½ cups**

Groceries

Chickpeas, Lemon, Garlic, Tahini, Apple Cider Vinegar, Cumin, Cayenne, Parsley, Scallions, Whole Wheat Bread, Lettuce, Grated Carrot, Sprouts.

Do Ahead

The humus will keep for 5 days refrigerated in a sealed container. Freezing will change the texture and is not ideal. The wrapped and sealed sandwich will stay fresh for 2 days. Make extra chickpeas for the Baked Falafel, Garbanzo & Zucchini Bisque, Mediterranean Chickpeas & Pasta Salad or the Indian Almond Pilaf.

Hot Tips

The tahini gives the humus an authentic flavor and richness, but you can reduce or omit it for a practically fat-free spread. You can use basil or cilantro instead of the parsley for variety, and add some grated ginger to spice it up.

Meal Balance

This is a very delicious balanced meal in one portable sandwich. You could elaborate your meal with a warming Sumptuous Soup and/or vegetables from Veggie Ventures. This makes a great dip for crudités, crackers and chips.

Humus was unknown to me until my travels brought me to the fascinating ancient city of Jerusalem. The sights, sounds and aromas of Israel are reflected in their cuisine.

1-2 Garlic cloves
1½ cups Chickpeas* (cooked or canned)
Grated zest and juice of ½-1 lemon (to taste)
¼ cup Tahini **
1 tablespoon Apple Cider Vinegar (to taste)
1-2 teaspoons Tamari**
1 teaspoon Cumin
½ teaspoon Sea Salt, or to taste
¼ teaspoon Cayenne and/or Pepper, to taste
1 large sprig Parsley, minced
1 Scallion, minced
Whole Wheat Bread
Grated Carrot, Sprouts
Boston, Curly or Romaine Lettuce

1. Purée the garlic in a food processor until minced. Add the chickpeas with some of the cooking liquid, water or vegetable stock, and the remaining ingredients, up to and including the pepper, and process until smooth.
2. Pulse to mix in the parsley and scallions. Adjust seasonings to taste.
3. Spread some humus on 1 slice of bread and sprinkle grated carrot and sprouts onto the humus. They will stick to the humus and will not fall out of the sandwich as easily. Place your lettuce and other slice of bread on top. Serve immediately, or wrap each sandwich individually in plastic, and store in a larger sealed container to ensure freshness.

* See STAPLES
** See GLOSSARY

TOFU EGG SALAD SANDWICH

Prep Time: 20   **Cook Time: 0**   **Makes: 4**

Groceries

Silken Tofu, Apple Cider or Rice Vinegar, Mustard Powder, Turmeric, Carrot, Green and Red Pepper, Scallions, Peanut or Sunflower Butter, Parsley.

Do Ahead

Make the Tofu Egg Salad and stored refrigerated for 4 days, or frozen for 3 months in a sealed container, before using in a sandwich. The assembled sandwich stays fresh for 2 days, wrapped well and refrigerated in a sealed container. Freezing will change the texture.

Hot Tips

The Peanut and Sunflower Butter are equally high in fat, and can be omitted - but the small amount in this recipe goes a long way in giving a rich egg-like flavor and texture. This recipe can be made into a luscious potato salad by substituting the 1 package of mashed tofu with 1 cooked and diced potato.

Meal Balance

The whole grain bread is complemented by the soy protein and nut butter, and is balanced with fresh vegetables in a portable complete meal. This is also great wrapped in Chapatis or stuffed in Pita with vegetables.

You will be amazed at how much this recipe resembles the version we have grown to love that some of us may need, or prefer to avoid. Tahini can be substituted for the peanut or sunflower butter, only it is a little more bitter, and may be noticed.

1 - 10.5 oz. package Silken Tofu* Extra Firm
½ tablespoon Peanut or Sunflower Butter*
½ tablespoon Apple Cider or Rice Vinegar*
½ teaspoon each Tamari* and Sea Salt
¼ teaspoon each Mustard Powder, Turmeric
1/8 teaspoon Pepper or to taste
1 small Carrot, grated
¼ small Green, finely diced
¼ small Red Pepper, finely diced
1 large Scallion, finely sliced
1 tablespoon Italian Parsley, minced
Fresh Lettuce leaves, washed and patted dry
8 slices Whole Grain Bread

1. Purée ½ of the tofu with the nut butter, vinegar, tamari, sea salt, mustard, turmeric and pepper until smooth.
2. In a large bowl, mash the other ½ of the tofu with a potato masher briefly, leaving lumps of texture. Combine the purée and mix in the carrot, peppers, scallions and parsley. Adjust seasonings to taste.
3. Place a lettuce leaf on each slice of bread to prevent the bread from getting soggy from the Tofu Egg Salad. Spread ±¼ cup of the salad on 1 leaf, then place the other leaf and bread slice on top. Wrap in wax paper or plastic wrap for a portable meal, or slice and serve immediately with a Sumptuous Soup or Savory Stew.

* See GLOSSARY

CHAPTER 2

DISH IT UP

Spectacular Salads

Sumptuous Soups

Savory Stews

GREEK SALAD WITH TOFETA

Prep Time: 15   **Cook Time: 0**   **Serves: 4**

Groceries

Tofu, Tomatoes, Black Olives, Lemon, Red Wine or Balsamic Vinegar, Garlic, Oregano, Red Onion, Italian Parsley, Romaine Lettuce.

Do Ahead

Marinate the tofu refrigerated in a sealed container up to 5 days in advance, occasionally turning the tofu to evenly distribute the flavor. Prepare the vegetables fresh before serving as the tomatoes become soggy in the dressing after awhile.

Hot Tips

To reduce fat omit the oil. Leave the tofu in slabs and serve one per person, or dice into ½" cubes, toss with the tomatoes and vegetables and serve over lettuce leaves.

Meal Balance

This is a marriage made in heaven with the Seitan Souvlaki. Barley Soup with Mushrooms and Leeks is a great way to round out a light balanced meal. Serve this dish with various grain and pasta entrées for a full course meal. Otherwise, mix some cooked grains or pasta right into the salad to absorb the juices.

After enjoying Greek salads in restaurants from Corfu to Athens, and from Crete to Rhodes, one can safely say they have experienced the real thing. Here's our tofu interpretation.

Tofeta
1 pound (454 gr.) firm Tofu pressed**
¼ cup Extra Virgin Olive Oil
¼ cup Lemon Juice (1 Lemon)
2 tablespoons Red Wine or Balsamic Vinegar
2 Garlic Cloves, crushed
1 teaspoon dried Oregano or 1 tbsp. fresh
½ teaspoon Sea Salt, or to taste
¼ teaspoon Pepper, or to taste

4 vine ripened medium Tomatoes, diced 1"
6 oz (±¾ cup) Black Olives (Kalamata)
¼ cup Red Onion, sliced into thin rounds
¼ cup Italian Parsley, minced
6 large leaves Romaine Lettuce, well drained

1. Slice the tofu into 6 slabs, ½" thick. Mix remaining Tofeta ingredients (dressing) into a flat dish with straight sides (just large enough to lay the tofu slabs side by side so that they are covered in the liquid as much as possible). Marinate tofu 1 hour or more, turn the tofu to coat both sides.
2. Drain the tofu and set aside. Combine the dressing with the tomatoes, olives, red onion (reserving 6 beautiful rounds) and the parsley (reserving 1 tablespoon).
3. Place a whole lettuce leaf on each plate and divide the tomato mixture among the servings. Place a slab of tofu on top and garnish each with red onion and parsley.

Variation: **Tofu Kebabs** - 1" cube the tofu and marinate as above. Place on skewers with a variety of vegetables and grill on the barbecue, basting and turning each side until golden brown.

* See GLOSSARY
** See Tofu in TRICKS OF THE TRADE

CAESAR SALAD
WITH DULSECHOVIES & CROUTONS

Prep Time: 20   **Cook Time: 15**   **Serves: 4**

Groceries

Romaine Lettuce, Whole Grain
Bread, Dulse, Tahini, Garlic, Rice
Syrup, Umeboshi Paste, Lemon,
Mustard, Capers, Garlic Powder,
Basil, Oregano.

Do Ahead

Refrigerate the croutons stored in
a sealed container for several
weeks, or 3 months frozen. The
dressing keeps for 2 weeks
refrigerated in a jar or sealed
container. Wash and drain the
lettuce and refrigerate up to 2
days in a plastic bag or sealed
container.

Hot Tips

Make extra dressing for other
salads and cooked vegetables.
Assemble the salad just before
serving as it quickly becomes limp
once the dressing is added. Allow
the bread to dry out for a day
exposed to air so that it absorbs
the olive oil and flavor of the
herbs. To eliminate fat, omit the
oil in the croutons and the tahini
in the dressing—but the flavor will
not be as fabulous.

Meal Balance

Rich, yet a light and refreshing.
The Lasagna with Tofu Ricotta or
Pizza with Pizzazz are perfect
main meals to serve with this.

"This dressing is out of this world!", to quote the president of Real Food Daily in Santa Monica. Reddish purple dulse has a sea-like flavor and replaces anchovies, but make it without if desired.

Croutons
2 slices dry Whole Grain Bread, cubed ½-¾"
2 tablespoons Extra Virgin Olive Oil
¼ teaspoon each Garlic Powder and Sea Salt
¼ teaspoon each dried Basil and Oregano
Caesar Dressing
2 large or 4 small Garlic Cloves, minced
2 tablespoons Lemon Juice (½ Lemon)
1 tablespoon Tahini*
2 teaspoons Rice Syrup*
1 teaspoon Umeboshi Paste*
1 teaspoon Stone Ground Mustard*
½ teaspoon Pepper or to taste

8 large leaves Romaine Lettuce, drained
¼ cup Dulse*, rinsed briefly, chopped ½"
1 tablespoon Capers*

1. Preheat oven to 350°F. Toss the bread
with the remaining crouton ingredients to coat
evenly. Spread on a baking tray (scraping all the
seasonings from the bowl onto the bread) and bake
for 10 minutes, or until crispy-golden.
2. Blend the dressing ingredients in a food
processor (or a mortar and pestle or suribachi)
until smooth. Adjust seasonings to taste.
3. Chop or tear the lettuce into bite-size
pieces into a large bowl and mix the dressing
evenly with the lettuce. Combine half of the
capers and 1 cup of the croutons with the
lettuce and dressing. Divide among plates and
serve garnished with a few croutons and
capers.

* See GLOSSARY

MEDITERRANEAN CHICKPEAS & PASTA

Prep Time: 25   **Cook Time: 0**   **Serves: 6**

Groceries

Chickpeas, Vegetable Shells or Spiral Pasta, Green, Red and Yellow Pepper, Celery, Carrot, Red Onion, Italian Parsley, Garlic, Basil, Oregano, Marjoram, Apple Cider and Balsamic Vinegar,

Do Ahead

The dressing will store for 2 weeks refrigerated in a glass jar. Refrigerate cooked chickpeas and pasta in sealed containers for up to 4 days before using in the recipe. Wash the vegetables and refrigerate in a plastic bag or sealed container up to 5 days in advance. The salad will keep for 5 days refrigerated (made with fresh ingredients),and 3 months frozen, but the texture changes.

Hot Tips

Double the dressing and use on various fresh leafy green salads, cooked vegetables and to make grain and pasta salads in a snap. To eliminate fat, omit the oil - It will still be delicious. You can use various beans and pasta instead of chickpeas and shell or spiral pasta.

Meal Balance

This is grains, beans and vegetables in one. Enjoy!

Colors galore, delightful dressing, crisp and refreshing vegetables and tender, chewy chickpeas - this is a big hit at barbecues.

Mediterranean Dressing
1 Garlic Clove, finely minced
¼ cup Extra Virgin Olive Oil
¼ cup Apple Cider Vinegar
¼ cup Balsamic Vinegar
2 tablespoons Lemon Juice (±½ lemon)
2 tablespoons fresh* Basil, minced
1 teaspoon fresh* Marjoram
1 teaspoon fresh* Oregano
1 teaspoon Sea Salt
¼ teaspoon Pepper

1 Celery, sliced thin diagonally
1 Carrot, grated
1/3 of a large Red Onion, sliced
¼ Green Pepper, julienne
¼ Red Pepper, julienne
¼ cup Italian Parsley, minced
6 cups Veg. Shells or Spiral Pasta, cooked**
2 cups Chickpeas, cooked*** (or canned)

1. Combine dressing ingredients and let the flavors marry and develop while you...
2. Chop the vegetables. Mix the vegetables, chickpeas and pasta with the dressing and refrigerate for 1 -3 hours before serving. It will taste better the second day or so as the dressing marinates with the other ingredients.

* Use 1 teaspoon dried for each 1 tablespoon fresh.
** ±16 oz. raw - see PASTA in STAPLES
*** See COOKING BEANS chart in STAPLES

FAST & FUN
HOT PASTA SALAD

Prep Time: 10 **Cook Time: ±5** **Serves: 4-6**

Groceries

Pasta, Carrot, Celery, Chinese Cabbage, Red Cabbage, Romaine, Ginger, Scallions, Cilantro or Italian Parsley, Basil, Apple Cider or Balsamic Vinegar, Tamari, Mustard, Toasted Sesame Oil (optional).

Do Ahead

Wash the vegetables and refrigerate in a plastic bag or sealed container up to 3 days in advance. Store the salad in the refrigerator for 3 days in a sealed container.

Hot Tips

Salting the vegetables in Step 1 is optional. On the other hand, you may prepare the salad this way, serve it as a marinated salad, and leave out the pasta. Omit the oil for a fat-free dish. Substitute or include; other types of lettuce, bok choy, green and red peppers, zucchini, watercress, red onion, etc. Make this with various cooked grains instead of pasta.

Meal Balance

This is a balanced meal in a bowl. Make it more exciting add: cooked beans, tempeh, seitan or tofu; toasted nuts and seeds; raisins, etc. Have fun!

No left-overs in the fridge? NO time? This colorful, satisfying salad is a tasty, quick fix.

±16 ounces dry Pasta (any kind you like)
1 medium Carrot, grated
1 medium Celery, sliced thin diagonally
8 leaves Chinese Cabbage, julienne*
8 large leaves Romaine Lettuce, julienne
½ cup Red Cabbage, julienne
1 Scallion, sliced (white and green parts)*
¼ cup Cilantro or Italian Parsley, minced

Fast & Fun Dressing
2 tablespoons Lemon or Lime Juice
1 teaspoon fresh Ginger, grated
¼-½ cup Apple Cider, Balsamic and/or Brown Rice Vinegar (to taste)
1 tablespoon Tamari**, or to taste
1 teaspoon Basil (1 tbsp. fresh minced)
1 teaspoon Stone Ground Mustard** (opt.)
1 teaspoon Toasted Sesame Oil** (optional)

1. Bring 2-3 quarts of water to a boil. Stir in the pasta and cook until al dente, stirring occasionally to prevent sticking. Combine the dressing ingredients in a separate bowl.
2. Place the vegetables in a large colander, and pour the boiling pasta water, and the pasta evenly all over. This rinses tbriefly cooks the vegetables. Drain all the water from the colander.
3. Mix the pasta and vegetables with the dressing in a large bowl. Adjust seasonings to taste. Serve immediately and enjoy!

* See CUTTING TO THE CHASE
** See GLOSSARY

MOROCCAN COUSCOUS & VEGETABLES

Prep Time: 15   **Cook Time: 5**   **Serves: 4-6**

Groceries

Couscous, Green or Black Olives, Green, Red and Yellow Pepper, Carrot, Tomato, , Cilantro, Garlic, Lemon, Cumin, Paprika, Ginger.

Do Ahead

Make couscous and refrigerate up to 4 days in advance in a sealed container. Wash vegetables and refrigerate in plastic bags or sealed containers up to 2 days ahead.

Hot Tips

Eliminate fat by omitting the oil. If you do not mind a little fat, various seeds or nuts can be added for flavor and texture. Bulgur, quinoa and rice can be used instead of couscous (see COOKING WHOLE GRAINS chart).

Meal Balance

This is a light balanced dish as is, but you can elaborate by adding cooked chickpeas. If you have time, serve a Sumptuous Soup before and some lightly cooked green vegetables with for a complete meal. Couscous is not a whole grain, but a flour product —have whole grains at another meal during the day.

This authentically seasoned dish can be served as a hot entree if desired, instead of chilled.

3½ cups Vegetable Stock* or Water
½ teaspoon each Saffron, crushed, Sea Salt
1 Carrot, diced ½"
2 cups Couscous (preferably Whole Wheat)
2 small Tomatoes, diced ½"
½ each Green, Red and Yellow Pepper, diced
1 cup (1 small jar) Green or Black Olives
¼ cup Cilantro, minced
¼ cup Italian Parsley, minced

Moroccan Dressing
1/3 cup Lemon Juice
¼ cup Extra Virgin Olive Oil
2 Garlic Cloves, minced
1 teaspoon fresh Ginger, grated
½ teaspoon each Cumin, Paprika + Sea Salt
¼ teaspoon Pepper and Turmeric

1. Bring the stock or water to a low boil with the saffron. Add the sea salt and carrots and cook for 5 minutes or until tender-crisp. Meanwhile combine dressing ingredients.
2. Stir the couscous into the simmering saffron broth, add the dressing and set aside covered for 15 minutes to absorb all the liquid. Fluff couscous into a bowl with a fork to allow steam to escape, cool to room temperature. Chop the olives in ½ or ¼.
3. Mix with the remaining vegetables and chill for 1-3 hours before serving.

Variation: **Hot Moroccan Couscous**
Cook the tomatoes, bell peppers and olives in the broth with the carrots for 5 minutes. Stir in couscous and the dressing and set aside as above. Mix in the cilantro and parsley and serve.

* See Vegetable Stock in TRICKS OF THE TRADE

SPICY SZECHWAN
SOMEN & VEGETABLES

Prep Time: 15   **Cook Time: 0**   **Serves: 4-6**

Groceries

Somen, Soba or Udon Noodles, Chinese Cabbage, Mung Bean Sprouts, Green and Red Pepper, Carrot, Snow Peas, Watercress, Garlic, Ginger, Rice Syrup and Vinegar, Toasted Sesame Oil, Tamari, Dried Crushed Chili.

Do Ahead

Refrigerate dressing in a glass jar for 2 weeks. Cooked noodles store refrigerated for 4 days in a sealed container.

Hot Tips

To eliminate fat omit the oil. Assemble the salad just before serving as it will go limp soon afterwards. Chinese cabbage can be substituted with various types of lettuce - iceberg, romaine, etc.

Meal Balance

This is a grain and vegetable meal all in one. For additional protein, Tempeh Teriyaki or Marinated Tofu go well in this recipe. You may want a Sumptuous Soup before or a complementary side dish such as Dijon Ginger Glazed Butternut (see Veggie Ventures).

This is a pungent one that you can adjust to your taste buds' tolerance. Various oriental noodles such as glass noodles can be used for variety.

Szechwan Dressing
¼ cup Sesame or Peanut Oil
¼ cup Brown Rice Vinegar*
3 tablespoons Tamari*
2 tablespoon Rice Syrup*
1 large Garlic Clove, minced
1 tablespoon fresh Ginger, grated
1 tsp. each Sea Salt and Toasted Sesame Oil*
¼ teaspoon Dried Crushed Chili or to taste

3 cups Chinese Cabbage, fine julienne**
1 cup Mung Bean Sprouts
1 cup Snow Peas, whole or julienne
1 Carrot, grated or fine matchstick**
1 Celery, sliced thin diagonally
½ Green Pepper and ½ Red Pepper, julienne
½ bunch Watercress, chopped 1" sections
¼ cup Cilantro, minced
2 Scallions, finely sliced**
4 cups Somen Noodles, cooked***

1. Combine dressing ingredients and set aside so flavors can marry and develop while you chop the vegetables and cook the noodles. Cool the noodles before mixing.
2. Mix the dressing with the vegetables and noodles in a large bowl. Adjust seasonings to taste and serve.

* See GLOSSARY
** See CUTTING TO THE CHASE
*** (±16 oz. raw) See PASTA in STAPLES

JAPANESE NOODLES
WITH SHIITAKE & ARAME

Prep Time: 10   **Cook Time: 15**   **Serves: 4-6**

Groceries

Genmai or Udon Noodles, Shiitake Mushrooms, Arame, Carrot, Scallions, Ginger, Rice and Umeboshi Vinegar, Rice Syrup, Tamari, Toasted Sesame Oil.

Do Ahead

Cooked noodles keep 4 days refrigerated in a sealed container. Cooked arame and shiitake will store for 1 week refrigerated in sealed containers. The dressing can be made in larger batches and refrigerated in a glass jar for 2 weeks. The completed salad keeps 5 days refrigerated (made with fresh ingredients).

Hot Tips

Double the dressing and use on various fresh leafy green salads, cooked vegetables and to make grain and pasta salads in a snap. To eliminate fat, omit the oil - It will still be delicious. Various noodles; soba, somen, spaghetti can all be substituted.

Meal Balance

This is a nice light meal as is. You can make it more complete and substantial by adding seitan, Tempeh Teriyaki or Marinated Tofu. You can include a greater variety of steamed vegetables.

The black strands of arame dramatically contrast in both color and texture with the white cauliflower and noodles, artfully sliced, bright orange carrots and gorgeous green broccoli flowers.

½ cup dried Shiitake Mushrooms (1 cup fresh)
½ cup dry raw Arame*
2 teaspoons Tamari*
1 large Carrot, thin matchsticks**
1 cup Cauliflowerettes**
1 stalk Broccoli, flowerettes, stems sliced**
3 Scallions, sliced thin diagonally**
1 cup Watercress, chopped
4 cups Genmai or Udon Noodles, cooked***

Japanese Dressing
2 tablespoon fresh Ginger, grated
¼ cup Brown Rice Vinegar*
2 tbsp. Rice Syrup* and Umeboshi Vinegar*
1 tablespoon Toasted Sesame Oil**

1. Soak shiitake mushrooms in 1½ cups water for 10 minutes and soak the arame in 1 cup water for 5 minutes. Remove the tough stems from the mushrooms and slice into ¼" wide strips. Bring shiitake and arame to a boil in separate small pots over medium heat in their soaking water with 1 tsp. tamari, reduce heat and simmer 15 minutes, reduce liquid.
2. In a pot fitted with a steamer basket over boiling water, steam the vegetables until bright and tender-crisp. Mix dressing ingredients.
3. Combine the shiitake, arame, vegetables, noodles and dressing. Chill for 1-3 hours to let flavors marry and develop before serving.

* See GLOSSARY
** See CUTTING TO THE CHASE
*** ±16 oz raw - see PASTA in STAPLES

QUINOA TABOULI

Prep Time: 15   **Cook Time: 20**   **Serves: 4-6**

Groceries

Quinoa, Lemons, Limes, Garlic, Scallions, Cherry Tomatoes, Corn, Italian Parsley, Mint, Cumin, Pine Nuts.

Do Ahead

Refrigerate toasted pine nuts in a glass jar for several weeks. Toast extra to have on hand and use in the Spiced Basmati with Pine Nuts, and as a condiment if desired. The dressing can be made in larger batches and refrigerated in a glass jar for 2 weeks. Cooked quinoa stores up to 5 days refrigerated in a sealed container. The assembled salad will keep 5 days refrigerated (made with fresh quinoa).

Hot Tips

To eliminate fat, omit the oil and nuts. Use bulgur or couscous for variety in place of quinoa. Various fresh herbs; basil, cilantro, dill, etc., can be used instead of the mint and parsley. Freshly squeezed lemons and limes are preferred over bottled juices.

Meal Balance

A simple, complete meal in itself for hot weather. Perhaps serve a Sumptuous Soup before and steamed colorful vegetables on the side. Quinoa is a nutritious grain, and parsley is very high in minerals and vitamins.

Fresh mint and toasted cumin seeds are essential for the height of zest in this tabouli. Cherry tomatoes, corn and pine nuts are a burst of flavor, color and crunch.

2 cups Quinoa, washed and drained
2 Corn Cobs, niblets removed
1 teaspoon Sea Salt
¼ cup Pine Nuts
1 teaspoon Cumin Seeds
½-1 pint Cherry Tomatoes, quartered
½ cup Italian Parsley, minced
2 Scallions, sliced* (green and white parts)
1½ tablespoons fresh Mint, minced

Tabouli Dressing
1/3 cup Lemon Juice
¼ cup Extra Virgin Olive Oil
2 tablespoons Lime Juice
2 Garlic Cloves, minced
½ teaspoon Sea Salt or to taste
¼ teaspoon Pepper or to taste

1. Bring 3½ cups water to a boil with the quinoa. Add the corn and sea salt, reduce heat and simmer 20 minutes or until water is absorbed. Fluff with a fork into a bowl and allow steam to escape. Meanwhile...
2. Toast pine nuts and cumin seeds in a 350°F toaster oven** for 5-10 minutes, or until golden brown. Combine the dressing ingredients with the cumin seeds and add to the hot quinoa. Chill for 1-3 hours. Chop and then refrigerate the tomatoes, parsley and mint together into a separate bowl.
3. Mix the toasted pine nuts and chopped vegetables with the quinoa and dressing. Adjust seasonings to taste and serve.

* See CUTTING TO THE CHASE
** A conventional oven at 350°F is ideal if you are baking
   something else, otherwise too much energy is wasted.

FESTIVE INDONESIAN RICE

Prep Time: 15   **Cook Time: 50**   **Serves: 6**

Groceries

Long Grain, Short Grain and Sweet Brown Rice, Peanuts, Tempeh, Coconut, Scallions, Celery, Mung Bean Sprouts, Raisins, Green and Red Pepper, Red Onion, Garlic, Ginger, Peanut Butter, Apple Cider Vinegar, Cayenne.

Do Ahead

Thaw tempeh 1 hour before using. The peanuts and coconut can be toasted and stored separately in glass jars for several weeks. The dressing will keep for up to 10 days refrigerated in a glass jar. Sort, wash and soak the rice 1-4 hours for best results. Cooked rice keeps up to 5 days refrigerated.

Hot Tips

To eliminate fat; omit oil, peanut butter, peanuts, tempeh, coconut —it will just be less festive. ***Cool rice, then combine with baked tempeh, peanuts, coconut and raisins with the dressing and marinate 1-3 hours (with or without the vegetables) to let the flavors develop. Add vegetables just at the end for a crispier dish.

Meal Balance

This is definitely a complete balanced meal-in-a-bowl. You may want to add some fresh lightly cooked greens.

Let this dish carry your senses away somewhere between the Indian and South Pacific Oceans.

1 cup each Long and Short Grain Brown Rice
½ cup Sweet Brown Rice*
1 - 12 oz. package Tempeh*, cubed ½-¾"
2 tablespoons Toasted Sesame Oil*
2 tablespoons Tamari*
2 teaspoons Ginger Powder
½ cup Peanuts
1 cup dried unsweetened shredded Coconut
½ cup Raisins (Sultana or Thompson)
2 each Celery ribs and Scallions, sliced thin**
1 cup Mung Bean Sprouts
½ each Green and Red Pepper, julienned
1/3 large Red Onion, sliced thin ½ moons
½ cup Apple, Mango or Pineapple diced (opt)
¼ cup Cilantro or Parsley, minced

Indonesian Dressing
1/3 cup Apple, Mango or Pineapple Juice
½ cup Apple Cider Vinegar
3 tablespoons Peanut Butter
1 Garlic Clove, minced
1 teaspoon Sea Salt or to taste
¼-½ tsp. Cayenne, or to taste

1. Bring rice to a boil in 5 cups water over high heat. Add 2 teaspoons sea salt, reduce heat to low and simmer covered 50 minutes.
2. Preheat oven to 375°F. Toss the tempeh with the oil, tamari and ginger to coat evenly. Spread onto a baking tray and bake for 25 minutes or until golden brown. On separate trays, toast the peanuts for 10 minutes and the coconut for 2-3 minutes (watch the coconut carefully because it burns easily).
3. Combine dressing ingredients. Transfer rice to a large bowl to allow steam to escape (see Hot Tips***). Mix all ingredients and serve.

* See GLOSSARY
** See CUTTING TO THE CHASE

NATIVE AMERICAN WILD RICE

Prep Time: 10   **Cook Time: 50**   **Serves: 6**

Groceries

Long Grain, Short Grain, Wehani and Wild Rice, Sunflower Seeds, Corn, Carrot, Celery, Cilantro, Chives, Apple Cider Vinegar, Maple Syrup, Oregano, Mustard, Dried Crushed Chili, Sage.

Do Ahead

Store sunflower seeds refrigerated in a glass jar for several weeks. Toast extra to have on hand and use in Sun Seed Rice Patties and Sunflower Olive Oat Bread if desired. Sort, wash and soak the rice for 1 hour, up to overnight for best results. Refrigerate cooked rice for 5 days in a sealed container. The salad will keep for 5 days refrigerated made with fresh rice. Refrigerate dressing in a glass jar for 2 weeks.

Hot Tips

Omit the oil and seeds to cut fat. Double the dressing and use on various fresh leafy green salads, cooked vegetables and to make grain and pasta salads in a snap.

Meal Balance

This is a meal in a bowl although additional steamed greens may be enjoyed with it. Cooked beans, Seitan Chorizo, Marinated Tofu can be added for more protein and substance.

The delicate mauve chive flowers can be used if you have fresh chives in your garden. Snip at the top of the stem to disperse the cluster and mix into the salad and save some whole flowers for garnish.

1 cup Long Grain Brown Rice
1 cup Short Grain Brown Rice
¼ cup Wehani Rice
¼ cup Wild Rice
2 Corn Cobs, niblets
1 Carrot, sliced ½ moons
½ cup Sunflower Seeds
1 Celery, thinly sliced
2 tbsp. each Chives, Cilantro, Mint, minced

Native American Dressing
½ cup Apple Cider Vinegar
¼ cup Corn Oil
2 tablespoons Maple Syrup*
2 teaspoons Oregano
1 tsp. each Stoneground Mustard*, Sea Salt
½ tsp. each Crushed Dried Chili, ground Sage

1. Bring rice to a boil in 5 cups water over high heat. Add 2 teaspoons sea salt, reduce heat to low and simmer covered 40 minutes. Add the corn and carrots on top (without mixing the rice)and continue to cook for 10 minutes until tender-crisp and bright.
2. Meanwhile toast the sunflower seeds in a 350°F toaster oven** for 5-10 minutes, or until golden brown. Mix dressing ingredients.
3. Transfer cooked rice and vegetables to a large bowl to allow steam to escape and cool.
4. Combine rice and vegetables with celery, fresh herbs, dressing and sunflower seeds. Chill for 1-3 hours before serving so the flavors have a chance to marry and develop.

* See GLOSSARY
** A conventional at 350°F is ideal if you are baking
   something else, otherwise too much energy is wasted.

KASHMIR POTATO SALAD

Prep Time: 20   **Cook Time: 15**   **Serves: 6**

Groceries

Red Potatoes, Green and Red Apple, Radish, Celery, Peas, Pistachios, Cilantro, Silken Tofu, Apple Cider Vinegar, Soymilk, Rice Syrup, Curry, Cayenne.

Do Ahead

Refrigerated toasted cashews in a glass jar for several weeks. Toast extra to have on hand if desired. The dressing can be made in larger batches and refrigerated in a sealed container for 5 days. Cooked potatoes keep 2-3 days refrigerated.

Hot Tips

This tastes better the second day as the flavors have had a chance to marry and develop. Reduce fat by omitting the nuts, and use water instead of soymilk. The dressing can be heated and served as a sauce over many grain, pasta and vegetable dishes. Sweet potatoes can be used instead of the red, Yukon gold or white varieties.

Meal Balance

Potatoes are "a starch" but not as nutritious as whole grains with complex carbohydrates. You can replace all or part of the cooked potatoes with cooked brown rice; basmati, long or short grain. To balance the meal include some leafy greens, as a salad or lightly cooked (see Veggie Ventures).

New red potatoes and sweet peas, toasted pistachios, refreshing celery and pungent radish, crisp, juicy red and tart green apples, are all coated in a creamy curried tofu dressing.

6 medium Red Potatoes (Yukon Gold or White)
½ cup whole Cashews
1 Green Apple and 1 Red Apple, diced ½"*
4 Red Radishes, sliced thin ½ moons*
2 Celery ribs, sliced thin
1/3 cup fresh Peas (or Green Beans diced)
¼ cup Cilantro, minced (or Parsley)

Kashmir Dressing
1 - 10.5 (297 gr.) package Silken Tofu** Lite
2/3 cup Apple Cider Vinegar
2/3 cup Soymilk** (or potato cooking water)
2 tablespoons each Corn Oil, Rice Syrup**
1 tablespoon Curry Powder
1 teaspoon Sea Salt
¼ teaspoon Cayenne or Pepper to taste

1. Boil the potatoes whole in water to cover for 15 minutes or until tender when a skewer is inserted to the center. Toast cashews in a 350°F toaster oven*** for 5-10 minutes, or until golden brown. Meanwhile...
2. Purée all the dressing ingredients until very smooth. Adjust seasonings to taste.
3. Allow potatoes to cool before dicing. Mix all the chopped fruit and vegetables with the nuts and dressing. Chill for 1-3 hours. Mix again just before serving.

* See CUTTING TO THE CHASE
** See GLOSSARY
*** A conventional oven at 350°F is ideal if you're baking something else, otherwise too much energy is wasted.

HOT & SOUR SOUP

Prep Time: 10

Cook Time: 25

Serves: 6

Groceries

Shiitake Mushrooms, Apple Cider or Rice Vinegar, Sake, Ginger, Scallions, Snow Peas, Carrot, Tofu (opt.), Cornstarch, Toasted Sesame Oil.

Do Ahead

Wash and refrigerate the vegetables in plastic bags or sealed containers, ready to chop, up to 3 days in advance. The soup will keep refrigerated for 5 days, or frozen for 3 months.

Hot Tips

Café or white mushrooms may substitute the shiitake, although the flavor of the shiitake is more aromatic, and intense. Use fresh shiitake instead, if desired. You may use vegetable stock or water, in place of the sake if preferred. The toasted sesame oil adds authenticity, flavor and fragrance, but can be omitted to reduce fat.

Meal Balance

Make this into a meal-in-a-bowl; add broccoli for the last few minutes of cooking, until tender-crisp, and add cooked grains or pasta. Serve this before a meal based on grains or pasta and colorful vegetables (see Index and Menu Magician for possibilities).

* See Vegetable Stock in TRICKS OF THE TRADE.

No need to go out for authentic, gourmet Chinese food, when you can create it in your kitchen.

6 large, dried Shiitake Mushrooms
3 tablespoons Ginger, grated
6 cups Vegetables Stock* or Water
18 small Snow Peas (3 per person)
3 Scallions, sliced**, white part + greens
1 straight, slender Carrot sliced into flowers**
½ cup Apple Cider or Rice Vinegar***
¼ cup Sake, or Dry White Wine or Sherry
3 tablespoons Tamari***, or to taste
1½ teaspoons Sea Salt
½ lb. Tofu***, pressed and ½" cubed
2 tablespoons Cornstarch
1 teaspoon Toasted Sesame Oil*** (optional)

1. Reconstitute the shiitake in 2 cups of water for 10 minutes, or until tender. Remove the tough stems, and slice them into strips. Bring to a boil in a 3 quart pot over medium-high heat, with the soaking water. Reduce heat, cover, and simmer 10 minutes.
2. Add the ginger to 5½ cups of the stock or water. Strain it through a fine mesh strainer, into the pot. Squeeze the ginger fibers to extract the flavor and juice. Add the snow peas, white part of scallions, carrot flowers, vinegar, sake, tamari, sea salt and tofu, and bring to a gentle boil. Simmer for 5 minutes.
3. Dissolve cornstarch in remaining ½ cup of stock or water. Stir and simmer into the soup for 1 minute, until clear. Adjust seasonings to taste. Add the oil, if desired, and the scallion greens (except for 2 tablespoons). Serve, and garnish each bowl with a sprinkle of scallions.

* Salted stock reduces the amount of salt added to the soup.
** See CUTTING TO THE CHASE
*** See GLOSSARY

MISO SOUP WITH WAKAME

Prep Time: 10   **Cook Time: 15**   **Serves: 6**

Groceries

Wakame, Onion, Carrot, Daikon, Broccoli, Celery, Scallions, Miso.

Do Ahead

Wash and refrigerate the vegetables, ready to chop, in plastic bags or sealed containers up to 3 days in advance. The soup keeps 5 days refrigerated, and 3 months frozen.

Hot Tips

Do not *boil* the miso, simmer it for 3-4 minutes, or you destroy the medicinal effects of the beneficial bacteria. Use a barley or rice miso, of medium color—fermented for 24 to 36 months—for ideal flavor and health benefits (see Miso in H.H.I.H.). Substitute, or include more vegetables in the soup if desired.

Meal Balance

Add 1 cup of diced tofu during the last 5 minutes of cooking for additional protein and substance. Make this into a meal-in-a-bowl by adding cooked grains or pasta to the soup, and adjust seasonings to taste.

* See GLOSSARY
** See CUTTING TO THE CHASE

This is delicious served with almost any style of main grain or pasta dish. It is a calming, centering and wonderfully nourishing food. Many people have adopted the Japanese custom of starting their day with miso soup.

6" strip dried Wakame*
6 cups Water
1 medium Onion, sliced ½ moons
1 medium Carrot, sliced thin ½ moons
2" section Daikon, sliced thin ¼ or ½ moons
1 Broccoli stalk, flowerettes, stems diced**
1 medium Celery rib, Sliced thin
2 Scallions, sliced (white and green parts)**
±¼ cup Miso*, or to taste

1. Briefly rinse the wakame and soak it in 2 cups of water for 10 minutes. Meanwhile...
2. Bring the remaining 4 cups of water to a boil over medium-high heat with the onion, carrot and daikon. Reduce heat to low and cook for 5 minutes. Meanwhile...
3. Chop the wakame into ½" pieces. Add the wakame and its soaking water to the soup with the broccoli, celery and scallion whites. Return to a boil and cook for 5 minutes or until the broccoli is bright green and tender-crisp. Adjust liquid consistency to your liking.
4. Remove ½ cup of broth from the pot and dissolve the miso in it, removing any lumps. Add the dissolved miso to the soup and simmer for 3-4 minutes, adjusting seasonings to taste. Mix in the scallion greens and serve.

SHIITAKE BROTH
WITH NOODLES, TOFU & WATERCRESS

Prep Time: 10

Cook Time: 15   **Serves: 6**

Groceries

Shiitake Mushrooms, Somen, Soba or Udon Noodles, Kombu, tofu, Watercress, Scallions.

Do Ahead

You may cook and refrigerate the noodles up to 4 days in a sealed container. You may store the broth (without the noodles, tofu and vegetables) for 10 days refrigerated in a sealed container. The soup keeps for 5 days refrigerated, or 3 months frozen.

Hot Tips

Season the broth with a strong tamari flavor, a little saltier than you normally would for a soup because the noodles will absorb a lot of flavor. The kombu is optional, but it adds a delicate sea-like flavor.

Meal Balance

The whole wheat noodles, tofu and vegetables make a balanced, complete, oriental style meal-in-a-bowl. You can use Tempeh Teriyaki or seitan instead of tofu for variety. Simmer broccoli or other vegetables into the broth until tender-crisp if desired.

You will easily understand why this is such a favorite among Japanese food enthusiasts.

6 cups Water
6 large dried Shiitake Mushrooms (12 fresh)
6" long strip of dried Kombu* rinsed briefly
½ lb. Tofu*, pressed** and ½" cubed
1 straight, slender Carrot sliced into flowers***
¼-½ cup Tamari* or to taste
1 teaspoon fresh grated Ginger, or to taste
3 Scallions, sliced*** (white and green parts)
4 cups Udon Noodles, cooked****
¼-½ bunch Watercress, chopped 1"

1. Rinse and reconstitute dried shiitake and kombu in 6 cups of water for 10 minutes. Remove the tough stems and slice into ¼" strips. Bring water, shiitake and kombu to a boil over medium-high heat. Reduce heat and simmer for 10 minutes or until tender.
2. Add the tofu, carrot flowers, tamari, ginger, scallion whites and water if necessary for desired soup consistency and cook for 5 minutes. Adjust seasonings (see Hot Tips).
3. Distribute the noodles among bowls and sprinkle some of the watercress on top of each serving. Ladle the hot broth into each bowl distributing the shiitake mushrooms, tofu and carrot flowers among the servings. Garnish with scallion greens and serve.

* See GLOSSARY
** See Tofu in TRICKS OF THE TRADE
*** See CUTTING TO THE CHASE
**** See PASTA in STAPLES

BORSCH with FRESH DILL
& TOFU SOUR CREAM

Prep Time: 20   **Cook Time: 25**   **Serves: 6**

Groceries

Beets, Carrot, Celery, Cabbage, Leek, Parsnip, Turnip, Fresh Dill, Tomato Purée, Caraway and Dill Seeds, Apple Cider Vinegar, Maple Syrup, Tofu Sour Cream.

Do Ahead

Wash and refrigerate the vegetables in plastic bags or sealed containers up to 3 days ahead. Store the Tofu Sour Cream 5 days, refrigerated in a sealed container. The soup will keep for 5 days refrigerated, or 3 months frozen. Store the soup and Tofu Sour Cream separately.

Hot Tips

Tomato purée, maple syrup and vinegar are optional—they add more height and depth to the flavor (vegetable stock or water can be increased to make up the volume). Purée all or part of the soup, for a smooth as velvet deep red soup or a partially chunky-smooth soup.

Meal Balance

Perfect accompaniment for the Mushroom Vegetable Pie and Herbed Kale & Cauliflower with Poppy Seed Dressing. Plenty of root vegetables to balance a grain based meal with green vegetables on the side.

This soup makes a dramatic presentation served in wide shallow bowls, to expose the gorgeous green, fresh dill sprigs, sitting upon pure white Tofu Sour Cream, in flattering contrast to the deep red soup.

5 cups Vegetable Stock* or Water
3 medium Beets, diced ½"
1 medium Carrot and 1 Celery, diced ½"
1 medium Leek, diced* (white + green parts)
1 medium Parsnip and 1 Turnip diced ½"
1½ cups Cabbage, diced ½"
1 teaspoon each Caraway and Dill Seeds
1-2 teaspoons Sea Salt, or to taste
¼ teaspoon Pepper or to taste
1 cup Tomato Purée (or crushed or chopped)
1 tablespoon Apple Cider Vinegar
1 tablespoon Maple Syrup** (optional)
1 tablespoon Tamari**
2 tablespoon fresh Dill, minced
±1½ cups Tofu Sour Cream, see page 173
6 small perfect fresh dill sprigs for garnish

1. Bring stock** or water to a boil over medium-high heat with the first seven vegetables (except leek greens) and the seeds. Add sea salt and pepper, reduce heat, simmer for 20 minutes covered, or until tender.
2. Add the leek greens, tomato purée, vinegar, syrup, tamari, minced dill and more vegetable stock or water as necessary for the desired soup consistency. Return to a boil and simmer for 5 minutes.
3. Adjust seasonings to taste. Serve with a heaping spoonful of Tofu Sour Cream in each bowl topped with a sprig of dill.

* See Vegetable Stock in TRICKS OF THE TRADE.
  Salted stock reduces the amount of salt added to the soup.
** See GLOSSARY

TTERNUT & BROCCOLI BISQUE

10   **Cook Time: 20**   **Serves: 8**

A fat-free soup that is so delicious and naturally sweet - have an extra serving, and forgo dessert entirely.

Groceries

Butternut Squash, Broccoli, Sweet Potato or Carrot, Onion, Celery, Ginger, Coriander, Basil, Cayenne, Miso, Italian Parsley.

Do Ahead

Wash and refrigerate the vegetables, ready to chop, up to 4 days in advance. This soup keeps for 5 days refrigerated, or 3 months frozen.

Hot Tips

Do not peel the skin of the butternut squash or sweet potato (except for bruises), it becomes tender when cooked and is full of essential fiber. Delicatta squash may substitute for the butternut. Peel buttercup squash, only because the skin is green— otherwise leave the soup chunky (not puréed) and leave the skin on. Collard, kale or watercress may substitute for the broccoli. Use a light-medium or medium color miso for its balance of savory-sweetness, and it will not darken the soup.

Meal Balance

Turn this soup into a meal-in-a-bowl simply by adding cooked rice, various grains or pasta. It is rich in nutrients from both green and orange vegetables. Serve as the start to an Asian, Latin or Mediterranean flavored meal (see index for all the possibilities).

6 cups Vegetable Stock* or Water
1 Butternut Squash** (4 cups), diced
1 Sweet Potato or 2 Carrots (1½ cups) diced
1 medium Onion, diced
1 medium Celery rib, diced
1 tablespoon fresh Ginger, minced
1 teaspoon ground Coriander
1-2 teaspoons Sea Salt
1 stalk Broccoli**, flowerettes, stems diced
1 teaspoon dried Basil or 1 tablespoon fresh
¼ teaspoon Cayenne, or to taste (optional)
2 tablespoons light-medium Miso***, to taste
¼ cup Italian Parsley

1. Bring 6 cups of vegetable stock or water to a boil, in a 3 quart pot over medium-high heat, with the squash, sweet potato, onion, celery, ginger and coriander. Add the sea salt, reduce heat and simmer for 15 minutes or until tender.
2. Purée ¾ of the vegetables with some cooking liquid until very smooth. Return all the soup to the pot. Add the broccoli, basil (if using dried), cayenne and vegetable stock or water as necessary for desired consistency. Bring to a boil and simmer 2 minutes or until the broccoli is bright green and tender-crisp.
3. Dissolve the miso in the soup broth and simmer briefly. Adjust seasonings to taste, mix in the parsley and serve.

* See Vegetable Stock in TRICKS OF THE TRADE.
  Salted stock reduces the amount of salt added to the soup.
** See Winter Squash in CUTTING TO THE CHASE
*** See GLOSSARY

CREAM OF POTATO & LEEK

Prep Time: 15   **Cook Time: 25**   **Serves: 8**

Groceries

Potatoes or Parsnips, Leeks, Onion, Garlic, Rolled Oats, Thyme, Nutmeg, Soymilk, Italian Parsley.

Do Ahead

Wash and refrigerate the vegetables, ready to chop, in plastic bags or sealed containers up to 3 days in advance. The soup keeps 5 days refrigerated, and 3 months frozen.

Hot Tips

Choose the thin skinned potatoes and do not peel them (except for bruises), they are full of fiber and nutrients, and become tender once cooked. Purée all the soup for a silky smooth texture, or purée ½-¾ for a partially chunky-smooth soup. Use parsnips if you are avoiding potatoes, or night shade vegetables in general.

Meal Balance

This is very satisfying and quite filling. Serve it with a light grain or pasta dish and vegetables.

* See Vegetable Stock in TRICKS OF
  THE TRADE. Salt stock reduces the
  amount of salt added to the soup.

Chill this soup and you have a very healthy Vichyssoise. The oats create a rich creamy broth – omit them for a lighter consistency.

5 cups Vegetable Stock* or Water
3 large White Potatoes, (4 cups) diced
2 medium Leeks, white + green parts diced**
1 medium Onion, diced
2 large Garlic Cloves, minced
½ cup Rolled Oats
1 tablespoon dried Thyme, or 3 tbsp. fresh
2 teaspoons Sea Salt, or to taste
½ teaspoon Nutmeg
¼ teaspoon Pepper
½ cup Soymilk (optional)
1-2 tablespoons Tamari***, or to taste
¼ cup Italian Parsley, minced

1. Bring 5 cups of vegetable stock or water to a boil, in a 3 quart pot over medium-high heat, with the vegetables, herbs, spices (except the greens of the leeks and soymilk. Reduce heat to low and simmer for 20 minutes, until tender. Stir occasionally to prevent the oats from lumping on the bottom of the pot.
2. Purée ¾ of the vegetables in a food processor or blender with the soymilk, tamari and some of the cooking liquid until smooth.
3. Return the soup to the pot. Add the leek greens and more stock or water if necessary, for desired consistency. Simmer 5 minutes and adjust seasonings to taste. Stir in the parsley and serve.

** See CUTTING TO THE CHASE
*** See GLOSSARY

SPICY YUCATAN YAM SOUP

15   **Cook Time: 20**   **Serves: 8**

Groceries

Sweet Potato, Spanish Onion, Carrot, Celery, Garlic, Ginger, Bay Leaf, Oregano, Cumin, Coriander, Cilantro, Crushed Dried Chili, Cayenne, Tamari, Pure Coconut Milk (optional).

Do Ahead

Wash and refrigerate vegetables in sealed containers or plastic bags up to 3 days in advance. The soup keeps for 5 days refrigerated, or 3 months frozen.

Hot Tips

Increase the volume of liquid for a light soup, or decrease it for a thick sauce to serve over grains, pasta or vegetables. Do not peel the skin of the sweet potato (except for bruises), it is full of essential fiber, and becomes tender when cooked. Purée all the soup for a silky smooth texture, or purée ½-¾ for a partially chunky-smooth soup.

Meal Balance

This is packed with nutritious orange vegetables. Make this into a meal-in-a-bowl; simmer in chopped broccoli or leafy greens during the last few minutes of cooking, until bright in color and tender-crisp, and mix in cooked basmati rice, or various cooked grains or pasta and adjust seasoning to taste as the grains and pasta will absorb flavor.

The culinary style of the lush, beautiful Yucatan Peninsula in Mexico is inspiration for this soup. Replace the coconut milk with soymilk for a lower fat version, or water for fat-free!

5 cups Vegetable Stock* or Water
2 large Sweet Potatoes, (4 cups) diced
1 large Spanish Onion, diced
1 medium Carrots, diced
1 medium Celery ribs, diced
1 large Garlic Clove, minced
1 tablespoon fresh Ginger, minced
1 large Bay Leaf
1-2 teaspoons Sea Salt, or to taste
1 teaspoon each ground Coriander, Cumin
1 teaspoon dried Oregano
¼-½ Crushed Dried Chili, or to taste
¼ teaspoon Cayenne, or to taste
¼ cup Cilantro, minced (roots and greens)
1 cup Pure Coconut Milk
1-2 tablespoons Tamari**, or to taste

1. Bring 5 cups of vegetable stock or water to a boil, in a 3 quart pot over medium-high heat, with the vegetables. Add garlic, ginger, bay leaf, sea salt, herbs and spices. Add the cilantro roots, minced, if available. Reduce heat to low and simmer for 15 minutes.
2. Purée ¾ of the vegetables in a food processor or blender with the coconut milk, tamari and some of the cooking liquid until smooth.
3. Return the soup to the pot and add stock or water if necessary for desired consistency. Simmer for 5 minutes and adjust seasonings to taste. Stir in the cilantro greens and serve.

* See Vegetable Stock in TRICKS OF THE TRADE. Salted stock reduces the amount of salt added to the soup.
** See GLOSSARY

CREAM OF CARROT WITH CORIANDER

Prep Time: 10   **Cook Time: 20**   **Serves: 6**

Groceries

Carrots, Potatoes, Onion, Garlic, Ground Coriander, Miso, Fresh Coriander (Cilantro).

Do Ahead

Wash and refrigerate the vegetables in plastic bags or sealed containers up to 3 days in advance. The soup will keep for 5 days refrigerated, or 3 months frozen.

Hot Tips

If the fresh coriander comes with their roots still attached, mince them and cook in from the beginning with the vegetables. Use a miso that is medium-dark for the deep rich flavor. White or pale miso is a little too light and sweet and the very dark miso is too bitter, and will color the soup to a brownish orange. Potatoes may substitute the parsnips for variety and a delicate flavor.

Meal Balance

Grains or pasta based dishes, and some lightly cooked greens will balance and complete a nutritious meal (see index for all the possibilities).

This is perfect with a variety of ethnic styles - a colorful, savory, naturally sweet beginning to many meals from cuisines around the world.

5 cups Vegetable Stock* or Water
4-6 Carrots, (4 cups) chopped
2 small Parsnips, (1½ cups), chopped
1 large or Spanish Onion, chopped
1 Garlic Clove, minced
2 teaspoons ground Coriander
1-2 teaspoons Sea Salt or to taste
1 tablespoon medium-dark Miso** or to taste
4-5 sprigs fresh Coriander (Cilantro, minced

1. Bring vegetable stock or water to a boil over medium-high heat with the carrots, potatoes, onion, garlic and ground coriander. Add sea salt, reduce heat to low and simmer for 15 minutes or until the carrots and potatoes are tender.
2. Purée the vegetables in a food processor or blender with the miso and some cooking liquid until smooth.
3. Return the soup to the pot and add stock or water if necessary for desired consistency. Simmer for 5 minutes and adjust seasonings to taste. Stir in fresh coriander and serve.

* Salted stock reduces the amount of salt added to the soup. See Vegetable Stock in TRICKS OF THE TRADE.
** See GLOSSARY

HEARTY ♥ MINESTRONE

Prep Time: 15   **Cook Time: 30**   **Serves: 8**

Groceries

Navy Beans (cooked), Pasta, Onion, Celery, Carrot, Mushrooms, Squash, Zucchini, Cabbage, Spinach, Basil, Oregano, Thyme, Tomato Purée, Tamari, Italian Parsley.

Do Ahead

Wash and refrigerate the vegetables, ready to chop, up to 3 days sealed in plastic bags or sealed containers. You may cook and refrigerate the beans and pasta up to 4 days in advance. This soup keeps for 5 days (made with fresh beans and pasta) refrigerated. Make a double recipe and freeze for 3 months in serving-size containers.

Hot Tips

Vary the beans—use chickpeas, pinto, kidney, black, etc.— and vary the style of pasta for a new version every time you make the soup. Add cooked grains instead of pasta if desired. Tomato purée is optional—it adds dimension to the flavor—you may substitute vegetable stock or water.

Meal Balance

This is so complete and filling, all you may want is a salad or lightly cooked green vegetables on the side for a balanced meal (see Veggie Ventures and the index for all the possibilities.

A soup to nourish the heart and soul, and totally satisfy your appetite.

6-8 cups Water
1 medium Onion, Carrot + Celery, diced ½"
1 cup Squash*, diced ½"
4 oz. Mushrooms, quartered
1 cup Cabbage, diced ½"
1 medium Zucchini, diced ½"
1 cup Tomato Purée (or crushed or chopped)
2 teaspoons Sea Salt, or to taste
1 teaspoon dried Basil or 1 tbsp. fresh
½ teaspoon each dried Oregano and Thyme
1/8 teaspoon Pepper, or to taste
1 cup Navy Beans** + 1-2 cups cooking liquid
1 cup raw Pasta, or 2 cups cooked***
½ bunch fresh Spinach (or ½ 10 oz. package)
2 tablespoons Tamari****, or to taste
¼ cup Italian Parsley, minced

1. Bring water to a boil over medium- high heat with the onion, carrot, celery, squash and mushrooms. Reduce heat and simmer for 15 minutes, or until tender.
2. Add the cabbage, zucchini, tomato purée, sea salt, herbs, pepper and beans (including bean cooking liquid) and return to a boil. If you are using raw pasta, add it now. Simmer for 5 minutes or until pasta is cooked.
3. Add the spinach and tamari along with water if necessary for desired consistency. If using cooked pasta, add it now. Simmer for 5 minutes. Adjust seasonings to taste. Mix in the parsley and serve.

* Buttercup, Butternut or Delicatta (see Winter Squash in CUTTING TO THE CHASE)
** Cooked, see COOKING BEANS chart in STAPLES
*** See PASTA in STAPLES
**** See GLOSSARY

SUMMER CORN CHOWDER

Prep Time: 15   **Cook Time: 20**   **Serves: 6**

Groceries

Corn, Carrot, Onion, Celery, Red Potatoes, Summer Squash, Peas or Green Beans, Red Pepper, Ginger, Garlic, Miso, Cayenne, Scallions, Cilantro or Italian Parsley.

Do Ahead

You may wash and refrigerate the vegetables in plastic bags or sealed containers, ready to chop, up to 3 days in advance. The soup will keep refrigerated for 5 days, or frozen for 3 months.

Hot Tips

If the fresh coriander comes with their roots still attached, mince them and sauté with the onions. To eliminate fat omit the oil and sautéing step and simply boil everything together until tender. The light-medium miso is sweet and will keep the color and flavor light and summery.

Meal Balance

To make this into a meal-in-a bowl add cooked grains or pasta, and cooked beans if desired. Serve this as a beginning to a grain or pasta based meal. Add a salad or lightly cooked greens to balance this as a complete meal.

While fresh corn is abundant, this soup is a wonderful way to enjoy it.

6 Corn Cobs, niblets removed
2 small Red Potatoes, diced ½" (don't peel)
1-2 teaspoons Sea Salt, or to taste
1 tablespoon Corn Oil
1 large or Spanish Onion, diced
1 Garlic Clove, minced
1 tablespoon Ginger, minced
1 Carrot, 1 Celery and ½ Red Pepper, diced
1 small Summer Squash, diced
½ cup fresh Peas or Green Beans, diced
2 Scallions, sliced* (white and green parts)
¼ teaspoon Cayenne or to taste
1-2 tablespoon light-medium Miso**, to taste
¼ cup Cilantro or Italian Parsley

1. Bring 5 cups of vegetable stock*** or water to a boil over medium-high heat with the corn and potatoes. Add the sea salt, reduce heat, simmer 15 minutes, until tender.
2. Heat a stainless steel skillet over medium heat with the oil and sauté the onion, garlic and ginger until translucent (plus cilantro roots if available). Add the carrot, celery and red pepper and sauté until tender. Mix in the squash, peas, scallion whites and cayenne, and cook covered for 5 minutes.
3. Purée half of the corn and potatoes in a food processor or blender with the miso and some cooking liquid until smooth.
4. Return the soup to the pot with the sautéed vegetables (scrape all the juices from the skillet) and add stock or water as necessary for the desired soup consistency. Simmer 5 minutes and adjust seasonings to taste. Stir in the scallion greens and cilantro and serve.

* See Scallions in CUTTING TO THE CHASE
** See GLOSSARY
*** Salted stock reduces the amount of salt added to the soup.
    See Vegetable Stock in TRICKS OF THE TRADE.

MANALI LODGE LENTIL DAHL

Prep Time: 10   **Cook Time: 30**   **Serves: 8**

Groceries

Red Lentils, Onion, Carrot, Potato or Parsnip, Ginger, Bay Leaves, Curry, Cinnamon Sticks, Cayenne, Cilantro.

Do Ahead

You may cook and refrigerate the lentils in a sealed container up to 4 days before using in the recipe. Wash and refrigerate the vegetables in a plastic bag or sealed container up to 3 days in advance. The soup will keep for 5 days (made from fresh lentils) refrigerated and 3 months frozen.

Hot Tips

Cook extra lentils to use in the Red Lentil Paté. Increase the volume of liquid for a light soup or decrease it for a thick stew to serve over rice. To eliminate fat, omit the oil and sauté step, and simply boil everything together.

Meal Balance

Make this into a meal-in-a-bowl; simmer in chopped broccoli or leafy greens during the last few minutes of cooking, until bright in color and tender-crisp, and mix in cooked basmati rice, or various grains or pasta and adjust seasonings to taste as the grains and pasta will absorb flavor.

* See Vegetable Stock in TRICKS OF THE TRADE.

Trekking in the Himalayas restores one's humility. The lean, strong natives truly live in harmony with their environment. They served us this dish on a bed of rice, with steamed, freshly picked local spinach.

8 cups Vegetable Stock* or Water
2 cups Red Lentils, sorted and washed
2 large Bay Leaves
2 small Cinnamon Sticks
2 tablespoons Corn Oil**
2 tablespoons Curry Powder
1 tablespoon Ginger, minced
1 medium Onion, diced ½"
1 medium Carrot, diced ½"
1 medium Potato, diced ½" (or Parsnip)
2 teaspoons Sea Salt or to taste
¼ teaspoon Cayenne or to taste
¼ cup Cilantro, minced

1. In a 3 quart enamel coated or stainless steel pot bring 6 cups of vegetable stock or water to a boil over medium-high heat with the lentils, bay leaves and cinnamon sticks. Reduce heat to low and simmer 20 minutes.
2. Heat a skillet over medium heat with the oil and sauté the curry and ginger briefly to flavor the oil. Add the vegetables and sauté until tender, approximately 2 minutes.
3. Scrape the sautéed vegetables with all their juices into the lentils. Add stock or water to desired consistency with the sea salt and cayenne, return to a low boil and simmer for 5 minutes. Adjust seasonings to taste, add cilantro and serve.

* Salted stock reduces the amount of salt added to the soup.
** See TRICKS OF THE TRADE

LEBANESE LENTIL SOUP

Prep Time: 15   **Cook Time: 40**   **Serves: 8**

Groceries

Green Lentils, Onion, Garlic, Carrot, Celery, Mushrooms, Zucchini, Cinnamon, Basil, Bay Leaves, Dried Crushed Chili, Nutmeg, Rosemary, Thyme, Parsley, Tamari, Kombu (opt.).

Do Ahead

You may cook and refrigerate the lentils in a sealed container up 4 days in advance. Wash and refrigerate the vegetables, ready to chop, in plastic bags or sealed containers up to 3 days in advance. The soup keeps 5 days refrigerated and 3 months frozen.

Hot Tips

Eliminate fat by omitting the oil and sauté step—simply boil everything together. Make this into a stew simply by reducing the volume of liquid. Make extra lentils for the Laurentian Lentil Tortière. Substitute half or all the lentils with ground seitan for variety.

Meal Balance

Serve this legume based soup before your main dish of grains or pasta and include some lightly cooked green vegetables or a salad for a complete balanced meal (see Index for all the possibilities.

** See GLOSSARY

Lebanese chefs have a way with lentils, naturally balancing flavors and textures, herbs and spices in perfect harmony.

6 cups Vegetable Stock* or Water
1 cup Green Lentils, sorted and washed
2 Bay Leaves + 2" strip dried kombu** (opt.)
1 tablespoon Sesame Oil
1 medium Onion, 1 medium Carrot, diced ½"
2 medium Garlic Cloves, minced
1 medium Celery, diced ½"
1 teaspoon Sea Salt, or to taste
1 tsp. each dried Basil and ground Cinnamon,
½ tsp. each Rosemary (crushed), dried Thyme
¼ tsp. each Crushed Chili, Nutmeg, Pepper
1 medium Zucchini, diced ½"
4 oz. Mushrooms, sliced
2 tablespoons Tamari**, or to taste
¼ cup Italian Parsley, minced

1. Bring stock or water to a boil in a 3 quart pot with the lentils, bay leaves and kombu over medium-high heat. Reduce heat, simmer for 30 minutes or until the lentils are tender.
2. Heat a skillet over medium heat with the oil and sauté the onion, garlic, carrot and celery until tender, 2 minutes. Add zucchini and mushrooms with the sea salt, herbs and spices and cook for 2 minutes.
3. Scrape the sautéed vegetables and all their juices into the pot of lentils. Add the tamari and stock or water to desired consistency. Bring to a boil and simmer for 10 minutes. Adjust seasonings to taste. Mix in parsley and serve.

* See Vegetable Stock in TRICKS OF THE TRADE. Salted stock reduces the amount of salt added to the soup.

BARLEY with MUSHROOMS & LEEKS

Prep Time: 10   **Cook Time: 45**   **Serves: 8**

Groceries

Pearled or Pot Barley, Leeks, Mushrooms, Oregano, Dill or Italian Parsley, Scallions, Miso.

Do Ahead

Soak the barley for 1 hour, or overnight for quicker cooking and more tender, digestible grains. You may cook and refrigerate the barley in a sealed container up to 4 days in advance. Wash and refrigerate the vegetables, ready to chop, in plastic bags or sealed containers up to 3 days in advance. The soup keeps refrigerated 5 days, and 3 months frozen.

Hot Tips

Use Café, Shiitake or White mushrooms, or a combination. Do not *boil* the miso, simmer it for 3-4 minutes, or you destroy the medicinal effects of the beneficial bacteria. Use a barley or rice miso, of medium color, fermented for 24 to 36 months, for ideal flavor and health benefits (see Miso in H.H.I.H.). Substitute, or include more vegetables in the soup if desired.

Meal Balance

This is a light yet filling grain based meal-in-a-bowl. For a full course meal, serve this with one of the Fasta Pasta dishes and a salad, or lightly cooked green vegetables.

According to ancient wisdom, barley, mushrooms and leeks cleanse and stimulate and bring new creativity and energy into our lives, corresponding with spring, nature's time for new growth.

1 cup Pearled or Pot Barley, sorted, washed
2 cups Water
6 cups Vegetable Stock* or Water
8 ounces Mushrooms, sliced
2 medium Leeks, white + green parts sliced**
2 Scallions, white + green parts sliced**
1 tablespoon dried Oregano (or 3 tbsp. fresh)
1 teaspoon Sea Salt, or to taste
2 tablespoons Miso*** (medium color)
¼ cup fresh Dill or Italian Parsley, minced

1. Soak the barley in 2 cups of water in a 3 quart soup pot. Bring to a boil with the 6 cups of stock or water over medium-high heat. Reduce heat to low and simmer for 30 minutes, or until tender.
2. Add the mushrooms, white part of the leeks and scallions, dried oregano and sea salt. Return to a boil, simmer for 5 minutes.
3. Remove ½ cup of broth from the pot and dissolve the miso in it, removing any lumps. Add the dissolved miso and leek greens to the soup and simmer for 3-4 minutes, until bright green and tender. Adjust seasonings to taste. Mix in the fresh oregano (if using), scallion greens and dill and serve.

* See Vegetable Stock in TRICKS OF THE TRADE. Salted stock reduces the amount of salt added to the soup.
** See CUTTING TO THE CHASE
*** See GLOSSARY

SPLIT PEAS & VEGETABLES

Prep Time: 15   **Cook Time: 35**   **Serves: 8**

Groceries

Green Split Peas, Onion, Carrot, Celery, Parsnip, Squash, Basil, Bay Leaf, Sage, Thyme, Tamari, Italian Parsley, Toasted Sesame Oil, Kombu (opt.)

Do Ahead

You may cook and refrigerate the lentils in a sealed container up 4 days in advance. Wash and refrigerate the vegetables, ready to chop, in plastic bags or sealed containers up to 3 days in advance. The soup keeps refrigerated 5 days, and 3 months frozen.

Hot Tips

Eliminate fat by omitting the oil and sautéing step, simply boil the vegetables in with the puréed split peas. Cooking time for split peas will depend on their freshness, the older they are the longer they take to become soft. Soak the split peas several hours or overnight, and use the bay leaf and kombu to aid in the softening process. Use yellow split peas or lentils instead of green split peas for variety.

Meal Balance

This is a legume based soup that will balance a grain or pasta main meal. Include a salad or lightly cooked green vegetables to balance the orange root vegetables in the soup.

Mom's split pea soup was, "thick enough to stand your spoon in". In this recipe, fragrant oil and seasonings enhance the bouquet and depth of flavor, instead of the traditional ham bone.

2 cups Green Split Peas
2 large Bay Leaves + 2" strip dried Kombu
1 tbsp. each Corn Oil + Toasted Sesame Oil
1 medium Onion, 1 medium Carrot, diced ½"
1 medium Celery rib and 1 Parsnip, diced ½"
1 cup Squash**, diced ½"
1 teaspoon each dried Basil and Marjoram
½ teaspoon each ground Sage + dried Thyme
1 teaspoon Sea Salt, or to taste
2 tablespoons Tamari*, or to taste
¼ cup Italian Parsley, minced

1. Bring 8 cups <u>unsalted</u> stock*** or water to a boil, in a 3 quart pot, with the split peas, bay leaves and kombu (if using) over medium-high heat. Reduce heat and simmer for 30 minutes or until tender.
2. Heat a skillet over medium heat with the oil and sauté the vegetables until tender and browned, 5-10 minutes. Add the herbs and sea salt and cook for 5 minutes.
3. Remove the bay leaves. Purée the split peas in a food processor or blender with some of the cooking liquid until smooth. Return all the split peas and liquid to the pot.
4. Add the sautéed vegetables, and scrape all their juices into the pot. Add the tamari and more stock or water if necessary for desired consistency. Bring to a boil and simmer for 5 minutes. Adjust seasonings to taste. Mix in parsley and serve.

* See GLOSSARY
** Buttercup, Butternut or Delicatta (see Winter Squash in CUTTING TO THE CHASE)
*** See Vegetable Stock in TRICKS OF THE TRADE.

GARBANZO & ZUCCHINI BISQUE

Prep Time: 10   **Cook Time: 25**   **Serves: 6**

Groceries

Garbanzo Beans (Chickpeas), Zucchini, Onion, Garlic, Celery, Miso, Basil, Bay Leaves, Oregano, Rosemary, Italian Parsley.

Do Ahead

You may cook and refrigerate the beans up to 4 days in advance. Wash and refrigerate the vegetables in plastic bags or sealed containers up to 3 days in advance. The soup keeps refrigerated 5 days, and 3 months frozen.

Hot Tips

Pinto beans, white beans, lentils, etc. can be used in place of the garbanzo beans. You may purée all, part, or none of the soup for the consistency you desire. Use a light-medium or medium color miso for its balance of savory-sweetness—and it will not darken the soup too much.

Meal Balance

Serve this bean rich soup followed by Risotto Florentine, Grilled Vegetable Polenta, one of the Fasta Pasta dishes or one of the other harmoniously seasoned entrées. All you need are grains or pasta and a salad or lightly cooked green vegetables for a complete balanced meal.

This is a luxurious, rich soup, generously herbed and seasoned without being heavy - a perfect beginning to meals of Latin origin or with a Mediterranean flair.

6 cups Vegetable Stock* or Water
1 medium Onion, diced
1 medium Celery, diced
1 large or 2 small Garlic Cloves, minced
1 teaspoon Sea Salt, or to taste
3 medium Zucchini, diced
3 cups Garbanzo Beans cooked**
1 teaspoon dried Basil or 1 tablespoon fresh
½ teaspoon dried Oregano or ½ tbsp. fresh
½ teaspoon dried Rosemary or ½ tbsp. fresh
¼ teaspoon Pepper or to taste
2 tablespoons light-medium Miso***, to taste
¼ cup Italian Parsley, minced

1. Bring vegetable stock or water to a boil over medium-high heat with the celery, onion and garlic. Add the sea salt, reduce heat, and simmer 10 minutes.
2. Add zucchini, beans, herbs and pepper, return to a boil, and simmer for 10 minutes.
3. Purée half of the beans and vegetables in a food processor or blender with the miso and some cooking liquid until smooth.
4. Return the soup to the pot, with vegetable stock or water as necessary for the desired soup consistency. Simmer 5 minutes and adjust seasonings to taste. Stir in parsley and serve.

* See Vegetable Stock in TRICKS OF THE TRADE. Salted stock reduces the amount of salt added to the soup.
** See COOKING BEANS in STAPLES
*** See GLOSSARY

FRENCH ONION SOUP

Prep Time: 10   **Cook Time: 20**   **Serves: 6**

Groceries

Onion, Garlic, Basil, Tarragon, Thyme, Toasted Sesame Oil, Tamari, Italian Parsley.

Do Ahead

Peel and trim the onions and refrigerate in a plastic bag or sealed container up to 5 days in advance. The soup keeps for 5 days refrigerated, or 3 months frozen.

Hot Tips

To eliminate fat, omit the oil and sautéing step, simply boil all the ingredients together (except parsley) for 20 minutes.

Meal Balance

This is wonderful with the Tomato Leek Quiche or the Cauliflower Rizoulet Almandine. It is simple and versatile to serve with almost any cuisine's main grain or pasta dish. Complement the meal with colorful cooked vegetables or a salad (see Index for all the possibilities).

It is amazing how a simple soup, with so few ingredients, can taste so rich and satisfying. The flavor and texture of the corn and toasted sesame oil resemble the traditional butter and bacon drippings.

1 tablespoon Corn Oil*
1 tablespoon Toasted Sesame Oil*
3 medium Onions, sliced thin ½ moons
2 large Garlic Cloves, minced
1 teaspoon dried Basil
1 teaspoon dried Tarragon
1 teaspoon dried Thyme
1 teaspoon Sea Salt, or to taste
¼ teaspoon Pepper, or to taste
8 cups Vegetable Stock** or Water
¼ cup Tamari***, or to taste
¼ cup Italian Parsley, minced

1. Heat an enamel coated or stainless steel 3 quart soup pot over medium heat with the oil, and sauté the onions until browned and caramelized, 5-10 minutes. Add the garlic, herbs, sea salt and pepper and sauté for 2 minutes.
2. Add the stock or water and bring to a boil in the same pot with the sautéed vegetables. Reduce heat and simmer for 5 minutes. Adjust seasonings to taste. Mix in parsley and serve.

* See TRICKS OF THE TRADE
** See Vegetable Stock in TRICKS of the TRADE. Salted stock reduces the amount of salt added to the soup.
*** See GLOSSARY

GAZPACHO SEVILLANO

Prep Time: 20   **Cook Time: 0**   **Serves: 4**

Groceries

Tomatoes and/or Tomato Purée, Cucumber, Green Red Pepper, Red Onion, Garlic, Balsamic or Red Wine Vinegar, Tarragon, Basil, Cumin, Cayenne, Scallions, Cilantro or Italian Parsley.

Do Ahead

Prepare the soup and refrigerate for up to 5 days. There is no cooking involved in this recipe (although you may if desired). Freeze the soup for up to 3 months, although this changes the texture.

Hot Tips

Eliminate fat by omitting the oil. This soup tastes better after it has had a chance to marinate for a day or more. Use the high quality organic tomato purée for the best flavor, when vine ripened fresh tomatoes are not available.

Meal Balance

This is a light beginning to a meal with a Mediterranean or Latin flair. Serve with a grain or pasta entrée and a salad or lightly cooked green vegetables.

* See CUTTING TO THE CHASE
** See Vegetable Stock in TRICKS OF
    THE TRADE. Salted stock reduces the
    amount of salt added to the soup.

Perfect for hot and hazy weather - zesty, refreshing and full of character.

6 medium Tomatoes or 28 oz. Tomato Purée
1 large Cucumber, peeled, quartered, seeded*
1 small Green Pepper, quartered and seeded
1 small Red Pepper, quartered and seeded
1 small Red Onion, quartered
3 small Scallions, sliced (white + green parts)*
2 medium Garlic Cloves, chopped
¼ cup Olive Oil
3 tablespoon Balsamic or Red Wine Vinegar
1 tbsp. fresh Basil, minced or 1 tsp. dried
1 tbsp. fresh Tarragon, minced or 1 tsp. dried
1 teaspoon Sea Salt, or to taste
½ teaspoon ground Cumin
¼ teaspoon Pepper, or to taste
4 cups Vegetable Stock** or Water
2 tbsp. Cilantro or Italian Parsley, minced

1. Slice 5 of the tomatoes in half across and squeeze to remove the seeds, reserving the juices. Coarsely chop the 5 tomatoes, ¾ of the cucumber, ¾ of both the green and red peppers, and ¾ of the red onion into chunks.
2. Purée the tomato, cucumber, bell peppers and red onion chunks in a food processor or blender, with the white part of the scallions, garlic, oil, vinegar herbs, sea salt and spices. Purée with enough stock or water and tomato juices for a smooth soup-like consistency. Adjust seasonings to taste. Chill for 1 hour.
3. Seed the remaining tomato and dice fine, into ¼-½" cubes. Dice into ¼"-½" cubes; the remaining cucumber, green and red peppers, and the red onion. Serve the soup garnished with the diced vegetables, scallion greens and cilantro or parsley.

AWESOME AUTUMN VEGETABLES

Prep Time: 15   **Cook Time: 35**   **Serves: 6**

Groceries

Onion, Carrot, Parsnip, Corn, Rutabaga, Squash, Daikon (opt.), Rosemary, Sage, Italian Parsley, Arrowroot.

Do Ahead

Wash and refrigerate the vegetables in plastic bags or sealed containers up to 5 days in advance. The stew keeps for 5 days refrigerated, or for 3 months frozen.

Hot Tips

To save time and eliminate fat simply boil everything together—omit the oil and sautéing step. Chop the vegetables into 1" chunks for best stew consistency and cook them until very tender and sweet. To simplify you can reduce the variety of vegetables. Or, if desired, you can increase the selection of vegetables.

Meal Balance

Serve this with grains or pasta and some lightly cooked green vegetables, or a fresh leafy salad (see Veggie Ventures).

* Buttercup, Butternut or Delicatta (see Winter Squash in CUTTING TO THE CHASE)

The long, slow cooking creates enduring warmth, making this ideal in cold weather. Naturally sweet vegetables stabilize blood sugar levels, reducing cravings for desserts and sweets.

1 tablespoon Corn Oil
1 large or Spanish Onion, diced
1 teaspoon Sea Salt
½ teaspoon Rosemary, crushed
¼ teaspoon Sage
2 Corn Cobs, niblets removed
2 cups Squash, diced*
1 small Rutabaga, diced
1 cup Daikon Radish, diced (optional)
2 medium Parsnips, diced
2 medium Carrots, diced
±2½ cups Vegetable Stock** or Water
±2 tablespoons Arrowroot*** or Cornstarch
2 tablespoons Italian Parsley, minced

1. Heat an enamel coated or stainless steel heavy pot over medium heat with the oil, and sauté the onion until translucent, 2 minutes. Add the sea salt and herbs, cook for 1 minute.
2. Layer the vegetables in the order listed, on top of the sautéed onions, with enough stock or water to half cover the vegetables. Bring to a boil, reduce heat and simmer for 20 minutes or until very tender and sweet.
3. Adjust seasonings to taste. Dissolve arrowroot in 2 tablespoons of water, and simmer until clear and thickened. Mix in parsley and serve.

** See Vegetable Stock in TRICKS OF THE TRADE. Salted stock reduces the amount of salt added to the stew.
*** See GLOSSARY

BRAZILIAN BLACK BEANS

Prep Time: 15　　　　　　　　**Cook Time: 35**　　　　　　　　**Serves: 6**

Groceries

Black Beans, Coriander, Bay Leaves, Cumin, Ginger, Garlic, Aniseed, Rosemary, Thyme, Dried Crushed Chili, Green and Red Pepper, Onion, Carrot, Corn, Celery, Tamari.

Do Ahead

Cooked beans will store for up to 4 days refrigerated in a sealed container before cooking into the recipe. The stew keeps refrigerated for 5 days (made with fresh beans), or 3 months frozen, either as a whole, or in serving size containers.

Hot Tips

Save time and eliminate fat by simply boiling everything together—omit the oil and sautéing step.
You can substitute various beans in this recipe, and include more, or fewer vegetables, as desired. You can turn this into a soup by increasing volume of liquid and seasonings to taste.

Meal Balance

Serve this with Quinoa Polenta with Delicatta Squash, grains or pasta and some lightly cooked green vegetables or a fresh leafy salad (see Veggie Ventures).

* See GLOSSARY
** See COOKING BEANS chart
　in STAPLES

Bright yellow corn, orange carrot and vibrant red pepper complement the green pepper and celery, against the richly spiced black of the beans - truly reflecting the gaiety and brilliance of Brazil.

2 tablespoons Olive Oil
2 teaspoons Toasted Sesame Oil*
2 teaspoons Ginger, minced
2 tsp. each Cumin Seeds, crushed Rosemary
1 tsp. each Aniseed, Coriander, Thyme,
¼ tsp. each Dried Crushed Chili, Pepper
2 medium Bay Leaves
1 teaspoon Sea Salt or to taste
1 medium Onion, 1 Carrot + 1 Celery, diced
3 Garlic Cloves, minced
½ each Green and Red Pepper, diced
1 Corn Cob, niblets removed
4 cups Black Beans, cooked** (or canned)
± 4 cups Vegetable Stock*** or Water
1 tablespoon Tamari* or to taste
¼ cup Cilantro or Italian Parsley, minced

1. Heat an enamel coated or stainless steel pot over medium heat with the oil, and toast the ginger, herbs, spices, bay leaves and sea salt for 2 minutes to flavor the oil. Add the onion and garlic and sauté until tender, 2 minutes. Add the remaining vegetables and sauté until tender, approximately 5 minutes.
2. Add the beans (with their cooking juices) and enough stock or water to achieve a stew consistency and bring to a boil. Reduce heat and simmer for 25 minutes.
3. Add the tamari while simmering, adjust seasonings to taste and consistency to your liking (the beans will thicken up a lot as they cool and absorb the liquid). Mix in the cilantro or parsley and serve.

*** See Vegetable Stock in TRICKS OF THE TRADE. Salted stock reduces the amount of salt added to the stew.

JAMAICAN KIDNEY BEANS

Prep Time: 10

Cook Time: 25

Serves: 6

Groceries

Kidney Beans, Spanish Onion, Garlic, Tomato, Green Pepper, Maple Syrup, Mustard Powder, Thyme, Allspice, Marjoram, Bay Leaves.

Do Ahead

Cooked beans store up to 4 days refrigerated in a sealed container, before cooking into the recipe. Wash and refrigerate the vegetables in plastic bags or sealed containers up to 3 days in advance. The stew keeps for 5 days refrigerated (made with fresh beans), or 3 months frozen, either as a whole, or in serving size containers.

Hot Tips

Vary the vegetables, omit the tomatoes if desired, and include carrots, squash, sweet potato, etc. Rice syrup—up to double the volume as it is less sweet—may be used in place of maple syrup. Substitute any kind of beans for the kidney beans.

Meal Balance

Serve this with the Caribbean Risi e Bisi (see Chapter 4), or other grain or pasta dishes. Include green and orange vegetables, as salads or cooked, for a balanced meal.

This stew is spicy and sweet, reflecting the flavors of Jamaican cuisine. It is also fat-free - no oil or sauteing - simply boil and serve.

1 Spanish Onion, diced ½"
4 Garlic Cloves, minced
4 cups Tomatoes, chopped
1 large Bay Leaf
2 teaspoons Mustard Powder
1½ teaspoons Sea Salt, or to taste
1 teaspoon ground Allspice
1 teaspoon Marjoram
1 teaspoon Thyme
¼ teaspoon Pepper, or to taste
4 cups Kidney Beans, cooked* or canned
± 2½ cups Vegetable Stock** or Water
¼ cup Maple Syrup***
1 large Green pepper, diced

1. In an enamel coated or stainless steel 3 quart pot, place all the ingredients (except the green pepper), layering, in the order listed. Add enough stock or water for a stew-like consistency, and bring to a boil over medium-high heat. Reduce heat to low, and simmer covered for 20 minutes.
2. Add the green pepper, cover, and simmer for 2-5 minutes, or until bright green and tender-crisp. Adjust seasonings to taste and serve.

* See COOKING BEANS chart in STAPLES
** See Vegetable Stock in TRICKS OF THE TRADE. Salted stock reduces the amount of salt added to the stew.
*** See GLOSSARY

SUCCULENT SUCCOTASH

Prep Time: 10 **Cook Time: 35** **Serves: 6**

Groceries

Corn, Lima Beans, Onion, Garlic, Green Pepper, Sweet Potato, Zucchini, Cilantro or Italian Parsley, Basil, Marjoram, Paprika, Miso.

Do Ahead

Cook and refrigerate the beans in a sealed container, for 4 days, before adding to the recipe. Wash and refrigerate the vegetables in plastic bags, or sealed containers up to 3 days in advance. The stew keeps for 5 days refrigerated (made with fresh beans), or 3 months frozen.

Hot Tips

Use a miso that is medium-dark for the deep rich flavor. White or pale miso is a little too light and sweet, and the very dark miso is too bitter, and will turn the stew a brownish color. Substitute various beans and vegetables for variety.

Meal Balance

Serve this with grains or pasta (see Mainstream Meals and Fasta Pasta), and a salad, or lightly cooked green vegetables for a simple, balanced meal (see Veggie Ventures).

Traditional recipes are simply corn and lima beans. This version is colorful and textured with diced fragrant vegetables. Serve it with a hearty, robust grain, and a fresh, perky vegetable dish.

2 tablespoons Corn Oil
1 medium Onion, diced
1 medium Garlic Clove, minced
1 teaspoon Paprika
1 medium Sweet Potato, diced
6 Corn Cobs, niblets removed
1 medium Green Pepper + Zucchini, diced
1 teaspoon Basil (or 1 tablespoon fresh)
1 teaspoon Marjoram (1 tablespoon fresh)
1 teaspoon Sea Salt, or to taste
¼ teaspoon Pepper, or to taste
4 cups Baby Lima Beans, cooked*
±4 cups Vegetable Stock** or Water
2 tablespoons medium-dark Miso***
¼ cup Cilantro or Italian Parsley, minced

1. Heat an enamel coated or stainless steel pot over medium heat with the oil. Sauté the onion, garlic, sweet potato and paprika for 5 minutes, or until beginning to brown. Add the corn, green pepper and zucchini with the herbs, sea salt and pepper. Sauté for 2 minutes, or until tender.
2. Add the beans, and 3½ cups of the stock or water, and bring to a boil. Cover, reduce heat to low, and simmer for 25 minutes.
3. Meanwhile, mix the miso with the remaining ½ cup of liquid, and dissolve the lumps. Simmer with the beans and vegetables briefly, and adjust seasonings to taste. Stir in the cilantro or parsley and serve.

* See COOKING BEANS chart in STAPLES
** See Vegetable Stock in TRICKS OF THE TRADE. Salted stock reduces the amount of salt added to the stew.
*** See GLOSSARY

SOUTHERN BLACK EYED PEAS

Prep Time: 10   **Cook Time: 35**   **Serves: 6**

Groceries

Black Eyed Peas, Crushed Dried Chili, Garlic, Onion, Carrot, Celery, Scallions, Italian Parsley, Basil, Rosemary, Thyme, Bay Leaf.

Do Ahead

Cook and refrigerate black eyed peas in a sealed container, up to 4 days before using in the recipe. Wash and refrigerate the vegetables in plastic bags, or sealed containers up to 3 days in advance. The stew keeps for 5 days refrigerated (made with fresh peas), or 3 months frozen.

Hot Tips

Save time and eliminate fat by simply boiling everything together—omit the oil and sautéing step. You can substitute various beans in this recipe. Include more, or fewer vegetables, as desired. Turn this into a soup by increasing the volume of liquid, and seasonings to taste.

Meal Balance

Serve this with grains (see Mainstream Meals), or pasta (see Fasta Pasta), and some lightly cooked green vegetables or a fresh leafy salad (see Veggie Ventures).

The chili gives this a spicy lift. The garlic, herbs and black eyed peas, with aromatic vegetables become a Mardi Gras of flavors and aromas.

2 tablespoons Olive Oil
¼ teaspoon Crushed Dried Chili
1 medium Onion, diced
3 Garlic Cloves, minced
1 medium Carrot, diced
1 medium Celery rib, diced
2 Scallions*, sliced (white and greens)
1 large Bay Leaf
1½ teaspoons Sea Salt
1 teaspoon Basil (or 1 tablespoon fresh)
½ teaspoon Rosemary, crushed
½ teaspoon Thyme
¼ teaspoon Pepper
4 cups Black Eyed Peas, cooked** or canned
±4 cups Vegetable Stock*** or Water
¼ cup Italian Parsley, minced

1. Heat an enamel coated or stainless steel pot over medium heat with the oil, and sauté the chili, with the onion and garlic until translucent. Add the carrot, celery, scallion whites, sea salt, herbs and pepper and cook covered for 5 minutes, or until bright in color and tender.
2. Add the black eyed peas (with their cooking juices) and enough stock or water to achieve a stew consistency. Bring to a boil, reduce heat and simmer for 25 minutes.
3. Adjust seasonings to taste, and consistency to your liking (the beans will thicken up as they cool and absorb the liquid). Mix in the parsley and serve.

* See CUTTING TO THE CHASE
** See COOKING BEANS chart in STAPLES
*** See Vegetable Stock in TRICKS OF THE TRADE. Salted stock reduces the amount of salt added to the stew.

AZUKI BEANS & BUTTERCUP

Prep Time: 10   **Cook Time: 25**   **Serves: 6**

Groceries

Azuki Beans, Buttercup Squash, Scallions, Ginger, Miso.

Do Ahead

Cooked beans store up to 4 days refrigerated in a sealed container before cooking into the recipe. Wash and refrigerate the vegetables in plastic bags, or sealed containers up to 3 days in advance. The stew keeps for 5 days refrigerated (made with fresh beans), or 3 months frozen, either as a whole or in serving size containers.

Hot Tips

You can substitute any bean in this recipe and you can use butternut, delicatta squash or sweet potato instead of the buttercup for variety.

Meal Balance

Serve this with a grain or pasta dish, such as Spiced Basmati with Pine Nuts, Millet and Cauliflower, Thai Vegetable Fried Rice, Baked Rice Patties or Hazelnut Basil Barley Bread (see Mainsteam Meals and Fasta Pasta). Include lightly cooked green vegetables or a leafy green salad (see Veggie Ventures).

This is nourishing to the body and spirit. The naturally sweet, golden inner flesh of the buttercup squash marries with the delicate, earthy red azuki beans for a dish that is simply delicious and fat-free.

4 cups Buttercup Squash*, diced 1"
4 cups Azuki Beans, cooked**
±3 cups Vegetable Stock*** or Water
1 teaspoon Sea Salt or to taste
2 Scallions, sliced* (white and green parts)
1 tablespoon fresh Ginger, grated
1 tablespoon medium-dark Miso**** or to taste

1. In an enamel coated or stainless steel pot over medium heat, layer the squash, beans and cover with stock or water. Bring to a boil, reduce heat and cook for 5 minutes.
2. Add the sea salt and simmer for 15 minutes.
3. Add the scallion whites, ginger and miso and simmer for 5 minutes. Adjust seasonings to taste, mix in the scallion greens and serve.

* See Winter Squash, Scallions in CUTTING to the CHASE
** See COOKING BEANS chart in STAPLES
*** See Vegetable Stock in TRICKS OF THE TRADE. Salted stock reduces the amount of salt added to the stew.
**** See GLOSSARY

CHILI CON CARNE

Prep Time: 15   **Cook Time: 30**   **Serves: 6**

Groceries

Pinto Beans, Seitan, Tomatoes, Onion, Carrot, Celery, Green and Red Pepper, Basil, Cumin, Dried Crushed Chili, Oregano, Cinnamon, Tamari.

Do Ahead

Cooked beans store refrigerated for 4 days in a sealed container. Seitan keeps for weeks in its seasoned broth. Wash the vegetables and refrigerate in plastic bags or sealed containers up to 3 days in advance. The stew keeps refrigerated for 5 days (made with fresh beans), or 3 months frozen, either whole or in serving size containers.

Hot Tips

To save time and eliminate fat simply boil everything together for 30 minutes, omitting the oil and sautéing step. Pinto beans are sweeter and creamier than kidney beans, but you can use any variety you like. Be creative and mix two or more different kinds of beans.

Meal Balance

Lots of protein here with the beans and seitan. All you need are cooked grains or pasta to provide complex carbohydrates and absorb all the juices, with a salad, or lightly cooked green vegetables for a balance of nutrients (see Veggie Ventures).

You can make this without the seitan and it will still be delicious, just less meaty.

2 tablespoons Olive Oil
½-1 teaspoon Dried Crushed Chili (to taste)
1 large or Spanish Onion, diced
2 Garlic Cloves, minced
1 medium Carrot and 1 Celery, diced
1 medium Green and 1 Red Pepper, diced
1 large or 2 small Bay leaves
1 tablespoon each Basil, Cumin, Sea Salt
2 teaspoons each Cinnamon and Oregano
4 cups Pinto Beans, cooked*
3 cups Tomatoes, chopped
± 2 cups Vegetable Stock** or Water
1½ cups ground Seitan***
2 tablespoons Tamari****
¼ cup Italian Parsley, minced

1. Heat an enamel coated or stainless steel heavy pot over medium heat with the oil, and sauté the chili briefly. Add onion and garlic and sauté for 2 minutes to brown. Sauté in the carrot, celery, bell peppers, herbs, spices and sea salt and cook 5 minutes, until tender.
2. Add tomatoes, beans and enough stock or water for a stew consistency, bring to a boil and reduce heat to simmer for 20 minutes.
3. Mix in the seitan and tamari and simmer for 5 minutes. Adjust seasonings to taste and the consistency if necessary with more liquid. Mix in the parsley and serve *hot!*

* See COOKING BEANS chart in STAPLES
* See Vegetable Stock in TRICKS OF THE TRADE. Salted stock reduces the amount of salt added to the stew.
** See SPEEDY HOMEMADE SEITAN in STAPLES
*** See GLOSSARY

VITALITY STEW

Prep Time: 15   **Cook Time: 40**   **Serves: 6**

Groceries

Seitan, Tempeh, Onion, Garlic, Ginger, Celery, Carrot, Squash, Rutabaga, Parsnips, Burdock, Tamari, Arrowroot.

Do Ahead

The vegetables may be washed, chopped, sealed in plastic bags or containers and refrigerated up to 4 days in advance. Remove the tempeh from the freezer 1 hour before slicing and cooking. The stew keeps refrigerated for 5 days, or 3 months frozen, as a whole, or in serving size containers.

Hot Tips

Chop the vegetables into 1" chunks for best stew consistency and cook them until very tender and sweet. The root vegetables, seitan and tempeh combined with the oil and long, slow cooking adds strength, vitality and enduring warmth, making this ideal for physical activity and keeping warm in cold weather. Save time and reduce fat by chopping the vegetables small to cook quickly, and omit sautéing in oil—simply boil everything. Omit tempeh for a fat-free dish.

Meal Balance

Very substantial and hearty, and is balanced by green vegetables and whole grains or pasta to soak up all the juices.

This is a heart warming, nourishing dish for an active family with healthy appetites.

1 tablespoon Toasted Sesame Oil*
½ 12 oz. (340 gr.) package Tempeh*, cubed
1 medium Onion, diced
1 large Garlic Clove, minced
1 tablespoon fresh Ginger, minced
1 large Celery, diced
1 cup Cabbage, diced
2 cups Squash, diced**
1 cup Rutabaga, diced
1 large Parsnip, 1 large Carrot, diced
½ cup Burdock, diced ½" (optional)
2 cups Seitan***, cubed
2 cups Water
1 teaspoon Sea Salt
±4 cups Vegetable Stock**** or Water
± ¼ cup Tamari*
±3 tablespoons Arrowroot* or Cornstarch
¼ cup Italian Parsley, minced

1. Heat an enamel coated or stainless steel heavy pot over medium heat with the oil, and sauté the tempeh to brown all the sides for 5 minutes or so. Add the onion with the garlic and ginger and sauté until translucent.
2. Layer the remaining vegetables in the order listed, ending with the seitan water and sea salt. Bring to a boil, cover and reduce heat to simmer for 30 minutes or until tender.
3. Add enough stock or water to desired stew consistency. Mix the tamari and arrowroot, stir and simmer into the stew until clear and thickened. Adjust seasonings to taste, mix in the parsley and serve.

* See GLOSSARY
** Buttercup, Butternut and/or Delicatta (see Winter Squash in CUTTING TO THE CHASE)
*** See SPEEDY HOMEMADE SEITAN in STAPLES
****See Vegetable Stock in TRICKS OF THE TRADE. Salted stock reduces the amount of salt added to the stew.

TERRA-COTTA BAKED BEANS

Prep Time: 10   **Cook Time: 90**   **Serves: 6**

Groceries

Navy Beans, Onion, Garlic, Maple Syrup, Tomato Purée (opt.), Allspice, Mustard, Apple Cider Vinegar, Tamari, Seitan (opt.), Toasted Sesame Oil.

Do Ahead

Cook the beans and refrigerate in a sealed container, up to 4 days before adding to the recipe. The stew keeps refrigerated for 1 week (made with fresh beans), or 3 months frozen.

Hot Tips

To simplify and reduce fat you can omit the oil and sautéing the seitan—just bake everything all together. Great northern, navy and pinto beans can be substituted in this recipe. You can use any 2 quart casserole dish instead of Terra-cotta. The Terra-cotta casserole brings out a deep, earthy flavor.

Meal Balance

This is wonderful with the Hazelnut Basil Barley Bread, Millet & Cauliflower or Quinoa Polenta with Delicatta Squash, and a salad or lightly cooked green vegetables.

The traditional recipes are cooked for up to nine hours. We've sped up the process and traded ingredients for a lean and healthy version, with seitan filling in for meatiness.

1 tbsp. each Corn and Toasted Sesame Oil*
2 cups Seitan**, diced ½" (optional)
1 medium Onion, diced
2 Garlic Cloves, minced
1 cup Tomato Purée or Water
1/3 cup each Maple Syrup*, or to taste
¼ cup Tamari*, or to taste
2 tablespoons Apple Cider Vinegar
1 tablespoon Mustard Powder,
1 teaspoon Sea Salt, or to taste
½ teaspoon Allspice
¼ teaspoon Pepper or to taste
4 cups Navy Beans, cooked*** (or canned)
±3½ cups Vegetable Stock**** or Water

1. Preheat oven to 325°F. Soak a two quart Terra-cotta casserole in water. Heat a skillet over medium heat with the oil, and sauté the seitan for 5 minutes or until browned evenly. Add the onion and garlic and cook for 2 minutes, or until browned and tender. Stir in the remaining ingredients (except beans) and bring to a boil to deglaze the pan.
2. Drain the Terra-cotta and fill with the beans (along with their cooking juices), the skillet ingredients, (making sure you scrape all the browned goodness from the skillet), and enough stock or water for a stew consistency (the Terra-cotta loses moisture through the ceramic walls as they are not coated with enamel). Bake covered for 80 minutes. Adjust seasonings to taste, serve.

* See GLOSSARY
** See SPEEDY HOMEMADE SEITAN in STAPLES
*** See COOKING BEANS chart in STAPLES
**** See Vegetable Stock in TRICKS OF THE TRADE.
Salted stock reduces the amount of salt added to the stew.

SAVORY STRATFORD STEW

Prep Time: 10 **Cook Time: 30** **Serves: 6**

Groceries

Seitan (opt.), Potatoes, Onions, Carrots, Parsnips, Cabbage, Rosemary, Thyme, Sage, Flour, Tamari, Parsley.

Do Ahead

You may bake and refrigerate the seitan up to 1 week in a sealed container. Wash and refrigerate the vegetables in plastic bags or sealed containers, up to 3 days in advance. The stew keeps refrigerated for 1 week (made with freshly baked seitan), or 3 months frozen.

Hot Tips

To save time and reduce fat you can omit the oil and baking step and simply boil everything for 30 minutes or until tender. This way is still delicious, just a little less rich and savory. You can use cooked beans, tempeh or tofu instead of the seitan, or use none for a savory vegetable stew.

Meal Balance

This is so filling and satisfying and all you really need is a salad or lightly cooked greens. Grains or pasta will provide whole grain goodness and soak up the extra sauce.

You will immediately be swept away to a jolly pub in an English town, surrounded by rolling green pastures and country estates.

2 cups Seitan*, drained, patted dry, 1" cubed
¼ cup Whole Wheat Pastry Flour
2 tablespoons Corn Oil
2 medium Onions, diced
3 large Potatoes, diced
2 large Carrots, 2 large Parsnips, diced
1 teaspoon Rosemary, crushed
1 teaspoon each Sage, Sea Salt and Thyme
2 cups Water
±2½ cups Vegetable Stock** or Water
3 tablespoons Tamari*** (to taste)
¼ cup Parsley, minced

1. Toss the seitan with the flour to coat and save the extra flour. Heat an enamel coated or stainless steel heavy pot over medium heat with the oil, and brown the seitan evenly, 5 minutes. Remove and set aside.
2. In the same pot, sauté the vegetables for 2 minutes, until the onions are tender. Add the flour and cook for 2 minutes, until browned.
3. Add the seitan, herbs, sea salt and water, plus enough stock or water for a stew consistency and bring to a boil. Reduce heat and simmer covered 20 minutes, until tender.
4. Add the tamari and adjust seasonings and consistency as desired. Mix in parsley and serve.

* See SPEEDY HOMEMADE SEITAN in STAPLES
** See Vegetable Stock in TRICKS OF THE TRADE. Salted stock reduces the amount of salt added to the stew.
*** See GLOSSARY

30 MINUTES OR LESS!

The following recipes (except for the Meat Balls) can be made from start to finish in 30 minutes or less.

The noodles or pasta is usually listed at the end of each recipe, to be added and heated through with the vegetables and sauces, etc. Alternatively, when there's no cooked pasta on hand, bring a pot of water to a boil while when you begin preparing the meal, and cook the pasta in the process. By the time you're finished sauteing, stir frying or simmering, simply add the noodles or pasta (or cooked grains for variety) and voila!

CHAPTER 3

FASTA PASTA

International Favorites

PASTA PRIMAVERA

Prep Time: 20   **Cook Time: 15**   **Serves: 6-8**

Groceries

Vegetable Spiral Pasta, Onion, Garlic, Carrot, Cauliflower, Red and Green Pepper, Mushrooms, Celery, Broccoli, Snow Peas, Basil, Oregano, Parsley, Tomato Purée (optional).

Do Ahead

Cooked pasta can be stored up to 4 days refrigerated in a sealed container. The vegetables may be washed and trimmed and stored for 2 days refrigerated in a sealed container or plastic bags.

Hot Tips

Have all the vegetables cut and ready in little piles on a large plate or in bowls before you begin cooking. Timing is crucial so nothing is overcooked or undercooked. Keep the heat high to cook quickly while sautéing, and cover the skillet occasionally to create steam. Use ¼ cup water to sauté instead of oil—to cut fat and calories.

Meal Balance

This is a great one-dish balanced meal! Pasta, a grain product, is full of complex carbohydrates, and the vegetables provide an abundance of nutrients. For more distinct vibrant color, omit the tomato purée.

* See CUTTING TO THE CHASE
** (±12oz. raw) See PASTA in STAPLES

You can simplify this recipe if you like and reduce the variety of vegetables. Each time, vary the choice of vegetables for a whole new experience.

1-2 tablespoons Olive Oil
1 Onion, sliced ½ moons
2 Garlic Cloves, minced
1 Carrot, sliced diagonal ½ moons
1 cup Cauliflowerettes*
2 cups Mushrooms, quartered
1-2 teaspoons Sea Salt, or to taste
1 teaspoon Basil
½ teaspoon Oregano
¼ teaspoon Pepper, or to taste
¼ Green Pepper, julienne
¼ Red Pepper, julienne
1 cup Broccoli flowerettes*
1 Celery Rib, sliced thin diagonally
½ cup Snow Peas, whole or sliced
1-2 cups Tomato Purée (optional)
4 cups Vegetable Spiral Pasta cooked **
¼ cup Italian Parsley, minced

1. In a skillet over medium heat, add olive oil, sauté the onion and garlic 1 minute, until tender. Add the vegetables, one at a time; carrots, cauliflower and mushrooms, sautéing each vegetable briefly before adding the next.
2. Add the seasonings, a little water to create some juice and steam, and cover the skillet for 1 minute. Sauté in the peppers and broccoli, cover and steam briefly. Mix in the celery and snow peas.
3. Add the tomato purée (if using) to the vegetables. Simmer everything for a few minutes, until the broccoli, celery and snow peas are bright green and tender-crisp.
4. Mix in the pasta, heat through, and adjust seasonings to taste. Add parsley and serve.

WOK AROUND THE CLOCK

Prep Time: 15 **Cook Time: 10** **Serves: 4**

Groceries

Somen Noodles, Onion, Carrot, Bok Choy, Shiitake Mushrooms, Basil, Parsley, Tamari, Arrowroot.

Do Ahead

The vegetables can be washed and refrigerated in plastic bags or sealed containers up to 3 days in advance. The cooked somen will keep for 4 days refrigerated in a sealed container. The completed cooked recipe keeps refrigerated for 3-4 days (made with fresh noodles).

Hot Tips

Have your vegetables already chopped when you begin cooking so that each vegetable can be added quickly, one after the other. The bok choy should be bright green and the carrots bright orange, both tender-crisp. Use ¼ cup of water instead of oil for a fat-free alternative.

Meal Balance

This is a perfectly balanced light and quick meal as is, and you can make it more substantial by adding seitan, tempeh, tofu or cooked beans (see index for all the possibilities). The Dijon Ginger Glazed Butternut or Roasted Rutabaga Salad are wonderful accompaniments.

When you are in the mood for something easy, fast and tasty, this one delivers. You can use regular mushrooms instead of the shiitake, and broccoli in place of bok choy if this is more convenient for you.

1 tablespoon Olive Oil
1 Onion (large or 1 Spanish), sliced ½ moons
1 Carrot, sliced matchsticks*
4 oz. Shiitake Mushrooms, quartered or sliced
1-2 cups Water or Vegetable Stock
1 teaspoon Sea Salt, or to taste
3-4 Bok Choy leaves, julienned*
±2 tablespoons Tamari** or Sea Salt to taste
1-2 tablespoons Arrowroot or Cornstarch
4 cups Cooked Somen Noodles*** (±12oz. raw)
2 sprigs of fresh Basil, minced or ½ tsp. dried
2 sprigs of Italian Parsley, minced

1. Heat a stainless steel wok or skillet over medium heat, add the oil and sauté the onion for 1 minute, or until tender. 2. Add the carrots and shiitake mushrooms along with water and sea salt. Sauté briefly, and then cover for a moment to create steam.
3. Mix in the bok choy white parts, cover for 1 minute. Add the greens and the tamari.
4. Dissolve 1 tablespoon of arrowroot in 1 tablespoon of water to thicken each cup of liquid remaining in your wok. Push the vegetables to one side, stir the arrowroot into the liquid and cook briefly until clear.
5. Incorporate your noodles well with everything to heat them through, and adjust seasonings to taste. Mix in the basil and parsley, and serve.

Variations: Various styles of pasta or cooked grains can be substituted for the somen noodles.

* See CUTTING TO THE CHASE
** See GLOSSARY
*** See PASTA in STAPLES

SPICY PEANUT SAUCE
WITH VEGETABLES & GENMAI NOODLES

Prep Time: 15   **Cook Time: 5**   **Serves: 4**

Groceries

Genmai Noodles, Garlic, Ginger, Toasted Sesame Oil, Peanut Butter, Maple Syrup, Tamari, Cayenne, Onion, Broccoli, Carrot, Mushrooms.

Do Ahead

The peanut sauce keeps refrigerated for 10 days or 3 months frozen, in a sealed container.

Hot Tips

Extra peanut sauce will never go to waste, it can be served with grains, pasta and many vegetable dishes. Don't bother trying to reduce fat by omitting the oil, this small amount is a drop in the bucket compared to the peanut butter, and it adds an aromatic fragrant quality. Just resign yourself to enjoying this dish. Use various pastas and other Oriental style noodles for variety; Udon, Somen, Soba, etc.

Meal Balance

Noodles provides complex carbohydrates for energy. The peanut sauce is very satisfying, and adds protein and richness— all to be balanced with fresh colorful Veggie Ventures and a Sumptuous Soup or Savory Stew, if desired.

Low to zero fat this is not, but fabulous...definitely.

1 cup smooth Peanut Butter*
2-3 Garlic Cloves, minced
2 teaspoons fresh Ginger, minced
¾ cups Vegetable Stock or Water
1/3 cup Maple Syrup*
2 tablespoons Tamari*, or to taste
1 tablespoon Toasted Sesame Oil*
½ teaspoon Sea Salt, or to taste
½ teaspoon Cayenne or to taste
1 medium Onion, sliced ½ moons
1 Carrot, sliced diagonally ½ moons**
4 oz. Mushrooms quartered
4 cups Genmai Noodles, cooked***
2 Scallions, minced (white and green parts)**
¼ cup Cilantro or Parsley, minced

1. Spicy Peanut Sauce: Purée the peanut butter with next eight ingredients until smooth. Adjust seasonings to taste.
2. Heat a wok over medium-high heat with ¼ cup water. Sauté the onion until tender, then add the carrot, broccoli and mushrooms and cook covered for 2 minutes, or until bright in color and tender-crisp.
3. Add the peanut sauce with the scallion whites and simmer on low for 1 minute. Mix in the noodles to heat through. Add the scallion greens and cilantro and serve.

* See GLOSSARY
** See CUTTING TO THE CHASE
*** (±12 oz. raw) See PASTA in STAPLES

SUNBURST VEGETABLES
WITH CORN ANGEL HAIR

Prep Time: 15   **Cook Time:**   **Serves: 4**

Groceries

Corn Angel Hair Pasta, Bok Choy, Nappa Cabbage, English Cucumber, Carrot, Leek, Red Radish and Cabbage, Celery, Watercress, Apple Cider Vinegar, Arrowroot.

Do Ahead

Vegetables may be washed, ready to cut, refrigerated for 3 days in plastic bags or sealed containers. Cooked pasta keeps refrigerated for 4 days in a sealed container.

Hot Tips

Vegetables are steamed together, or added at intervals, depending on their cooking time. They should be tender-crisp. The Vinegar Sauce turns the vegetables into a rainbow of vibrant colors. Complimentary colors of the yellow pasta with the purple red cabbage is gorgeous. Corn elbows or spaghetti are also very attractive.

Meal Balance

The corn pasta is a grain product which is complemented by the vegetables for a balanced and satisfying light meal. Additions of Tofu Cheese or Tofeta will add protein and wonderful dimensions of taste and texture.

This is a favorite summer lunch dish. Serve it often, and vary the pastas and vegetables, using what's fresh and in season.

4 large leaves of Bok Choy, julienned*
4 large leaves of Nappa Cabbage, julienned*
1 large Leek, julienned*
1 large Carrot, fine matchsticks*
1 large Celery Rib, sliced thin diagonally
2" section of English Cucumber, ½ moons*
4 Red Radishes, quartered*
1/3 cup Red Cabbage, fine julienned*
1/3 cup Apple Cider or Rice Vinegar**
2 teaspoons Umeboshi Vinegar**
4 teaspoons Arrowroot**
4 cups Corn Pasta, cooked*** (±12 oz. raw)
¼ cup fresh Dill, minced

1. Place 2 cups of water in a pot with a steamer basket. Bring the water to a boil over medium high heat and steam the bok choy and nappa white parts 1-2 minutes, to tender-crisp. Add and steam the bok choy and nappa greens until bright green and wilted. Remove and set aside in a bowl. Steam the leek white parts partially before adding the greens. Remove as above. Steam carrot, celery and cucumber. Remove. Steam the red radish and red cabbage, remove as above.
2. Measure the remaining cooking liquid and add water if necessary to equal 1 cup. Mix the vinegar with the arrowroot until dissolved and simmer for 1 minute with the measured liquid, or until clear. Add the pasta to heat through. Combine the steamed vegetables with the pasta and dill and serve.

* See CUTTING TO THE CHASE
** See GLOSSARY
** See PASTA in STAPLES

TOFU CACCIATORE
WITH VEGETABLE BOWTIES

Prep Time: 15 **Cook Time: 20** **Serves: 4**

Groceries

Tofu, Vegetable Bowties, Onion, Green Pepper, Mushrooms, Garlic, Marjoram, Oregano, Poultry Seasoning, Thyme, Italian Parsley, Tomatoes, Apple and Lemon Juice.

Do Ahead

Marinate the tofu for up to 3 days refrigerated in a sealed container. The vegetables may be prepared, ready for chopping, and refrigerated in plastic bags or a sealed container up to 3 days in advance.

Hot Tips

You can substitute various pasta or grains. Flouring and baking is optional. To simplify and save time, omit these steps, although this yields a better consistency. To reduce fat, sauté the vegetables in ¼ cup of water instead of the oil.

Meal Balance

The Cream of Carrot Soup with Fresh Coriander, Butternut & Broccoli or Garbanzo & Zucchini Bisque precede this dish wonderfully. Fresh greens, a salad or cooked vegetables will balance this meal.

Various pastas combine fabulously with this family favorite. Substitute seitan or tempeh for the tofu for variety if you prefer something meatier.

1 lb. (454 gr.) Tofu, pressed*
1 cup apple juice
¼ cup Lemon Juice (1 Lemon)
2 medium Garlic Cloves, minced
3/4 teaspoon each Marjoram, Oregano, Poultry Seasoning and Thyme
1/8 teaspoon Pepper, or to taste
1½ teaspoons Sea Salt, or to taste
¼ cup Whole Wheat Pastry Flour
1 tablespoon Olive Oil
1 medium Onion + Green Pepper, diced
8 oz. Mushrooms, quartered
4 cups chopped Tomatoes (or 28 oz. can)
4 cups Vegetable Bowties Pasta cooked**
¼ cup Italian Parsley, minced

1. Slice the tofu in ½, into 2 slabs (to expose as much surface as possible) and place in a shallow flat dish. Marinate the tofu in the apple and lemon juice, garlic, herbs, pepper and ½ teaspoon sea salt, for 1 hour or more.
2. Preheat oven to 375°F. Drain the tofu and cube ½"-¾", reserve the marinade. Toss the tofu in the flour to coat. Bake on an oiled baking tray for 15 minutes. Meanwhile...
3. Heat a skillet over medium heat with the oil and sauté the onion, green pepper and mushrooms 2 minutes, until tender and browned. Add the left over flour and cook 2 minutes. Add tomatoes, 1 cup of water, the marinade, 1 tsp. sea salt and tofu and cook 10 minutes covered. Mix in the pasta to heat through with the parsley (except 1 tbsp. for garnish). Adjust seasonings to taste and serve.

* See Tofu in TRICKS OF THE TRADE
** (±12 oz. raw) See PASTA in STAPLES

WHOLE GRAINS = MORE ENERGY GAINED & SAVED

Whole grains offer the most vitality compared to other sources of complex carbohydrates. When you place a whole grain in water, it will sprout in a day or two. Once grains have been ground into flour, rolled, puffed, flaked or cracked, they no longer sprout. They have lost their life force.

As an added benefit to the natural energy we gain from eating whole grains and natural whole foods, the environment is saved by all the energy and waste that would go into processing and packaging. A win-win situation!

CHAPTER 4

MAINSTREAM MEALS

Gourmet Grains & Breads

Casseroles, Pies & Quiche

Sensational Seitan

GRAINS ON THE GO

Prep Time: 5   **Cook Time: 45**   **Serves: 6-8**

Groceries

Short Grain Brown Rice, Sweet Brown Rice, White Thai Jasmine Rice, Bulgur, Quinoa.

Do Ahead

Sort, wash and soak the short and sweet rice with the quinoa for 1 hour or overnight (do not soak bulgur or white rice). Cooked grains keep refrigerated for 5 days in a sealed container. Freezing is possible for 3 months although it changes the texture.

Hot Tips

For variety, substitute amaranth, barley, basmati rice, kamut, kasha, millet, spelt, wheat berries, wehani rice or wild rice for the quinoa. Use simply 1 variety of rice, such as basmati, long, medium or short grain (sweet rice is too glutinous to use in large proportions), combined with 1 other grain.

Meal Balance

Serve with vegetables for a basic, simple balanced meal. Add a Super Sauce or Savory Stew with beans or seitan, tempeh or tofu. A Sensational Seitan dish is also a perfect accompaniment.

This is a wonderful combination, instead of plain rice or grains, and makes enough to use in many recipes over the course of several days, so there's always something ready to whip up a meal with. Add delicious whole grains to salads, soups and stir fries, in nori maki or shaped into patties.

1 cup Quinoa
1 cup Short Grain Brown Rice
1 cup Sweet Brown Rice
9¾ cups Water
1 cup Thai Jasmine White Rice
1 cup Bulgur
2½ teaspoons Sea Salt

1. Sort*, wash* and soak* the quinoa, short grain and sweet rice in the water for 1 hour or overnight. Use a 3 quart enamel coated or stainless steel, heavy bottom pot.
2. Bring the soaked grains in their soaking water to a boil over medium-high heat. Stir in the white rice, bulgur and sea salt. Cover, reduce heat to low, simmer for 45 minutes.
3. Remove from heat, remove the lid and place a bamboo mat over the pot**. Let the grains sit for 5 minutes before transferring to a serving dish***.

Note: This yields a large volume of cooked grains. If you prefer, use ½ the volume of ingredients, or, select fewer varieties of grains, to total 2 or 3 cups of grain, and adjust the sea salt and water volume accordingly (see COOKING WHOLE GRAINS chart for cooking times of various grains and water measurements).

* For complete directions see STAPLES.
** The bamboo mat allows steam to escape so the grains do not become soggy.
*** This lets scorched grains at the bottom of the pot soften for easy removal. See REMOVING GRAINS FROM THE POT in STAPLES.

JAPANESE GOMOKU RICE

Prep Time: 15   **Cook Time: 60**   **Serves: 4-6**

Groceries

Brown Rice, Burdock, Carrot, Shiitake, Dried or Fresh Lotus Root, Kombu (opt.), Seitan, Scallions.

Do Ahead

Roast the rice and store refrigerated in a glass jar for several weeks. Soak the shiitake and dried lotus up to 4 hours, or refrigerate in a sealed container for 2 days. The rice keeps refrigerated for 3 days, or 3 months frozen.

Hot Tips

Roasting the rice adds a nutty flavor. You may soak the rice instead for 4 hours or overnight and cook as indicated. Tempeh or cooked beans may substitute the seitan. Various vegetables may be included; celery, green and red pepper, parsnips, squash, etc. Use long or medium grain rice. Use up to ½ the volume in white rice for a lighter version. Millet or quinoa may substitute the rice, and will take only 25 minutes to cook.

Meal Balance

This becomes a balanced meal with a serving of lightly cooked green vegetables, or a fresh green salad. For a full course meal, serve a Sumptuous Soup or Savory Stew, and a Veggie Venture.

Gomoku means "Five variety". You may include more than five additions, or fewer - this combination is a Japanese favorite.

5 Dried Shiitake Mushrooms (or fresh)
¼ cup Dried Lotus Root* (or fresh)
2" piece dry Kombu**, cleaned (optional)
±4 cups Water
2 cups Short Grain Brown Rice**, sorted
1 medium Carrot, diced ½"
½ cup Burdock, diced ½"
½ cup Seitan***, diced ½"
2 medium Scallions, minced white + greens
1½ teaspoons Sea Salt, or to taste

1. Soak the shiitake, lotus and kombu in the water for 10 minutes, or until reconstituted.
2. Wash and drain the rice in a fine mesh strainer over a sponge to absorb all the excess water. Heat a cast iron or stainless steel skillet over medium-low heat, stirring for 10 minutes, or until golden and fragrant.
3. Save the soaking water and add extra water to equal 4 cups. Remove the tough stems from, and ½" dice the shiitake. Dice the lotus and kombu into ½" pieces.
4. Place all the ingredients (except scallion greens) in an enamel coated or stainless steel pot and bring to a boil over medium-high heat. Add sea salt, cover and reduce heat to low. Simmer for 50 minutes.
5. Remove the pot from the heat, remove the lid and place a bamboo mat over the pot. Let the grains sit for 5 minutes before transferring to a serving dish. Mix in scallion greens as you transfer the grains to a serving dish****.

* Available in Asian grocers and natural food stores.
** See GLOSSARY
*** See SPEEDY HOMEMADE SEITAN in STAPLES
**** See REMOVING GRAINS FROM THE POT

RICE UNDER PRESSURE
& TAMARI ROASTED SEEDS

Prep Time: 10   **Cook Time: 45**   **Serves: 4-6**

Groceries

Brown Rice, Sweet Rice, Sunflower Seeds, Tamari.

Do Ahead

Sort, wash and soak the rice 1 hour or overnight. Roast the seeds (make extra for the Sunflower Olive Oat Bread) and refrigerate in a glass jar for several weeks. Pressure cooked rice keeps refrigerated for 5 days in a sealed container, or 3 months frozen, although the texture will change.

Hot Tips

For variety, substitute amaranth, basmati rice, kamut, kasha, millet, quinoa, spelt, sweet rice, wheat berries, wehani or wild rice. Use simply 1 variety of rice, such as basmati, long, medium or short grain, (sweet rice is too glutinous to use in large proportions). Use pumpkin or sesame seeds, or various nuts instead of sunflower seeds. Releasing the pressure gauge results in fluffier rice. If you let the pressure come down slowly by itself, the rice will be heavier.

Meal Balance

This will become a simple balanced meal with a side portion of colorful vegetables.

Create elaborate gourmet feasts, or simple daily meals around delicious whole grains. Tamari roasted seeds add crunch and wonderful flavor.

2 cups Short Grain Brown Rice*, sort, wash**
½ cup Barley, sorted, washed**
3¾ cups Water
1¼ teaspoons Sea Salt
1 cup Sunflower Seeds, sorted and washed
1 tablespoon Tamari*

1. Soak the rice in the water for 1 hour or more, directly in the pressure cooker.
2. Add the sea salt, close the lid and bring to a boil over medium-high heat. Once the pressure gauge is hissing quietly, reduce heat to low. Simmer for 40 minutes. Touch the pressure gauge occasionally to make sure the pressure is still up. The pot should make a steady, faint hissing sound. Meanwhile...
3. Preheat oven to 350°F. In a bowl, mix the seeds with the tamari to coat evenly. Spread the seeds on a baking tray and bake for 10 minutes, or until golden brown and the tamari has baked dry. Cool, place in a dish.
4. Remove the pot of cooked rice from the heat, and release the pressure gauge to bring down the pressure quickly. Remove the lid and place a bamboo mat over the pot***. Let the grains sit for 5 minutes before transferring to a serving dish****. Mix the seeds with the rice or serve them on the side as a garnish.

* See GLOSSARY
** For complete directions see STAPLES.
*** The bamboo mat allows steam to escape so the grains do not become soggy.
**** This lets scorched grains at the bottom of the pot soften for easy removal. See REMOVING GRAINS FROM THE POT in STAPLES.

CONFETTI VEGETABLE RICE
WITH **WHEAT BERRIES**

Prep Time: 20   **Cook Time: 50**   **Serves: 4-6**

Groceries

Medium Grain Brown Rice, Wheat Berries, Corn, Red Pepper.

Do Ahead

Sort, wash and soak the wheat berries overnight. Or, instead of soaking, precook the wheat berries for 20 minutes before cooking with the rice. This recipe keeps refrigerated for 3 days in a sealed container, or 3 months frozen, although the texture will change.

Hot Tips

For variety, substitute amaranth, barley, kasha, millet, quinoa, wehani or wild rice for the wheat berries. Use other varieties of rice, such as basmati, long, or short grain, (sweet rice is too glutinous to use in large proportions). Use carrots, celery, yellow pepper, fresh peas and diced green and/or yellow beans instead of, or with the corn and red pepper.

Meal Balance

This simply needs fresh cooked greens or a salad to complete a simple balanced meal. Include beans or bean products, sauces and soups or stews to round out a full course meal if desired.

This is a very bright, colorful rice dish with yellow corn and red peppers. Wheat berries add a nutty flavor and chewy texture.

½ cup Wheat Berries, Spelt or Kamut
2 cups Medium Grain Brown Rice*, washed**
5 cups Water
1¼ teaspoons Sea Salt
1 Corn Cob, niblets removed
½ cup Red Pepper, diced ¼"

1. Sort, wash and soak** the wheat berries overnight with the rice. (Alternatively, instead of soaking, bring the wheat berries to a boil in 1 cup of the water, and simmer covered for 20 minutes. Add wheat and cooking water to the rice and 4 cups water. Cook as below.)
2. Bring the wheat berries and rice to a boil in an enamel coated or stainless steel pot. Add the sea salt, reduce heat to low and simmer covered for 40 minutes.
3. Add the corn and red pepper, and cook covered for 10 minutes more.
4. Remove the pot from the heat, remove the lid and place a bamboo mat over the pot***. Let the grains sit for 5 minutes before serving****.

* See GLOSSARY
** For complete directions see STAPLES.
*** The bamboo mat allows steam to escape so the grains do not become soggy.
**** This lets scorched grains at the bottom of the pot soften for easy removal. See REMOVING GRAINS FROM THE POT in STAPLES.

SWEET RICE & CHESTNUTS

Prep Time: 15   **Cook Time: 60**   **Serves: 4-6**

Groceries

Dried Chestnuts, Short Grain and Sweet Brown Rice.

Do Ahead

Soak the chestnuts and rice separately for 4 hours or overnight. The cooked rice and chestnuts keep refrigerated for 5 days in a sealed container, or 3 months frozen.

Hot Tips

Roast the chestnuts in a dry cast iron or stainless steel skillet before soaking for a nuttier flavor. Use various grains such as barley, millet, quinoa or long or medium grain brown rice instead of the short grain.

Meal Balance

Serve with colorful vegetables for a simple meal. Have a bean and/or vegetable based Sumptuous Soup or Savory Stew, and a Veggie Venture to complete a balanced feast.

This is a very rich and sweet rice dish that almost doubles as a dessert. It's wonderful as a base for holiday stuffing recipes.

1 cup Dried Chestnuts* (or fresh), washed
±6 cups Water
2 cups Short Grain Brown Rice**, washed
1 cup Sweet Brown Rice**, sorted, washed
2 teaspoons Sea Salt, or to taste

1. Soak the chestnuts for 4 hours or overnight in 3 cups of water. Soak the rice in 3 cups of water for 4 hours or overnight.
2. Strain and measure the chestnut soaking water, and add extra water to equal 3 cups. Split the chestnuts open to check for bruised or inedible pieces, and break them into small pieces, (for two reasons; so people do not pick out and eat all the whole chestnuts, and so the chestnuts and their flavor are distributed evenly throughout the dish).
3. Bring the water, chestnuts and rice to a boil over medium high heat in an enamel coated or stainless steel pot. Add sea salt, cover and reduce heat to low. Simmer for 50 minutes.
4. Remove the pot from the heat, remove the lid and place a bamboo mat over the pot***. Let the grains sit for 5 minutes before transferring to a serving dish****.

* Available in Asian grocers and natural food stores.
** See GLOSSARY
*** The bamboo mat allows steam to escape so the grains do not become soggy.
**** This lets scorched grains at the bottom of the pot soften for easy removal. See REMOVING GRAINS FROM THE POT in STAPLES.

RISOTTO FLORENTINE

Prep Time: 15   **Cook Time: 35**   **Serves: 4-6**

Groceries

Arborio Rice, Basil, Celery, Garlic, Onion, Mushrooms, Carrot, Kale, Arugula (opt.).

Do Ahead

The vegetables can be washed and ready to chop, stored refrigerated in plastic bags or sealed containers for 2 days. Extra servings keep refrigerated for 5 days in a sealed container.

Hot Tips

You can be creative with many different vegetables to transform this recipe each time you make it. Many cooks suggest to cook the rice to "al dente", which is fine. For best results in terms of health and digestibility, here the rice is cooked until tender. To reduce fat and save time, boil everything together from the beginning, and omit sautéing in oil.

Meal Balance

This will be very satisfying as a complete meal in itself with the grains and both root and leafy green vegetables. Add seitan, tempeh, tofu or cooked beans to turn this into a heartier entrée. A simple Sumptuous Soup followed by a Luscious, Light and Lean dessert will turn this into a balanced feast.

This dish is usually cooked with spinach. Kale and arugula offer beautiful color, great texture and wonderful flavor, as well as higher nutritional value, while keeping within traditional ingredients.

1 tablespoon Olive Oil
1 medium Onion, diced
2 Garlic Cloves, minced
1 Carrot and 1 Celery, diced
4 oz. Mushrooms, quartered
2 cups Arborio Rice (or white short grain rice)
4 cups Vegetable Stock* or Water
2 teaspoons Basil or 2 tablespoons fresh
1½-2 teaspoons Sea Salt
4-6 leaves Kale, stems and leaves chopped**
6-8 leaves Arugula, chopped "1 (or Spinach)
¼ cup Italian Parsley, minced

1. Heat an enamel coated or stainless steel heavy pot over medium-high heat, with the oil and sauté the onion, garlic, carrot, celery and mushrooms until tender and beginning to brown. Mix in and roast the rice until golden, approximately 5 minutes.
2. Stir in the stock or water, basil and sea salt and bring to a boil. Reduce heat to low and simmer covered for 20 minutes.
3. Add the kale stems, cover and cook for 1 minute. Add the kale leaves and arugula, cover and cook for 1 minute, or until bright green and tender crisp. Mix in the parsley and serve***.

Variation: Substitute barley, bulgur, couscous, millet, quinoa and other varieties of rice for the arborio rice (see COOKING WHOLE GRAINS chart for cooking times and water measurements).

* See Vegetable Stock in TRICKS OF THE TRADE. Using salted vegetable stock will reduce the quantity of added salt.
** See Kale in CUTTING TO THE CHASE
*** See REMOVING GRAINS FROM THE POT in STAPLES.

INDIAN ALMOND PILAF

Prep Time: 10   **Cook Time: 40**   **Serves: 4**

Groceries

Brown Basmati or Long Grain Rice, Chickpeas, Peas or Green Beans, Carrot, Almonds, Raisins, Cardamom, Crushed Dried Chili, Cinnamon, Clove, Cumin, Turmeric, Cilantro, Mint.

Do Ahead

Toast almonds and store refrigerated in a glass jar for several weeks (make extra to have on hand and use in Peach Couscous Cake). You can add 4-5 cups of cooked rice or grains (which keep refrigerated for up to 5 days) at the end, instead of adding raw rice in the beginning. The pilaf keeps refrigerated for 5 days (made with fresh rice), in a sealed container.

Hot Tips

To reduce fat, omit the nuts and oil completely, and simply boil everything together. You can substitute various nuts and seeds for the almonds, and use lentils or other beans in place of the chickpeas for variety.

Meal Balance

Whole grains, beans, vegetables and nuts are satisfying. A simple steamed green or salad is all you need for a balanced meal. Serve Manali Lodge Lentil Dahl or the Cream of Carrot with Coriander Soup for a full course meal.

This dish creates an image of a restaurant in Calcutta we dined at - a miniature palace inside, where we enjoyed authentic dishes. Ghee and white rice is upgraded in this version, to corn oil and brown rice, for healthier results.

½ cup Whole Almonds (not blanched)
2 tablespoons Corn, Peanut or Sesame Oil
2 cups Brown Basmati Rice
1 teaspoon Cumin Powder
½ teaspoon each Crushed Chili, Turmeric
¼ tsp. each Cardamom, Cinnamon and Clove
3½ cups Vegetable Stock* or Water
1-1½ teaspoons Sea Salt, to taste
1 medium Carrot, diced
1 cup fresh Peas (or Green Beans, diced)
1 cup Chickpeas, cooked** (or canned)
½ cup Sultana or Thompson Raisins
2 tablespoons Cilantro or Parsley, minced
1 tablespoon fresh Mint, minced

1. . Toast the almonds in a 350°F toaster oven*** for 5-10 minutes, or until fragrant and golden brown. Meanwhile...
2. Heat an enamel coated or stainless steel pot over medium heat with the oil and sauté the rice for ±5 minutes, until golden. Stir in the spices and toast until fragrant, 2 minutes.
3. Add the stock or water and bring to a boil. Add the sea salt, and remaining ingredients (except cilantro and mint). Reduce heat to low and simmer for 30 minutes or until liquid is absorbed. Mix in the cilantro and mint and serve****.

* See Vegetable Stock in TRICKS OF THE TRADE. Salted stock reduces the amount of salt added to the stew.
** See COOKING BEANS chart in STAPLES
*** A conventional oven at 350°F is ideal if you are baking something else, otherwise too much energy is wasted.
**** See REMOVING GRAINS FROM THE POT In STAPLES.

SPICED BASMATI with PINE NUTS

Prep Time: 10

Cook Time: 40

Serves: 4-6

Groceries

Basmati Rice, Pine Nuts, Bay Leaf, Anise or Fennel Seeds, Coriander Seeds, Cinnamon Stick, Cumin Seeds.

Do Ahead

Toast pine nuts and store refrigerated in a glass jar for several weeks (make extra to have on hand and use in the Quinoa Tabouli).

Hot Tips

Extra cooked rice can be used in the Thyme Efficient Meat Loaf, Sun Seed Rice Patties and various stir fries. Omit the pine nuts to eliminate fat if desired. (** A conventional oven preheated to 350°F is perfect if you are baking something else, otherwise too much energy is wasted toasting such a small amount)

Meal Balance

This is a whole grain dish that you can serve with various fresh, colorful vegetables, sauces, stews and salads. Make a complete meal by starting with a Sumptuous Soup, or include a Savory Stew or Sensational Seitan with it. A serving of beans, or a bean product will provide added protein (see index for all the possibilities).

This versatile rice dish is spiced in such a way, that it marries well with Latin, Middle Eastern and Far Eastern cuisines.

1/3 cup Pine Nuts
1 teaspoon Anise or Fennel Seeds
1 teaspoon each Coriander and Cumin Seeds
5¼ cups Vegetable Stock* or Water
1 Bay Leaf and 1 Cinnamon Stick
3 cups Brown Basmati Rice
1½ teaspoons Sea Salt or to taste

1. Toast the Pine Nuts with the Anise, Coriander, and Cumin in a 350°F toaster oven (see Hot Tips**) for 5-10 minutes, or until golden brown. Meanwhile...
2. Bring the water to a boil over medium-high heat with the bay leaf, cinnamon and rice. Add the sea salt, toasted nuts and seeds. Reduce heat to low and simmer for 35 minutes or until all the liquid is absorbed**.

Variations: **Ethnic Diversity**
1. Substitute various nuts and seeds for the pine nuts - almonds, cashews, hazelnuts, pistachios, walnuts, pumpkin seeds, sesame seeds and sunflower are all ideal.
2. Try other whole (seed) herbs and spices such as caraway, cardamom, celery, clove, dill, fenugreek, mustard and poppy seeds.
3. Dried herbs such as basil, chervil, marjoram, mint, oregano, parsley, rosemary, sage, savory, tarragon and thyme.
4. Powdered versions of some of the above herbs and spices can be used. Try also; allspice, curry, mace, nutmeg, pepper, saffron, turmeric.

* See Vegetable Stock in TRICKS OF THE TRADE. Salted stock reduces the amount of salt added to the stew.
** See REMOVING GRAINS FROM THE POT in STAPLES.

PAELLA VALENCIA

Prep Time: 15   **Cook Time: 55**   **Serves: 4-6**

Groceries

Tempeh, Long Grain Rice, Red and Green Pepper, Spanish Onion, Garlic, Carrot, Celery, Peas (opt.), Tomatoes (opt.), Cilantro, Basil, Chili, Oregano, Cumin, Tamari.

Do Ahead

The baked tempeh can be refrigerated in a sealed container for 5 days. Extra servings of the Paella keep refrigerated 5 days (made with fresh baked tempeh), or 3 months frozen, although this will change the texture.

Hot Tips

Don't mix the rice while cooking so it can absorb the liquid in the bottom of the pan. Turmeric can be used instead of Saffron with good results in terms of color, but there will be a subtle flavor difference. Cooked rice (4-5 cups) can be added to the dish at the end with the peas instead of using raw at the start. To save time and reduce fat, omit baking the tempeh and sautéing the ingredients in oil, boil all together for 45 minutes.

Meal Balance

Here's a Latin staple that reflects the traditional grain, bean and vegetable based diet in many cultures around the world. Add freshly steamed green vegetables or a salad for a balanced meal.

Having the real thing was a treat I looked forward to while en route to the Spanish Riviera. Here we substitute chicken or seafood with Tempeh.

1 teaspoon dried Saffron, crushed
4 cups Vegetable Stock* or Water
1 12 oz. package Tempeh**, diced ½"
3 tablespoons each Olive Oil and Tamari**
2 Dried Whole Chilies and 2 Garlic Cloves
1 Spanish Onion, 1 Carrot, 1 Celery, diced
½ Green Pepper, ½ Red Pepper, diced
2 cups Long Grain Brown Rice (raw)
2 tsp. each Basil, Cumin, Oregano, Sea Salt
2 large Tomatoes, diced (optional)
Cayenne or Pepper to taste
½ cup fresh Peas or diced Green Beans
¼ cup Italian Parsley, minced

1. Bring saffron and stock to a simmer, cover and keep hot. Preheat oven to 375°F. Toss the tempeh with 2 tbsp. oil and the tamari to coat. Bake 15 minutes on a baking tray.
2. Heat a wide deep heavy bottom stainless steel skillet over medium-high heat, with the remaining oil and sauté the chili and garlic until browned to flavor the oil, then discard. In the same pan, sauté the onion, carrot, celery and peppers, 5 minutes, until the onion is translucent. Add and roast the rice, 5 minutes. Add the herbs, sea salt, tomatoes (if using) and the hot saffron-stock. Bring to a boil, simmer covered 30 minutes on low heat.
3. Add peas and baked tempeh, cover, cook 15 more minutes. Adjust seasonings to taste. Mix in the parsley, reserving a little to sprinkle on top as a garnish.

Variation: You can use seitan or tofu instead of tempeh if desired. Other varieties of rice may be substituted for the long grain.

* See Vegetable Stock in TRICKS OF THE TRADE
** See GLOSSARY

JAZZY JAMBALAYA

Prep Time: 15

Cook Time: 55

Serves: 4-6

Groceries

Long Grain Brown Rice, Seitan, Toasted Sesame Oil, Onion, Bay Leaves, Celery, Green Pepper, Garlic, Tomatoes (opt.), Thyme, Dried Crushed Chili, Clove, Scallions.

Do Ahead

Bake the seitan and refrigerate for 1 week in a sealed container. Extra servings of Jambalaya can be refrigerated for 5 days (made with fresh baked seitan) or frozen for 3 months, although the texture will change.

Hot Tips

You can make this with cooked rice; add 4-5 cups at the end with the seitan to heat through. To reduce fat and time, boil all the ingredients together, omit sautéing seitan and vegetables in the oil. The quantity of stock or water may vary, depending on the juiciness of the tomatoes and the amount of moisture loss from the pot you are using.

Meal Balance

With this dish all you need is leafy greens - as a salad or lightly cooked - to balance the meal (see Veggie Ventures). Tempeh or tofu instead of seitan will provide soybean protein if you prefer.

Spicy foods are native to hot climates. Chilies and cayenne disperse body heat, from inside the body, out to the surface, so although initially you feel hot, spices are cooling.

2 tablespoons Corn Oil*
2 teaspoons Toasted Sesame Oil*
2 cups Seitan, drained, patted dry, diced ¾"
¼ teaspoon Crushed Dried Chilies
1 medium Onion, diced
2 Celery ribs, diced
½ each Green and Red Pepper, diced
2 cups Tomatoes, diced (optional)
2 Garlic Cloves and 2 Scallions**, minced
2 Bay Leaves and 2 teaspoons Thyme
¼ teaspoon each Cayenne and Clove powder
2 cups Long Grain Brown Rice (raw)
±3 cups Vegetable Stock*** or Water
¼ cup Italian Parsley, minced

1. Heat a heavy enamel coated or stainless steel pot over medium-high heat with the oil and brown the seitan as evenly as possible. Set seitan aside in a bowl. In the same pot,
2. Add the chili and onion and sauté until golden brown. Sauté the celery and bell peppers until tender. Mix in the tomatoes (if using, otherwise add 1 extra cup liquid), garlic, scallion whites, herbs, spices, rice, stock or water and the browned seitan.
3. Bring to a boil, reduce heat to low and simmer for 40 minutes or until liquid is absorbed. Mix in scallion greens and parsley and serve****.

* See TRICKS OF THE TRADE
** See CUTTING TO THE CHASE
*** See Vegetable Stock in TRICKS OF THE TRADE. Salted
   stock reduces the amount of salt added to the stew.
**** See REMOVING GRAINS FROM THE POT in STAPLES.

CARIBBEAN RISI E BISI

Prep Time: 5   **Cook Time: 45**   **Serves: 4-6**

Groceries

Long Grain Brown Rice, Pigeon Peas or Green Peas, Garlic, Scallion, Thyme, Coconut Milk (optional).

Do Ahead

Soak the rice for 1 hour in the water. The cooked dish keeps refrigerated for 5 days in a sealed container, or 3 months frozen.

Hot Tips

Eliminate fat by substituting the coconut milk for vegetable stock or water. It will still be delicious, only less tropical-paradise tasting.

Meal Balance

Serve with a mixture of colorful vegetables for a simple meal. The Jamaican Kidney Beans, or Vegetable Seitan Curry is ideal accompaniment, for heartier appetites.

Every part of the world has their version of grains and beans, the staple foods for humanity. Natives in the Caribbean Islands serve this every week.

2 cups Long Grain Brown Rice
3 cups Water
2 cups Pure Coconut Milk
1 cup fresh or frozen Peas or Pigeon Peas
1 large Garlic Clove, minced
1 large Scallion*, white + green parts minced
1 teaspoon dried Thyme (or 1 tbsp. fresh)
1 teaspoon Sea Salt, or to taste
¼ teaspoon Pepper

1. Bring the rice to a boil over medium-high heat, with the water, coconut milk, peas, garlic, white part of the scallion and the dried thyme.
2. Mix in the sea salt and pepper, reduce heat to low, and simmer covered for 40 minutes.
3. Transfer to a serving dish**, mixing in the scallion greens (and fresh thyme, if using).

* See CUTTING TO THE CHASE
** See REMOVING GRAINS FROM THE POT in STAPLES.

THAI VEGETABLE FRIED RICE

Prep Time: 15   **Cook Time: 10**   **Serves: 4-6**

Groceries

Brown Thai Jasmine Rice, Lemon Grass (optional), Ginger, Garlic, Onion, Carrot, Celery, Red Pepper, Cabbage, Broccoli, Corn, Scallions, Cilantro, Dried Crushed Chilies.

Do Ahead

Wash the vegetables, ready to chop and refrigerate in sealed containers up to 3 days in advance. Cooked rice keeps up to 5 days refrigerated. Extra servings of this dish will keep refrigerated for 5 days (made with fresh cooked rice).

Hot Tips

Have all the vegetables chopped before you begin cooking so you don't overcook some vegetables while waiting for the others to be added. To reduce fat, sauté in ¼ cup of water instead of oil. This dish will be very spicy with the full ¼ teaspoon of chili. As an option, season with pepper or cayenne at the end to taste.

Meal Balance

This is a balanced grain and vegetable dish in one. For extra protein; add tempeh (at the beginning); cooked beans, or tofu (at the end). Serve lightly cooked, leafy greens or a salad with this if desired.

In Bangkok local natives at their food stalls serve up all kinds of grilled and stir fried vegetables with rice. If you find fresh cilantro with roots attached, mince and cook them in with the garlic.

1 tablespoon Peanut or Sesame Oil
1 tablespoon Ginger, minced
1 tablespoon Lemon Grass, minced (optional)
2 Garlic Cloves, minced
¼ teaspoon Crushed Dried Chilies
1 medium Onion, diced
1 Carrot and 1 Celery, diced
½ Red Pepper, diced
1 teaspoon Sea Salt and ½ cup Water
2 cups Cabbage, diced
1 stalk Broccoli, flowerettes, stems diced*
1-2 Corn Cobs, niblets removed
2 Scallions, sliced*(whites and greens)
2 tablespoons Tamari** or to taste
4 cups White Thai Jasmine Rice, cooked***
¼ cup Cilantro, minced (or Italian Parsley)

1. Heat a large stainless steel wok over medium-high heat with the oil and sauté the ginger, lemon grass, garlic and chili to flavor the oil. Add the onion, carrot, celery and red pepper and sauté until tender, 2 minutes.
2. Add the salt and water and bring to a boil. Add the cabbage, broccoli, corn and scallion whites, cover and cook for two minutes or until bright green and tender-crisp.
3. Add tamari to the juices and mix the rice in with the vegetables, cover and heat through. Adjust seasoning to taste. Mix in the cilantro or parsley and serve****.

* See CUTTING TO THE CHASE
** See GLOSSARY
*** See COOKING WHOLE GRAINS chart
**** See REMOVING GRAINS FROM THE POT in STAPLES.

SUN SEED RICE PATTIES

Prep Time: 15   **Cook Time: 35**   **Makes: 8**

Groceries

Brown Rice, Tofu, Seitan, Carrot, Pumpkin, Sunflower or Sesame Seeds, Scallion, Parsley.

Do Ahead

Make extra toasted seeds to have on hand and store them in a glass jar for several weeks. Cooked rice will keep refrigerated for up to 5 days in a sealed container. You may assemble and refrigerate the patties up to 3 days in advance before baking. Once baked, they keep refrigerated for 5 days (made with fresh grains), or 3 months frozen.

Hot Tips

You can use various cooked grains; barley, bulgur, millet, quinoa, and varieties of rice. For a fat-free patty omit the seeds and tofu, and double the seitan.

Meal Balance

These patties are portable, mini, balanced meals with whole grains, soy product, seeds and vegetables. A lightly cooked green vegetable or salad will keep this simple and delicious. Heartier meals can be created by adding a Savory Stew or Sensational Seitan dish, or by beginning your meal with a Sumptuous Soup.

These are very attractive in a wholesome way. Serve them topped with a Super Sauce, for a gourmet main course.

¼ cup Pumpkin, Sesame or Sunflower Seeds
3 cups Brown Rice, cooked*
1 cup Seitan**, grated
1 cup crumbled Tofu***
½ cup Carrot, grated
2 small or 1 large Scallion, minced
¼ cup Italian Parsley, minced
Sea Salt and Pepper to taste

1. Preheat oven to 350°F. Wash and drain the seeds. Spread on a baking tray and bake for 10 minutes, or until golden brown. Meanwhile...
2. In a food processor grind half of the rice to a sticky ball. In a large bowl, combine all the rice with the remaining ingredients. Adjust seasonings to taste. Mix in the toasted seeds (whole or coarsely ground if desired).
3. Moisten your hands with water and shape the mixture into patties, 3" diameter and ½" thick. Bake on an oiled baking tray until golden and cooked through to the center, approximately 25 minutes.

* See BROWN RICE in STAPLES
** See SPEEDY HOMEMADE SEITAN in STAPLES
*** See GLOSSARY

PEANUTTY PATTIES

Prep Time: 15   **Cook Time: 45**   **Makes: 8**

Groceries

Millet, Carrot, Sweet Potato, Italian Parsley, Scallion, Peanuts, Peanut Butter.

Do Ahead

Toast extra peanuts, and store refrigerated in a glass jar for several weeks, to have on hand. Wash and refrigerate the vegetables in a plastic bag, up to 3 days in advance. The patties will keep refrigerated for 5 days, and frozen 3 months.

Hot Tips

In place of the peanuts and peanut butter, you may use almonds and almond butter, sunflower seeds and sunflower butter, or sesame seeds and sesame butter or tahini. To eliminate fat, omit the nuts and nut butter, and roll the patties in bread crumbs. Substitute quinoa, bulgur or couscous for, or use in combination with the millet. Use buttercup or butternut squash, cauliflower, corn and/or parsnips in place of the above vegetables.

Meal Balance

Serve with plenty of colorful vegetables for a balanced meal. A Sumptuous Soup, Savory Stew, Sensational Seitan and/or a Super Sauce can turn the meal into a full course feast.

These were created with kids in mind. We have disguised, and turned "unappealing food" - healthy grains and vegetables - into attractive, fun food. Adults enjoy them as much as, if not more than children do.

½ cup Millet, sorted, washed and drained
1 Carrot, grated or diced fine
1 small Sweet Potato, (1½ cups) diced ½"
½ teaspoon Sea Salt
½ cup Whole Raw Peanuts
1 Scallion, minced
2 tablespoon Italian Parsley, minced
2 tablespoons Peanut Butter*

1. Preheat oven to 350°F. Bring 1½ cups of water to a boil over medium-high heat with the millet, carrots and sweet potato. Add sea salt, cover, reduce heat to low, simmer for 25 minutes, until tender and water is absorbed.
2. Meanwhile, toast the peanuts on a baking tray in the oven 5-10 minutes, until golden brown. Coarsely grind them in a food processor, or chop them finely with a knife.
2. Add the scallion, parsley and peanut butter to the millet and vegetables. Mash with a potato masher to completely incorporate the peanut butter and mix everything together.
3. When the mixture is cool enough to handle, shape into patties or croquettes with moist hands. Roll and press the patties in the ground peanuts. Place patties on the baking tray and bake for 20 minutes. This will intensify their flavor, make them more firm, and a deeper golden brown. Alternatively, you may omit the baking step and serve as is.

* See GLOSSARY

MILLET & VEGETABLES

Prep Time: 15   **Cook Time: 25**   **Serves: 4-6**

Groceries

Millet, Onion, Carrot, Celery, Cauliflower, Corn (opt.), Squash or Sweet Potato, Garlic, Basil, Marjoram, Rosemary, Miso.

Do Ahead

Vegetables may be washed and refrigerated for up to 3 days in plastic bags or sealed containers. Extra servings will keep refrigerated for 5 days or frozen for 3 months (although this changes the texture somewhat).

Hot Tips

Cook this recipe the evening or morning before you plan to serve it and let it cool and set in a loaf dish. To heat for serving, bake whole, or slice it into ½" thick slabs which can be grilled (see Grilled Vegetable Polenta), steamed or baked. Various vegetables, cooked beans, toasted nuts or seeds, herbs and spices may be added.

Meal Balance

Perfect dish for a Super Sauce poured on top. This nutritious grain and vegetable meal-in-one could become a heartier meal with a Sumptuous Soup served before, and a Savory Stew or Sensational Seitan with it. Serve also with freshly cooked leafy green vegetables or a salad.

This is perfect for those days when you want quick cooking grains that will at once satisfy and nourish. When time is of the essence, steamed broccoli completes the meal perfectly.

2 cups Millet, sorted, rinsed and drained
6 cups Vegetable Stock* or Water
1 large Onion, diced ¼"
1 Carrot, diced ¼"
1 Celery, diced ¼"
1 Corn Cob, niblets removed (optional)
2 cups Cauliflower, chopped
2 cups Squash** or Sweet Potato, diced
1 teaspoon each Basil, Marjoram, Sea Salt
Pepper to taste (optional)
1½ teaspoons Sea Salt, or to taste
¼ cup Italian Parsley, minced

1. Bring millet to a boil with the water over medium-high heat, with the remaining ingredients (except parsley). Reduce heat to low, simmer covered 20 minutes or until tender.
2. Mix in the parsley and serve. Or make a loaf or patties as in the variations.

Variations:
Millet & Vegetable Loaf
Preheat oven to 350°F. Once boiled, transfer to an oiled loaf dish and bake 30 minutes, until the edges are golden brown and the center is set.

Millet & Vegetable Patties
Shape the mixture, once cooled enough to handle, into patties. Eat as is or bake in a pre-heated 350°F oven until golden or to reheat.

* See Vegetable Stock in TRICKS OF THE TRADE. Salted stock reduces the amount of salt added to the stew.
** Buttercup, Butternut or Delicatta (see Winter Squash in CUTTING TO THE CHASE)

MILLET & CAULIFLOWER

Prep Time: 5 **Cook Time: 25** **Serves: 4**

Groceries

Millet, Cauliflower

Do Ahead

Cauliflower can be washed (and chopped if this is convenient), refrigerated in a sealed container for up to three days. Extra servings will keep for five days refrigerated or three months frozen (the texture will change).

Hot Tips

This may seem quite soft and mushy just after cooking, but it will firm up a lot after a few minutes, as it sits and cools. You can shape this into patties for another meal or for lunch the next day. Reheat the patties by baking or fry them (see Grilled Vegetable Polenta).

Meal Balance

Millet is a very nutritious grain. For a simple light meal all you need are some steamed greens or a salad. Heartier appetites can be satisfied by a Sumptuous Soup or Savory Stew served before, or include a Sensational Seitan dish on the side.

To quote a successful home-maker and mother of young boys, "This is definitely a children's favorite, they make volcanoes on their plate with it". Like mashed potatoes, only healthier, it is perfect with Mushroom Onion Gravy and other Super Sauces.

3 cups Vegetable Stock* or Water
1 cup Millet, sorted, washed, drained
3 cups Cauliflower, chopped ½" chunks
½-1 teaspoon Sea Salt, or to taste

1. Bring water to a boil over medium-high heat with the millet and cauliflower. Add the sea salt, reduce to low and simmer covered for 20-25 minutes, or until tender.
2. Mash the millet and cauliflower with a potato masher and serve.

Variations:
Millet & Cauliflower Loaf
Preheat oven to 350°F. Various vegetables, cooked beans, toasted nuts or seeds, herbs and spices may be added. Once boiled, transfer to an oiled loaf dish and bake for 30 minutes, until the edges are golden brown and the center is set.

Millet & Cauliflower Patties
Shape the mixture, once cooled enough to handle, into patties. Eat as is or bake in a preheated 350°F oven until golden or to reheat.

Millet & Cauliflower Nori Rolls
Once it has cooled, spread and roll 1-1½ cups into a nori sheet for a portable meal (see Nori Rolls in TRICKS OF THE TRADE).

* See Vegetable Stock in TRICKS OF THE TRADE. Salted stock reduces the amount of salt added to the stew.

KASHA & CARAWAY

Prep Time: 15   **Cook Time: 25**   **Serves: 4**

Groceries

Kasha, Bulgur, Onion, Carrot, Mushrooms, Squash, Caraway, Coriander, Sage, Tamari.

Do Ahead

Wash the vegetables, ready to chop and store refrigerated in a sealed container up to 3 days in advance. Extra cooked servings will keep refrigerated for 5 days in a sealed container, or frozen for 3 months (although the texture changes somewhat).

Hot Tips

You can cook this recipe the evening or morning before you plan to serve it, transfer it to a loaf dish and let it cool and set. To heat for serving, bake whole, or slice it into ½" thick slabs, which can be grilled (see Grilled Vegetable Polenta), steamed or baked. This also makes great patties! See Millet & Vegetables.

Meal Balance

This is a hearty, warming fat-free grain dish that is wonderful with a Super Sauce and freshly cooked green vegetables or a salad. You could serve a Sumptuous Soup before, and/or a Savory Stew or Sensational Seitan with it for a full course meal.

Kasha's robust flavor harmonizes with the mellow, nutty flavor of bulgur. The vegetables add color, taste and texture, with the savory seasonings.

3½ cups Vegetable Stock* or Water
1 Onion, diced
1 Carrot, diced
2 cups Squash**, diced
½ cup Kasha, sorted rinsed and drained
¼ cup Tamari***, or extra Sea Salt to taste
½ teaspoon each ground Caraway, Coriander
½ teaspoon Sage
¼-½ teaspoon Sea Salt, or to taste
Pepper to taste (optional)
1 cup Bulgur or Couscous
¼ cup Italian Parsley, minced

1. Bring water to a boil over medium-high heat with the vegetables. Reduce heat to a low boil and simmer for 10 minutes covered.
2. Stir in the kasha and next six ingredients (up to and including pepper). Return to a boil, cover, simmer 15 minutes, until tender.
3. Stir bulgur and parsley into the mixture (if there is much moisture loss with the pot you are using, add ¼-½ cup of water or vegetable stock with the bulgur, or it may be too dry) and remove from heat. Let stand covered for 15 minutes to absorb all the liquid. Adjust seasonings to taste and serve.

Variation: **Kasha & Caraway Loaf**
Transfer the cooked mixture to an oiled loaf pan and bake in a pre-heated 350°F for 30 minutes, until browned and set.

* See Vegetable Stock in TRICKS OF THE TRADE. Salted stock reduces the amount of salt added to the stew.
** Buttercup, Butternut or Delicatta (see Winter Squash in CUTTINGTO THE CHASE)
*** See GLOSSARY

COUSCOUS with VEGETABLES

Prep Time: 15   **Cook Time: 15**   **Serves: 4-6**

Groceries

Couscous, Onion, Garlic, Carrot, Celery, Red Pepper, Zucchini, Winter Squash, Lemon Juice, Basil, Parsley, Tamari, Pine Nuts/Walnuts (opt).

Do Ahead

Vegetables may be washed, ready to chop, refrigerated in plastic bags or sealed containers for up to 3 days. Couscous is an instant grain, but can be prepared up to 3 days in advance, and stored refrigerated in a sealed container.

Hot Tips

If you want to create a sauce with the vegetables, simply add 2 tbsp. arrowroot diluted in 2 cups water, simmer in at the end until clear with the tamari. Add an extra ±½ tsp. sea salt, or ±¼ cup tamari (to taste) to season the extra liquid. For a fat-free dish omit the oil and nuts, sauté in ¼ cup of water instead.

Meal Balance

This is light and nutritious one-dish balanced meal. The couscous is a flour product so have whole grains at another meal in the day. Cooked beans such as chickpeas, kidney or pinto beans can be cooked in with the vegetables for added protein, rich texture and flavor.

This is a very colorful dish that makes a beautiful presentation. Use whole wheat couscous for higher nutritional value.

2 cups Couscous
2 tablespoons Olive Oil
½ cup Pine Nuts or Walnuts
1 Onion, diced
2 Garlic Cloves, minced
1 Red Pepper and 2 Celery ribs, diced ½"
2 cups Squash, diced ½"
2 Carrots, sliced ½ moons
2 Zucchini, sliced ½ moons
½-1 teaspoon Sea Salt or to taste
¼ teaspoon Pepper or to taste
2-4 tablespoons Tamari** or to taste
2 teaspoons Lemon Juice
¼ cup each fresh Basil, minced
¼ cup Italian Parsley, minced

1. Bring vegetable stock* or water to a boil, stir in the couscous, cover and remove from heat. Let set for 15 minutes to absorb the liquid. Remove lid and fluff couscous with a fork into a large serving platter. Meanwhile...
2. Heat a skillet over medium-high heat with the oil and sauté the nuts with a pinch of salt until golden brown. Remove and set aside.
3. In the same skillet sauté the onion and garlic until tender. Add the remaining vegetables, sea salt and pepper with ¼ cup of water. Cover and cook the vegetables in their juices for 10 minutes, or until tender.
4. Stir lemon juice and tamari into the juices, adjust seasonings to taste. Add basil, parsley (except 1 tbsp. of each), and serve over the couscous topped with the toasted nuts. Garnish with remaining basil and parsley.

* See Vegetable Stock in TRICKS OF THE TRADE
** See GLOSSARY
*** Buttercup, Butternut or Delicatta (see Winter Squash in CUTTING TO THE CHASE)

GRILLED VEGETABLE POLENTA

Prep Time: 15   **Cook Time: 35**   **Serves: 4-6**

Groceries

Cornmeal, Winter Squash or Sweet Potato, Carrot, Green and Red Pepper, Celery, Italian Parsley, Basil, Oregano, Tamari.

Do Ahead

Vegetables may be washed and refrigerated in a sealed container for up to 3 days. Cook this recipe the evening or morning before you plan to serve it, and let it cool and set in a loaf dish.

Hot Tips

When it's time to reheat, you can either a) bake it whole as a loaf, b) steam the slices over boiling water, or c) bake the slices in a 375°F oven on a baking tray. These alternate cooking methods eliminate frying in oil = fat-free.

Meal Balance

This grain and vegetable dish will be a light balanced meal with a salad or freshly cooked green vegetables. For a hearty full course meal, serve a Sumptuous Soup before, and a Savory Stew or Sensational Seitan with it.

* See Vegetable Stock in TRICKS OF THE TRADE. Salted stock reduces the amount of salt added to the stew.

** Buttercup, Butternut or Delicatta (see Winter Squash in CUTTING TO THE CHASE)

*** See GLOSSARY

You can serve this recipe directly in a bowl instead of setting it in a loaf dish, slicing and frying it. This is great served with one of the Super Sauces.

1½ cups Cornmeal
1 Carrot, diced ¼" 1 Celery, diced ¼"
1 cup Squash** or Sweet Potato, diced ¼"
¼ each Green and Red Pepper, diced ¼"
½ teaspoon each Basil and Oregano
1 teaspoon Sea Salt
1/8 teaspoon Pepper or to taste
¼ cup Italian Parsley, minced
Olive Oil
Tamari**

1. Bring 2½ cups of vegetable stock* or water to a boil over medium heat with the diced vegetables, and cook for 5 minutes, or until tender-crisp. Meanwhile...
2. Stir the cornmeal with a whisk into 2 cups of water, dissolve the lumps and then whisk into the boiling water with the herbs, sea salt and pepper. Return to a boil, simmer on low heat for 15 minutes stirring occasionally to prevent it from lumping on the bottom.
3. Stir in the parsley and pour it into an oiled 8" by 8" baking dish. Let it cool and set until firm. (See Hot Tips.) Slice into ½" thick slabs.
4. Heat a skillet brushed with olive oil over medium-high heat and fry the polenta slices on one side until golden brown, about 3-5 minutes. Sprinkle ¼-½ teaspoon tamari on the top of each slice. Turn the slices over, being careful not to break them and fry the other side. Sprinkle tamari on top. Serve with minced parsley garnish.

THREE GRAIN JOHNNYCAKE

Prep Time: 5   **Cook Time: 45**   **Serves: 6-8**

Groceries

Cornmeal, Millet, Quinoa, Soymilk, Baking Powder.

Do Ahead

Cook the grains and transfer to a baking dish the evening or morning before you plan to serve it. Simply bake it as indicated to reheat, and serve. The baked grains will keep refrigerated for 5 days, or frozen for 3 months, either whole or in serving-size containers.

Hot Tips

To eliminate fat, substitute water for the soymilk. It will be less rich and creamy, but still delicately delicious.

Meal Balance

Serve this simple grain dish with a Savory Stew or Super Sauce. Complement and balance the meal with colorful lightly cooked vegetables or a salad, see Veggie Ventures.

Johnnycake is a real "down home" southern dish of cornmeal, cooked in milk, dotted with butter, and baked. This intercontinental-vegan version blends corn of North America, millet of Asia, quinoa of South America and soymilk, baked golden with a glaze of corn oil.

3 cups Water
½ cup Millet, sorted, washed and drained
½ cup Quinoa, sorted, washed and drained
1½ teaspoons Sea Salt
1 cup Cornmeal (fine ground)
2 cups Soymilk* or Water
1 teaspoon Baking Powder
1-2 tablespoons Corn Oil (optional)

1. Bring 3 cups of the water to a boil over medium heat, with the millet and quinoa. Reduce heat to low, add sea salt, cover and simmer for 10 minutes. Meanwhile,
2. Preheat oven to 350°F. In a bowl, whisk the cornmeal and soymilk together. Whisk the cornmeal mixture into the millet and quinoa and return to a boil. Cover, reduce heat to low, and simmer for 5 minutes. Stir occasionally to prevent lumping on the bottom. Oil a 2 quart baking dish.
3. Mix the baking powder evenly into the cooked grains. Pour and scrape the grains into the baking dish. Drizzle the corn oil on top. Smooth the top with a spatula. The oil helps it become browned and crispy on top, and gives it a rich buttery flavor. Bake for 30 minutes.

Variation: Make this with 2 cups of Cornmeal instead of the combination of 3 grains. Bring water to a boil, add salt, then continue with step 2 as above.

* See GLOSSARY

HAZELNUT-BASIL BARLEY BREAD

Prep Time: 10   **Cook Time: 65**   **Makes: 1**

Groceries

Barley Flour, Barley Flakes (opt.), Hazelnuts, Basil, Soymilk, Lemon Juice, Baking Powder, Baking Soda, Flax Seeds (opt.).

Do Ahead

Toast extra hazelnuts and store refrigerated in a glass jar for several weeks. Combine the dry ingredients and store covered for several days. Wet ingredients can be refrigerated for up to 3 days in a sealed container. The bread tastes better after it has cooled and the flavors have married and intensified. It lasts 1 week refrigerated in a sealed container, or frozen 3 months.

Hot Tips

Toasting nuts or seeds enhances and intensifies their flavor and aromatic qualities (optional). Substitute other dried or fresh herbs for variety. Substitute other nuts, or completely omit them to reduce fat. Flax seeds cooked in water have a similar consistency as egg whites. They give the bread a lift and additional nutrition.

Meal Balance

Serve a Sumptuous Soup before, or a Savory Stew with, including a salad or lightly cooked green vegetables, see Veggie Ventures.

This is wonderful with many different soups and stews, from Summer Corn Chowder to Savory Stratford Stew. Try it, you'll love it.

1 cup Barley Flakes* + 1 cup Hazelnuts
2 tablespoons Flax Seeds
3 cups Barley Flour
2 tablespoons Baking Powder
1 teaspoon each Baking Soda and Sea Salt
¼ cup fresh Basil, minced (4 teaspoons dried)
2 cups Soymilk
¼ cup Lemon Juice
2 tablespoons Olive Oil

1. Preheat oven to 350°F. Toast barley flakes on a baking tray until golden brown, 10 minutes. Toast hazelnuts on a baking tray 10 minutes, until golden brown. In a small pot, bring 1 cup water to a boil with the flax seeds, simmer on low covered 5 minutes. Remove from heat, set aside. Meanwhile...
2. In a large bowl, combine the flour, baking powder and soda, sea salt, and dried basil (if using). In a separate bowl, combine the fresh basil (if using), soymilk, lemon juice and oil.
3. Remove the skins from the hazelnuts, they rub off easily. Grind the toasted barley flakes to a coarse meal-flour and mix into the dry ingredients with the whole toasted hazelnuts. Add the flax seeds and water into the wet ingredients, and then mix this into the dry.
4. Transfer the mixture to an oiled loaf pan and bake uncovered for 55-65 minutes, until golden brown and a skewer inserted comes out clean. Allow the loaf to sit at room temperature for 10 minutes or so before removing from the pan. Slice and serve.

* These are rolled barley grains, not puffed cereal. You may substitute 1 cup of barley flour for the flakes.

SUNFLOWER OLIVE OAT BREAD

Prep Time: 10　　　　**Cook Time: 65**　　　　　　　**Makes: 1**

Groceries

Oat Flour, Oat Flakes, Sunflower Seeds, Olives, Soymilk, Lemon Juice, Baking Powder, Baking Soda, Flax Seeds (optional).

Do Ahead

Toast extra seeds and store refrigerated in a glass jar for several weeks, to have on hand for other recipes. Combine the dry ingredients and store covered for several days. Wet ingredients can be refrigerated for up to 3 days in a sealed container. The bread tastes better after it has cooled and the flavors have married and intensified. It keeps 1 week refrigerated in a sealed container, or frozen 3 months.

Hot Tips

Toasting nuts or seeds before using them in a recipe enhances and intensifies their flavor and aromatic qualities (optional). The seeds can be substituted with other varieties, or completely omitted to reduce fat. The flax seeds become as egg whites and give a lift to the bread, and are very nutritious.

Meal Balance

Serve a Sumptuous Soup before, or a Savory Stew with, and a salad or lightly cooked green vegetables (see Veggie Ventures) with this grain rich bread.

This aromatic bread is wonderful with everything!

1½ cups Rolled Oats*
1 cup Sunflower Seeds
1 cup Water
2 tablespoons Flax Seeds
3 cups Whole Wheat Pastry Flour
2 tablespoons Baking Powder
1 teaspoon Baking Soda
½ teaspoon Sea Salt
2 cups Soymilk
¼ cup Lemon Juice
2 tablespoons Olive Oil
¾-1 cup (1 small jar) Black or Green Olives

1. Preheat oven to 350°F. Toast the rolled oats on a baking tray until golden brown, 10 minutes. Toast sunflower seeds on a baking tray for 10 minutes, until golden brown. In a small pot, bring water to a boil on medium heat with the flax seeds, simmer for 5 minutes. Remove from heat, set aside.
2. In a large bowl, combine the flour, baking powder, baking soda and sea salt. In a separate bowl, combine the soymilk, lemon juice and oil.
3. Grind the toasted rolled oats to a coarse meal-flour and mix into the dry ingredients with the whole toasted sunflower seeds. Add flax seeds and water into the wet ingredients. Chop the olives in ½ or ¼, or leave whole if desired and mix with the wet ingredients. Combine the wet with the dry ingredients.
4. Transfer the mixture to an oiled loaf pan and bake uncovered for 55-65 minutes, until golden brown and a skewer inserted comes out clean. Allow the loaf to sit at room temperature for 10 minutes or so before removing from the pan. Slice and serve.

* These are old fashioned rolled oats, not the quick cooking variety. You may substitute 1½ cups of oat flour for the rolled oats.

ANASAZI SKILLET BREAD

Prep Time: 10   **Cook Time: 35**   **Makes: 1**

Groceries

Cornmeal, Whole Wheat Pastry Flour, Cilantro, Anasazi Beans, Carrot, Sweet Potato, Dandelion or Watercress, Lemon Juice, Dried Crushed Chilies, Soymilk, Corn, Baking Powder and Soda.

Do Ahead

Prepare the vegetables, ready to chop, and refrigerate in a sealed container for up to 3 days. Mix the dry ingredients in a bowl several days in advance. Store the wet ingredients in a sealed container, refrigerated, up to 3 days in advance. Once baked it keeps refrigerated for 5 days, or frozen for 3 months.

Hot Tips

For ideal slicability, let the bread cool for 10-15 minutes after removing it from the oven, or it will be very crumbly. Substitute various beans for anasazi. Use watercress instead of dandelion. If dandelions are available with their roots, mince the roots and sauté with the carrots. Use bean cooking liquid or water instead of soymilk to cut calories and fat.

Meal Balance

This grain, bean and vegetable dish is wonderful with a salad or lightly cooked greens for a simple, yet very satisfying meal.

Native American Indians prepared their meals in cast iron pots over a camp fire. Dried beans and ground corn were their staple, served with wild roots, squash, tubers and freshly picked greens. Here's our interpretation.

¼ cup Corn Oil
½ teaspoon Dried Crushed Chilies
1 cup Carrot, diced ¼"
1 cup Squash or Sweet Potato, diced ¼"
1 Corn Cob, niblets removed
1 cup Anasazi Beans, cooked* (or canned)
2 cups fine-medium ground Cornmeal
2 cups Whole Wheat Pastry Flour, (sift after)
1 tablespoon Baking Powder
1½ teaspoons each Baking Soda and Sea Salt
1 teaspoon each Oregano and Sage
2½ cups Bean Liquid, Soymilk** +/or Water
¼ cup Apple Cider Vinegar
1 cup packed Dandelion Greens, ½" chopped

1. Preheat oven to 350°F. Heat a cast iron skillet over medium heat with 1 tbsp. of the oil and sauté the chili, carrot, sweet potato and corn 5 minutes or until browned. 2. Combine the cornmeal, flour, baking soda and powder, sea salt and herbs in a bowl. In a separate bowl, combine the liquid, vinegar and the remaining oil. Mix the wet ingredients into the dry to form a batter.
3. Add the beans and dandelion to the skillet and cook covered 1 minute. Mix the batter in, smooth the top evenly and place the skillet in the oven. Bake for 30 minutes, until a skewer inserted comes out clean.

* See COOKING BEANS chart in STAPLES
** See GLOSSARY

KASHA WALNUT MEAT LOAF

Prep Time: 15   **Cook Time: 50**   **Serves: 4-6**

Groceries

Tofu, Kasha, Bulgur, Onion, Celery, Mushrooms, Garlic, Green Pepper, Walnuts, Miso, Thyme, Sage, Mustard, Nutmeg, Parsley.

Do Ahead

You can prepare the loaf and refrigerate, well sealed, for up to 3 days, before baking. Once baked it will keep for 5 days refrigerated (if made with fresh ingredients), or frozen for 3 months, either whole or in slices, in a sealed container.

Hot Tips

You can use leftover cooked grains instead of the bulgur and kasha to be more time efficient. The flavor and texture of kasha and bulgur are well suited to this dish.

Meal Balance

You have grains and soy bean goodness in one dish that become a complete balanced meal with freshly cooked green vegetables or a salad, along with naturally sweet orange vegetables such as squash and carrots (see Veggie Ventures, Sumptuous Soups or Savory Stews).

* See GLOSSARY

This is hearty, savory and satisfying. The Mushroom Onion Gravy or Bechamel Dijon Sauce makes it sing.

½ cup Walnut Halves
½ cup Kasha and ½ cup Bulgur
1 tablespoon Corn or Sesame Oil
1 medium Onion and 1 Celery, diced
4 oz. Mushrooms, diced
½ Green Pepper, diced
2 Garlic Cloves, minced
1 teaspoon each Thyme and Mustard Powder
½ teaspoon each Sage and Sea Salt
¼ teaspoon each Nutmeg and Pepper
½ pound (454 gr.) Tofu* Extra Firm
1/3 cup Ketchup* (optional)
2 tablespoons medium-dark Miso*

1. Preheat oven to 350°F. Toast walnuts on a baking tray for 10 minutes. Bring 2 cups of water to a boil over medium-high heat, with the kasha. Reduce heat to low, cover and simmer for 10 minutes. Stir in the bulgur and remove from heat. Set aside covered.
2. Meanwhile, heat a skillet over medium-high heat with the oil. Sauté the onion, celery, mushrooms, green pepper and garlic, until tender and browned, 5 minutes. Add the herbs, spices and sea salt, cook 1 minute.
3. In a food processor, grind the tofu with the ketchup, miso and walnuts until fairly smooth, with some texture remaining. Combine the tofu mixture with the kasha and bulgur from Step 1, and the sautéed vegetables from Step 2.
4. Transfer the mixture to an oiled loaf pan (9" by 5") and bake for 45 minutes, or until browned, and a skewer inserted comes out clean.

LASAGNA WITH SPINACH & TOFU RICOTTA

Prep Time: 20   **Cook Time: 55**   **Serves: 6**

Groceries

A "10" Tomato Sauce, Tofu, Spinach, Lasagna Noodles, Tahini, Miso, Apple Cider Vinegar, Rice Syrup.

Do Ahead

The Noodles can be precooked and refrigerated for 3 days in a sealed container. Tofu Ricotta can be made up to 5 days in advance (without the spinach). The cooked Lasagna will keep refrigerated for 5-7 days. Freeze the lasagna in serving-size portions, well wrapped and sealed for 3 months.

Hot Tips

Omit the tahini to reduce the fat, but you lose some of the creamy-cheese-like taste, reminiscent of ricotta cheese. Have the tofu mixture as the top layer if you prefer instead of tomato sauce.

Meal Balance

The Caesar Salad goes fabulously with this dish. Fresh greens as a salad, steamed or one of the other Veggie Ventures turns this into a balanced meal. Ground seitan or tempeh can be mixed into the tomato sauce for a meaty-sauce which provides more protein and substance.

Proudly serve this as a traditional favorite that everyone will enjoy. For variety, try the Carrot Beet Basil Sauce in place of tomato sauce.

1 10 oz. package Spinach or 1 large bunch
1 pound (454 gr.) Tofu*, extra firm
¼ cup Tahini*
¼ cup Miso*, (light color)
3 tablespoons Apple Cider Vinegar (to taste)
2 tablespoons Rice Syrup*
1 teaspoon Sea Salt
±4 cups of A "10" Tomato Sauce, page 155
9 Whole Wheat Lasagna Noodles, cooked**

1. Wash and drain the spinach. Cook it in a pot over medium-low heat, covered, with only the moisture left on the leaves from washing. After 1-2 minutes the spinach will be wilted and bright green. Let it cool. Squeeze out and save the liquid, finely chop the spinach.
2. Tofu Ricotta: Purée the tofu, tahini, miso, vinegar, syrup and sea salt, with the saved spinach juice. Add more water or vegetable stock if necessary to achieve a thick, creamy, pourable, spreadable consistency.
3. Preheat oven to 350°F. Mix the chopped spinach with the Tofu Ricotta.
4. Oil a 9" by 13" baking dish and spread 1 cup tomato sauce over the bottom. Lay 3 noodles side by side over the sauce, then spread ±1½ cups of the tofu mixture evenly all over the noodles. Repeat the layers; sauce, noodles, tofu, and then repeat the layers again. Spread a top layer of tomato sauce evenly all over. Bake uncovered for 55 minutes, until the edges begin to brown and the center is no longer shiny.

* see GLOSSARY
** see PASTA in STAPLES

SHEPHERD'S PIE
WITH CAULIFLOWER PARSNIP TOPPING

Prep Time: 20   **Cook Time: 50**   **Serves: 6-8**

Groceries

Tempeh or Seitan, Cauliflower, Parsnips, Shiitake Mushrooms, Bulgur, White Miso, Soymilk, Corn and Toasted Sesame Oil, Onion, Garlic, Green Pepper, Corn, Rosemary, Sage, Thyme, Nutmeg, Tamari.

Do Ahead

The filling may be refrigerated 5 days in a sealed container. The topping is best made when you are completing the recipe, once refrigerated, it becomes too stiff to spread. The baked dish keeps refrigerated for 1 week or frozen for 3 months, either in serving-size sections or as a casserole.

Hot Tips

To reduce fat; use seitan instead of tempeh, omit step 1, and sauté in ¼ cup water instead of the oil. Substitute 2 large potatoes, peeled, for the cauliflower and parsnips if desired. Substitute or combine lentils or other varieties of beans with the tempeh.

Meal Balance

The combination of bulgur as a grain, with the complete soy protein in the tempeh, plus all the vegetables add up to a one dish meal!

Aromatic shiitake mushrooms enhance the flavor and texture of this popular dish.

1 12 oz. pk. Tempeh* or 3½ cups Seitan**
3 tablespoons Corn Oil
1/3 cup each Tamari*, Soymilk*, White Miso*
3 cups each Cauliflower, Parsnips chopped
½ cup raw Bulgur** (or 1 cup cooked grain)
1 teaspoon Toasted Sesame Oil*
1 large Onion and 1 Green pepper, diced
2 Garlic Cloves, minced
8 oz. fresh Shiitake Mushrooms***, sliced
2 tsp. each crushed Rosemary, Salt, Thyme
¼ teaspoon each Nutmeg, Pepper (to taste)
¼ cup Balsamic Vinegar
3 Corn Cobs, niblets removed

1. Preheat oven to 425°F. Cube tempeh ½" dice and toss with 2 tbsp. corn oil and 3 tbsp. tamari. Bake 15 minutes on a baking tray.
2. Bring cauliflower and parsnips to a boil in 1 cup of water, add ¾ tsp. salt, cook 10 min.
3. Boil 1 cup of water, add bulgur, let set.
4. Filling: Heat a skillet with 1 tbsp. corn oil, toasted sesame oil and sauté the onion, green pepper, garlic and mushrooms until browned. Add the herbs, spices, remaining tamari and sea salt, the vinegar, and cook 5 minutes. Crumble the tempeh with your fingers and add to the sautéed vegetables with the bulgur. Adjust seasonings to taste. Oil a 9" by 13" casserole. Spread the mixture into the base. Top with corn niblets.
5. Topping: Purée the cauliflower, parsnips, cooking liquid, soymilk, miso until smooth. Spread topping evenly over corn and bake uncovered 15 minutes at 425°F. Reduce heat, bake at 350°F 20 minutes, until golden.

* see GLOSSARY
** see STAPLES
*** or 12 dried mushrooms, reconstituted.

BROCCOLI & CAULIFLOWER RIZOULET ALMANDINE

Prep Time: 15   **Cook Time: 45**   **Serves: 6-8**

Groceries

Rice, Broccoli, Cauliflower, Silken Tofu, Miso, Tahini, Apple Cider Vinegar, Thyme, Nutmeg, Almonds or Bread Crumbs.

Do Ahead

Both the cooked rice and the tofu purée will keep refrigerated for 5 days in a sealed container. Wash the cauliflower (ready to chop) and refrigerate in plastic bags or a sealed container for up to 5 days. The baked dish keeps refrigerated for 5 days, or frozen for 3 months, either whole or in serving-size portions.

Hot Tips

The Almandine topping is very delicious, but to reduce fat use the bread crumbs, or no topping. You can add carrots, parsnips, squash, etc., if desired. Other grains can be used instead of rice. Use a light-medium color miso. The tahini may be omitted to reduce fat, but it adds flavor and richness.

Meal Balance

This has a substantial proportion of grains, soy goodness and essential nutritional vegetables. Serve with a fresh salad or lightly cooked colorful vegetables.

When I first made this at Ecos Cafe in Toronto, it began as a creative way to use up extra cooked rice. The dish sold out with rave reviews. A year later in Santa Monica, restaurant patrons again polished it off, and some came back for seconds.

2 cups Broccoli, chopped into 1" pieces
2 cups Cauliflower, chopped into 1" pieces
2 - 10.5 oz. (297 gr.) packages Silken Tofu*
1/3 cup each Miso* and Tahini*
2-3 tablespoons Apple Cider Vinegar, to taste
1 teaspoon each Tarragon and Thyme
½-1 teaspoon Sea Salt, to taste
¼ teaspoon each Nutmeg and White Pepper
1 cup coarse ground Almonds/Bread Crumbs
3 cups Brown Rice, cooked**

1. Steam the broccoli for 2 minutes or until bright green and tender-crisp over 1 cup of boiling water. Set aside in a bowl. Steam the cauliflower and set aside in the bowl. Reserve steaming water. Preheat oven to 375°F.
2. Purée the tofu with the miso, tahini, vinegar, herbs, spices and sea salt and the reserved steaming water until smooth.
3. Combine the tofu purée and rice with the steamed vegetables. Adjust seasonings to taste. Transfer mixture to an oiled 9" by 13" baking dish and bake for 40 minutes or until golden brown and the center is set.

Variation:
Broccoli Cauliflower Quiche Almandine
Fill two 8" pie dishes with the Whole Wheat Crust, page 247. Fill each crust with ½ of the above mixture and sprinkle with almonds (optional). Bake as above. Decorate with steamed Broccoli and Cauliflower-ettes.

* See GLOSSARY
** See BROWN RICE in STAPLES

QUINOA POLENTA
WITH DELICATTA SQUASH

Prep Time: 10   **Cook Time: 45**   **Serves: 6**

Groceries

Quinoa, Cornmeal, Delicatta Squash, Basil, Cilantro, Ginger, Marjoram, White Miso, Soymilk.

Do Ahead

The casserole may be assembled and refrigerated up to 2 days before baking. Once baked, it keeps refrigerated for 5 days and frozen for 3 months, in serving size portions or whole in the baking dish.

Hot Tips

Use all Quinoa or all Cornmeal if desired (see COOKING WHOLE GRAINS chart for water measurements). Butternut squash may be used in place of Delicatta, or use Buttercup (but peel the green skin). For variety, 1 cup of cooked beans, seitan, tempeh, or Tofu Cheese can be mixed into the polenta.

Meal Balance

With the whole grain goodness of the quinoa and cornmeal, and the nutrient rich squash, all you need is a side dish of freshly cooked green vegetables or a salad to balance this dish. The above tips for variety offer added protein, substance and texture.

This is a colorful, two layer casserole of delicately spiced grains and pureed sweet squash - ideal with boldly spiced dishes like Chili Con Carne.

1 cup Quinoa
6 cups Delicatta Squash, ½" diced*
½ cup finely ground Cornmeal
1½ teaspoons Sea Salt
1 teaspoon Basil
½ teaspoon Marjoram
¼ teaspoon Pepper or to taste
¼ cup Cilantro or Italian Parsley, minced
½ cup White Miso**
½ cup Soymilk**
2 teaspoons Ginger powder

1. Bring 2 cups of water to a boil with the quinoa, and simmer on low for 15 minutes. In another pot, bring the squash to a boil in ¼ cup of water, simmer 10 minutes, to tender.
2. Preheat oven to 350°F. Mix the cornmeal in with 1½ cups water, and whisk it into the quinoa with the sea salt, basil, marjoram and pepper. Return to a low boil, simmer for 5 minutes stirring occasionally to prevent it from sticking at the bottom. Stir in cilantro and pour into an oiled 9" by 13" baking dish.
3. Purée the squash and cooking water with the miso, soymilk and ginger until very smooth. Spread over the grain mixture evenly. (The grains will seem a little soft at this point but will firm up completely once baked and set at room temperature.)
4. Bake uncovered for 30 minutes or until golden brown. Let it set at room temperature for 15 minutes or more for sliceable servings.

* see Winter Squash in CUTTING TO THE CHASE
** see GLOSSARY

SAVORY COUNTRY PIE

Prep Time: 15   **Cook Time: 55**   **Makes: 1**

Groceries

Seitan, Carrot, Celery, Onion, Potato, Mushroom, Peas or Green Beans, Marjoram, Thyme, Parsley, Miso, Flour, Whole Wheat Crust.

Do Ahead

Make the dough fresh before assembling for best results. The filling can be refrigerated for 5 days before baking in the crust. Once baked, the pie keeps refrigerated for 1 week (made with fresh filling), or 3 months frozen, well wrapped and sealed.

Hot Tips

Make 2 miniature pies by rolling the dough into 5" circles. For portable turnovers, fold the dough over the filling, crimp and bake. Make a double or triple recipe and freeze the extra pies to have on hand. You'll be glad you did. To reduce fat, omit the oil and tossing the seitan in flour. Sauté the vegetables in ¼ cup water, add seitan with the miso.

Meal Balance

The seitan and crust provide a satisfying portion of grain products. (Have whole grains at another meal during the day.) Enjoy the pie with a salad or steamed green vegetables to balance the hearty root vegetables.

Tempeh can substitute for the seitan with delicious results, or use tofu for a light, meaty texture.

1½ cups Seitan*, drain, pat dry, dice ½"
3 tablespoons Whole Wheat Flour
1 tablespoon Corn Oil
1 Onion, diced ½"
1 Carrot, 1 Celery, 1 Potato, diced ½"
4 oz. Mushrooms, quartered
¼ cup fresh Peas or Green Beans, diced
1 teaspoon each Marjoram and Thyme
1 teaspoon Sea Salt, or to taste
1/8-1/4 teaspoon Pepper, to taste
1-2 tablespoons medium-dark Miso**(to taste)
1½ cups Water or Vegetable Stock
¼ cup Parsley, minced
1 Whole Wheat Crust***, page 247

1. Preheat oven to 350°F. Prepare the dough for the crust and cover with plastic.
2. Filling: a) Toss the seitan with the flour to coat evenly (save extra flour). Heat a skillet over medium-high heat with the oil and fry the seitan to brown. Remove and set aside.
b) In the same skillet add the onion, carrot, celery, potato and mushrooms and sauté until browned. Add remaining flour and toast for 2 minutes. Add peas, herbs, salt and pepper, cook covered for 5 minutes. Add miso dissolved in water, simmer for 5 minutes. Add parsley, and adjust seasonings to taste.
3. Place the base crust in a 2" deep, 9" pie dish. Add the filling. Cover with the top crust, crimp edges and pierce steam vents. Bake for 35 minutes, or until golden brown.

Variation: **Savory Vegetables**
Omit the crust. Dissolve 1 tbsp. arrowroot in 1 cup water + 2 tbsp. tamari. Simmer with miso in step 2 b). Serve over grains or pasta.

* See SPEEDY HOMEMADE SEITAN
** See GLOSSARY
*** See Pie Crusts in STAPLES

LAURENTIAN LENTIL TORTIÈRE

Prep Time 20   **Cook Time: 55**   **Makes: 1**

Groceries

Lentils, Whole Wheat Crust, Corn and Toasted Sesame Oil, Bay Leaf, Onion, Celery, Garlic, Cumin, Cinnamon, Thyme, Sage, Clove.

Do Ahead

Extra filling can be made in large batches and frozen for up to 3 months, in a sealed container. Prepare the dough fresh (raw dough will not refrigerate or freeze well, the oil separates from the dough). The baked pie keeps refrigerated for 1 week or frozen for 3 months, in a sealed container.

Hot Tips

To save time and fat, omit the oil and instead of sautéing, cook the vegetables, herbs, spices and seasonings directly in with the lentils during the last 15 minutes of cooking. For portable turnovers, roll the dough into 6" circles and fill each with ¼ cup of filling. Fold dough over, crimp, pierce steam vents and bake.

Meal Balance

This is a very savory , satisfying main dish. Balance this with a fresh salad or one of the Veggie Ventures. If you'll be eating the turnovers on the run, bring along carrot, celery and cucumber sticks for vegetables.

Whether you make pies or turnovers, you must experience eating this with the Chunky Fruit Ketchup, the way it is traditionally enjoyed.

1 cup Brown/Green Lentils, sorted, washed
1 Potato, ½" diced (optional)
1 Bay Leaf and a 1" piece Kombu*, optional
1½ teaspoons Sea Salt
2 tsp. each Corn** and Toasted Sesame** Oil
1 Onion and 1 Celery, finely diced
2 Garlic Cloves, minced
1-1½ teaspoons Cumin, to taste
½ teaspoon each Cinnamon, Thyme, Sage
¼ teaspoon each Clove, Nutmeg, Pepper
1-2 tablespoons Tamari*, to taste
1 Whole Wheat Crust***, page 247

1. Bring 2½ cups water to a boil with the lentils, potato, bay leaf and kombu. Reduce heat and simmer, covered for 25 minutes, until tender. Meanwhile...
2. Preheat oven to 350°F. In a skillet, sauté the onion, celery, garlic and spices in the oil 5 minutes, or until browned. Add sautéed vegetables to the cooked lentils. Adjust seasonings to taste, remove bay leaves, purée ¾ of filling. Mix purée with rest of the filling.
3. Prepare the dough. Roll 2/3 of dough between sheets of wax paper into a 10" diameter circle, ±1/6" thick, and transfer to a 9" pie dish. Spread 2 cups of filling evenly into the base crust. Roll the remaining 1/3 of dough into a 9" circle, 1/8" thick and place on top of the base and filling. Crimp the edges together and pierce steam vents in a decorative pattern on top.
Bake for 30 minutes, or until golden brown.

* See GLOSSARY
** SEE TRICKS OF THE TRADE
***See Pie Crusts in STAPLES

MUSHROOM VEGETABLE PIE

Prep Time: 25   **Cook Time: 45**   **Makes: 1**

Groceries

Mushrooms, Tofu, Cabbage, Carrots, Onion, Scallion, Basil, Caraway, Mustard, Miso, Apple Cider Vinegar, Flour, Lemon Juice, Tahini, 1 Whole Wheat & Rye Crust, Tofu Sour Cream.

Do Ahead

The Tofu-Vegetable filling can be stored refrigerated for 3 days, or 3 months frozen in a sealed container. Make the dough fresh just before assembling. The baked pie will keep for 5 days refrigerated or 3 months frozen, well sealed in a container.

Hot Tips

The pie tastes even better the second or third day. Spread the filling out as evenly as possible, so when you add the Tofu Sour Cream, it goes on smoothly. ***Use a pale-medium color miso as a dark miso will change the color of the filling, and a white miso is too delicate in flavor.

Meal Balance

The crust provides a small portion of grain product (have whole grains at another meal in the day). Serve with the Borsch if desired. Have the Herbed Kale & Cauliflower with Poppy Seed Dressing, or steamed greens, a salad or colorful mixed vegetables to balance the meal.

This is an attractive, healthy vegetarian version of the traditional Russian favorite.

1 Whole Wheat & Rye Crust*, page 247
1 tablespoon Corn Oil
10 whole Mushroom caps + 2 cups sliced
1 teaspoon Caraway Seeds
1 Onion, finely diced
1 cup each Carrot and Cabbage, finely diced
1 Scallion, white and greens finely diced
1 tsp. each Basil, Mustard Powder, Sea Salt
¼ teaspoon Pepper, or to taste
¼ cup Whole Wheat Pastry Flour
½ pound (454 gr.) Tofu**
2 tbsp. each Miso***, Rice Vinegar**, Tahini**
1/3 cup Tofu Sour Cream, see page 173
¼ teaspoon Paprika

1. Preheat oven to 350°F. Prebake a 9" pie crust 10 minutes. Heat a skillet over medium heat with the oil, sauté the mushroom caps 2 min., until their liquid is released. Strain and set the mushrooms aside, and save the juices.
2. Filling: a) In the same skillet toast the caraway seeds until fragrant, then sauté the onions, cabbage, carrots, sliced mushrooms for 2 minutes. Add scallion whites, herbs, salt, pepper, flour, cook 5 minutes covered. b) Purée the tofu, vinegar, tahini, miso, the mushroom juices and ±¼ cup vegetable stock or water until smooth. Mix into the sautéed vegetables, with the scallion greens. Adjust seasonings to taste. Spread into the pie crust.
3. Bake for 25 minutes, until pale golden and set in the center. Remove from the oven.
4. Spread Tofu Sour Cream over the filling. Place nine mushrooms around the edge near the crust, and one mushroom in the center. Sprinkle with paprika, bake 10 minutes more.

* See Pie Crusts in STAPLES
** See GLOSSARY

TOMATO LEEK QUICHE

Prep Time: 15   **Cook Time: 55**   **Makes: 1**

Groceries

Tomatoes, Leek, Silken Tofu, Lemon Juice, Sunflower Butter, White Miso, Garlic, Basil, Tarragon.

Do Ahead

The filling can be refrigerated 3 days in a sealed container before baking in the crust. The crust dough needs to be made fresh (raw dough will not refrigerate or freeze well, the oil separates from the flour). The quiche keeps refrigerated for 5 days, or frozen for 3 months, wrapped and sealed.

Hot Tips

Choose perfect small tomatoes and slice in ½ moons to decorate the top, placing the cut edge of the tomato against the crust. Ask your farmer or grocer which are the tastiest tomatoes available. The sunflower butter has a richer egg-like taste than tahini. Use an 8" dish for a deeper filling; a 9" or 10" results in a more shallow quiche.

Meal Balance

This is a filling yet light main course. Serve a Sumptuous Soup before, and enjoy with freshly cooked colorful vegetables or a salad. The crust is a small portion of grain product, have whole grains at another meal during the day.

The red tomato pattern on top turns the creamy tones of the tofu filling into a bright attractive dish. Place a healthy sprig of fresh tarragon or Italian parsley in the center just before serving.

1 Toasted Oats & Whole Wheat Crust*
1 tablespoon Olive Oil
1 large or 2 small Leeks, diced**
2 Garlic Cloves, minced
2 cups Tomatoes, chopped
1 teaspoon dried Basil or 1 tbsp. fresh
1 teaspoon dried Tarragon or 1 tbsp. fresh
½ teaspoon Sea Salt or to taste
¼ teaspoon Pepper or to taste
¼ cup Whole Wheat Pastry Flour
1 - 10.5 oz. pk. Silken Tofu*** Extra Firm
3 tbsp. each Lemon Juice and White Miso***
3 tbsp. Sunflower Butter*** or Tahini***
±¼ cup Soymilk*** or Water as needed
2 Plum Tomatoes, sliced into thin ½ moons**

1. Preheat oven to 350°F. Prebake pie crust for 10 minutes, until pale golden. Meanwhile,
2. Heat a skillet with the oil over medium-high heat and sauté the leek whites and garlic until golden. Add the chopped tomatoes, the leek greens, dried tarragon, sea salt, pepper and flour and cook covered for 2 minutes. (Add fresh herbs now if using.) Meanwhile…
3. Purée the tofu, lemon juice, white miso, sunflower butter and enough liquid to achieve a thick, smooth and creamy consistency. (If the tomatoes are very juicy, reduce soymilk or water in the tofu purée.) Mix the tofu purée with the sautéed vegetables, adjust seasonings to taste. Spread evenly into the pie crust and bake for 35 minutes, or until center is set.
4. Remove from the oven and place the tomato slices around the edge of the crust. Bake for 10 minutes more.

* See Pie Crusts in STAPLES, page 247
** See CUTTING TO THE CHASE
*** See GLOSSARY

FRITTATA FIRENZE

Prep Time: 10   **Cook Time: 35**   **Serves: 6-8**

Groceries

Zucchini, Green and Red Pepper, Red Onion, Garlic, Silken Tofu, Tofu, Basil, Oregano, Lemon Juice, Balsamic Vinegar, White Miso, Rice Syrup, Peanut and Sunflower Butter, Parsley, Cornstarch.

Do Ahead

Prepare the vegetables and refrigerate in a sealed container up to 2 days in advance. Chop all the vegetables before cooking so that you can sauté quickly. The tofu purée can be made 2 days in advance. The baked Frittata will keep refrigerated for 5 days (made with fresh ingredients), or 3 months frozen, but is best enjoyed fresh.

Hot Tips

You may include various vegetables, tomatoes and/or add seitan, tempeh (see index) or cooked beans for variety. To reduce fat; omit the oil and sauté in ¼ cup of water, and omit the nut and seed butters, but this also reduces flavor.

Meal Balance

This is wonderful with a grain based soup or salad (see index) to balance the cheesy soybean products. Fresh steamed greens, mixed vegetables or a salad will balance this nicely.

This tofu-vegetable "omelet" transports your senses to friendly Italian restaurants. Buon Appetito!

1 pound fresh Tofu* Firm
1 - 10.5 oz. package Silken Tofu* Extra Firm
½ cup White Miso*
¼ cup Lemon Juice or Vinegar
2 tablespoons Sunflower Butter* or Tahini*
2 tbsp. each Peanut Butter*, Umeboshi Paste*
¾ cup Vegetable Stock**, Soymilk* or Water
1 tablespoon Olive Oil
1 medium Onion + 1 medium Zucchini, diced
1 large Garlic Clove, minced
½ Green Pepper + ½ Red Pepper, diced
1 teaspoon each Basil, Oregano
¼ tsp. each Pepper and Sea Salt, or to taste
½ cup Whole Wheat Pastry Flour
¼ cup Italian Parsley, minced

1. Preheat oven to 350°F. Process the 1 lb. tofu to a fine texture. Add the silken tofu with the next six ingredients (from miso to stock, soymilk or water) until smooth.
2. Heat a 10" cast iron skillet over medium-high heat with the oil and sauté the onion, garlic, zucchini and bell peppers 4 minutes, until tender. Reduce heat, mix in remaining ingredients (reserving 1 tablespoon of parsley for garnish), coating the vegetables with flour.
3. Combine the tofu purée with the sautéed ingredients in the skillet and adjust seasonings to taste. Smooth the top with a spatula. Bake directly in the skillet, uncovered, for 30 minutes, or until set and golden brown. Let set at room temperate for 10-15 minutes if desired, to allow the center to firm up. Serve sprinkled with parsley.

* See GLOSSARY
** See Vegetable Stock in TRICKS OF THE TRADE. Salted stock reduces the amount of salt added to the stew.

SEITAN PARMIGIANA

Prep Time: 25 **Cook Time: 35** **Serves: 4-6**

Groceries

Seitan, A "10" Tomato Sauce, Silken Tofu, Tahini, Miso, Garlic Powder, Basil, Oregano, Flour, Soymilk.

Do Ahead

The tomato sauce will store refrigerated for 10 days. The Tofu Parmigiana will keep refrigerated for 1 week or 3 months frozen. You can flour and fry the seitan and store refrigerated for 5 days before baking with the sauces.

Hot Tips

You can reduce fat and omit the flouring and frying of the seitan, it will be delicious, but you lose out on experiencing the authenticity. Place the fried cutlets fairly close together in a flat dish, leaving enough space between so you can determine where one cutlet ends and the other begins. You will be happy you did when it comes time to serve out portions.

Meal Balance

This is very rich and satisfying. Serve with grains, pasta or rice to soak up extra sauce if desired. Otherwise, have whole grains at another meal during the day. Serve this with the Caesar Salad for a real gourmet treat, lightly cooked greens or mixed vegetables (see Veggie Venture).

This dish will amaze, and may even fool your hardest-to-please-customers. Not as fast and low to zero fat as some recipes, but definitely fabulous!

¼ cup Whole Wheat Pastry Flour
1 teaspoon each Basil, Oregano, Sea Salt
¼ teaspoon Pepper
8 Seitan* Cutlets (slice slabs ¼" to 1/3" thick)
¼ cup Soymilk** or Water
¼ cup Olive Oil
1 - 10.5 oz. (297 gr.) package Silken Tofu**
±1/3 cup Tahini**
±1/3 cup light-medium color Miso**
¼-½ teaspoon Garlic Powder
½-1 cup Water
2 cups of A "10" Tomato Sauce, see pg. 155

1. In a bowl, combine the flour, herbs, sea salt and pepper. Dip both sides of the seitan cutlets in the soymilk and then to coat in the flour mixture. Preheat oven to 375°F.
2. Heat a large skillet over medium-high heat with one tablespoon of the oil and fry four cutlets on one side until golden brown. Add another tablespoon of oil and fry the other side. Repeat with the remaining four cutlets.
3. Tofu Parmigiana: Purée the tofu with tahini, miso, garlic powder and enough water to achieve a very smooth consistency, pourable and thick, with a cheesy taste.
4. Place the fried cutlets in an oiled baking dish and pour the tomato sauce equally over each cutlet. Ladle some Tofu Parmigiana over the sauce. (The extra Tofu Parmigiana can be saved to use on Pizza with Pizzazz or Tijuana Tostadas.) Bake uncovered for 15 minutes or until the tofu is golden on top.

* See SPEEDY HOMEMADE SEITAN in STAPLES
** See GLOSSARY

SEITAN BOURGUIGNON

Prep Time: 15   **Cook Time: 30**   **Serves: 4-6**

Groceries

Seitan, Flour, Onions, Mushrooms, Garlic, Thyme, Toasted Sesame Oil, Tomato Paste (opt.), Red Wine (opt.).

Do Ahead

The seitan can be baked and stored refrigerated for 5 days in a sealed container. The cooked dish will keep refrigerated for 5 days (made with freshly cooked seitan) or three months frozen.

Hot Tips

You can eliminate fat by: omitting step 1, add the seitan in at the end without baking it, and sauté the vegetables in ¼ cup of water instead of the oil. Baking the seitan improves the texture and flavor, and the oils add a savory richness to the dish.

Meal Balance

Serve this with a grain, pasta or rice to soak up all the sauce and complete the grain portion of the meal. Balance this with lightly cooked colorful vegetables or a fresh green salad.

This is a favorite at our cooking school when we hold the seitan making classes. So close, yet so far from the traditional recipe.

4 cups Seitan*, drained, patted dry, 1" cubed
¼ cup Unbleached White Flour
½ teaspoon Sea Salt
¼ teaspoon Pepper
1 tablespoon Corn Oil**
1 teaspoon Toasted Sesame Oil**
18 Pearl Onions (or 3 medium diced 1")
8 oz. Café Mushrooms, sliced
1 large Garlic Clove, minced
1 teaspoon Thyme
1½ cups Red Wine ***
1½ cups Vegetable Stock**** or Water
¼ cup Tamari**
1 tablespoon Tomato Paste (optional)
2 tablespoons Arrowroot** or Cornstarch

1. Preheat oven to 375°F. In a large bowl, toss seitan cubes with the flour, sea salt and pepper to coat. Bake on a baking tray for 15 minutes or until golden brown. Meanwhile...
2. Heat a large skillet over medium-high heat with the oil and brown the onions, 5 minutes. Add the mushrooms, garlic, thyme, sea salt and pepper and sauté for 2 minutes with the flour left over from step 1.
3. Add the wine and baked seitan and simmer covered for 15 minutes. Combine the remaining ingredients well to dissolve lumps and stir into the skillet with the vegetables. Simmer on low until clear and thickened. Adjust seasonings to taste and serve.

* See SPEEDY HOMEMADE SEITAN in STAPLES
** See GLOSSARY and TRICKS OF THE TRADE
*** You may use white or rosé wine, veg. stock or water instead of the red wine with delicious results.
**** See Vegetable Stock in TRICKS OF THE TRADE. Salted stock reduces the amount of salt added to the stew.

SEITAN VEGETABLE CURRY

Prep Time: 15 **Cook Time: 30** **Serves: 4-6**

Groceries

Seitan, Garlic, Onion, Carrots, Potatoes, Peas or Green Beans, Lemon or Lime, Curry, Cumin, Coriander, Dried Crushed Chili, Coconut, Coconut Milk, Cilantro, Arrowroot or Cornstarch.

Do Ahead

The seitan can be deep fried (if you do this step) and refrigerated for 3 days in a sealed container. The dish keeps refrigerated for 5 days or 3 months frozen in sealed containers, as a whole or in serving-size portions.

Hot Tips

To eliminate fat and save time: omit deep frying the seitan, sautéing the vegetables in oil, the coconut and the nut milk. Simply bring everything (without the flour) to a boil in vegetable stock or water and simmer until tender, ±30 minutes, and thicken at the end with arrowroot.

Meal Balance

This is very substantial. Serve with pasta or whole grains—to soak up the sauce—such as the Spiced Basmati with Pine Nuts or Curried Almond Pilaf, keeping within the culinary theme. Lentil Dahl is perfect as a start, and a salad, lightly cooked greens (see Veggie Ventures) will refresh and balance the meal.

Don't be afraid of deep frying, coconut or coconut milk. Having high quality rich food occasionally keeps you from looking for satisfying foods of lesser goodness. We give the authentic, rich and delicious version, and a fat-free one - you choose.

Vegetable Oil for deep frying (optional)
2 cups Seitan*, drained, patted dry, cubed ½"
1 tablespoon Corn or Sesame Oil
¼ cup dried unsweetened shredded Coconut
1-2 tablespoons Curry Powder (to taste)
1 teaspoon each ground Coriander, Cumin
¼ teaspoon Crushed Dried Chili
1 large or Spanish Onion, diced
2 Carrots and 2 Potatoes, diced
½ cup Chickpea Flour
½ cup Peas or diced Green Beans
1 cup Coconut Milk, Soymilk** or Water
±4 cups Vegetable Stock*** or Water
1½ teaspoons Sea Salt or to taste
Juice of 1 lime or ½ Lemon
¼ cup Cilantro, minced

1. Heat oil to 375°F. Deep fry seitan until golden brown, crispy. Drain on paper towels.
2. Heat a heavy pot over medium-low heat with the oil, and toast the coconut with the spices for 2 minutes, until golden, fragrant. Add the onion, carrots, potatoes and sauté 2 minutes. Mix in the flour, lower the heat and cook covered for 5 minutes. Add the peas, coconut milk and stock or water and bring to a boil. Simmer 15 minutes covered.
3. Add the lime juice and adjust seasonings to taste. If necessary, adjust consistency by adding liquid, and/or thicken with 1-2 tbsp. dissolved arrowroot or cornstarch.

* See SPEEDY HOMEMADE SEITAN in STAPLES
** See GLOSSARY
*** See Vegetable Stock in TRICKS OF THE TRADE.
  Salted stock reduces quantity of salt added to the stew.

BARBECUE SEITAN RIBS

Prep Time: 10   **Cook Time: 35**   **Serves: 4-6**

Groceries

Seitan, Onion, Garlic, Ketchup, Lemon Juice, Maple Syrup, Apple Cider Vinegar, Mustard, Oregano, Paprika, Tarragon, Crushed Dried Chili.

Do Ahead

The sauce can be made in advance and refrigerated in a sealed container for 10 days, or frozen for 3 months. The baked dish will keep refrigerated for 10 days (made with fresh sauce) or frozen for three months.

Hot Tips

To save time and reduce fat, omit the oil and simply combine all the ingredients, place directly in the baking dish and bake covered for 30 minutes. Then remove the cover and bake for 10 minutes to caramelize the sauce. Tempeh or frozen tofu can be used instead of seitan for variety. Lime juice may be used instead of lemon.

Meal Balance

Serve this over a bed of cooked grains or noodles with a salad or some lightly steamed greens (see Veggie Ventures). You may add ½ cup of cooked beans; kidney or pinto, chickpeas, lentils, etc., in with the seitan for additional protein, to complement the seitan and your grain portion.

This tastes even better the second or third day as the flavors have had a chance to marry and intensify.

1 tablespoon Olive Oil
1 small Onion, finely diced
1 Garlic Clove, minced
1/8-1/4 teaspoon Crushed Dried Chili
1 cup natural Ketchup*
½ cup Vegetable Stock** or Water
¼ cup each Lemon Juice + Maple Syrup*
2 tablespoons Apple Cider Vinegar*
1 tablespoon Tamari*
1 teaspoon Mustard Powder
1 teaspoon each Oregano and Tarragon
½ teaspoon each Paprika and Sea Salt
2 cups Seitan**, sliced into "ribs" - ½" thick by 1" wide and 3" long
1-2 sprigs Cilantro or Italian Parsley, minced

1. Barbecue Sauce Preheat oven to 350°F. Heat a skillet over medium-high heat with the oil and sauté the onion with the garlic and chili 2 minutes, or until tender and browned. Add the remaining ingredients (except seitan and cilantro) and bring to a boil. Reduce heat and simmer for 5 minutes.
2. Place seitan in an oiled 8" by 8" baking dish and add the sauce. Cover with foil and bake for 25 minutes. Remove the cover during the last 10 minutes to caramelize the sauce if desired. Serve over cooked grains or pasta garnished with cilantro.

* See GLOSSARY
** See Vegetable Stock in TRICKS OF THE TRADE. Using
   salted stock reduces the quantity of salt added to the dish.
*** See SPEEDY HOMEMADE SEITAN in STAPLES

SEITAN PEPPER STEAK

Prep Time: 5   **Cook Time: 15**   **Serves: 6**

Groceries

Seitan, Onion, Garlic, Green Pepper, Mustard, Sage, Thyme, Tahini, Tamari, Arrowroot.

Do Ahead

Wash and refrigerate the vegetables in plastic bags or sealed containers, up to 3 days in advance. Bake the seitan and refrigerate for up to 5 days before using in the recipe. The recipe keeps refrigerated for 5days (made with freshly baked seitan), or 3 months frozen.

Hot Tips

Eliminate fat by omitting the tahini and baking step, and sauté the vegetables in ¼ cup of water instead of the corn oil. Simply cook the seitan in with the sautéed vegetables. This fat-free version is still very delicious, only less rich and steak-like.

Meal Balance

This is a very substantial portion of fat-free, concentrated wheat protein. Serve with grains or pasta to soak up the sauce, and a variety of colorful vegetables, (see Index and Menu Magician for all the possibilities).

This is meaty and delectable – when you want something you can really sink your teeth into. Serve with the Bechamel Dijon Sauce or Mushroom Onion Gravy for a savory, rich entree.

6 Seitan Steaks*, slices - ½" thick, 3"-4" long
1 tablespoon each Dijon Mustard** + Tahini**
1 teaspoon Thyme
½ teaspoon each Pepper and Sage
3 tablespoons Tamari**
2 tablespoons Corn Oil
1 medium Onion, sliced ½ moons
1 Garlic Clove, minced
1 medium Green Pepper, julienne
2 cups Vegetable Stock*** or Water
2 tablespoons Arrowroot* or Cornstarch
2 tablespoons Curly or Italian Parsley, minced

1. Preheat oven to 350°F. Drain the seitan steaks, and pat dry on paper towels. In a large bowl, combine the mustard, tahini, thyme, pepper, sage and 2 tablespoons of the tamari. Coat the seitan steaks evenly in the mixture. Transfer to a baking tray and bake for 15 minutes. Meanwhile...
2. Heat an enamel coated or stainless steel skillet over medium-high heat, with the oil. Sauté the onion for 5 minutes, or until browned. Add the garlic and green pepper and sauté for 2 minutes, until tender. Add 1¾ cups of the stock or water and bring to a boil. Cover, reduce heat, simmer 5 minutes.
3. Dissolve arrowroot in the remaining ¼ cup of liquid and tamari. Stir and simmer with the vegetables until clear and thickened. Transfer the seitan steaks to serving plates and serve topped with the vegetable sauce, garnished with parsley.

* See SPEEDY HOMEMADE SEITAN in STAPLES
** See GLOSSARY
*** See Vegetable Stock in TRICKS OF THE TRADE.
    Salted stock reduces amount of salt added to the soup.

CHAPTER 5

VEGGIE VENTURES

Vegetables Galore

Super Sauces

SIMPLE STEAMED GREENS

Prep Time: 5 **Cook Time: 5** **Serves: 4**

Groceries

Cabbage, Kale, Garlic, Apple Cider Vinegar, Tamari.

Do Ahead

Wash and refrigerate the vegetables, ready to chop, in a sealed container or plastic bag for up to 2 days. Serve freshly cooked greens on a daily basis. Leftovers are not ideal both in terms of flavor and nutrition.

Hot Tips

Slice and cook the kale stems and mix them with the kale leaves— they are naturally sweet and delicious and add a color and texture. The stems are less nutritious than the leaves, but have more fiber and strengthening qualities.

Meal Balance

We should eat one to two cups of dark green vegetables daily. They provide calcium, iron and vitamin C, as well as vibrant color to our meals. Serve with grains or pasta for a simple balanced meal. The orange vegetables in the Cream of Carrot with Coriander Soup, Butternut and Broccoli Bisque, Awesome Autumn Vegetables or Vitality Stew will balance the greens.

Quick and easy to prepare, and abundant with healthful benefits, this really brightens and livens up meals.

1 small Garlic Clove
1 cup Water
4 cups Cabbage, diced 1"
8 Kale leaves, stems sliced, leaves chopped
2 tablespoons Apple Cider Vinegar
1 tablespoon Tamari*

1. Mince the garlic and add it to the water. Bring to a boil over medium heat, in a small pot with a steamer basket. Steam the cabbage for 5 minutes, or until tender and a brighter green. Transfer to a serving platter to cool. Make a neat pile with the cabbage.
2. Steam the kale stems for 1-2 minutes. Add the kale leaves and steam for 1-2 minutes more, or until bright green and wilted. Transfer to the serving dish to cool. Place the kale around the cabbage, creating a border.
3. There should be a small amount of water left in the pot, to this, add the vinegar and tamari. Drizzle the liquid mixture over the steamed greens and serve.

Variation:
Simple Steamed Squash**
Steam sliced squash for 5 to 10 minutes, (depending on the variety and the thickness of the slices), until tender when pierced with a fork or skewer. Serve as is, or with a Super Sauce.

* See GLOSSARY
** Buttercup, Butternut or Delicatta (see Winter Squash in CUTTING TO THE CHASE)

BEAUTIFUL BOILED SALAD

Prep Time: 15   **Cook Time: 10**   **Serves: 6-8**

Groceries

Broccoli, Carrots, Cauliflower, Rutabaga, Red Radishes, Nappa Cabbage, Brussels Sprouts, Umeboshi Vinegar, Italian Parsley.

Do Ahead

Wash the vegetables and refrigerate, ready to chop, in a sealed container or plastic bag for up to 3 days in advance. Once cooked, the vegetables will keep refrigerated for up to 2 days.

Hot Tips

Cook each vegetable to perfection, remove with a slotted spoon and transfer immediately to a large platter to cool, spreading the vegetables to allow steam to escape. Do not rinse or submerge the vegetables in cold water as this dilutes the flavor and nutrients.

Meal Balance

This vegetable dish contains vitamin rich green, yellow and orange vegetables. A simple grain or pasta dish will balance the meal.

* See CUTTING TO THE CHASE
** See GLOSSARY

Serve this colorful vegetable medley with the Dillicious Tofu, Green Goddess, Lemon Soy, or Poppy Seed Dressing. Also, Tahini Lemon Sauce on the side makes a great dip!

2 cups Cauliflower, flowers and stems sliced*
4 cups Nappa Cabbage, sliced*
3 cups Broccoli, flowers and stems sliced*
1 cup Carrots, sliced 1/6" thick flowers*
1 cup Rutabaga, sliced 1/6" thick triangles*
6 medium Brussels Sprouts, quartered*
6 Red Radishes, quartered*
1½ teaspoons Umeboshi Vinegar**
2 tablespoons Italian Parsley, minced

1. Bring 1" of water (±2 cups) to boil over medium-high heat in a 2 quart stainless steel pot. Boil each vegetable in the order listed, until bright in color, tender and still slightly crisp. Boil the cauliflower for 1-3 minutes, remove with a slotted spoon and spread out to cool on the serving platter. Continue with the remaining vegetables, except radishes. The cooking time will depend on each vegetable and the size they are cut.
2. After cooking the Brussels sprouts, keep 2 tablespoons of liquid in the pot. (Pour the remaining vegetable cooking liquid into a container and save to use in soups, stews, etc.) Add the umeboshi vinegar to the pot and cook the radishes covered for 1-2 minutes. They will be tender and bright red from the vinegar. Remove them with a slotted spoon and spread out to cool on the platter.
3. Mix the red radish and umeboshi juices, with the vegetables and the parsley and serve.

PARTY VEGETABLE ROLLS

Prep Time: 15 **Cook Time: 10** **Serves: 2-4**

Groceries

Nappa Cabbage, Collard or Romaine Lettuce, Watercress, Carrot, Red and Yellow Pepper, Red Cabbage, , Umeboshi Vinegar, (Sushi Mat).

Do Ahead

You may wash the vegetables and refrigerate in sealed containers or plastic bags up to 2 days in advance, fresh is best. Serve freshly cooked greens on a daily basis, leftovers are not ideal both in terms of flavor and nutrition.

Hot Tips

These are very simple to make and you can add the Marinated Tofu or Tempeh Teriyaki, cooked noodles or rice as fillings (see Nori Maki and Nori Rolls). Squeeze the sushi mat as you roll the vegetables, for a tight roll, so that when you slice it into rounds, the fillings do not fall out.

Meal Balance

These bundles of nutritious vegetables balance a grain or pasta main dish. Make these into a meal in themselves, with the addition of grains or noodles, and seitan, tofu or tempeh.

Artistic colorful vegetables rolled into neat and portable finger food - ideal for buffets, picnics, and to dress up everyday meals.

4 large Nappa Cabbage Leaves, whole
4 large Collard or Romaine Leaves, whole
½ bunch Watercress, whole
1 Carrot, 7" long, quartered lengthwise
¼ Red Pepper, sliced in long strips, ¼" thick
¼ Yellow Pepper, sliced long strips, ¼" thick
1½ teaspoons Umeboshi Vinegar**
2 large Red Cabbage Leaves, ¼" thick strips

1. Bring ½" of water to a boil, in a pot with a steamer basket. Steam the nappa leaves for 1-2 minutes, until tender. Remove and cool the leaves on a plate.
2. Remove the center stems from the collard leaves by slicing along where the leaf and stem meet. Steam the leaves for 1-2 minutes, until bright green and tender. Remove, cool.
3. Steam the watercress 1-2 minutes, or until bright green and tender-crisp. Remove, cool. Steam the carrot, red and yellow peppers for 3-4 minutes, or until bright in color and tender-crisp. Remove and cool as above.
4. Steam the red cabbage for 2 minutes, until bright in color and tender-crisp. Transfer to a bowl and mix with the umeboshi vinegar. The cabbage turns a beautiful, bright purple.
5. Spread the collard leaves open flat on a sushi mat. Lay the nappa leaves open flat on top. Place the watercress in a line (parallel with, and 1" above the bottom edge of the mat). Lay the carrot, red and yellow peppers and the red cabbage along this line. Roll up jelly-roll fashion*** (beginning from the bottom edge, tightly encasing the vegetables inside the leaves). Slice roll into 1" rounds. Serve rounds, cut side up.

* See GLOSSARY
** For complete rolling instructions see Nori Rolls in TRICKS
  OF THE TRADE

WATERCRESS
WITH LEMON-SOY DRESSING

Prep Time: 5   **Cook Time: 2**   **Serves: 4-6**

Groceries

Watercress, Lemon, Tamari, Mirin or Sake or White Wine.

Do Ahead

This needs to be made and eaten fresh.

Hot Tips

Substitute broccoli, Brussels sprouts, Chinese cabbage, collard, dandelion, nappa cabbage, kale and rapini for variety.

Meal Balance

These greens complete a meal of grains or pasta, with orange or yellow vegetables, such as in a soup, stew, main entrée or salad. (See Index for all the possibilities.)

Mirin has a strong, sweet, fermented flavor and is a Japanese culinary treasure. Used sparingly, it turns good recipes into great.

2 bunches of Watercress, chopped 1"

Lemon Soy Dressing
¼ cup Lemon Juice (1 Lemon)
1½ tablespoons Tamari*
2 teaspoons Mirin*

1. Bring ¼" to ½" water to a boil over medium-high heat, in a pot with a steamer basket. Reduce heat to medium-low and steam the watercress for 2 minutes or until bright green and wilted.
2. Combine the dressing ingredients.
3. Mix the watercress with the dressing and serve. Alternatively, you may serve the dressing on the side and drizzle it on as desired.

* Mirin is a fermented rice liquid seasoning (similar to sake wine) available in natural food stores and Japanese grocers.

SIZZLING BOK CHOY
& BEAN SPROUTS

Prep Time: 5   **Cook Time: 5**   **Serves: 4-6**

Groceries

Bok Choy, Mung Bean Sprouts, Red Pepper, Garlic, Ginger, Tamari, Toasted Sesame Oil.

Do Ahead

Wash the bok choy and refrigerate, ready to chop, in a sealed container or plastic bag up to 2 days in advance. Buy fresh mung bean sprouts and use within 2 days. Make fresh greens daily as they are not ideal as left-overs, both in terms of flavor and nutrition.

Hot Tips

Eliminate fat by omitting the oil, simply sauté the vegetables in ¼" of water in a skillet. Steam the sprouts and bok choy greens briefly so they are bright in color and tender-crisp.

Meal Balance

We should eat 1-2 cups of dark green vegetables every day. They provide iron, calcium and vitamin C, as well as vibrant color. For a simple, light meal serve with a main grain or pasta dish. Include a soup, stew or salad that has beans and root vegetables for a hearty balanced meal (see the Index for all the possibilities, and Leafy Greens in H.H.I.H.).

Ancient wisdom values dark leafy green vegetables for their healing powers. They enhance flexibility of the body and mind, and are especially beneficial to the liver and gall bladder functions.

1 tablespoon Toasted Sesame Oil*
1 Garlic Clove, minced
1-2 teaspoons fresh Ginger, minced
¼ medium Red Pepper, julienned
1 medium head of Bok Choy, sliced**
3 cups Mung Bean Sprouts
2 tablespoons Tamari*

1. Heat a stainless steel skillet or wok over medium- high heat with the oil and sauté the garlic and ginger for 1 minute. Add the red pepper and sauté until tender.
2. Add the white part of the bok choy and sauté for 1 minute. Cover and steam for 2 minutes, or until tender-crisp. Add the mung bean sprouts and sauté for 1 minute.
3. Add the tamari and bok choy greens and sauté until bright green and wilted. Serve immediately.

* See GLOSSARY
** See CUTTING TO THE CHASE

QUICK KOREAN KIMCH'I

Prep Time: 20   **Cook Time: 0**   **Serves: 4-6**

Groceries

Chinese Cabbage, Carrot, Celery, Cucumber, Red Cabbage, Red Onion, Red Radishes, Scallions, Garlic, Ginger, Crushed Dried Chili.

Do Ahead

Slice the vegetables and marinate with spices and sea salt refrigerated for up to 5 days in a covered bowl.

Hot Tips

Many vegetables may be included or substituted; bok choy, broccoli, cauliflower, daikon, nappa cabbage, rutabaga, turnips, zucchini, etc.

Meal Balance

This salad is ideal when you want refreshing raw vegetables, without the bitterness and bite. The sea salt and spices bring out the natural sweetness, and the vegetables retain their nutrients, while the excess water is drawn away. Serve with grains or pasta for a simple light meal, or include this as a side dish in a complete balanced meal based on grains, beans and vegetables.

* See CUTTING TO THE CHASE

Traditional Kimch'i - highly spiced, pickled, raw vegetables - takes two to four days to marinate. This quick version is colorful and crisp, with a hint of spice, that can be increased if desired.

6-8 cups of Chinese Cabbage, julienned*
1 medium Carrot, grated or fine matchstick*
1 Celery, sliced thin diagonally
1 cup Cucumber, sliced thin ½ moons
½ cup Red Cabbage, sliced fine
½ medium Red Onion, sliced fine
5 Red Radishes, sliced thin ½ moons*
1 Scallion, sliced thin*
1 small Garlic Clove, minced
1 teaspoon Ginger, grated
Pinch Crushed Dried Chili
1-2 tablespoons Sea Salt

1. This will seem like a lot of vegetables, and a lot of sea salt. The vegetable volume shrinks significantly as the salt draws the water from the vegetables, and the salt will be rinsed (if necessary) at the end. Place sliced vegetables in a large bowl and mix with the remaining ingredients. Combine enough sea salt to draw the water out of the vegetables. When you hold up a handful of vegetables and squeeze, water should drip out.
2. Set aside covered with an inverted plate for 1 hour or more. (You may marinate the vegetables with spices and sea salt, covered in the brine that accumulates for up to 5 days refrigerated in a covered bowl).
3. Squeeze the liquid from a small amount of the marinated vegetable mixture to see how salty it is. Rinse in cold water and strain in a fine mesh strainer if it tastes too salty. Otherwise, strain the excess liquid and serve.

TRI-COLOR ANTIPASTO

Prep Time: 15   **Cook Time: 5**   **Serves: 4-6**

Groceries

Broccoli, Cauliflower, Red Bell Pepper, Balsamic or Red Wine Vinegar, Lemon, Garlic, Basil, Oregano, Maple or Rice Syrup.

Do Ahead

Wash and refrigerate the vegetables in a plastic bag or sealed container, up to 3 days in advance (broccoli should be as fresh as possible). This dish will keep refrigerated for 2 days.

Hot Tips

Eliminate fat by omitting the oil. Make interesting combinations by adding and/or substituting; Broccoflower, Brussels Sprouts, Carrots, Celery, Green and Yellow Bell Peppers, Green and Yellow Zucchini, Mushrooms, Black or Green Olives, Kidney Beans, Chickpeas, etc.

Meal Balance

This dish will complement a grain or pasta entrée. You may also serve a Sumptuous Soup, Savory Stew or other Veggie Ventures with orange and yellow vegetables, such as carrots, rutabaga, squash and/or sweet potatoes, to balance the meal.

In Italy, huge spreads of antipasto dishes adorn buffet tables. The range of colorful ingredients and vegetables is overwhelming. This one is simply beautiful and delicious.

2 cups Cauliflowerettes*
1 Red Pepper, ½" thick julienned
1 stalk Broccoli, flowerettes, stems sliced*

Italian Dressing
¼ cup Extra Virgin Olive Oil
¼ cup Balsamic or Red Wine Vinegar
2 tablespoons Lemon Juice (½ Lemon)
1 large Garlic Clove, minced
1 tablespoon Maple or Rice Syrup**
1 tablespoon fresh Basil, minced (1 tsp. dried)
2 teaspoons Oregano, minced (½ tsp. dried)
½ teaspoon Sea Salt, or to taste
Pepper to taste

1. Bring ¼-½" of water to a boil over medium-high heat, in a large pot with a steamer basket. Reduce heat to medium and steam the cauliflower for 5 minutes, or until tender-crisp. Remove and cool on a plate.
2. Steam the red pepper and broccoli for 3-4 minutes or until the broccoli is bright green and tender-crisp. Remove, cool on a plate.
3. Blend the dressing ingredients in a blender or food processor for 30 seconds, or whisk in a bowl. Combine the vegetables with the dressing and serve immediately, or chill and marinate for 30 minutes before serving.

* See CUTTING TO THE CHASE
** See GLOSSARY

BRUSSELS SPROUTS WITH LEMONY MISO MUSTARD DRESSING

Prep Time: 5   **Cook Time: 5**   **Serves: 4**

Groceries

Brussels Sprouts, Lemon, Stone Ground Mustard, White Miso, Italian Parsley.

Do Ahead

Make the dressing and refrigerate for 1 week in a sealed container. Wash and trim the Brussels sprouts, and refrigerate up to 1 week in a plastic bag or sealed container. Steamed Brussels sprouts keep refrigerated for 2 days in a sealed container, although it is ideal to enjoy them freshly cooked, for the most flavor and nutrition.

Hot Tips

For variety, substitute broccoflower, broccoli, cauliflower, collard, kale, leek, zucchini, etc. for the Brussels sprouts.

Meal Balance

Serve as a complement to a grain or pasta based meal. See Index and Menu Magician for all the possibilities.

These humble miniature cabbages become hearty vegetables that rise to any occasion with this tangy, pungent dressing.

±20 Brussels Sprouts, washed and trimmed

Lemony Miso Mustard Dressing
1/3 cup Lemon Juice (1½ Lemons)
1 tablespoon Stone Ground Mustard*
1 tablespoon White Miso* (or pale color)
1 tablespoon Italian Parsley, minced

1. Slice the Brussels sprouts into halves or quarters lengthwise. Bring ¼" of water to a boil in a pot with a steamer basket. Steam the Brussels sprouts for 5 minutes or until tender and bright green.
2. Mix the remaining ingredients in a large bowl. Add the Brussels sprouts to the dressing and mix to coat evenly. Serve hot or chilled as a salad.

* See GLOSSARY

GUACAMOLE
WITH CHERRY TOMATOES

Prep Time: 15   **Cook Time: 0**   **Makes: ±4 cups**

Groceries

Avocados, Tomatoes, Onion, Scallions, Garlic, Lemon, Jalapeno Chili, Cilantro, Cayenne.

Do Ahead

Ideally, make this just before serving. Exposure to the air turns avocados brown. To help prevent this, you can place the avocado pits back into the guacamole, and cover the dish in plastic wrap. Store for up to 3 days refrigerated.

Hot Tips

Use very, perfectly ripe avocados for the best flavor and texture. The black pebbled variety has a delicate buttery taste. Leave some chunks when you mash the avocados for an interesting texture. This is quite high in fat, compared to most fruits and vegetables, so enjoy in moderation.

Meal Balance

Serve this condiment with the Funtastic Fajitas and Tijuana Tostadas, along with the Carrot Salsa. This is a great party dip with chips and tortillas.

The red and yellow cherry tomatoes add vibrant color, and a juicy burst of tangy sweetness, against the hot bite of the jalapeno chili, tamed by buttery, rich avocados.

4 ripe Avocados, pitted and peeled
4-6 Red Cherry Tomatoes, quartered
4-6 Yellow Cherry Tomatoes, quartered
1 small Red Onion, (1/3 cup) minced
1 medium Scallion, minced
¼ cup Cilantro*, minced
¼ cup Lemon Juice (1 Lemon)
2 Garlic Cloves, minced
½ Jalapeno Chili**, seeded and minced
½ teaspoon Sea Salt
Cayenne to taste (optional)

1. Mash the avocados with a fork until partially smooth, leaving some chunks.
2. Mix all the ingredients together.
3. Adjust seasonings to taste and serve.

* See GLOSSARY
** See TRICKS OF THE TRADE

HERBED KALE & CAULIFLOWER

Prep Time: 10   **Cook Time: 15**   **Serves: 4-6**

Groceries

Kale, Cauliflower, Basil, Nutmeg.

Do Ahead

You may wash and refrigerate kale and cauliflower in a sealed container or plastic bag for to 2 days in advance, fresh is best. Serve freshly cooked greens on a daily basis, leftovers are not ideal both in terms of flavor and nutrition.

Hot Tips

Eliminate fat by sautéing the vegetables in ¼" of water instead of the oil. Broccoli, Brussels sprouts, Chinese lettuce, collard, dandelion, head cabbage, nappa cabbage, rapini and watercress may substitute for the kale and/or cauliflower. Use various herbs instead of the basil for variety.

Meal Balance

Serve this as your green vegetable portion, with grains or pasta. A soup, stew or one of the other Veggie Ventures with orange vegetables completes and balances the meal. You may include a side dish of beans, or bean products.

Buy fresh, crisp, dark green kale - ask your grocer or farmer which day the greens are delivered. Serve this with the Green Goddess or Poppy Seed Dressing, or one of the international vinaigrettes.

1-2 tablespoons Corn Oil*
1 Garlic Clove, minced
2 cups Cauliflower, cut into flowers**
1½ teaspoons dried Basil, or 1½ tbsp. fresh
½ teaspoon Sea Salt
¼ teaspoon Nutmeg
2 lb. Kale, stems sliced, leaves chopped**

1. Heat an enamel coated or stainless steel skillet over medium heat with the oil and sauté the garlic for 1 minute.
2. Add the cauliflower, dried basil, sea salt and nutmeg and ¼ cup of water. Cover the skillet and cook for 2 minutes.
3. Add the kale stems, cover and steam for 1 minute. Add the kale leaves, cover and steam for 1 minute or until bright green and tender. The water may have evaporated, but serve any remaining juices with the meal.

* See TRICKS OF THE TRADE
** See CUTTING TO THE CHASE

ORIENTAL GINGERED CABBAGE

Prep Time: 5   **Cook Time: 15**   **Serves: 4-6**

Groceries

Green and Red Cabbage, Ginger, Coriander Seeds, Fennel Seeds, Mustard Seeds, Lime (optional).

Do Ahead

Wash the whole cabbage and refrigerate in a plastic bag or sealed container for several weeks. Once the cabbage has been cut (remove wedge slices as needed), refrigerate unused portion, sealed as above. Exposure to air will cause the cut edges to blacken after several days. Simply slice off the exposed layer and use the rest. The cooked cabbage keeps refrigerated for 5 days.

Hot Tips

Use the seeds instead of ground spices, for authenticity and because the ground spices will turn the dish a brownish color.

Meal Balance

Serve this with an Asian flavored meal of grains or pasta, and perhaps a Sumptuous Soup or Savory Stew to add orange vegetables for balance. You may also include another side dish of dark leafy greens. Turn this into a meal in itself by adding cooked rice or pasta at the end. Heat through and adjust seasonings to taste.

The red cabbage brightens up the sweet green cabbage, and the spices turn this humble vegetable into a culinary experience.

1 teaspoon Coriander Seeds
1 teaspoon Yellow Mustard Seeds
1 teaspoon Fennel Seeds
1 tablespoon Peanut or Sesame Oil
1 tablespoon fresh Ginger, minced
4 cups Green Head Cabbage, thinly sliced
¼ cup Water
1 teaspoon Sea Salt
1 cup Red Cabbage, thinly sliced
1 tablespoon Lime Juice (optional)

1. Grind the spices coarsely, in a mortar and pestle, spice grinder or suribachi*.
2. Heat a stainless steel skillet or wok over medium heat with the oil and sauté the ginger for 1 minute. Add the spices and sauté for 2 minutes. Add the green cabbage, water and sea salt and sauté until beginning to wilt, 1 minute. Cover and cook for 10 minutes, or until tender.
3. Add the red cabbage, cover and cook for 1-2 minutes, or until bright purple and tender. Mix in the lime juice if using, and serve.

* A Japanese ceramic bowl with grooves and a wooden pestle (a mortar and pestle of sorts), available in natural food stores and Japanese specialty shops.

CAULIFLOWER AU GRATIN

Prep Time: 5   **Cook Time: 25**   **Serves: 4-6**

Groceries

Cauliflower, Tahini, Umeboshi Paste.

Do Ahead

Wash cauliflower and refrigerate in a sealed container or plastic bag up to 5 days in advance. The tahini and umeboshi mixture keeps refrigerated for several weeks in a sealed container.

Hot Tips

Steam the cauliflower with just enough water— too much water will dilute the flavor of the cauliflower juices, and too little will not be enough to mix with the tahini and umeboshi paste. Substitute or combine broccoli, Brussels sprouts, cabbage, carrots, parsnips, potatoes, rutabaga and/or squash for variety.

Meal Balance

This dish completes a balanced meal of grains or pasta and beans, served with fresh leafy greens.

Tahini is rich and creamy, while umeboshi is salty and tangy, and in combination they taste like cheese. To save time, you can serve the sauce separately as a dip for vegetables, instead of baking it with the cauliflower.

1 small head of Cauliflower
¼ cup Tahini*
2 tablespoons Umeboshi Paste*

1. Preheat oven to 375°F. Cut the center stem from the top flower clusters of the cauliflower, trim and use the stem in another recipe such as a soup, stew or stir fry. Separate the flower clusters into smaller sections. Bring ¼-½" of water to a boil over medium-high heat, in a small pot with a steamer basket. Reduce heat to medium and steam the cauliflower for 5 minutes, or until tender.
2. Meanwhile, combine the tahini and umeboshi to a smooth paste in a bowl (a mortar and pestle or a suribachi** works well).
3. Place the cauliflower in a shallow baking dish or casserole. Add the cauliflower cooking water to the tahini-umeboshi paste and blend to a sauce-like consistency. Pour and spread the sauce over the cauliflower and bake uncovered for 20 minutes, or until golden.

* See GLOSSARY
** A Japanese ceramic bowl with grooves and a wooden pestle (a mortar and pestle of sorts), available in natural food stores and Japanese specialty shops.

CHOCTAW STEWED CORN

Prep Time: 10   **Cook Time: 10**   **Serves: 4-6**

Groceries

Corn, Onions, Green and Red Pepper, Tomatoes, Crushed Dried Chili, Apple Cider Vinegar, Maple Syrup, Arrowroot, Lettuce.

Do Ahead

Wash the bell peppers and refrigerate in a plastic bag or sealed container. Keep the corn cobs in their husk, until ready to use, to preserve their flavor and freshness.

Hot Tips

Eliminate fat by omitting the oil, and simply stew the vegetables in ¼ cup water. The Boston lettuce has perfect cup shaped leaves for serving, and the curly lettuce also holds a filling well. Romaine lettuce works if you use the curved inner leaves, rather than the flat outer leaves.

Meal Balance

Corn on the cob is a vegetable. (Dried corn; cornmeal, corn flour, etc., are considered grain products.) Serve this with a main grain dish, perhaps Anasazi Skillet Bread, or a pasta dish such as Paella Valencia. (See Mainstream Meals and Index for all the possibilities.) Have a salad or lightly cooked greens on the side.

Choctaw Indians originally called this stewed corn dish, Matache, meaning "spotted". They introduced it to the Cajuns, who are reknown for their cooking.

2 tablespoons Corn Oil
¼ teaspoon Dried Crushed Chili, or to taste
2 medium Onions, finely diced
½ Green Pepper, diced ¼"
½ Red Pepper, diced ¼"
4 cups Corn Niblets, cut from fresh cobs
2 ripe, medium Tomatoes, diced (opt.)
1 teaspoon Sea Salt, or to taste
½ cup Water
1 tablespoon Arrowroot*
¼ cup Apple Cider Vinegar
¼ cup Maple Syrup*
Cayenne or Pepper to taste (optional)
6 Green or Red Curly or Boston lettuce leaves

1. Heat an enamel coated or stainless steel skillet over medium-high heat with the oil and chili. Sauté onions for 2 minutes, until tender and beginning to brown.
2. Add the peppers and corn, and sauté for 2 minutes. Add the tomatoes, sea salt and water. Cover, reduce heat to low, and simmer for 5 minutes. Meanwhile, dissolve the arrowroot in the vinegar and syrup.
3. Stir the arrowroot mixture into the sautéed vegetables, and simmer briefly, until clear and thickened. Adjust seasonings to taste. Serve in lettuce leaves.

* See GLOSSARY

CALIFORNIA CARROT SALSA

Prep Time: 10   **Cook Time: 0**   **Serves: 6-8**

Groceries

Carrots, Green Pepper, Cilantro, Scallions, Jalapeno Chili, Apple Juice, Lemon, Cumin, Apple Cider and Umeboshi Vinegar.

Do Ahead

Wash the carrots, green pepper and scallions and refrigerate in plastic bags or sealed containers several days in advance, and the cilantro up to 2 days. The salsa will keep refrigerated for 5 days.

Hot Tips

Finely grating the carrots, then puréeing in a food processor, results in a smooth consistency. This makes for greater contrast in color and texture with the chunks of diced green pepper and scallions. You may grate the carrot coarsely, omit the purée step, and leave the texture of the whole salsa more chunky.

Meal Balance

Serve this condiment with the Frittata Firenze, Funtastic Fajitas and Tijuana Tostadas, along with the Guacamole. This is a great party dip with chips and tortillas.

This condiment is ideal accompaniment to the Funtastic Fajitas and Tijuana Tostadas, although it will add excitement to any meal.

6 medium Carrots, finely grated and puréed
1 small-medium Green Pepper, minced
2 medium Scallions, minced
¼-½ cup Cilantro*, minced
1 Jalapeno** Chili, seeded and minced
½ cup Apple Juice
2 tablespoons Lemon Juice (½ Lemon)
1 tablespoon Apple Cider Vinegar
1 tablespoon Umeboshi Vinegar*
1½ teaspoons ground Cumin
½ teaspoon Sea Salt

1. Combine all the ingredients.
2. Adjust seasonings to taste.
3. Serve immediately, or chill for 30 minutes before serving.

* See GLOSSARY
** See TRICKS OF THE TRADE

MARINATED CARROTS & ZUCCHINI

Prep Time: 10   **Cook Time: 5**   **Serves: 4-6**

Groceries

Carrots, Green and Yellow Zucchini, Garlic, Balsamic or Red Wine Vinegar, Lemon, Mustard, Maple Syrup, Tarragon, Thyme.

Do Ahead

Wash the vegetables and refrigerate in a sealed container up to 3 days in advance. The vinaigrette keeps refrigerated for 2 weeks in a glass jar. This recipe improves after it marinates overnight, or a minimum of 1-3 hours. Prepare this the day before you plan to serve it. It keeps refrigerated for 3 days in a sealed container.

Hot Tips

Eliminate fat by omitting the oil. Substitute various vegetables for the carrot and zucchini; green, red and yellow bell peppers, celery, cauliflower, red radish, green and yellow beans and rutabaga. Serve this dish hot; simply heat the vinaigrette in a pot for 1 minute, mix with the steamed vegetables and serve.

Meal Balance

Serve this with your main grain or pasta dish along with a salad or lightly cooked leafy green vegetables. A Latin or Mediterranean flavored meal is an ideal accompaniment.

This is a refreshing vegetable dish. It's easy to prepare, and adds color and zest to meals.

2 medium Carrots, cut into logs*
2 medium Green Zucchini, cut into logs*
2 medium Yellow Zucchini, cut into logs*

French Vinaigrette
¼ cup of Extra Virgin Olive Oil
¼ cup Balsamic or Red Wine Vinegar
2 tablespoons Lemon Juice (½ Lemon)
1 large Garlic Clove, finely minced
1 teaspoon Stone Ground Mustard**
1 teaspoon Maple Syrup**
1 teaspoon dried Tarragon or 1 tbsp. fresh
½ teaspoon dried Thyme or ½ tbsp. fresh
½ teaspoon Sea Salt
Pepper to taste
2 tablespoons Italian Parsley, minced

1. Bring ¼"-½" of water to a boil over medium-high heat, in a small pot with a steamer basket. Steam the carrots, covered for 3-4 minutes or until bright orange and tender-crisp. Transfer to a bowl to cool. Steam the zucchini for 2 minutes or until bright in color and tender-crisp. Transfer to the bowl to cool.
2. Combine the vinaigrette ingredients and mix with the steamed vegetables. Chill for 1 hour or more, and serve.

Variation:
Grilled Marinated Tofu & Vegetables
Marinate cubed tofu with the vegetables (cut into cubes) overnight. Place them on a skewer and grill on the barbecue, basting and turning on each side for 1-2 minutes, or until golden brown.

* See Cutting To The Chase
** See GLOSSARY

SPAGHETTI SQUASH
WITH MARJORAM

Prep Time: 5 **Cook Time: 45** **Serves: 4-8**

Groceries

Spaghetti Squash, Marjoram, Garlic.

Do Ahead

You may cut and season the squash, ready to bake up to 1 day in advance. Baked squash will keep refrigerated for 4 days in a sealed container.

Hot Tips

Eliminate fat by omitting the oil—but the oil improves the flavor and texture and quickens the cooking time. You may use acorn, buttercup or delicatta squash in place of spaghetti.

Meal Balance

This completes a balanced meal with a Mediterranean flavored grain or pasta entrée, and a salad or lightly cooked green vegetables.

Brighten up your pasta meal! The texture of the golden inner flesh resembles spaghetti. It becomes complete meal when combined with hot cooked pasta - the tri-color vegetable spaghetti is very attractive - and served with a Super Sauce such as A "10" Tomato, Alfredo with Portabella Mushrooms, Carrot Beet Basil, Venetian Vegetable or Zesty Squash.

1 Spaghetti Squash
1 Garlic Clove
1 tablespoon Extra Virgin Olive Oil
1 teaspoon dried Marjoram or 1 tbsp. fresh
¼ teaspoon Sea Salt, or to taste

1. Preheat oven to 350°F. Cut the squash into half across the middle. Scoop out the seeds. Cut each half into 2, 3 or 4 wedges (depending on the size of the servings required). Place the squash into a 9" by 13" baking dish, inner-flesh side up, outer-skin side down, and try not to overlap the wedges. Fill the baking dish with ½" of water.
2. Slice the garlic in half and rub the cut sides of the garlic over the insides and cut surfaces of the squash. Rub the olive oil over the same areas. Sprinkle the marjoram, and then the sea salt evenly over the squash.
3. Cover the dish with foil and bake for 45 minutes or until tender. The water may have evaporated, but serve any remaining juices with the meal.

BUTTERNUT SQUASH
WITH DIJON GINGER SAUCE

Prep Time: 5   **Cook Time: 35**   **Serves: 4-6**

Groceries

Butternut Squash, Dijon Mustard, Ginger, Rice Syrup.

Do Ahead

You may wash, chop and refrigerate the butternut squash in a sealed container up to 2 days in advance. Prepare the sauce and refrigerate in a sealed container up to 5 days in advance. Baked squash will keep refrigerated 4 days in a sealed container.

Hot Tips

Eliminate fat by omitting the oil— but the oil improves the flavor and texture and quickens the cooking time. You may use acorn, buttercup or delicatta squash in place of butternut, and/or you may substitute carrots, onions, parsnips or rutabaga. Use maple syrup instead of rice syrup, in this case, reduce syrup by half. Double the sauce ingredients and serve over grains or pasta

Meal Balance

This is rich and satisfying, and makes a complete balanced meal with a light grain or pasta entrée, and a salad or lightly cooked green vegetables.

The delicate rice syrup, pungent mustard and spicy ginger enhances and excites the naturally sweet butternut squash.

1 Butternut Squash, (4 cups) thick ½ moons*
¼ cup Water

Dijon Ginger Sauce
3 tablespoons Rice Syrup**
2 tablespoons natural Dijon Mustard
1 tablespoon fresh grated Ginger
1 tablespoon Corn Oil***
½ teaspoon Sea Salt

1. Preheat oven to 350°F. Oil a 9" by 13" baking dish.
2. Place the squash in a large bowl with the remaining ingredients and mix to coat evenly. Lay the squash in the baking dish, try not to overlap the slices. Scrape all the juices from the bowl onto the squash.
3. Cover the dish with foil and bake for 35 to 45 minutes or until bubbling and tender.

* See Winter Squash in CUTTING TO THE CHASE
** See GLOSSARY
*** See TRICKS OF THE TRADE

ROSEMARY ROASTED POTATOES

Prep Time: 5   **Cook Time: 30**   **Serves: 6**

Groceries

Red Potatoes, Rosemary, Garlic, Italian Parsley.

Do Ahead

You may wash the potatoes and refrigerate in a sealed container or plastic bag, ready to bake up to 1 week in advance. Roasted Potatoes will keep refrigerated for 4 days in a sealed container.

Hot Tips

Crush dried rosemary coarsely, not to a powder, just partially grind the twigs. Eliminate fat by omitting the oil—but the oil improves the flavor and texture and quickens the cooking time— the potatoes will be dry without it. You may use Yukon gold or white potatoes, acorn, buttercup or delicatta squash in place of red potatoes, and/or substitute carrots, parsnips and rutabaga if desired.

Meal Balance

A perfect side dish that adds a wonderful dimension and substance to a balanced meal of grains, beans and vegetables. Potatoes are full of nutrition and starch, but not considered a substitute for the complex carbohydrates in whole grains.

So simple to prepare, and the results will receive rave reviews.

6 medium Red Potatoes, diced ¾"
1 large Garlic Clove, minced
2 tablespoons Olive Oil
1 tablespoon dried Rosemary, or 3 tbsp. fresh
½ teaspoon ground Sage
½ teaspoon Paprika
½ teaspoon Sea Salt, or to taste
¼ teaspoon Pepper, or to taste
¼ cup Italian Parsley, minced

1. Preheat oven to 350°F. Place the potatoes into a large bowl and sprinkle the remaining ingredients on top (reserving 1 tablespoon of parsley). Mix well to coat evenly.
2. Spread the potatoes onto a baking tray and scrape the seasonings from the bowl onto the potatoes. Bake for 30 minutes or until golden brown on the edges and tender through to the center.
3. Serve garnished with the remaining parsley.

BARBECUE GOLDEN POTATOES

Prep Time: 5   **Cook Time: 10**   **Serves: 6**

Groceries

Potatoes, Cayenne, Cumin, Garlic Powder, Ginger Powder, Paprika, Tahini.

Do Ahead

You may wash the potatoes and refrigerate in a sealed container or plastic bag, ready to bake up to 1 week in advance. Baked or barbecued potatoes will keep refrigerated for 4 days in a sealed container.

Hot Tips

Eliminate fat by omitting the oil and tahini but the chips will be dry and crisp, and less flavorful. Sweet potatoes or regular white potatoes, and winter squash are delicious substitutes for the Yukon potatoes. Use carrots, parsnips and rutabaga for variety in place of potatoes.

Meal Balance

Potatoes add wonderful dimension and substance to a balanced meal of grains, beans and vegetables. They are full of nutrition and starch, but not considered a substitute for the complex carbohydrates in whole grains.

This is a fun and spicy side dish that looks so festive - golden flesh potatoes seasoned with bright red cayenne and paprika, and blazed with grill marks.

6 medium Yukon Gold Potatoes, sliced
1 tablespoon Corn Oil*
1 tablespoon Tahini**
½ teaspoon ground Cumin
½ teaspoon Garlic Powder
½ teaspoon Ginger Powder
½ teaspoon Paprika
½ teaspoon Sea Salt
¼ teaspoon Cayenne

1. If an outdoor or indoor barbecue is not available, preheat oven to 350°F. Slice the potatoes into ¼" thick round discs and place in a large bowl.
2. Sprinkle the remaining ingredients over the potatoes and mix to coat evenly.
3. Grill the potatoes on the barbecue, each side until golden brown and tender. Alternatively, spread on a baking tray (scrape all the seasonings from the bowl onto the potatoes) and bake for 10 minutes or until golden brown and tender.

* See TRICKS OF THE TRADE
** See GLOSSARY

CINNAMON SWEET POTATOES

Prep Time: 5   **Cook Time: 30**   **Serves: 4**

Groceries

Sweet Potatoes, Cinnamon.

Do Ahead

Wash the potatoes and refrigerate in a sealed container, several days before slicing. Baked sweet potatoes will keep refrigerated for 3 days in a sealed container.

Hot Tips

Eliminate fat by omitting the oil but the potatoes will be dry and crisp, and less flavorful. Yukon Gold or regular white potatoes, and winter squashes are delicious substitutes for the sweet potatoes.

Meal Balance

Sweet potatoes add hearty, wonderful substance to a balanced meal of grains, beans and vegetables. The are full of nutrition, starch and Vitamin A (see Beta Carotene in H.H.I.H.).

Make a double recipe - this is a fast and fun favorite with kids, teens and adults!

4 medium Sweet Potatoes
2 tablespoons Corn Oil
1½ teaspoons Cinnamon
½ teaspoon Sea Salt

1. Preheat oven to 350°F. Slice the sweet potatoes into 1/3" to ½" thick rounds.
2. Place the sweet potatoes in a large bowl and sprinkle the remaining ingredients on top. Mix well to coat evenly, and transfer to two baking trays. Spread the slices out, so that none are overlapping.
3. Bake for 30 minutes, uncovered, or until golden brown and caramelized on the bottom, and tender. Serve immediately.

ROASTED RUTABAGA SALAD

Prep Time: 5 | **Cook Time: 35** | **Serves: 4-6**

Groceries

Rutabaga, Garlic, Ginger, Apple Cider Vinegar, Italian Parsley, Basil, White Miso.

Do Ahead

You may cut and season the rutabaga, ready to bake up to 1 day in advance. Baked rutabaga will keep refrigerated for 4 days in a sealed container.

Hot Tips

This tastes better the second day after it has had a chance to marinate in the dressing. Eliminate fat by omitting the oil— but the oil improves the flavor and texture and quickens the cooking time. You may substitute or combine carrots, onions, parsnips. You may use acorn, buttercup, butternut or delicatta squash in place of the rutabaga. The maple syrup is sweeter than the rice syrup; add according to taste.

Meal Balance

This is a rich and satisfying yellow vegetable dish, and makes a complete balanced meal with a light grain or pasta entrée, and a salad or lightly cooked green vegetables.

Warming winter salads are rich and hearty. You will feel grounded and well nourished after enjoying this dish.

1 Rutabaga (8 cups), ½" thick triangles*
¼ cup Olive Oil
½ teaspoon Sea Salt, or to taste

<u>Roasted Roots Dressing</u>
¼ cup Apple Cider Vinegar
1 small Garlic Clove, minced
2 tablespoons White Miso** (or pale color)
2 tablespoons Italian Parsley, minced
1-2 tablespoons Maple or Rice Syrup
1 tablespoon fresh Basil, minced (1 tsp. dried)
1/8 teaspoon Pepper, or to taste

1. Preheat oven to 350°F. In a large bowl, toss the rutabaga with the oil and sea salt to coat evenly. Spread into a 9" by 13" baking dish, and scrape all the oil and salt from the bowl onto the rutabaga. Cover with foil and bake for 35 minutes, or until tender.
2. Meanwhile, combine the remaining ingredients. Mix with the cooked rutabaga and serve hot. (You may cool it to room temperature, and chill the mixture for a cooling salad if desired.)

* See CUTTING TO
  THE CHASE
** See GLOSSARY

BRAISED BURDOCK
& SESAME SEEDS

Prep Time: 10   **Cook Time: 20**   **Serves: 4-6**

Groceries

Burdock, Sesame Seeds, Toasted Sesame Oil, Ginger, Cayenne, Brown Rice Vinegar, Tamari, Scallions.

Do Ahead

Toast the sesame seeds and refrigerate in a glass jar for several weeks to have on hand, (use in Sesame Sauce with Soba Noodles and Sun Seed Rice Patties). The cooked burdock keeps refrigerated for 5 days in a sealed container.

Hot Tips

Substitute carrots, parsnips and rutabaga for the burdock if desired. Eliminate fat by omitting the oil and seeds—and you will have a simple spicy burdock dish.

Meal Balance

Serve this with a main grain or pasta dish, such as the Sweet & Sour Vegetables with Seitan & Udon Noodles, Japanese Noodles with Shiitake and Arame. The Miso Soup with Wakame makes a perfect beginning to the meal, and a salad or lightly cooked green vegetables will balance the burdock roots.

Need vitality, strength and stamina? Burdock extract is used as medicine to boost immunity, detoxify blood and heal the sex organs. The best way to receive these benefits is to enjoy it naturally, as delicious food.

¼ cup tan Sesame Seeds, sorted, washed
1 tablespoon Toasted Sesame Oil
±3 cups Burdock, matchsticks*
1 tablespoon Ginger, minced
1/8 teaspoon Crushed Dried Chili, or to taste
1 cup Water
1 tablespoon Brown Rice Vinegar**
4 Scallions, sliced (white + green parts)*
1-2 tablespoons Tamari**, or to taste

1. Preheat oven to 350°F. Heat an enamel coated or stainless steel skillet over medium heat with the oil. Sauté the burdock with the ginger and chili for 2 minutes, or until tender. Add the water and vinegar and bring to a boil. Reduce heat and simmer for 15 minutes. Meanwhile...
2. Toast the sesame seeds on a baking tray for 10 minutes, or until golden brown.
3. Add the scallion whites and tamari to the burdock and cook for 1 minute. Add the scallion greens and remove from the heat.
4. Place the sesame seeds in a food processor and grind to a coarse meal. Mix the seeds with the burdock and serve.

* See CUTTING TO THE CHASE
** See GLOSSARY

ARAME WITH
AROMATIC VEGETABLES

Prep Time: 15   **Cook Time: 35**   **Serves: 4-6**

Groceries

Arame, Onion, Carrot, Parsnip, Burdock, Shiitake Mushrooms, Ginger, Toasted Sesame Oil, Scallions, Tamari.

Do Ahead

Soak the shiitake and arame for up to 30 minutes, or soak and refrigerate in a sealed container up to 5 days in advance. The cooked recipe keeps refrigerated for 5 days in a sealed container, or 3 months frozen.

Hot Tips

Substitute various mushrooms for the shiitake; café, oyster, portabella, etc. Celery, corn, daikon, green and yellow beans, rutabaga, zucchini may be included. Fresh cilantro may be added at the end with the scallions. Garlic and other spices may be added with the ginger for variety. Brown cubed seitan or tempeh in the skillet before adding the ginger, and cook with the vegetables. Alternatively, add cubed fresh tofu at the end with the tamari.

Meal Balance

This is a side dish, to be eaten with rice and vegetables. The Azuki Beans & Buttercup are a perfect bean side dish.

This dark and mysterious dish is a very rich and delicious way to enjoy sea vegetables, and wins over the most fussy customers.

5 Dried Shiitake Mushrooms* (or fresh)
1 cup dry Arame*
2 cups Water
1 tablespoon Toasted Sesame Oil*
1 tablespoon Ginger, minced
1 large Onion, ½ moons
1 large Burdock, matchsticks**
1 large Carrot, matchsticks**
1 large Parsnip, matchsticks**
2 tablespoons Arrowroot*
¼ cup Tamari*
1 large Scallion, sliced white + green parts**

1. Soak the dried shiitake in 1 cup water for 10 minutes, or until reconstituted. Squeeze the water from the shiitake (save the water), remove the tough stems and slice into thin strips. Soak the arame in 1 cup water for 10 minutes. Chop the arame into 2" pieces.
2. Heat a cast iron or stainless steel skillet over medium heat with the oil, and sauté the ginger for 1 minute. Sauté the onion until tender, 1 minute. Add the shiitake, burdock, carrot, parsnip and sauté 5 minutes.
3. Spread the arame over the vegetables, with the soaking water and bring to a boil. Reduce heat, cover, simmer for 20 minutes.
4. Dissolve the arrowroot in the tamari and stir into the liquid. Cook until clear and thickened. Add the scallion whites and adjust consistency and seasonings to taste. Mix in scallion greens and serve.

* See GLOSSARY
** See CUTTING to the CHASE

RUBY RED RADISHES

Prep Time: 10　　　　　　**Cook Time: 5**　　　　　　**Serves: 4-6**

Groceries

Red Radishes, Rice and Umeboshi Vinegar, Arrowroot, Black Sesame Seeds (optional).

Do Ahead

Wash the radishes and refrigerate in a plastic bag or a sealed container, up to 2 days in advance with the greens. Radishes without the greens will keep for 1 week. Cooked radishes keep refrigerated for 3 days. Consume the cooked greens within 1 day. Toast extra sesame seeds and refrigerate in a glass jar for several weeks, to use as a garnish for grains, pasta, porridge, salads, etc.

Hot Tips

You may substitute Beets with Tops, Carrots with Tops and Daikon with Tops in place of the radishes. In these cases, simply steam the roots, instead of cooking directly in the umeboshi vinegar. Combine the umeboshi vinegar and cook with the other ingredients.

Meal Balance

Serve this with a main entrée of grains or pasta, and a Sumptuous Soup or Savory Stew using orange and yellow vegetables, as an added course. The radish greens are very high in calcium, iron and vitamins.

Make this dish when fresh radish greens are available. The bright greens bordering the brilliant red roots is gorgeous -a festive presentation for every occasion.

1 bunch Red Radishes with fresh Green Tops
½ cup of water
2 teaspoons Umeboshi Vinegar*
1½ teaspoons Arrowroot*
2 tablespoons Rice Vinegar*
1 teaspoon Toasted Black Sesame Seeds (opt)

1. Trim the greens from the roots where they meet. Clean the greens and chop into 1" pieces. Wash the radishes and trim the long thin roots from the round part of the root. Cut a ½" deep cross into the top of each radish, keeping the radish whole. This is to quicken cooking time, and allow the center to cook more evenly.
2. Bring the water and umeboshi vinegar to a boil over medium heat, with the radishes (use a heavy bottom stainless steel pot that is large enough for the radishes to sit at the bottom without overlapping). Cover and reduce heat to low, and cook for 4-5 minutes, or until tender when inserted with a skewer.
3. Meanwhile, dissolve the arrowroot in rice vinegar. Steam the greens on top of the radishes for 1 minute or until bright green and tender-crisp. Remove just the greens, and place them around the periphery of a serving platter. Add the arrowroot mixture to the radishes and cooking juices, and simmer stirring until clear and thickened. Place in the center of the platter and serve.

* See GLOSSARY

A "10" TOMATO SAUCE

Prep Time: 20

Cook Time: 25   **Makes: 10 cups**

Groceries

Tomatoes, Carrot, Onion, Garlic, Celery, Green and Red Pepper, Mushrooms, Scallions, Italian Parsley, Basil, Oregano, Thyme, Marjoram or Rosemary.

Do Ahead

Wash and refrigerate the vegetables, ready to chop, in a sealed container or plastic bag for up to 3 days. The sauce keeps for 2 weeks refrigerated, or 3 months frozen.

Hot Tips

Some Italian Chefs believe that tomato sauce should simmer for hours, even days. It becomes sweeter, and the long cooking balances the acidity. This is a very delicious quick version, using high quality tomatoes. Use fresh, vine ripened tomatoes in equal volume when available.

Meal Balance

Use in either the Lasagna with Tofu Ricotta, the Spaghetti & Meatballs or Seitan Parmigiana. Serve over the Grilled Polenta or Sun Seed Rice Patties. Make instant simple meals: heat the sauce, add cooked grains or pasta and serve with steamed broccoli and cauliflower.

* See SPEEDY HOMEMADE SEITAN
** See GLOSSARY

These "10" vegetables create a colorful sauce with character, and the range of flavors blend into a symphony of taste.

4 - 28 ounce cans Organic Tomato Purée
28 ounces Water
1 large Carrot, grated or diced
1 Spanish or large Onion, diced
8 ounces Mushrooms, quartered or sliced
1 Green and 1 Red Pepper, diced
2 Celery, diced
6 Scallions, chopped
6 large Garlic Cloves, minced
2 tablespoons dried Basil or ¼ cup fresh
2 teaspoons dried Oregano or 2 tbsp. fresh
2 teaspoons dried Marjoram or Rosemary
2 teaspoons dried Thyme or 2 tbsp. fresh
1 tablespoon Sea Salt, or to taste
½ teaspoon Pepper, or to taste
½ cup Italian Parsley, minced

1. Pour the tomato purée into a 6 quart heavy bottom pot. Fill one of the empty tomato cans with water, to rinse out the remaining tomato purée, and then pour this liquid into the other empty cans to rinse them out, before adding the water to the sauce. Bring to a boil over medium heat with the remaining ingredients, except parsley and fresh herbs, if using. Add dried herbs now.
2. Reduce heat to low and simmer for 25 minutes, stirring occasionally to prevent scorching at the bottom. Adjust seasonings to taste. Mix in the parsley and serve.

<u>Variation</u>: **Meaty Tomato Sauce**
Reduce Sea Salt to 2 teaspoons. Add 2 cups ground Seitan*, and ¼ cup Tamari** during the last 5 minutes of cooking. Adjust seasonings to taste.

ZESTY SQUASH SAUCE

Prep Time: 10   **Cook Time: 20**   **Serves: 4-6**

Groceries

Butternut Squash, Carrot, Ginger, Garlic, Cumin, Basil, Cayenne, Miso, Soymilk (opt.), Dill, Cilantro or Italian Parsley.

Do Ahead

Wash the vegetables (except the squash) and refrigerate, ready to chop, in a sealed container or plastic bag for up to 3 days. The sauce will keep refrigerated for 5 days, or 3 months frozen.

Hot Tips

Peel the squash for a silky smooth sauce, although the cooked skin becomes tender, and purées very well. Leave the peel on for more fiber and nutrients. Use a light-medium or medium color miso for its balance of savory-sweetness, and it won't darken the sauce. Vegetable stock or water is fat-free, soymilk adds fat and calories. Delicatta may substitute the Butternut, or use Buttercup, but peel the skin.

Meal Balance

There is an abundance of Vitamin A in the carrots and squash. This completes a meal of grains or pasta, and green vegetables. Serve with Spaghetti & Meatballs, Sun Seed Rice Patties, various grains and pasta entrées (see Index and Menu Magician for all the possibilities).

A beautiful orange, ultra rich and creamy, fat-free sauce to pour over grains, pasta and vegetables - turning simple meals into haute cuisine.

2 cups Water
3 cups Butternut Squash, ½" diced*
1 medium Carrot, ½" diced
1 medium Onion, ½" diced
1 tablespoon Ginger, minced
1 Garlic Clove, minced
1 teaspoon Sea Salt, or to taste
±1 cup Vegetable Stock**, Water or Soymilk
1 teaspoon Basil (or 1 tbsp. fresh, minced)
1 teaspoon ground Cumin
Pinch of Cayenne, or to taste
1 tablespoon light-medium Miso***
2 tablespoons fresh Dill, Cilantro or Italian Parsley, minced

1. Bring the water to a boil over medium-high heat, with the squash, carrot, onion, ginger, garlic and sea salt. Reduce heat to low and simmer covered for 10 minutes, or until very tender.
2. Purée the vegetables in a blender or food processor, with stock, water or soymilk as necessary, to achieve a completely smooth sauce-like consistency. Return the sauce to the pot, and add the remaining ingredients, except the fresh herbs.
3. Bring to a gentle boil over medium heat. Reduce heat to low and simmer for 5 minutes. Add the fresh herbs and serve.

* See Winter Squash in CUTTING TO THE CHASE)
** See Vegetable Stock in TRICKS OF THE TRADE. Salted stock reduces the amount of salt added to the stew.
*** See GLOSSARY

VENETIAN VEGETABLE SAUCE

Prep Time: 10 **Cook Time: 20** **Serves: 4-6**

Groceries

Onion, Garlic, Green Pepper, Mushrooms, Carrots, Parsnip, Celery, Balsamic Vinegar, Basil, Italian Parsley, Rosemary.

Do Ahead

Wash the vegetables and refrigerate, ready to chop, in a sealed container or plastic bag for up to 3 days. The sauce will keep refrigerated for 5 days, or 3 months frozen.

Hot Tips

Eliminate fat by omitting the oil, and sauté the vegetables in ¼ cup of water. Use 1 cup of red wine, in place of 1 cup of the stock or water. ***Use a medium color miso for its balance of savory-sweetness, and it will not darken the sauce (see Miso in GLOSSARY).

Meal Balance

There are plenty of minerals, nutrients and vitamins in all these vegetables. This sauce balances a meal of grains or pasta, and green vegetables. Serve with Spaghetti & Meatballs, Sun Seed Rice Patties, various grains and pasta entrées (see Index and Menu Magician for all the possibilities).

The farmers in the fertile countryside near Venice grow these fragrant vegetables, and by cooking, transform them into art.

2 tablespoons Olive Oil
1 medium-large Onion, diced
2 Garlic Cloves, minced
2 Celery, diced
½ medium Green Pepper, diced
4 ounces Mushrooms, quartered or sliced
2 tsp. Oregano (or 2 tbsp. fresh, minced)
2 cups Butternut Squash, diced ½"*
1 medium Carrot + Parsnip, diced ½"
½ teaspoon Sea Salt, or to taste
¼ teaspoon Pepper, or to taste
3 cups of Vegetables Stock** or Water
1 tablespoon medium Miso***, or to taste
¼ cup Italian Parsley

1. Heat an enamel coated or stainless steel skillet over medium heat, with 1 tablespoon of the oil. Sauté the onion, garlic, celery, green pepper, mushrooms and dried oregano, for 2 minutes, or until tender and beginning to brown (fresh oregano goes in at the end, if using). Transfer to a bowl and set aside.
2. In the same skillet, add the remaining oil and sauté the squash, carrot and parsnip, with the sea salt and pepper, for 2 minutes. Add the stock or water and bring to a boil covered. Reduce heat to low and simmer for 10 minutes, or until tender.
3. Purée the vegetables and liquid from step 2, in a blender or food processor, with the miso until smooth. Return the purée to the skillet, and add the sautéed vegetables from Step 1. Bring to a gentle boil, simmer 1 minute, and adjust seasonings to taste. Mix in parsley, and fresh oregano if using, and serve.

** See Winter Squash in CUTTING TO THE CHASE
* See Vegetable Stock in TRICKS OF THE TRADE. Using salted stock reduces the amount of salt added to the sauce.

CARROT BEET BASIL SAUCE

Prep Time: 10   **Cook Time: 20**   **Serves: 4-6**

Groceries

Carrots, Beet, Onion, Garlic, Celery, Bay Leaf, Basil, Balsamic Vinegar, Umeboshi Paste.

Do Ahead

Wash the vegetables and refrigerate, ready to chop, in a sealed container or plastic bag for up to 3 days. The sauce will keep refrigerated for 5 days, or 3 months frozen.

Hot Tips

Eliminate fat by omitting the oil, and sauté the step 2 vegetables in ¼ cup of water. When the proportion of beet is larger, the sauce will be a bright red beet sauce. When the proportion of carrot is larger, the sauce will be orange. Don't overcook the sauce or it will lose its red color. Use 1 cup of red wine, in place of 1 cup of the stock or water.

Meal Balance

Serve this sauce on grains, pasta and vegetables. The orange vegetables balance a meal of grains or pasta, and a salad or lightly cooked green vegetables.

Love tomato sauce? Can't have tomatoes? Even if you can have tomatoes, this is a deep red, wonderful tasting sauce, to accompany any cooking style, for all occasions.

3 cups Vegetable Stock* or Water
6 medium Carrots, (3 cups) diced ½"
1 small Beet, (½ cup) diced ¼"
1 Bay Leaf
½ teaspoon Sea Salt
1 tablespoon Olive Oil
1 medium Onion, diced
1 Garlic Clove, minced
2 Celery, diced
1 tablespoon Balsamic Vinegar
1 teaspoon Umeboshi Paste**
3 tablespoons (packed) fresh Basil, minced or
1 tablespoon dried Basil

1. Bring stock or water to a boil over medium-high heat with the vegetables and bay leaf. Reduce heat to low, add sea salt, cover and simmer for 20 minutes, or until tender.
2. Meanwhile, heat an enamel coated or stainless steel skillet over medium heat, with the oil. Sauté the onion, garlic and celery for 5 minutes, or until tender and beginning to brown. (If using dried basil, add it now.)
3. Purée the vegetables in Step 1 in a blender or food processor, with enough cooking liquid to achieve a very smooth consistency. Blend in the vinegar and umeboshi paste.
4. Pour and scrape all the puréed vegetables, and cooking liquid into the skillet with the sautéed vegetables. Bring to a gentle boil, simmer for 1 minute, and adjust seasonings to taste. Mix in the fresh basil and serve.

---

* See Vegetable Stock in TRICKS OF THE TRADE. Using salted stock reduces the amount of salt added to the soup.
** See GLOSSARY

BÉCHAMEL DIJON SAUCE

Prep Time: 5   **Cook Time: 10**   **Serves: 4-6**

Groceries

Unbleached White Pastry Flour, Soymilk, White Miso, Dijon Mustard.

Do Ahead

Make the sauce and refrigerate for up to 1 week in a sealed container.

Hot Tips

A simpler, oil-free version is possible; omit the flour and oil, dissolve 2 tablespoons of cornstarch in the soymilk, and simmer until thickened with the miso and mustard. Still very creamy and tasty, but less rich and luxurious.

Meal Balance

Serve over grains or pasta and vegetables. It is heavenly on the Grilled Vegetable Polenta, Kasha Walnut Meat Loaf, Seitan Pepper Steak, or Sun Seed Rice Patties. Turn simple grains and pasta with vegetables into a gourmet dinner.

This is one of the recipes I loved to make as a teenager - before changing to a vegetarian diet - usually served with fish, scallops or shrimp. Here, Dijon mustard adds character, and the miso and soymilk render a lovely, smooth resemblance to the original sauce.

¼ cup Corn Oil
½ cup Unbleached White Flour
¼ cup White Miso* (or pale color)
2 tablespoons Dijon Mustard*
¼ teaspoon Sea Salt
1/8 teaspoon White Pepper (or Black)
1/8 teaspoon Nutmeg (optional)
2 cups Soymilk* or Water (or a combination)

1. Heat an enamel coated or stainless steel skillet over medium heat with the oil. Add the flour and cook for 5 minutes, stirring the flour with a whisk to prevent scorching.
2. Add the miso, mustard, sea salt, pepper and nutmeg to the flour, and smooth out the lumps with the whisk. Add ¼ cup of soymilk and/or water and whisk until smooth. Add ½ cup more of soymilk and whisk until smooth. Gradually add the remaining soymilk, stirring constantly. Simmer for 1 minute. Adjust seasonings to taste, and serve.

* See GLOSSARY

MUSHROOM ONION GRAVY

Prep Time: 5   **Cook Time: 10**   **Serves: 4**

Groceries

Onion, Mushrooms, Toasted Sesame Oil, Tamari, Arrowroot or Cornstarch, Italian Parsley.

Do Ahead

Wash the vegetables and refrigerate, ready to chop, in a sealed container or plastic bag for up to 3 days. Puff up the plastic bag containing the mushrooms with air, to keep them dry. The gravy keeps refrigerated for 1 week, or 3 months frozen.

Hot Tips

Eliminate fat by sautéing the vegetables in ¼ cup of water instead of the oil. The toasted sesame oil adds a deep savory flavor, but the gravy will still be delicious without it. Substitute or use a combination of oyster, portabella, shiitake or white mushrooms, instead of the café for variety.

Meal Balance

Serve over the Pepper Seitan Steak, Kasha Walnut Meat Loaf, Sun Seed Rice Patties, Millet and Cauliflower, Kasha and Caraway, and many other grain and pasta dishes.

This gravy is dark, rich and savory, yet very quick and simple to make.

1 tablespoon Corn Oil*
1 teaspoon Toasted Sesame Oil*
1 medium Onion, sliced thin ½ moons
2 cups Café Mushrooms, sliced or quartered
½ teaspoon dried Thyme
¼ teaspoon ground Sage
4 cups Vegetable Stock or Water
4 tablespoons Arrowroot** or Cornstarch
¼-½ cup Tamari**, to taste
2 tablespoons Italian Parsley, minced

1. Heat a skillet over medium-high heat with the oil, and sauté the onion and mushrooms until tender and beginning to brown, 5 minutes.
2. Add the herbs and stock or water and bring to a boil. Reduce heat and simmer for 2 minutes covered.
3. Dissolve the arrowroot in the tamari and mix in, stirring while simmering, until clear and thickened. Adjust seasonings to taste. Serve garnished with parsley.

* See TRICKS OF THE TRADE
** See GLOSSARY

CHUNKY FRUIT KETCHUP

Prep Time: 20   **Cook Time: 25**   **Makes: ±9 cups**

Groceries

Tomatoes, Apples, Pear, Peach, Onions, Green and Red Pepper, Apple Cider Vinegar, Apple Juice, Maple Syrup, Tomato Paste, Ginger, Clove, Cinnamon Sticks, Allspice, Nutmeg.

Do Ahead

Combine the spices and store in a small sealed container. You may refrigerate the liquid ingredients in a sealed container up to 5 days in advance. The ketchup keeps refrigerated for months in a sealed container, freezing changes the texture.

Hot Tips

Use a firm apple that will not dissolve when cooked such as; Cortland, Empire or Spartan. The texture should resemble a chunky, sauce-like chutney, not thick and smooth like bottled ketchup. If pears and peaches are not in season, use extra apples. Traditionally this recipe cooks for 1 hour on medium heat, and another hour on low.

Meal Balance

Serve this like a chutney or salsa on grain and grain products or protein rich main dishes.

This is essential accompaniment for the Laurentian Lentil Tortiere - the fruity, tangy, sweetness complements the hearty, whole wheat crust and savory, meaty filling.

6 ripe medium Tomatoes, diced
2 medium Onions, diced
2 medium Apples, diced
1 medium Pear, diced
1 medium Peach, diced
½ medium Green Pepper, diced
½ medium Red pepper, diced
1 cup Apple Cider Vinegar
1 cup Apple Juice
1 cup Maple Syrup
1 5.5 ounce can Tomato Paste
1 tablespoon fresh Ginger, grated
2 Cinnamon Sticks
1 teaspoon each Allspice and Sea Salt
½ teaspoon each Nutmeg and Pepper
¼ teaspoon ground Cloves

1. Bring all the ingredients to a boil in an enamel coated or stainless steel pot, over medium heat. Stir occasionally to prevent lumping and scorching on the bottom.
2. Reduce heat to low and simmer, covered, for 25 minutes. Adjust seasonings to taste. Serve hot or chilled.

CHAPTER 6

TOFU TRANSFORMATIONS

Cheeses, Dips & Dressings

Sauces, Spreads & Toppings

Creams & Frostings

MISO AGED TOFU CHEESE

Prep Time: 1-4 days   **Cook Time: 0**   **Makes: 1 lb.**

Groceries

Tofu, Miso, Garlic Powder, Ginger Powder.

Do Ahead

This whole recipe is a Do Ahead. Refrigerate the aged tofu for 2 weeks in a sealed container (tofu must be covered with the miso paste, and not exposed to air). Take sections of tofu as needed, then recover the exposed cut side with the miso paste that you remove from the piece you took.

Hot Tips

Poach and press the tofu for ideal flavor and texture (see Tofu in TRICKS OF THE TRADE). Use a well-aged miso, 18-24 months fermentation period. White miso will not give the same rich and robust character. Add various herbs and spices to create many flavors of gourmet cheese. Scrape the miso from the aged tofu and use in sauces, soups and stews to add a rich cheesy flavor.

Meal Balance

Slice the cheese and use on bread, crackers, rice cakes, tortillas, etc. Slice it into slabs and use as a sandwich filling. Crumble or cube it and add to pasta dishes, salads and stir fries. Soy products are complemented by grains such as breads and pastas. Serve vegetables to balance the meal.

Use it as you would cheese!

1 pound fresh Tofu* (firm or extra-firm)
1 cup Barley or Rice Miso**
1 tablespoon Garlic Powder
1 tablespoon Ginger Powder
¼-½ cup of water

1. Poach (optional), and then press (recommended) the tofu for 1 hour.
2. In a bowl, food processor or mortar and pestle, combine the remaining ingredients to a smooth paste. The water volume will depend on the thickness of the miso. The texture should be a spreadable paste, thick enough to coat the tofu without sliding off.
3. Slice the tofu into 2 large slabs (this is to expose the center of the tofu, to cover it with the miso paste). Spread the miso paste ¼" thick all over the tofu, covering the sides and edges, so that none of the tofu is exposed to air.
4. Place the tofu in a dish with sides higher than the height of the tofu. Place a clean thin cotton cloth over the dish. The towel should be thin enough to allow the tofu to breathe, but there should be no holes; it should be a finely woven cloth. Set the tofu aside for 1 to 4 days at room temperature (up to 2-3 days in hot Summer weather). The longer time results in a stronger aged flavor.

* See TRICKS OF THE TRADE
** See GLOSSARY

TOFU CAMEMBERT

Prep Time: 1-4 days   **Cook Time: 0**   **Makes: 10.5 oz.**

Groceries

Silken Tofu, White Miso, Onion Powder, Mustard Powder.

Do Ahead

This whole recipe is a Do Ahead. Refrigerate and age the tofu 1-4 days, and store for up to 2 weeks in a sealed container (tofu must be covered with the miso paste, and not exposed to air). Take sections of tofu as needed, then recover the exposed cut side with the miso paste that you remove from the piece you took.

Hot Tips

Scrape the miso from the aged tofu and use in sauces, soups and stews to add a rich cheesy flavor. Use the Lite silken tofu to reduce fat, but the Camembert will not be as rich and creamy. Silken tofu is ideal in recipes requiring a smooth texture, such as Brie or Camembert. Fresh tofu is preferable in recipes that require texture, such as cream cheese or ricotta.

Meal Balance

Slice the cheese and spread on bread, crackers, rice cakes, tortillas, etc. Slice it into slabs and spread as a sandwich filling. The silken tofu is too soft to crumble or cube. Soy products are complemented by grains such as breads and pastas. Serve vegetables to balance the meal.

And you thought you had to give up the finer things in life.

1 - 10.5 oz. package Silken Tofu*, Extra Firm
¾ cup White Miso* (or light-medium color)
2 teaspoons Onion Powder
2 teaspoons Mustard Powder
±¼ cup Water

1. Drain the tofu carefully, to keep it from falling apart. Slice it into 3 large slabs (this is to expose the center of the tofu, to cover it with the miso paste), and wrap in paper towels to dry. Set aside for 1 hour.
2. Meanwhile, combine the remaining ingredients to a smooth paste. The water volume will depend on the thickness of the miso. The texture should be a spreadable paste, thick enough to coat the tofu without sliding off. Spread the miso paste ¼" thick all over the tofu slices, covering the sides and edges, so none of the tofu is exposed to air.
3. Place the tofu slices (either stacked together or side by side), in a dish with sides higher than the height of the tofu. Place a clean thin cotton cloth over the dish. The towel should be thin enough to allow the tofu to breathe, but there should be no holes; it should be a finely woven cloth. Refrigerate the tofu for 1 to 4 days. The longer time results in a stronger aged flavor.

Variations: Add various herbs and spices to create many flavors of gourmet cheese.

* See GLOSSARY
  PS The tofu isn't available round as in the photo.

GREEN GODDESS DRESSING

Prep Time: 10   **Cook Time: 0**   **Makes: 2 cups**

Groceries

Silken Tofu, Italian Parsley, Scallions, Garlic, Lemon, Apple Cider and Umeboshi Vinegar, Maple or Rice Syrup, Soymilk (optional).

Do Ahead

The flavor improves after 1-2 days. Store refrigerated in a sealed container for up to 1 week, or 3 months frozen.

Hot Tips

For lower fat use silken tofu LITE and water instead of soymilk. When using rice syrup, double the volume (or to taste) as it is less sweet than maple syrup. Substitute apple cider vinegar for the umeboshi vinegar, and add ¼ teaspoon of sea salt (or to taste), to compensate. Silken tofu is ideal in recipes requiring a very smooth texture, such as sour cream or yogurt. Fresh tofu is preferable for recipes that require texture, such as cream cheese, ricotta, and for spreads.

Meal Balance

This delicious dressing has a substantial amount of tofu for calcium and protein, and the parsley contains an abundance of nutrients. Serve it with grains, pasta and vegetables, and especially on salads.

To achieve a beautiful green color, use very fresh, green parsley and scallions, and puree the dressing literally for one to two minutes.

1 - 10.5 oz. (297 gr.) package Silken Tofu*
1/3 cup, packed, Italian Parsley, minced
¼ cup, packed, Scallions, minced
1 Garlic Clove, minced
¼ cup Lemon Juice (1 Lemon)
2 tablespoons Apple Cider Vinegar
1 tablespoon Umeboshi Vinegar*
1 tablespoon Maple or Rice Syrup*
½ teaspoon Sea Salt, or to taste
Pepper to taste
Soymilk* or Water as necessary

1. Purée all the ingredients in a food processor or blender for 1-2 minutes, with enough liquid to achieve a creamy, smooth consistency. Adjust seasonings to taste. Serve immediately or chill for 1-3 hours to let the flavors marry and intensify.

Variations: **Green Goddess Dip**
Reduce the soymilk or water for a thicker consistency.

Add or substitute either basil, chives, cilantro, dill, fennel, Italian parsley, marjoram, oregano, rosemary, tarragon or thyme for the Italian parsley and scallions.

Note: You may add the parsley and scallions after puréeing the dressing, to keep it white, with flecks of green.

* See GLOSSARY

DILLICIOUS TOFU DRESSING

Prep Time: 10   **Cook Time: 0**   **Makes: ±2 cups**

Groceries

Tofu, Lemon, Apple Cider and Umeboshi Vinegar, Tahini, Maple or Rice Syrup, Dill.

Do Ahead

The flavor improves after 1-2 days. Store refrigerated in a sealed container for up to 1 week, or 3 months frozen. You may poach the tofu before using in the recipe, if desired (see Tofu in TRICKS OF THE TRADE).

Hot Tips

Reduce fat by omitting the tahini—but it will be less rich tasting. For variety, substitute basil, chives, cilantro, fennel, Italian parsley, marjoram, oregano, rosemary, tarragon or thyme for the dill. When using rice syrup, double the volume, or to taste, as it is less sweet than maple syrup. Substitute apple cider vinegar for the umeboshi vinegar, add ¼ teaspoon of sea salt, or to taste, to compensate. Silken tofu may be used instead.

Meal Balance

Serve this dressing on grains, pasta, salads, vegetables, etc. It adds soy protein, complementing grains and vegetables. You may still have beans in the same meal if desired.

Serve this with the Beautiful Boiled Salad, Herbed Kale & Cauliflower, Simple Steamed Greens or any green salad.

½ pound (454 gr.) Tofu
¼ cup Lemon Juice (1 Lemon), or to taste
2-3 tablespoons Tahini*
2 tablespoons Apple Cider Vinegar
1 tablespoon Umeboshi Vinegar*
2 teaspoons Maple or Rice Syrup*
Water as necessary
2 tablespoons fresh Dill, minced

1. Purée the tofu in a food processor with the remaining ingredients, and enough water to achieve a creamy, very smooth consistency. There should be no grainy quality left in the tofu. Depending on the brand of tofu, this may require puréeing for 1-2 minutes.
2. Adjust seasonings to taste. Serve immediately, or chill for 1-3 hours before serving.

Variations: **Dillicious Tofu Dip**
Reduce the water for a thicker consistency.

Add or substitute either basil, chives, cilantro, fennel, Italian parsley, marjoram, oregano, rosemary, tarragon or thyme for the dill.

* See GLOSSARY

POPPY SEED DRESSING

Prep Time: 5 **Cook Time: 5** **Makes: ±1 cup**

Groceries

Silken Tofu Lite, Poppy Seeds, Garlic, Apple Cider and Umeboshi Vinegar, Italian Parsley.

Do Ahead

Toast extra poppy seeds to have on hand, and use in the Lemon Poppy Seed Muffins. The dressing keeps for 1 week refrigerated in a sealed container, or frozen for 3 months.

Hot Tips

Toasting seeds intensifies their flavor and aromatic qualities. The Lite silken tofu is lower in fat and calories than regular silken tofu. Do not purée the seeds too long with the other ingredients, unless you want a black tinted dressing. Substitute apple cider vinegar for the umeboshi vinegar, and add ¼ teaspoon of sea salt, or to taste, to compensate. Silken tofu is ideal in recipes requiring a very smooth texture, such as sour cream or yogurt. Fresh tofu is preferable in recipes that require texture, such as cream cheese or ricotta, and for spreads.

Meal Balance

Serve over grains, pasta, salads and cooked vegetables. This small amount of soy doesn't interfere with a bean dish in the same meal.

This is very light and creamy. The black seeds contrast with the white tofu and make for a dramatic presentation, especially served with brightly colored vegetables.

1 tablespoon Poppy Seeds
1 large Garlic Clove
½ of a 10.5 oz. package Silken Tofu* Lite
1 tablespoon Apple Cider Vinegar
1 tablespoon Umeboshi Vinegar*
½ cup Water
1 tablespoon Italian Parsley, minced

1. Toast the poppy seeds in a 375°F toaster oven** for 5 minutes, or until fragrant and a golden tinge appears.
2. Mince the garlic in a blender or food processor. Add and purée the tofu, vinegar and water until smooth
3. Pulse briefly to mix in the seeds and parsley. Adjust seasonings to taste. Serve immediately, or chill for 1-3 hours to let the flavors marry and intensify.

<u>Variation</u>: **Poppy Seed Dip**
Reduce or omit the water content for a thicker consistency.

* See GLOSSARY
** A conventional at 375°F is ideal if you are baking something else, otherwise too much energy is wasted.

TOFU TZATZIKI

Prep Time: 5   **Cook Time: 0**   **Serves: 4**

Groceries

Silken Tofu, Cucumber, Garlic, Lemon, Dill (optional).

Do Ahead

This keeps refrigerated for 1 week in a sealed container. Freezing will cause the water and cucumber to separate, resulting in a very watery tzatziki.

Hot Tips

Use this as a base for party dips and salad dressings. Various fresh herbs can substitute for the dill. For lower fat content, use the silken tofu LITE. Silken tofu is ideal in recipes requiring a very smooth texture, such as sour cream or yogurt. Fresh tofu is preferable for recipes that require texture, such as cream cheese or ricotta, and for spreads.

Meal Balance

This healthy soy product complements grains and vegetables in a balanced meal. It's ideal with Seitan Souvlaki, served with pita bread or on rice, and vegetables. It's wonderful with the Baked Falafel and Kentucky Un-Fried Seitan.

Many have said, "this is the best Tzatziki" they have ever tried - many not knowing it was tofu.

1 medium Cucumber, peeled and seeded
1 Garlic Clove
¼ cup of Lemon Juice (1 Lemon)
1 - 10.5 oz. (297 gr.) package Silken Tofu*
½ teaspoon Sea Salt
1 tablespoon fresh Dill, minced (optional)

1. Grate the cucumber and place in a bowl.
2. Place the garlic in a food processor and grind to mince. Add the lemon juice, tofu and sea salt and purée until smooth. Scrape the sides of the bowl and purée completely
3. Mix the purée with the cucumber and the dill. Adjust seasonings to taste. Serve immediately, or chill for 1 hour before serving.

* See GLOSSARY

CREAMY CHEESY SAUCE

Prep Time: 5

Cook Time: 0

Makes: ±2 cups

Groceries

Silken Tofu or Silken Tofu Lite, Garlic, Mustard Powder, Apple Cider Vinegar, Tamari.

Do Ahead

Store refrigerated for 1 week in a sealed container, or frozen for 3 months.

Hot Tips

Omit the olive oil to reduce fat and calories if desired—it adds flavor and aromatic qualities. Silken tofu is ideal in recipes requiring a very smooth texture, such as sour cream or yogurt. Fresh tofu is preferable in recipes that require texture, such as cream cheese or ricotta, and for spreads.

Meal Balance

Use as a sauce or topping on grains, patties, loaves, pasta, salads and vegetables. Use is as a base for creamy salad dressings, or reduce the water volume and use is as a dip or spread.

This is an elegant sauce or topping for entrees, such as Tijuana Tostadas. Turn a vegetable and pasta stir fry into a rich, scrumptious main course.

1 Garlic Clove
1 - 10.5 oz. package Silken Tofu* (Lite opt.)
2 tablespoons Apple Cider Vinegar
2 tablespoons Tamari*
1 tablespoon Extra Virgin Olive Oil
½ teaspoon Mustard Powder
±½ cup Water

1. Mince the garlic in a blender or food processor. Add the remaining ingredients and purée, with enough water to achieve a creamy, smooth sauce-like consistency. Adjust seasonings to taste and serve.

Note: You may heat it up in a pot on the stove over medium heat until it begins to simmer. Or, heat it up directly in the skillet or wok during the last few minutes of cooking a dish such as; Pasta Primavera, Wok Around the Clock, Penne Putanesca with Rapini, Spaghetti with Meat Balls, Miso Onion Bell Pepper Sauce with Spinach Fettuccini, Tofu Cacciatore with Vegetable Bowties—turning it into a Creamy Cheesy Pasta Primavera.

* See GLOSSARY

TAHINI LEMON SAUCE

Prep Time: 5　　　　　　　　**Cook Time: 0**　　　　　　　**Makes: ±3 cups**

Groceries

Silken Tofu Lite, Tahini, Lemon, Garlic, Cumin, Paprika, Cayenne, Italian Parsley, Scallions.

Do Ahead

Store refrigerated in a sealed container for up to 1 week, or frozen for 3 months.

Hot Tips

The Lite silken tofu extends the recipe and lowers the fat content, compared to regular tofu, or an all-tahini recipe, while retaining the creamy, smooth texture. Use freshly squeezed lemons, not bottled juice. Silken tofu is ideal in recipes requiring a very smooth texture, such as sour cream or yogurt. Fresh tofu is preferable in recipes that require texture, such as cream cheese or ricotta, and for spreads.

Meal Balance

There is an abundance of calcium in this recipe from the tahini, tofu and parsley. The soy protein complements grains and vegetables to round out a balanced meal.

Serve this with the Baked Falafel for perfect companionship. It is also wonderful with the Kentucky Un-Fried Seitan and various grains, pasta, salads and vegetables.

2 Garlic Cloves
1 - 10.5 oz. package Silken Tofu* Lite
1 cup Tahini*
1½ cups Lemon Juice (±3 Lemons)
1½ teaspoons Sea Salt, or to taste
1 teaspoon Cumin
½ teaspoon Paprika
Cayenne to taste
±¾ cup Water
¼ cup Italian Parsley, minced
¼ cup Scallions, minced (white + green parts)

1. Mince the garlic in a blender or food processor. Purée the remaining ingredients, except parsley and scallions, until smooth. Scrape the sides of the bowl and purée completely, adding enough water to achieve a thick, but pourable consistency.
2. Pulse in the parsley and scallions to mix. Adjust seasonings to taste. Serve immediately, or chill for 1-3 hours to let the flavors marry and intensify.

Variations:
Orange Almond Dip or Dressing
Substitute almond butter for the tahini, and orange juice for the lemon juice. Reduce or omit the water for a thicker, dip consistency.

Orange Almond Sauce
Add extra water and purée to a sauce-like consistency. Adjust seasoning to taste.

Tahini Lemon Dip
Reduce or omit the water for a thicker consistency.

* See GLOSSARY

TOFU CREAM CHEESE SPREAD

Prep Time: 10   **Cook Time: 0**   **Makes: ±3 cups**

Groceries

Tofu, Lemon Juice, Apple Cider and Umeboshi Vinegar, Tahini, Rice Syrup, Miso.

Do Ahead

Store refrigerated for 1 week in a sealed container, or 3 months frozen.

Hot Tips

Use a light-medium color miso. You may use up to ¼ cup of white miso, which is sweet and delicate in flavor. Dark miso is bitter and will turn the spread a darker color. Substitute apple cider vinegar for the umeboshi vinegar, add ¼ teaspoon of sea salt, or to taste, to compensate. Fresh tofu is preferable in recipes that require texture, such as cream cheese or ricotta, and for spreads. Use silken tofu in recipes requiring a very smooth texture, like sour cream .

Meal Balance

Serve as a spread on bagels, bread, crackers, rice cakes, tortillas, etc., (see Bagels and Tofu Cream Cheese with Mock-Lox). This is full of calcium (see Tofu in H.H.I.H) and the soy protein balances the complex carbohydrates in grains and grain products. Add colorful fresh vegetables to complete a balanced meal.

Heaven on earth is Tofu Cream Cheese Spread on fresh, warm, toasted bagels.

1 pound Tofu*, (poached**, optional)
2 tablespoons Miso*
1 tablespoon Lemon Juice
1 tablespoon Apple Cider Vinegar
1 tablespoon Umeboshi Vinegar*
1 tablespoon Rice Syrup*
1 tablespoon Tahini*
¼ teaspoon Sea Salt, or to taste
±¼ cup Water

1. Purée all the ingredients, adding enough water to achieve a smooth, grain-free texture. Scrape the sides of the bowl and purée completely. Adjust seasonings to taste and serve immediately, or chill for 1-3 hours to let the flavors marry and intensify.

Variation:
Herbs & Garlic Cream Cheese Spread
Add 1 small Red Onion, (1/3 cup) minced, and 1 tablespoon each of fresh minced Basil, Oregano and Thyme (or 1 teaspoon of each dried).

* See GLOSSARY
** See TRICKS OF THE TRADE

TOFU MOZZARELLA

Prep Time: 5   **Cook Time: 5**   **Makes: ±2 cups**

Groceries

Mochi, Silken Tofu, , Cashew Butter, White Miso.

Do Ahead

Store refrigerated for 1 week in a sealed container, or 3 months frozen.

Hot Tips

Use the Lite silken tofu for less fat and calories, although it is less rich and creamy, and less like Mozzarella. Use cashew butter instead of tahini as it is sweeter, less bitter. Omit the nut or seed butters to reduce fat if desired, if you don't mind sacrificing the taste and texture. Silken tofu is ideal in recipes requiring a very smooth texture, such as sour cream or yogurt. Fresh tofu is preferable in recipes that require texture, such as cream cheese or ricotta, and for spreads.

Meal Balance

Use as you would Mozzarella Cheese, as a topping on grain and pasta dishes, vegetables, etc. This makes a wonder sauce. The soy product complements a grain or pasta main dish, served with vegetables for a balanced meal.

This turns golden, and the flavors heighten as it bakes. Turn Pizza into Pizzazz, and Seitan Parmigiana into a sensuous, gourmet experience with this topping.

¾ cup Mochi*, grated
½ cup Water
½ of a 10.5 oz. package Silken Tofu**
3 tablespoons Cashew Butter, or Tahini**
5 tablespoons White Miso** (or light color)

1. Simmer the mochi in the water over low heat for 5 minutes, until dissolved.
2. Purée with the remaining ingredients in a blender or food processor (adding soymilk or water if necessary) to achieve a creamy, smooth, pourable, thick, sauce-like consistency. Adjust seasonings to taste and pour over various recipes before baking.

* Sweet rice pounded and dried into cakes. Available in natural food stores.
** See GLOSSARY

TOFU SOUR CREAM

Prep Time: 5　　　　　**Cook Time: 0**　　　　　**Makes: ±1½ cups**

Groceries

Silken Tofu or Silken Tofu Lite, Lemon.

Do Ahead

Store refrigerated for 1 week in a sealed container, or frozen for 3 months.

Hot Tips

Omit the oil to reduce calories and fat—it adds richness and texture. The Lite silken tofu is lower in fat and calories, but less creamy. Silken tofu is ideal in recipes requiring a very smooth texture, such as sour cream or yogurt. Fresh tofu is better for recipes that have texture, such as cream cheese or ricotta, and for spreads.

Meal Balance

Use as you would sour cream, as a topping in soups, salads, main dishes. Use is as a base for an unlimited variety of dips, salad dressings and sauces.

This simple, versatile recipe is a natural in the Borsch and Mushroom Vegetable Pie. Serve it on baked potatoes, sprinkled with Tempeh Bacon Bits and fresh chives.

1 - 10.5 oz. package Silken Tofu (Lite)
2 tablespoons Safflower Oil
2-3 tablespoons Lemon Juice, or to taste
¼ teaspoon Sea Salt, or to taste

1. Purée the ingredients until smooth. Adjust seasonings to taste. Serve immediately in various recipes.

Note: Certain oils may be too yellow to use, such as corn or canola, or too fragrant and strong in flavor, such as olive or sesame. Use an oil that is pale in color and neutral in flavor.

* See GLOSSARY

VANILLA TOFU CREAM

Prep Time: 5   **Cook Time: 0**   **Makes: ±2 cups**

Groceries

Silken Tofu, Maple Syrup, Vanilla Powder.

Do Ahead

Store refrigerated for 5 days in a sealed container, or frozen for 3 months.

Hot Tips

Use extra firm silken tofu for a thicker whipped cream, the soft variety yields a sauce-topping. The Lite silken tofu is lower in fat and calories, but less creamy. Silken tofu is ideal in recipes requiring a very smooth texture, such as sour cream, whipped cream or yogurt. Fresh tofu is preferable in recipes that require texture, such as cream cheese, ricotta, spreads or icing. When using rice syrup, double the volume, or to taste as it is less sweet than maple syrup. Vanilla powder is preferable over liquid extract, as it will not darken the tofu whipped cream.

Meal Balance

Use on desserts as a topping. Serve after a balanced meal based on grains or pasta and vegetables.

This is light and creamy - ideal to serve on cakes and pies, compotes, crisps and kantens.

1 - 10.5 oz. pk. Silken Tofu* Extra Firm (Lite)
¼ cup Maple or Rice Syrup*
2 tablespoons Vanilla Powder or Extract

1. Purée the ingredients with soymilk or water, if desired, to achieve a creamy smooth topping. Adding more soymilk or water turns this into a sauce to pour on desserts, rather than served as a dollop of topping.

Variations:
Gourmet Tofu Cream
Add ¼-½ teaspoon of liquid extract; almond, anise, banana, brandy, coconut, coffee, lemon, mint, orange, pineapple, raspberry, strawberry, walnut, etc.

Silky Tofruity Pudding
Add and purée 1 cup of fresh fruit (peeled and/or seeded); apple, apricot, banana, blueberry, cherry, cranberry, kiwi, mango, melon, orange, papaya, peach, pear, raspberry, strawberry, etc.

Vanilla Tofu Sauce
Add ¼ cup of Soymilk or Water and purée until smooth and creamy, adding more liquid if necessary to achieve a sauce-like consistency. Serve over any dessert for a luscious treat.

* See GLOSSARY

VANILLA TOFU FROSTING

Prep Time: 5 **Cook Time: 0** **Makes: ±3 cups**

Groceries

Tofu, Maple Syrup, Vanilla Powder, Almond Extract, Lemon Extract.

Do Ahead

Store refrigerated for 1 week in a sealed container, or frozen for 3 months.

Hot Tips

Fresh tofu is better for recipes that have texture, such as icing, cream cheese, ricotta or spreads. Silken tofu is ideal in recipes requiring a very smooth texture, such as sour cream, whipped cream or yogurt. Maple syrup is preferable over rice syrup as it results in a sweeter, thicker icing. When using rice syrup, double the volume, or to taste as it is less sweet than maple syrup. Vanilla powder is preferable over liquid extract, as it will not darken the tofu icing, and keeps it thicker.

Meal Balance

Spread over cakes, cupcakes and muffins as you would any frosting. Serve after a balanced meal of grains or pasta and vegetables.

* See GLOSSARY
** See Tofu in TRICKS OF THE TRADE

My mother, a professional pastry chef, creates masterpieces with this on birthday, special occasion and wedding cakes. It doesn't fool anyone or compare to commercial dairy and sugar based icings, the taste and texture is uniquely delicious.

1 lb. fresh Tofu* Extra Firm, (poached**, opt.)
¾ cup Maple or Rice Syrup
2 tablespoons Vanilla Powder
½-1 teaspoon Almond Extract (to taste)
½-1 teaspoon Lemon Extract (to taste)
¼ teaspoon Sea Salt

1. Purée the ingredients in a food processor until smooth. Scrape the bowl and purée completely. Spread on various desserts.

Note: A new blade on the food processor yields a smoother, grain-free texture, in less time than a worn out blade. Change your blade every few years or so, depending on frequency of use.

Variations:
Gourmet Tofu Frostings
Add ½-1 teaspoon of liquid extract, either; anise, banana, brandy, coconut, coffee, lemon, mint, orange, pineapple, raspberry, strawberry, walnut, etc.
You may add food coloring to match the flavors; green with mint, yellow with lemon, orange with orange, red with raspberry or strawberry, etc.

Tofruity Puddings
Add 2 cups of fresh fruit (peeled and/or seeded); Apple, Apricot, Banana, Blueberry, Cherry, Cranberry, Kiwi, Mango, Melon, Orange, Papaya, Peach, Pear, Raspberry, Strawberry, etc.

CHOCOLATY TOFU FROSTING

Prep Time: 5   **Cook Time: 0**   **Makes: ±3 cups**

Groceries

Tofu, Maple Syrup, Carob Powder, Vanilla Powder, Almond or Hazelnut Butter (optional), Almond Extract.

Do Ahead

Store refrigerated for 1 week in a sealed container, or frozen for 3 months.

Hot Tips

Fresh tofu is preferable in recipes that require texture or thickness, such as frosting, cream cheese, ricotta or spreads. Silken tofu is ideal in recipes requiring a very smooth texture, such as sour cream, whipped cream or yogurt. Maple syrup is preferable over rice syrup as it results in a sweeter, thicker icing. When using rice syrup, double the volume, or to taste as it is less sweet than maple syrup. Vanilla powder results in a slightly thicker tofu frosting, compared to the liquid extract. Use cocoa power instead of carob if desired, but it is higher in fat and contains caffeine. Omit the almond or hazelnut butter to reduce fat and calories, but it adds flavor, richness and texture.

Meal Balance

Spread over cakes, cupcakes and muffins as you would any frosting or icing.

This is very rich and decadent, yet guilt-free! Make the Dark & Delicious Chocolaty Frosting simply by increasing the carob powder and maple syrup.

1 lb. fresh Tofu* Extra Firm, (poached**, opt.)
1 cup Maple Syrup*
½ cup Carob Powder*
2 tbsp. Almond or Hazelnut Butter (optional)
2 tablespoons Vanilla Extract or Powder
1 teaspoon Almond Extract (optional)
¼ teaspoon Sea Salt

1. Purée the ingredients in a food processor until smooth. Scrape the bowl and purée completely. Spread on various desserts.

Note: A new blade on the food processor yields a smoother, grain-free texture, and in less time than a worn out blade. Change your blade every few years or so, depending on the frequency of use.

Variations:
Dark & Delicious Chocolaty Frosting
Add an extra ¼ cup of Carob Powder, and up to ¼ cup of Maple Syrup, or to taste.

Swiss Mocha Frosting
Reduce the Carob Powder to 2 tablespoons. Add ¼ to 1/3 cup of Grain Coffee Powder, or to taste.

* See GLOSSARY
** See Tofu in TRICKS OF THE TRADE

BREAKFAST BENEFITS

Eating gets your body's metabolism going. Meals eaten in the beginning of the day have more time to be burned off compared to food eaten later.

Get in the habit of eating porridge regularly, and a fun brunch occasionally. Have a nourishing lunch, and a lighter, smaller meal toward the end of the day, no later than three hours before bedtime. This way you'll be hungry by morning!

CHAPTER 7

BREAKFAST
FOR BUSY BODIES

Porridge to Pancakes
Scrambled to Fried
Tea Breads to Muffins

OATS & AMARANTH WITH RAISINS

Prep Time: 5

Cook Time: 35

Serves: 6-8

Groceries

Rolled Oats, Amaranth, Raisins, Cinnamon Stick (optional).

Do Ahead

Make the porridge the evening before serving. Reheat portions in the morning, and refrigerate the rest. Refrigerate for 5 days in one sealed container, or individual serving size containers. It keeps frozen for 3 months, although the texture changes.

Hot Tips

Toasting the oats and amaranth is optional, it adds a hearty, nutty flavor. Add the raisins during the last 10 minutes. Cooking them from the beginning will make them dissolve and become mushy. You may add them as a garnish, without cooking them if desired. Cooking the porridge longer gives a creamier texture.

Meal Balance

Serve with your favorite tea or coffee for breakfast.

Make several mornings' worth of porridge. If you make delicious combinations that you really enjoy, you won't mind having it again the next day. With a little creativity, you need not repeat the same porridge for several weeks, or even months.

3 cups Old Fashioned Rolled Oats*
½ cup Amaranth*
±14 cups Water
1 Cinnamon Stick (optional)
2 teaspoons Sea Salt, or to taste
½-1 cup Raisins

1. Heat an enamel coated or stainless steel 5 quart pot over medium-high heat. Toast the oats and amaranth, moving them constantly with a wooden spoon for 5 minutes, or until golden and fragrant.
2. Add the water and cinnamon stick and bring to a boil. Add the sea salt, cover and reduce heat to low. Simmer for 20 minutes, or longer if desired, stirring occasionally to prevent lumping on the bottom. Add water as necessary, if the texture becomes thicker than desired.
3. Mix in the raisins and cook for 10 minutes more. Remove the cinnamon stick and serve. Cool extra porridge to room temperature before refrigerating in sealed containers.

Variation:
Oats & Kasha with Dried Apples
Substitute Kasha for the amaranth. Substitute dried apples (cut with scissors into ½" pieces) for the raisins.

---

* It is not necessary to sort or wash rolled oats or packaged amaranth before cooking.

BARLEY & QUINOA with APRICOTS

Prep Time: 10   **Cook Time: 60**   **Serves: 6-8**

Groceries

Pearled or Pot Barley, Quinoa, Cinnamon Stick (optional), Apricots.

Do Ahead

Sort, wash and soak the barley and quinoa several hours. Make the porridge the evening before serving. Reheat portions in the morning, and refrigerate the rest. Refrigerate 5 days in one sealed container, or individual serving size containers. It keeps frozen for 3 months, although the texture changes.

Hot Tips

Add the apricots during the last 15 minutes. Cooking them from the beginning will make them dissolve and become mushy. You may add them as a garnish, without cooking them if desired. Cooking the porridge longer gives a creamier texture.

Meal Balance

Serve with your favorite tea or coffee for breakfast.

Whole grains cooked into a hot creamy porridge for breakfast gives stable, enduring energy for hours. Processed dry cereal and bread don't provide as much nutrition and vitality.

2 cups Pearled or Pot Barley, sorted, washed*
1 cup Quinoa, sorted, washed*
±14 cups Water
1 Cinnamon Stick (optional)
2 teaspoons Sea Salt, or to taste
½-1 cup Dried Apricots, chopped ½" pieces

1. Soak the barley and quinoa in the water for several hours (1-8 hours, or overnight).
2. Bring to a boil with the soaking water, in an enamel coated or stainless steel 5 quart pot over medium-high heat. Add the sea salt and cinnamon stick, cover and reduce heat to low. Simmer for 45 minutes, or longer if desired, stirring occasionally to prevent lumping on the bottom. Add water as necessary, if the texture becomes thicker than desired.
3. Mix in the apricots and cook for 15 minutes more. Remove the cinnamon stick and serve. Cool extra porridge to room temperature before refrigerating in sealed containers.

Variation:
Creamy Sweet Brown Rice & Currants
Substitute 2 cups of Short Grain Brown Rice and 1 cup of Sweet Brown Rice for the barley and quinoa. Substitute currants for the apricots.

* See STAPLES for complete instructions.

MILLET & CORNMEAL WITH DATES

Prep Time: 5

Cook Time: 30

Serves: 6-8

Groceries

Millet, Cornmeal, Dates, Cinnamon Stick (optional).

Do Ahead

Make the porridge the evening before serving. Reheat portions in the morning, and refrigerate the rest. Refrigerate 5 days in one sealed container, or individual serving size containers. It keeps frozen for 3 months, although the texture changes.

Hot Tips

Toasting is optional, if desired, simply boil for 25 minutes instead of 20. Add the dates during the last 5 minutes. Cooking them from the beginning will make them dissolve and become mushy. You may add them as a garnish, without cooking them if desired. Cooking the porridge longer gives a creamier texture.

Meal Balance

Serve with your favorite tea or coffee for breakfast.

Toasting the grains before boiling adds a hearty, nutty flavor and a wonderful aroma that fills your home.

2 cups Millet, sorted, washed and well drained
1 cup Cornmeal*
±14 cups Water
1 Cinnamon Stick (optional)
2 teaspoons Sea Salt, or to taste
½-1 cup Dried Dates, chopped ½" pieces

1. Heat an enamel coated or stainless steel 5 quart pot over medium-high heat. Toast the millet and cornmeal, moving them constantly with a wooden spoon for 5 minutes, or until golden and fragrant.
2. Add the water and cinnamon stick and bring to a boil. Add the sea salt, cover and reduce heat to low. Simmer for 20 minutes, or longer if desired, stirring occasionally to prevent lumping on the bottom. Add water as necessary, if the texture becomes thicker than desired.
3. Mix in the dates and cook for 5 minutes more. Remove the cinnamon stick and serve. Cool extra porridge to room temperature before refrigerating in sealed containers.

Variation:
Cream of Wheat & Teff with Peaches
Substitute 1 cup of Teff* for the millet. Substitute 2 cups of cream of wheat* for the cornmeal. Substitute dried peaches, cut with scissors into ½" pieces, for the dates, except cook from the beginning with the teff.

* Do not wash before soaking and/or cooking.

INTERNATIONAL PANCAKES

Prep Time: 5   **Cook Time: 30**   **Makes: 8**

Groceries

Whole Wheat Pastry Flour, Apple Juice, Cooked Grains (leftovers-opt.), Baking Powder and Soda. Optional; Buckwheat and Rye Flour, Caraway, Allspice, Poppy Seeds, Cinnamon.

Do Ahead

Keep the dry ingredients covered in a bowl, in a cool dry place up to 5 days in advance. Use up leftover grains that are several days old, and if the grains have begun to sour, this adds a wonderful sourdough flavor. Extra pancakes store refrigerated for 5 days, or frozen for 3 months, in a sealed container.

Hot Tips

The first pancake usually sticks. Once the skillet gets well heated and oiled, the rest of the pancakes cook perfectly. Place them on a plate, with another plate inverted to cover, and keep them in a warm oven while you prepare the rest of the pancakes, and the meal.

Meal Balance

This is a "treat" grain product, not recommended as daily fare, for optimum health. Serve with Ravishing Raspberry Coulis, Orange Almond Sauce, Favorite Fruit Sauce or Lemon Maple Raisin Sauce.

Serve for breakfast or brunch with all the fixin's!

2 cups Whole Wheat Pastry Flour
2 teaspoons Baking Powder
½ teaspoon each Baking Soda and Sea Salt
1 cup Apple Juice
½-1 cup Water, as necessary
½ cup Cooked Grains (leftovers - optional)
Corn, Safflower or Sesame Oil as necessary

1. Combine the first 4 dry ingredients in a bowl. Mix in the apple juice and enough water for a smooth, pourable batter. Add the cooked grains and adjust consistency. The grains will cause the batter to thicken up as it sits, add more liquid as necessary.
2. Heat a cast iron or stainless steel skillet over medium heat. Brush the skillet with oil and ladle 1/8 of the batter onto the skillet. Tilt the skillet if necessary to spread the batter, and fry for a few minutes on one side, until golden brown. Turn the pancake with a spatula, and fry the other side. Continue with remaining batter, oiling the skillet as needed.

Variations:
Cinnamon Maple Oatmeal Pancakes
Substitute ½ cup of Quick Cooking Rolled Oats for ½ cup of the flour. Reduce the apple juice to ±¾ cup. Add 3 tablespoons of Maple Syrup, and 1 tablespoon of Cinnamon.

German Poppy Seed Pancakes
Substitute ½ cup of Rye Flour for ½ cup of the wheat flour. Substitute Soymilk for the Water. Add 1 tbsp. of Toasted Poppy Seeds.

Russian Buckwheat Pancakes
Substitute ½ cup of Buckwheat Flour for ½ cup of the wheat flour. Add 1 teaspoon Ground Caraway, and ¼ teaspoon Allspice.

FOUR GRAIN GRIDDLE CAKES

Prep Time: 5   **Cook Time: 30**   **Makes: 8**

Groceries

Barley Flour, Cornmeal, Rolled Oats, Whole Wheat Pastry Flour, Baking Powder and Soda, Silken Tofu, Lemon Juice, Maple Syrup.

Do Ahead

Keep the dry ingredients covered in a bowl, in a cool dry place up to 5 days in advance. You may add leftover grains that are several days old, and if the grains have begun to sour, this adds a wonderful sourdough flavor. Extra griddle cakes store refrigerated for 5 days, or frozen for 3 months, in a sealed container.

Hot Tips

The first griddle cake usually sticks. Once the skillet gets well heated and oiled, the rest of the griddle cakes cook perfectly. Place them on a plate, with another plate inverted to cover, and keep them in a warm oven while you prepare the rest of the griddle cakes, and the meal.

Meal Balance

This is a "treat" grain product, not recommended as daily fare, for optimum health. Serve with Ravishing Raspberry Coulis, Orange Almond Sauce, Favorite Fruit Sauce or Lemon Maple Raisin Sauce.

These are hearty and wholesome. You may also cook this as one large skillet cake, that you may slice and serve topped with a fruity sauce.

½ cup Barley Flour
½ cup Cornmeal
½ cup Rolled Oats
½ cup Whole Wheat Pastry Flour
1 tablespoon Baking Powder
½ teaspoon each Baking Soda and Sea Salt
1 - 10.5 oz. pk. Silken Tofu* Extra Firm Lite
1 cup Apple Juice
±1 cup Water, as necessary
2 tablespoons Lemon Juice (±½ Lemon)
Corn, Safflower or Sesame Oil as necessary

1. Combine the first seven dry ingredients in a bowl. Purée the tofu with the next three liquid ingredients, adding enough water for a smooth, pourable consistency. Add the dry ingredients to the purée and blend to mix. The grains will cause the batter to thicken up as it sits, add more liquid as necessary. The batter should be thicker than pancakes.
2. Heat a cast iron or stainless steel skillet over medium-low heat. Brush the skillet with oil and ladle 1/8 of the batter onto the skillet. Fry for a few minutes on one side, until golden brown. Turn the griddle cake with a spatula, and fry the other side. Continue with remaining batter, oiling the skillet as needed.

Variation: **Four Grain Skillet Cake**
Preheat oven to 350°F. Oil a cast iron skillet and heat it in the oven for 10 minutes. Pour the batter into the skillet and bake for 20 minutes, or until golden brown and a skewer inserted comes out clean.

* See GLOSSARY

SCRAMBLED TOFU MISH MASH

Prep Time: 15   **Cook Time: 10**   **Serves: 4-6**

Groceries

Tofu, Corn, Onion, Green Pepper, Tofu Wieners, Turmeric.

Do Ahead

Crumble the tofu, grate the corn, and store refrigerated in a sealed container up to 1 day in advance. The Scramble keeps refrigerated for 4 days, or frozen for 3 months.

Hot Tips

Crumble the tofu with your fingers for ideal results, and it's also a good workout for your fingers. Grate the corn on a flat or box grater, and get all the juices and pulp from the niblets. Turmeric adds an appetizing yellow color (like eggs). Reduce fat by sautéing in ¼ cup of water instead of oil.

Meal Balance

This has a substantial amount of soy to balance grains or grain products. Serve with bagels or toast. Round out the brunch with International Whole Wheat Pancakes or Tofu French Toast, Home Fried Potatoes and Tempeh Bacon.

Many Montrealers will recognize the origins of this dish. Pass this recipe off as creative scrambled eggs to unsuspecting friends and family members.

1 pound fresh Tofu*, crumbled fine
4 Corn Cobs, grated
¼ teaspoon Turmeric
1 tablespoon Corn, Safflower or Sesame Oil
1 medium Onion, diced ½"
2 Tofu Wieners, diced ½" diagonally
½ Green Pepper, diced ½"
½-1 teaspoon Sea Salt, or to taste
¼ teaspoon Pepper, or to taste

1. Combine the tofu with the corn and turmeric, and set aside in a bowl.
2. Heat a stainless steel skillet over medium heat, with the oil and sauté the onion and tofu wieners for 5 minutes, until beginning to brown. Add the green peppers, sea salt and pepper and sauté for 2 minutes, until tender-crisp.
3. Mix in the tofu-corn mixture, cover and cook for 3 minutes to heat through. Adjust seasonings to taste, and serve.

Variation: **Sunday Scrambled Tofu**
Omit the onion, tofu wieners and green pepper, and serve as you would scrambled eggs.

* See GLOSSARY

TURKISH MENEMEN

Prep Time: 15   **Cook Time: 10**   **Serves: 4-6**

Groceries

Tofu, Corn, Onions, Tomatoes, Crushed Dried Chili, Miso, Apple Cider Vinegar, Tahini, Italian Parsley, Mint.

Do Ahead

Crumble the tofu, and grate the corn, and store refrigerated in a sealed container up to 1 day in advance. The Menemen keeps refrigerated for 4 days, or frozen for 3 months.

Hot Tips

Crumble the tofu with your fingers for ideal results, and it's also a good workout for your fingers. Grate the corn on a flat or box grater, and get all the juices and pulp from the niblets. The turmeric adds an appetizing yellow color (like eggs). Reduce fat by sautéing in ¼ cup of water instead of oil, and omit the tahini if you don't mind sacrificing some richness and flavor. Use a light-medium miso, the white or pale miso is too delicate and sweet, and the dark miso is too bitter and will darken the dish.

Meal Balance

Scrambled eggs will never be the same after you experience this. Serve with bagels or toast—in Turkey they always serve it with toast. This has a substantial amount of soy to balance grains or grain products.

Side is a small tourist town on the Turkish Riviera, where one can enjoy the culinary delights, while taking in scenes of ancient ruins and Mediterranean sunsets. The Hotel Chef let me in his kitchen to learn the secret of this popular dish. This version creatively substitutes the eggs.

1 pound fresh Tofu*, crumbled fine
4 Corn Cobs, grated
1/3 cup Miso* (light-medium color)
¼ cup Tahini*
3 tablespoons Apple Cider Vinegar
¼ teaspoon Turmeric
1 tablespoon Corn, Safflower or Sesame Oil
¼ teaspoon Crushed Dried Chili
1 medium Onion, diced ½"
6 medium Tomatoes**, diced
½-1 teaspoon Sea Salt, or to taste
¼ teaspoon Pepper, or to taste
¼ cup each Italian Parsley, fresh Mint, minced

1. Combine the tofu with the corn, miso, vinegar, tahini and turmeric, and set aside.
2. Heat a stainless steel skillet over medium heat. Add the oil, and sauté the chili with the onion for 2 minutes, or until tender. Add the tomatoes, sea salt and pepper, and sauté for 2 minutes, until tender.
3. Mix in the tofu mixture, cover and cook for 3 minutes to heat through. Add parsley and mint, adjust seasonings to taste, serve.

* See GLOSSARY
** Use vine ripened tomatoes for best results.

TOFU FRENCH TOAST

Prep Time: 10   **Cook Time: 30**   **Makes: 8**

Groceries

Silken Tofu, Whole Grain Bread, Vanilla Extract, Turmeric, Soymilk (optional).

Do Ahead

Purée the batter and refrigerate in a sealed container up to 3 days in advance, or freeze for 3 months. Soak the bread for 15 minutes, several hours, or overnight. When soaking for more than 1 hour, cover the dish with plastic wrap and refrigerate. Tofu French Toast keeps refrigerated for 5 days in a sealed container.

Hot Tips

The Lite silken tofu is lower in fat and calories, but less creamy. Use water instead of soymilk to reduce fat and calories. Bake the battered bread on a baking tray in a preheated 350°F oven for 20 minutes or until golden brown. This is a lower fat version than frying. When frying, only turn the bread once: fry one side, turn, fry the other side. Frequent turning may cause the bread to fall apart, especially if it is a light, delicate bread.

Meal Balance

This combines whole grain products with soybean products providing substantial nutritional value.

Top with the Favorite Fruit Sauce or Lemon Maple Raisin Sauce. Add a dollop of Vanilla Tofu Cream for a treat.

1 - 10.5 oz. package Silken Tofu* (Lite)
1 teaspoon Pure Vanilla Extract
½ teaspoon Sea Salt, or to taste
¼ teaspoon Turmeric
1-2 cups Soymilk or Water, as necessary
8 slices Whole Grain Bread
Corn, Safflower or Sesame Oil as necessary

1. Purée all the ingredients, except the bread, adding enough soymilk or water to achieve a creamy, smooth, pourable, thick consistency.
2. Place the bread in a large shallow dish such as a large rectangle baking dish. Use two dishes if necessary so that the slices are not overlapping. Pour ½ of the batter over the bread to cover completely. Poke holes in the bread using a fork so the batter absorbs all the way through to the center, otherwise the bread will still be dry inside after frying. Turn the bread slices over and pour the remaining batter on top to coat the bread completely. Poke again, set aside to soak.
3. Heat a cast iron or stainless steel skillet over medium heat. Brush the skillet with oil and fry the battered bread on each side for 3-5 minutes, or until golden brown and a crust has formed. Serve immediately or keep warm in a low oven, in a covered dish.

* See GLOSSARY

HOMEFRIED POTATOES

Prep Time: 10   **Cook Time: 20**   **Serves: 4**

Groceries

Spanish Onion, Potatoes, Garlic, Italian Parsley.
Optional: Cilantro, Ginger, Basil, Oregano, Rosemary, Chives, Dill, Tarragon, Thyme, Caraway Seeds.

Do Ahead

Cook, cool and refrigerate the potatoes whole, in a sealed container for up to 3 days. Fried potatoes keep refrigerated for 5 days in a sealed container.

Hot Tips

Make extra potatoes for the Kashmir Potato Salad, or use in the Cauliflower Au Gratin instead of, or in combination with the cauliflower.

Meal Balance

This is *THE* side dish in a great brunch, with Tofu French Toast and/or International Whole Wheat Pancakes. Not limited to brunch, the potatoes are full of nutrients and add a wonderful dimension to any meal.

Potatoes lend themselves to a great variety of ethnic flavors, and have no culinary boundaries. Happy travels.

4 medium Potatoes (thin skinned white)
2 tablespoons Corn Oil*
1 Spanish or large Onion, diced ¾"
1 large Garlic Clove, minced
½ teaspoon Sea Salt, or to taste
Pepper to taste
2 tablespoons Italian Parsley, minced

1. Place the potatoes in a pot with water to just cover, and bring to a boil on high heat. Reduce heat, boil gently for 15 minutes, or until tender when pierced. Drain and dice the potatoes into ¾" cubes.
2. Heat a skillet over medium heat with the oil, and sauté the onion 2 minutes, until tender. Add potatoes, garlic, salt and pepper and sauté 5 minutes, to brown. Adjust seasonings to taste, mix in parsley and serve.

Variations:
Asian Homefries - Use Peanut or Sesame oil instead of corn oil. Sauté 1 tsp. each of minced Ginger and Curry Powder with the garlic. Substitute Cilantro for the parsley.

French Homefries - Add 1 teaspoon dried Tarragon or Thyme with the garlic, or add 1 tablespoon fresh at the end. Substitute Chives for the parsley.

Hungarian Homefries - Add 1 teaspoon of Caraway Seeds with the onions. Substitute the parsley with minced fresh Dill.

South American Homefries - Use Olive Oil instead of corn oil. Add ¼ tsp. Crushed Dried Chili and 1 tsp. of Cumin Seeds with the garlic. Use Cilantro instead of parsley.

TEMPEH CANADIAN BACON

Prep Time: 5   **Cook Time: 25**   **Makes: ±24 slices**

Groceries

Tempeh, Maple Syrup, Toasted Sesame Oil, Umeboshi Vinegar, Tamari.

Do Ahead

Thaw tempeh 1 hour before using. Marinate the tempeh refrigerated in a sealed container up to 5 days. The Tempeh Bacon keeps refrigerated for 10 days in a sealed container, or frozen for 3 months.

Hot Tips

If you omit the oil to reduce fat, you lose crucial flavoring, especially from the toasted sesame oil.

Meal Balance

This complete soybean product complements grains and grain products. Use in the Club Sandwich with Grilled Tofu and Tempeh Bacon or in Somen Nori Maki, in place of the Tempeh Teriyaki. It makes a great topping on the Pizza with Pizzazz, in casseroles, stews, any way you like to use bacon. Use the bacon bits on salads.

This adds savory heartiness to a festive brunch. The possibilities for use is unlimited.

1 - 12 ounce package Tempeh*
3 tablespoons Water
1 tablespoon Umeboshi Vinegar*
1 tablespoon Maple Syrup*
1 tablespoon Tamari*
1 teaspoon Toasted Sesame Oil**
2 teaspoons Corn Oil**

1. Slice the tempeh into strips the length of the block, 1/6" thick. Lay the tempeh in a flat dish with straight sides, so the marinade covers the tempeh.
2. Combine the water, vinegar, syrup, tamari and toasted sesame oil. Mix with the tempeh and turn the tempeh to coat both sides. Marinate for 1 hour or more.
3. Heat a stainless steel skillet over medium-high heat with the corn oil. Drain the tempeh, saving the marinade. Fry the tempeh on each side for 5 minutes, or until golden brown. Add the marinade with extra water if necessary to just cover the tempeh. Reduce heat to low, cover the skillet and simmer for 15 minutes, to caramelize the marinade.

Variation: **Tempeh Bacon Bits**
Bake the marinated tempeh in a preheated 350°F oven for 20 minutes, or until very well browned. Crumble the tempeh, once cooled enough to handle, into bits.

* See GLOSSARY
** See TRICKS OF THE TRADE

BARBADOS BANANA BREAD

Prep Time: 20   **Cook Time: 70**   **Makes: 1 Loaf**

Groceries

Unbl. White Flour, Banana, Pineapple (opt.), Coconut and Walnuts (opt.), Baking Powder and Soda, Maple Syrup, Soymilk, Apple Juice, Allspice, Vanilla.

Do Ahead

Toast the coconut and walnuts and refrigerate in glass jars for several weeks. Toasting is optional. Sift the flour after measuring. Combine the dry ingredients and store in a covered bowl in a cool dry place. Mix and refrigerate the liquid ingredients in a sealed container up to 3 days in advance. Mash bananas fresh. The bread keeps refrigerated for 5 days, or 3 months frozen.

Hot Tips

To reduce fat omit the coconut and walnuts. Depending on the flour, you may need to add a little extra soymilk or apple juice if the batter is too thick. Use Whole Wheat Pastry Flour instead for more fiber and nutrition, but a less light result.

Meal Balance

This can follow a balanced meal, or have it as a snack between meals. Enjoy slices plain or toasted, with jams and spreads or with a sauce or topping (see Index for all the possibilities).

This tropical fruity, nutty loaf is like having a Caribbean vacation, if only with your senses, for a few moments.

½ cup Walnuts, toasted and chopped (opt.)
¼ cup unsweetened dried shredded Coconut
3 cups Unbleached White Flour
1½ tablespoons Baking Powder
1 tsp. Baking Soda
1 teaspoon Allspice
¼ teaspoon Sea Salt
1 cup Apple Juice
½ cup Maple Syrup*
¼ cup Corn Oil
¼ cup Soymilk*
½ tablespoon Pure Vanilla Extract
2 *very ripe* mashed Bananas
½ cup fresh Pineapple, diced (optional)
½ cup Raisins (optional)

1. Preheat oven to 350°F. Toast the walnuts on a baking tray for 10 minutes, until golden brown. Chop coarsely. Toast the coconut on a separate tray for 2-5 minutes or until pale golden (watch it!). Oil and flour a loaf pan**.
2. Combine the first seven dry ingredients in a large bowl. Mix the next five liquid ingredients in a separate bowl. Mix the bananas, pineapple and raisins (if using) with the liquid evenly. Add this to the dry ingredients using a whisk, blending completely so no lumps of flour remain. Pour the batter into the loaf pan.
3. Bake for 60 minutes, or until a skewer inserted comes out clean.
4. Cool on a rack for 20 minutes. Remove the pan and serve the bread warm, or cool on the rack to room temperature before storing.

* See GLOSSARY
** Use a 9" X 5" loaf pan. You may also use a bundt pan or two 8" cake pans; decrease baking time to ±45 minutes.

SWEET & FRUITY CORN BREAD

Prep Time: 15   **Cook Time: 45**   **Makes: 1 Loaf**

Groceries

Cornmeal, Whole Wheat Pastry Flour, Dried Fruit, Fresh Fruit, Soymilk, Lemon, Apple Juice, Baking Powder and Soda, Cinnamon, Allspice.

Do Ahead

Soak and refrigerate the dried fruit in the juice up to 5 days in advance, in a sealed container. Sift the flour after measuring. Combine the dry ingredients and store in a covered bowl in a cool dry place 5 days in advance. Refrigerate the fresh fruit and liquid ingredients separately in sealed containers up to 2 days ahead. The bread keeps refrigerated 4 days, or 3 months frozen.

Hot Tips

Use water instead of soymilk to reduce fat and calories, but the soymilk adds richness. For variety use a 10" round pie dish instead of making a loaf. Dice the fresh fruit and the large dried fruit (all but the raisins) into equal ½" pieces for an even consistency.

Meal Balance

This makes a nutritious dessert or scrumptious, portable snack.

Turn these into muffins, if desired, simply by scooping the batter into oiled muffin molds. Vary the dried and fresh fruit for a delicious new experience each time.

1 cup Dried Fruit; Apricots, Dates, Raisins, etc.
½ cup Apple Juice
2 cups Cornmeal, finely ground
2 cups Whole Wheat Pastry Flour
1 tablespoon each Cinnamon, Baking Powder
1 teaspoon each Baking Soda and Sea Salt
½ teaspoon Allspice
2 cups Soymilk* or Water
¼ cup each Lemon Juice and ¼ cup Corn Oil
2 cups of ½" diced Fresh Fruit**

1. Dice the dried fruit, except raisins, into ½" pieces. Soak the dried fruit in the apple juice for 30 minutes or more. Preheat oven to 350°F. Oil and flour a large loaf pan.
2. Combine the next seven dry ingredients in a large bowl. Combine the next three liquid ingredients in a separate bowl, and mix them with the dry, until no lumps of flour remain. Fold in the fresh fruit.
3. Scrape everything from the bowl into the loaf pan, and smooth the top. Bake for 45 minutes, or until golden brown and a skewer inserted comes out clean.
4. Cool on a rack for 20 minutes. Remove the pan and serve the bread warm, or cool on the rack to room temperature before storing.

* See GLOSSARY
** Use apples, apricots, bananas, blueberries, cherries, cranberries, kiwis, mangos, melon, nectarines, oranges, papayas, peaches, pears, raspberries, strawberries, etc.

OATMEAL CURRANT SCONES

Prep Time: 10   **Cook Time: 20**   **Makes: 8-12**

Groceries

Whole Wheat Pastry Flour, Rolled Oats, Baking Powder and Soda, Maple Syrup, Soymilk, Lemon Juice, Currants.

Do Ahead

Sift the flour after measuring. Combine the dry ingredients and store in a covered bowl in a cool dry place 5 days in advance. The scones keep refrigerated for 4 days, or 3 months frozen in a sealed container.

Hot Tips

The lemon juice will make the soymilk appear curdled, but this is simply the protein separating, so don't panic. Barley flour may be used instead of wheat flour with wonderful moist results.

Meal Balance

This makes a great breakfast treat or a healthy grain snack food between meals. Have balanced meals during the day, including whole grains and/or pasta and colorful vegetables.

These scones can be served for breakfast or brunch, and are perfect at "tea time", as enjoyed in England.

1½ cups Whole Wheat Pastry Flour
½ cup Rolled Oats
1 tablespoon Baking Powder
½ teaspoons Baking Soda
½ teaspoon Sea Salt
2 tablespoons Maple Syrup*
2 tablespoons Corn Oil**
3/4 - 7/8 cup Soymilk*
1 tablespoon Lemon Juice
½ cup Currants

1. Preheat oven to 375°F. Oil a baking tray.
2. Combine the first five dry ingredients in a large bowl. Mix the next four liquid ingredients together, and add the currants. Add the liquid ingredients to the dry, and mix completely so no lumps of flour remain. The consistency should be stiff enough so the batter holds its scooped shape, without much spreading.
3. Using an oiled ice cream scoop, drop the batter onto the baking tray. Bake for 20 minutes, or until golden and a skewer inserted comes out clean. Serve hot.

Variation: Substitute raisins or various dried fruits in place of the currants. Add ½ cup of nuts and/or seeds (toasted if desired).

* See GLOSSARY
** See TRICKS OF THE TRADE

ORANGE DATE
FAT-FREE WHEAT-FREE MUFFINS

Prep Time: 10   **Cook Time: 45**   **Makes: 18 large**

Groceries

Barley Flour, Baking Powder and Soda, Silken Tofu Lite, Apple Sauce, Flax Seeds, Cinnamon, Orange Marmalade, Vanilla, Maple Syrup, Dates.

Do Ahead

Combine the dry ingredients and store in a covered bowl in a cool dry place 5 days in advance. Purée the liquid ingredients and refrigerate in a sealed container up to 2 days in advance. The muffins keep refrigerated for 4 days, or 3 months frozen.

Hot Tips

The flax seeds become gluey, like egg whites, and add lightness to the muffins, but can be omitted if desired. The tofu also adds lightness. Omit either the flax or tofu, not both, or the muffins will be very dense.

Meal Balance

This makes a great breakfast treat or a healthy grain snack food between meals. Have balanced meals during the day, including whole grains and/or pasta and colorful vegetables.

Healthy and marvelous! There is no oil or nuts, and the highly nutritious flax seeds and tofu add lightness, and only a fraction of a gram of fat.

2 tablespoons Flax Seeds
6 cups Barley Flour, sift after measuring
3 tablespoons Baking Powder
1 tablespoon Cinnamon
1 tablespoon Vanilla Powder or Extract
1 teaspoon Baking Soda
½ teaspoon Sea Salt
1 - 10.5 oz. pk. Silken Tofu* Extra Firm Lite
1 cup each Apple Sauce** and Maple Syrup*
2 cups (2 small jars) Orange Marmalade**
1½ cups dried Dates, ½" diced

1. Preheat oven to 350°F. Oil the muffin trays. Bring the flax seeds to a boil with ½ a cup of water. Reduce heat and simmer for 5 minutes. Set aside to cool.
2. Combine the next six dry ingredients in a large bowl. Purée the tofu, apple sauce, syrup and 1¼ cups water in a blender or food processor until smooth. Add the flax seeds and their cooking water, and the puréed tofu mixture, to the dry ingredients (scrape all the flax liquid, and the purée to get all the juices). Mix until no lumps of flour remain. Fold in the dates and marmalade evenly. (The consistency should be stiff enough so the batter holds its scooped shape, without spreading or running into the muffin beside.) Using an ice cream scoop, distribute the batter among the muffin molds.
3. Bake for 45 minutes, or until a skewer inserted comes out clean. Cool on racks 20 minutes. Remove muffins from the pans and serve warm, or cool to room temperature before wrapping or storing.

* See GLOSSARY
** Use sugar-free, unsweetened or fruit sweetened.

WILD BLUEBERRY PECAN OAT MUFFINS

Prep Time: 10 **Cook Time: 45** **Makes: 18 large**

Groceries

Barley Flour, Baking Powder and Soda, Cinnamon, Silken Tofu Lite, Apple Sauce, Flax Seeds, Vanilla, Maple Syrup, Pecan, Blueberries.

Do Ahead

Toast the pecans and refrigerate in a glass jar for several weeks. Combine the dry ingredients and store in a covered bowl in a cool dry place. Purée the liquid ingredients and refrigerate in a sealed container for up to 2 days in advance. The muffins keep refrigerated for 4 days, or 3 months frozen.

Hot Tips

Toasting the pecans adds to their flavor, but is optional. Omit the pecans to reduce fat. The flax seeds add lightness to the muffins, but can be omitted if desired. The tofu also adds lightness.

Meal Balance

This makes a great breakfast treat or a healthy, grain based snack food.

Make these low fat, wheat-free muffins when wild blueberries are in season for best results.

1 cup Pecans, toasted and chopped
2 tablespoons Flax Seeds
4 cups Barley Flour, sift after measuring
2 cups Rolled Oats*
3 tablespoons Baking Powder
1 tbsp. each Cinnamon and Vanilla Powder
1 teaspoon Baking Soda
½ teaspoon Sea Salt
1 - 10.5 oz. pk. Silken Tofu** Extra Firm Lite
1 cup each Apple Sauce***, Maple Syrup**
4 cups fresh Blueberries, or 3 cups frozen

1. Preheat oven to 350°F. Toast the pecans on a baking tray for 10 minutes, until golden brown. Chop coarsely. Oil the muffin trays. Bring the flax seeds to a boil with ½ a cup of water. Reduce heat, simmer for 5 minutes.
2. Combine the next seven dry ingredients in a large bowl. Purée the tofu, apple sauce, syrup and 1¼ cups water in a blender or food processor until smooth. Add the flax seeds and their cooking water, and the puréed tofu mixture, to the dry ingredients (scrape all the flax liquid, and the purée to get all the juices). Mix until no lumps of flour remain. Fold in the blueberries and pecans evenly. (Consistency should be stiff enough so the batter holds its scooped shape, without spreading into the muffin beside.) Using an ice cream scoop, distribute the batter among the muffin molds.
3. Bake for 45 minutes, or until a skewer inserted comes out clean. Cool on racks 20 minutes. Remove muffins from the pans and serve warm, or cool to room temperature before wrapping or storing.

** See GLOSSARY
*** Use sugar-free, unsweetened or fruit sweetened.

CRANBERRY APPLE MUFFINS

Prep Time: 15 | **Cook Time: 45** | **Makes: 18 large**

Groceries

Barley Flour, Baking Powder and Soda, Cinnamon, Silken Tofu Lite, Apple Sauce, Flax Seeds, Vanilla, Maple Syrup, Apples, Cranberries.

Do Ahead

Sift the flour after measuring. Combine the dry ingredients and store in a covered bowl in a cool dry place. Purée the liquid ingredients and refrigerate in a sealed container up to 2 days in advance. Muffins keep 4 days refrigerated, or 3 months frozen.

Hot Tips

Use a firm apple that will not dissolve when cooked such as; Cortland, Empire or Spartan. The flax seeds become gluey, like egg whites, and add lightness to the muffins, but can be omitted. The tofu also adds lightness.

Meal Balance

This makes a great breakfast treat or a healthy grain snack food between meals. Have balanced meals during the day, including whole grains and/or pasta and colorful vegetables.

These fat-free, wheat-free muffins are chock full of fruit, and delicately spiced.

1¾ cups Water
2 tablespoons Flax Seeds
6 cups Barley Flour, sift after measuring
3 tablespoons Baking Powder
1 tablespoon Cinnamon
1 tablespoon Vanilla Powder or Extract
1 teaspoon Baking Soda
½ teaspoon each Allspice and Sea Salt
1 - 10.5 oz. pk. Silken Tofu* Extra Firm Lite
1 cup Apple Sauce**
1 cup Maple Syrup*
2 cups Apples, ½" diced
2 cups Cranberries, fresh or frozen

1. Preheat oven to 350°F. Bring the flax seeds to a boil with ½ a cup of the water. Reduce heat and simmer for 5 minutes. Set aside to cool. Oil the muffin trays.
2. Combine the next seven dry ingredients in a large bowl. Purée the tofu, apple sauce, syrup and the 1¼ cups water in a blender or food processor until smooth. Add the flax seeds and their cooking water, and the puréed tofu mixture, to the dry ingredients (scrape all the flax liquid, and the purée to get all the juices). Mix completely so no lumps of flour remain. Fold in the apples and cranberries evenly. (The consistency should be stiff enough so the batter holds its scooped shape, without spreading or running into the muffin beside.) Using an ice cream scoop, distribute the batter among the muffin molds.
3. Bake for 45 minutes, or until a skewer inserted comes out clean. Cool on racks for 20 minutes. Remove muffins from the pans and serve warm, or cool to room temperature before wrapping or storing.

* See GLOSSARY
** Use sugar-free, unsweetened or fruit sweetened.

LEMON POPPY SEED MUFFINS

Prep Time: 15

Cook Time: 45

Makes: 18 large

Groceries

Barley Flour, Baking Powder and Soda, Cinnamon, Silken Tofu Lite, Apple Sauce, Flax Seeds, Vanilla, Maple Syrup, Lemons, Poppy Seeds.

Do Ahead

Toast the poppy seeds (make extra) and refrigerate in a glass jar for several weeks. Combine the dry ingredients and store in a covered bowl in a cool dry place. Purée the liquid ingredients and refrigerate in a sealed container up to 2 days ahead. The muffins keep refrigerated for 4 days, or 3 months frozen.

Hot Tips

Toasting the poppy seeds adds to their flavor. The flax seeds become gluey, like egg whites, and add lightness to the muffins, but can be omitted. The tofu also adds lightness.

Meal Balance

This makes a great breakfast treat or a healthy, portable snack between meals. Have balanced meals during the day, including whole grains and/or pasta and colorful vegetables.

These fat-free, wheat-free muffins are both light and tangy with lemon, while aromatic and nutty with poppy seeds.

1 cup Poppy Seeds, toasted
2 tablespoons Flax Seeds
6 cups Barley Flour, sift after measuring
3 tablespoons Baking Powder
1 tablespoon Cinnamon
1 tablespoon Vanilla Powder or Extract
1 teaspoon Baking Soda
½ teaspoon Sea Salt
1 - 10.5 oz. pk. Silken Tofu* Extra Firm Lite
1 cup each Apple Sauce** and Maple Syrup*
½ cup Lemon Juice (±2 Lemons)

1. Preheat oven to 350°F. Toast the poppy seeds on a baking tray for 10 minutes, or until fragrant and tinged golden brown. Bring the flax seeds to a boil with ½ a cup of water. Reduce heat and simmer for 5 minutes. Set aside to cool. Oil the muffin trays.
2. Combine the next seven dry ingredients in a large bowl, with the poppy seeds. Purée the tofu, apple sauce, syrup, lemon juice and ¾ cup of water in a blender or food processor until smooth. Add the flax seeds and their cooking water, and the puréed tofu mixture, to the dry ingredients (scrape all the flax liquid, and the purée to get all the juices). Mix completely so no lumps of flour remain. (The consistency should be stiff enough so the batter holds its shape, without spreading into the muffin beside.) Using an ice cream scoop, distribute the batter among the muffin molds.
3. Bake for 45 minutes, or until a skewer inserted comes out clean. Cool on racks for 20 minutes. Remove muffins from the pans and serve warm, or cool to room temperature before wrapping or storing.

* See GLOSSARY
** Use sugar-free, unsweetened or fruit sweetened.

CHAPTER 8

DIETER'S DREAM DESSERTS

Baking for the Health of It
Energy Booster Snacks
Luscious, Light & Lean

GOLD MEDAL CARROT CAKE

Prep Time: 20 **Cook Time: 55** **Makes: One 9" Cake**

Groceries

Whole Wheat Pastry Flour, Carrots, Banana (opt.), Walnuts, Cinnamon, Baking Powder, Maple Syrup, Soymilk, Apple Juice.

Do Ahead

Toast the walnuts and refrigerate in a glass jar for several weeks (toasting is optional). Sift the flour after measuring. Combine the dry ingredients and store in a covered bowl in a cool dry place up to 5 days in advance. Mix and refrigerate the liquid ingredients in a sealed container up to 3 days in advance. Grate carrots and mash the banana fresh. The cake keeps refrigerated for 4 days, or 3 months frozen.

Hot Tips

Reduce fat by omitting the walnuts, and a few calories by omitting the raisins. Depending on the flour, you may need to add a little extra soymilk or apple juice if the batter is too thick.

Meal Balance

This can follow a balanced meal or be a snack between meals. Serve with a sauce or topping such as; Favorite Fruit Sauce, Lemon Maple Raisin Sauce, Vanilla Tofu Cream or spread the cake with frosting (see Index).

My best buddy claims that Mom's carrot cake, (and my massages), helped him win the Gold Medal in the Hammer Throwing Event at the 1976 Canada Games. He held the Canadian Record for seven years. This is an even healthier version.

1 cup Walnuts, toasted + chopped (optional)
4 cups Whole Wheat Pastry Flour
2 tablespoons Baking Powder
1 tablespoon Cinnamon
2 teaspoons Baking Soda
½ teaspoon Sea Salt
2 cups Apple Juice
1 cup Maple Syrup*
½ cup Corn Oil
½ cup Soymilk*
2 cups Carrots, grated
1 Banana, mashed (optional)
½ cup Raisins (optional)

1. Preheat oven to 350°F. Toast the walnuts for 10 minutes, or until golden brown. Chop coarsely. Oil and flour two 9" cake pans**.
2. Combine the first six dry ingredients in a large bowl. Mix the next four wet ingredients in a separate bowl, and add to the dry ingredients. Use a whisk to blend until no lumps of flour remain. Fold in the carrots, banana and raisins evenly. Equally distribute the batter into cake pans. Bake 45 minutes, or until a skewer inserted comes out clean.
3. Cool on racks for 30 minutes. Remove the pans, and cool the cakes on the racks to room temperature. Serve slices with a fruit or tofu based sauce or topping, or spread the cake with lemon flavor Vanilla Tofu Frosting.

* See GLOSSARY
** Use one large bundt pan or loaf pan if desired; the baking time will need to be increased to ±1 hour.

HAPPY BIRTHDAY VANILLA CAKE

Prep Time: 10

Cook Time: 35   **Makes: One 8" Cake**

Groceries

Unbleached White Flour, Baking Powder, Maple Syrup, Soymilk, Apple Juice, Vanilla.

Do Ahead

Sift the flour after measuring. Combine the dry ingredients and store in a covered bowl in a cool dry place 5 days in advance. Mix and refrigerate the liquid ingredients in a sealed container up to 3 days in advance. The cake keeps refrigerated for 5 days, or 3 months frozen.

Hot Tips

Depending on the flour, you may need to add a little extra soymilk or apple juice if the batter seems too thick. Vanilla powder helps keep the cake slightly whiter, using the powder may require liquid compensation with a little extra apple juice. Use a pale colored oil with neutral flavor.

Meal Balance

This can follow a balanced meal of grains or pasta and vegetables, or have it as a snack between meals. Serve with a sauce or topping such as; Favorite Fruit Sauce, Lemon Maple Raisin Sauce, Vanilla Tofu Cream. Spread the cake with Vanilla or Chocolaty Tofu Frosting.

A cake made without butter, eggs, milk and sugar? Unbelievable! The results are pleasantly surprising in a very wholesome way.

4 cups Unbleached White Flour
2 tablespoons Baking Powder
½ teaspoon Sea Salt
2 cups Apple Juice
1 cup Maple Syrup*
½ cup Safflower Oil
½ cup Soymilk*
2 tablespoons Pure Vanilla Extract or Powder

1. Preheat oven to 350°F. Oil and flour two 8" cake pans.
2. Combine the first three dry ingredients in a large bowl. Mix the remaining ingredients in a separate bowl, and add to the dry ingredients. Use a whisk to blend completely so no lumps of flour remain. Pour and equally distribute the batter into the cake pans.
3. Bake for 35 minutes or until a skewer inserted comes out clean. The center will no longer be shiny, and the cake will come away from the edges of the pan.
4. Cool on racks for 30 minutes. Remove the pans and cool the cakes on the racks to room temperature. Serve with a fruit or tofu based sauce or topping, or spread with tofu icing.

Variation:
Happy Birthday Vanilla Cup Cakes
Pour the batter into muffin trays containing individual paper cup cake molds. Reduce the baking time to ±25 minutes, or until a skewer inserted comes out clean. Spread with Chocolaty, Gourmet, Swiss Mocha or Vanilla Tofu Frosting (see Index).

* See GLOSSARY

DARK & DELICIOUS CAROB CAKE

Prep Time: 15   **Cook Time: 35**   **Makes: One 8" Cake**

Groceries

Whole Wheat Pastry Flour, Carob Powder, Baking Powder, Maple Syrup, Soymilk, Apple Juice, Vanilla.

Do Ahead

Sift the flour after measuring. Combine the dry ingredients and store in a covered bowl in a cool dry place 5 days in advance. Mix and refrigerate the liquid ingredients in a sealed container up to 3 days in advance. The cake keeps refrigerated for 5 days, or 3 months frozen.

Hot Tips

Depending on the flour, you may need to add a little extra soymilk or apple juice if the batter seems too thick. Use Unbleached White Flour instead for a lighter cake, although you reduce the fiber and nutrition. Use cocoa powder if you want the caffeine and a little extra fat.

Meal Balance

This can follow a balanced meal of grains or pasta and vegetables, or have it as a snack between meals. Spread the cake with Dark & Delicious Chocolaty Frosting. Serve with a sauce or topping such as; Favorite Fruit Sauce, Lemon Maple Raisin Sauce, Vanilla Tofu Cream.

This looks too rich to eat, yet it's full of healthy ingredients.

4 cups Whole Wheat Pastry Flour
½ cup Carob Powder
2 tablespoons Baking Powder
½ teaspoon each Baking Soda and Sea Salt
2 cups Apple Juice
1¼ cups Maple Syrup*
½ cup each Safflower Oil and Soymilk*
2 tablespoons Pure Vanilla Extract

1. Preheat oven to 350°F. Oil and flour two 8" cake pans.
2. Combine the first four dry ingredients in a large bowl. Mix the remaining ingredients in a separate bowl. Using a whisk, add the liquid to the dry ingredients, Blend completely so no lumps of flour remain. Pour and equally distribute the batter into the cake pans.
3. Bake for 35 minutes, or until a skewer inserted comes out clean. The center will no longer be shiny, and the cake will come away from the edges of the pan.
4. Cool on racks for 30 minutes. Remove the pans and cool the cakes on the racks to room temperature. Spread with tofu frosting, or serve with a fruit or tofu based sauce.

Variations:
Swiss Mocha Almond Cake
Reduce the carob powder to 2 tablespoons. Add ¼ cup Grain Coffee Powder or Instant Coffee. Add ½-1 cup toasted, chopped Almonds and ½ teaspoon each of Almond and Coffee Extract.

Dark & Delicious Carob Cup Cakes
Pour the batter into muffin trays containing individual paper cup cake molds. Reduce baking time to ±25 minutes, or until a skewer inserted comes out clean. Spread with Chocolaty or Vanilla Tofu Frosting.

* See GLOSSARY

APPLE CHERRY ALMOND FLAN

Prep Time: 20   **Cook Time: 55**   **Makes: One 9"**

Groceries

Apples, Cherries, Tofu, Rolled Oats, Whole Wheat Pastry Flour, Maple Syrup, Apple Sauce, Cinnamon, Ground Almonds, Arrowroot or Cornstarch, Lemon and Orange Extract.

Do Ahead

The crust can be baked 1 week in advance or frozen for 3 months, well wrapped in a sealed container. Make extra crusts to have on hand for the Carob Cream Pie and the Strawberry Delight Tofu Mousse Cake. The flan keeps refrigerated for 5 days (made with fresh filling), and frozen for 3 months.

Hot Tips

You may use a 10" pie dish instead of a flan dish if desired. Make sure you spread the crust evenly and press it up around the sides of your dish, so that when the filling is added, it is flush with the top of the crust.

Meal Balance

This healthy dessert contains whole grain and soy products, with only a little fat. Enjoy after a balanced meal based on whole grains or pasta and vegetables.

* See GLOSSARY

Use strawberries or red grapes when cherries are not available, with equally spectacular results.

Oat Crust ingredients, see recipe page 204
1 cup ground Almonds
1 teaspoon Cinnamon
1 pound (454 gr.) extra firm Tofu
1 cup Maple Syrup*
½ cup Apple Sauce
¼ cup Corn Oil*
1 tablespoon Arrowroot or Cornstarch
1 tablespoon Pure Vanilla Extract
½ teaspoon each Lemon and Orange Extract
¼ teaspoon Sea Salt
2 firm Red Apples, sliced in ¼" thin wedges
1 cup Cherries, pitted
Glaze, see page 214

1. Crust: Preheat oven to 350°F. Combine ground almonds and cinnamon with the Oat Crust ingredients. The texture of the dough should be crumbly, yet moist so it sticks together in a handful. Press into an oiled 9" flan dish, and bake 10 minutes. Cool to room temperature while preparing the filling.
2. Filling: Purée the next nine ingredients (from tofu to sea salt) in a food processor for 1 minute, until very smooth. Transfer to the baked pie shell and smooth the top evenly. Bake for 30 minutes. Prepare the glaze.
3. Lay the apple slices around the outer edge of the filling, overlapping them to fit. Place the cherries in the center. Pour the glaze evenly over the fruit. Bake for 15 minutes, or until a skewer inserted comes out clean. Let it set for 20 minutes at room temperature, or in a cool place before serving.

LATTICE TOP
APPLE APRICOT PIE

Prep Time: 20   **Cook Time: 45**   **Makes: One 9"**

Groceries

Whole Wheat Pastry Flour, Cinnamon, Apple Juice, Dried Apricots, Maple Syrup, Lemon, Vanilla, Allspice.

Do Ahead

Soak and refrigerate the dried apricots in the apple juice up to 5 days in advance, in a sealed container. Make the dough fresh, it gets tough after refrigeration for more than 30 minutes, and the oil separates from the dough. The pie keeps refrigerated for 5 days, or frozen for 3 months.

Hot Tips

Soaking the dried fruit produces a syrupy sweetness. For a lighter crust, partially or completely substitute unbleached white flour for the whole wheat. The whole wheat has more flavor, fiber and nutrition, and makes a darker crust. Use organically grown apples and leave the peel on for a healthier, heartier result. For variety, use various fruit.

Meal Balance

There is a substantial amount of grain product in this dessert, and you may consider this when planning the meal.

The lattice top is a beautiful, decorative presentation of a deep golden brown crust, and the tangy, sweet fruit filling is divine.

1 cup (packed) Dried Apricots, diced ¼"
½ cup Apple Juice
4 cups Apples*, diced ½"*
¼ cup Arrowroot, Cornstarch, or Flour
Zest of 1 Lemon + 2 tbsp. Lemon Juice
1 tablespoon Pure Vanilla Extract
2 teaspoons Cinnamon
½ teaspoon Allspice
¼ teaspoon Sea Salt
1½ cups Whole Wheat Pastry Flour
1 teaspoon Cinnamon
¼ teaspoon each Nutmeg and Sea Salt
1/3 cup Corn Oil**
±5 tablespoons Apple Juice or Water

1. Soak the apricots in the ½ cup of apple juice for ½ hour. Preheat oven to 450°F.
2. Combine the apricots, apples and the next seven ingredients in a bowl (arrowroot to salt).
3. Dessert Pie Crust: Combine the next four dry ingredients in a bowl. Mix in the corn oil until crumbly. Mix in enough apple juice to form a moist, pliable dough. Roll 2/3 of the dough between two sheets of wax paper with a rolling pin. Transfer to a 10" pie dish. Fill with the apple-apricot mixture. Roll the remaining dough between the wax paper, and slice it into ½" wide strips. Lay them in a crisscross pattern over the pie filling. Crimp the base crust with the ends of the lattice strips, around the edge of the pie.
4. Bake 10 minutes, reduce heat to 350°F and bake for 30 minutes more, or until bubbling and golden brown.

* See CUTTING TO THE CHASE
** See TRICKS OF THE TRADE

APPLE PEACH CRISP

Prep Time: 15   **Cook Time: 35**   **Makes: One 9" X 13"**

Groceries

Apples, Peaches, Whole Wheat Pastry Flour, Rolled Oats, Maple Syrup, Nuts (opt.), Raisins (opt.), Cinnamon, Allspice, Lemon.

Do Ahead

Combine the dry ingredients for the topping and filling separately and store in covered bowls in a cool dry place 5 days in advance. Dice the fruit fresh. This dessert keeps refrigerated for 5 days, or frozen for 3 months.

Hot Tips

Omit the nuts to reduce fat, but they add crunch and flavor. You may use; almonds, cashews, hazelnuts, pecans, walnuts, and/or seeds such as; pumpkin, sunflower or sesame. Use a firm apple that will not dissolve when cooked such as; Cortland, Empire or Spartan. Use organically grown apples and leave the peel for a healthier, heartier result. For variety, you may substitute various fruits for the apples and peaches.

Meal Balance

Serve this after a balanced meal based on whole grains or pasta and vegetables. There is a substantial amount of grain product in this dessert, and you may consider this when planning the meal.

The cinnamon spiced, hot and juicy apples and peaches complement the hearty, nutty crumble topping. Use one variety, or creatively combine various nuts and/or seeds for fun toppings.

8 medium Apples, ½" diced*
4 medium Peaches, ½" diced
1 cup Raisins (optional)
1/3 cup Maple Syrup**
¼ cup Arrowroot, Cornstarch, or Flour
Zest of 1 Lemon
2 tablespoons Lemon Juice
1 tablespoon Cinnamon
¼ teaspoon Sea Salt
1½ cups Whole Wheat Pastry Flour
1½ cups Rolled Oats
1 cup chopped Nuts; Almonds, Pecans, etc.
1 teaspoon Cinnamon
½ teaspoon Sea Salt
1/3 cup each Corn Oil** + Maple Syrup**

1. Preheat oven to 350°F. In a large bowl, mix the first nine ingredients (from apples to sea salt). Transfer and spread evenly into an oiled 9" by 13" baking dish.
2. Combine the next five dry ingredients in the large bowl. Mix in the oil and syrup until moist but crumbly. Sprinkle and spread evenly over the filling.
3. Bake for 35 minutes, until bubbling and golden brown on top. Let cool briefly before serving.

* See CUTTING TO THE CHASE
** See GLOSSARY

RASPBERRY OATMEAL SQUARES

Prep Time: 10   **Cook Time: 40**   **Makes: 8" X 8"**

Groceries

Whole Wheat Pastry Flour, Rolled Oats, Raspberries, Arrowroot or Cornstarch, Maple Syrup, Walnuts (opt.), Cinnamon, Vanilla.

Do Ahead

Toast the walnuts (make extra) and refrigerate in a glass jar for several weeks. Sift the flour after measuring. Combine the dry ingredients and store in a covered bowl in a cool dry place 5 days in advance. Make the raspberry filling and refrigerate in a sealed container up to 2 days in advance. The squares keep refrigerated for 5 days, or frozen for 3 months.

Hot Tips

Omit the walnut to reduce fat. You can substitute raspberry jam for the cooked fresh raspberries. Omit the arrowroot, cooking and thickening step. Use various fruits in place of the raspberries.

Meal Balance

Serve this after a balanced meal based on whole grains or pasta and vegetables. There is a substantial amount of grain product in this dessert, and you may consider this when planning the meal.

Chewy, fruity and nutty - these are a very nutritious portable snack. Top with Vanilla Tofu Cream for a fabulous dessert.

1 cup Walnuts, toasted and chopped
2 cups fresh Raspberries
½ cup Maple Syrup*
2 tablespoons Arrowroot* or Cornstarch
2 tablespoons Water
1 tablespoon Pure Vanilla Extract
2 cups Whole Wheat Pastry Flour
1 cup Rolled Oats
1½ teaspoons Cinnamon
½ teaspoon Sea Salt
½ cup Corn or Safflower Oil
½ cup Maple Syrup*

1. Preheat oven to 350°F. Toast the walnuts on a baking tray for 10 minutes, until golden brown. Chop medium-fine. Meanwhile...
2. In a small pot over medium heat, bring the raspberries and ½ cup of syrup to a low boil. Dissolve the arrowroot in the water, and stir into the raspberries. Simmer for 1 minute, until clear and thickened. Mix in the vanilla. Set aside to cool. Oil a 8" X 8" baking dish.
3. In a bowl, combine the next four dry ingredients with the walnuts. Mix in the oil and syrup until moist and sticky, but still somewhat crumbly. Press ½ of the flour-nut mixture evenly over the base the dish. Pour and scrape the raspberry mixture on top. Sprinkle and spread the remaining flour-nut mixture evenly over the filling.
4. Bake for 30 minutes, until golden brown on top. Let cool briefly before slicing and serving.

* See GLOSSARY

CAROB CREAM PIE
with OAT CRUST

Prep Time: 20   **Cook Time: 40**   **Makes: One 9"**

Groceries

Rolled Oats, Whole Wheat Pastry Flour, Silken Tofu, Carob Powder, Maple Syrup, Soymilk, Vanilla, Cinnamon, Almond Extract.

Do Ahead

The crust can be baked 1 week in advance or frozen for 3 months, well wrapped in a sealed container. Make extra crusts to have on hand for this recipe, the Apple Cherry Almond Flan and Strawberry Delight Tofu Mousse Cake. Prepare and refrigerate the filling up to 3 days in advance or freeze for 3 months in a sealed container. The pie keeps refrigerated for 1 week (made with fresh filling), and frozen for 3 months.

Hot Tips

Make sure you spread the crust evenly and press it up around the sides of your dish, so that when the filling is added, it is flush with the top of the crust.

Meal Balance

You have whole grain and soy products in this healthy treat, and there is only a little fat. So indulge moderately, and enjoy thoroughly.

This is so quick and easy to make, and always a big hit! Decorate it with Vanilla Tofu Frosting piped through a star tipped pastry bag, if desired.

Oat Crust
1 cup Rolled Oats*
1 cup Whole Wheat Pastry Flour
¼ cup Corn or Safflower Oil
±2 tablespoons Apple Juice or Water
¼ teaspoon Sea Salt

Carob Filling
1 - 10.5 oz. pk. Silken Tofu* Lite Extra Firm
2/3 cup Maple Syrup*
½ cup Carob Powder*
½ cup Soymilk*
1½ tablespoons Pure Vanilla Extract
1½ teaspoons Cinnamon
¼ teaspoon Almond Extract

1. Oat Crust: Preheat oven to 350°F. Combine all the ingredients adding enough juice or water to achieve a dough that is crumbly, yet moist and sticks together in a handful. Press into an oiled 9" pie dish. Bake for 10 minutes. Cool to room temperature. Meanwhile, prepare filling.
2. Carob Filling: Purée all the ingredients in a food processor for 1 minute or until very smooth. Pour into prebaked pie shell and smooth out the top evenly. Bake for 30 minutes or until center is set and no longer shiny.

Variation: **Rich Carob Pudding**
Omit the crust step and serve the puréed filling as a pudding.

* See GLOSSARY

CARROT RAISIN OATMEAL POWER BARS

Prep Time: 15   **Cook Time: 25**   **Makes: 8 Bars**

Groceries

Whole Wheat Pastry Flour, Rolled Oats, Carrots, Raisins, Maple Syrup, Tahini, Ginger, Cinnamon, Vanilla, Allspice.

Do Ahead

Combine the dry ingredients and store in a covered bowl in a cool dry place 5 days in advance. Mix and refrigerate the liquid ingredients up to 5 days in advance. Grate the carrots and ginger fresh. The bars keep refrigerated for 1 week, or 3 months frozen.

Hot Tips

Omit the tahini to reduce fat, but it adds a buttery richness. For variety, use dates, apricots and other dried fruit in place of the raisins.

Meal Balance

This is a very satisfying, portable snack between meals. It is ideal for traveling as it will not perish, and doesn't need refrigeration for up to 1 week or more. Have balanced meals during the day, including whole grains and/or pastas and colorful vegetables (dark green and orange especially).

These homemade power bars are delicious and nutritious, without chemicals and preservatives, sugar or other unwanted ingredients.

2 cups Whole Wheat Pastry Flour
2 cups Rolled Oats
1 tablespoon Cinnamon
½ teaspoon Allspice
½ teaspoon Sea Salt
1 cup Maple Syrup*
½ cup Corn Oil
½ cup Tahini*
1 tablespoon fresh Ginger, grated
1 cup Carrots, grated
1 cup Raisins

1. Preheat oven to 350°F. Combine the first five dry ingredients in a large bowl. Mix the next five wet ingredients in a separate bowl. Add the wet to the dry ingredients and mix well so no lumps of flour remain. Fold in the carrots and raisins evenly.
2. Oil a 8" by 8" baking dish. Scrape all the batter from the bowl into the dish and smooth the top. Bake for 25 minutes, or until golden brown and a skewer inserted comes out clean.
3. Cool to room temperature for 1 hour before slicing into bars.

Variation: **Carrot Raisin Oatmeal Cookies**
Make cookies simply by adding 2 teaspoons of Baking Powder to the dry ingredients. Spoon the cookies onto a baking tray, and bake for 15-20 minutes.

Note: The baking powder causes the cookies to rise and makes them lighter. (The power bars will be crumbly, and will not hold together in a firm bar with the baking powder.)

* See GLOSSARY

CARAMEL POPCORN BALLS

Prep Time: 5   **Cook Time: 10**   **Makes: 12**

Groceries

Popcorn, Barley Malt or Rice Syrup, Vanilla, (Pumpkin, Sesame or Sunflower Seeds - optional).

Do Ahead

Combine the dry ingredients and store in a covered bowl in a cool dry place 5 days in advance. The balls keep refrigerated for several weeks, individually wrapped or in 1 large sealed container.

Hot Tips

Barley malt has a heartier, more caramel flavor, compared to the delicate sweetness of rice syrup. Instead of using a candy thermometer to determine the temperature of the malt or syrup, boil it until it is thick and hangs in the air without dripping and pouring from a spoon or rubber scraper. The corn oil adds a buttery flavor, but omit it to eliminate fat if desired.

Meal Balance

This is a healthy whole grain snack that is low in calories, and the basic recipe is fat-free. It is ideal portable food, and great for traveling as it will not perish, and doesn't need refrigeration.

These are like the favorite store bought caramel popcorn balls we enjoy, only much healthier.

4 cups Popped Corn*
1 cup Barley Malt or Rice Syrup**
2 tablespoons Corn Oil (optional)
1 teaspoon Vanilla

1. Preheat oven to 250°F. Place the popped corn in a large stainless steel or heat proof bowl. Place the bowl in the oven to warm the bowl (so when you add the boiling malt, it doesn't harden when it comes in contact with a cold bowl. This ensures even mixing of the malt with the dry ingredients).
2. Bring the barley malt to a boil in a small pot over medium-high heat, for 5 minutes or to 265°F on a candy thermometer. Stir the malt and scrape the sides of the pot with a rubber scraper to prevent lumping. Mix the corn oil and vanilla with the malt. Pour and scrape all the malt mixture from the pot, and immediately mix with the dry ingredients in the bowl, to incorporate evenly. Wet your hands and roll the mixture into balls. Bake for 10 minutes on a baking tray.
3. Serve, or cool completely to room temperature before wrapping in plastic and storing in a sealed container.

Variations: Add to the dry ingredients:
Pumpkin Seed Caramel Popcorn Balls
Add ¾ cup of toasted Pumpkin Seeds.

Sesame Seed Caramel Popcorn Balls
Add ¼ cup of toasted Sesame Seeds.

Sunflower Seed Caramel Popcorn Balls
Add ½ cup of toasted Sunflower Seeds.

* Or begin with ½ cup popcorn kernels, and pop them
   in an air popper, or in a pot on the stove.
** See GLOSSARY

TOFU RICE NUT BALLS

Prep Time: 10   **Cook Time: 25**   Makes: ±18

Groceries

Tofu, Cooked Rice, Ground Almonds, Dried Coconut (opt.), Almond or Peanut Butter, Cinnamon, Maple Syrup.

Do Ahead

Cooked rice keeps up to 5 days refrigerated in a sealed container. The mixture may be refrigerated for up to 4 days before baking (made with freshly cooked rice). The baked balls keep for 1 week refrigerated in a sealed container (made with freshly cooked rice).

Hot Tips

Cooked Barley, Bulgur, Couscous, Millet or Quinoa, etc., may be used in combination or in place of rice. Toasted seeds and various nuts may be added, as well as raisins and other dried fruits. Omit the ground almonds and nut butter to reduce fat, if you don't mind sacrificing the flavor, richness and texture.

Meal Balance

This has whole grains, soy products and nuts combined into a satisfying, nutritious snack.

This recipe originated as a way to get children to enjoy brown rice and tofu, that is quick and simple enough so they can help with the preparation. It is a wonderful portable snack and party food.

½ pound Tofu* Extra Firm
½ cup Ground Almonds
1/3 cup Maple Syrup*
¼ cup Almond or Peanut Butter
1 teaspoon Cinnamon
¼ teaspoon Sea Salt
1½ cups cooked Brown Rice

1. Preheat oven to 350°F. Purée the tofu in a food processor until crumbly. Add the remaining ingredients (except rice) and process to mix. Add the rice and blend briefly, to form a stiff dough.
2. Oil a baking tray. With moistened palms, form the mixture into 1½" balls and place them on the baking tray. Bake for 25-30 minutes, or until a skewer inserted comes out clean. Serve warm or cooled.

* See GLOSSARY

CRISPY RICE SQUARES

Prep Time: 10   **Cook Time: 15**   **Makes: 12**

Groceries

Puffed Rice, Rice Syrup, Cinnamon, (Carob Chips, Nuts, Raisins, etc. - optional).

Do Ahead

Combine the dry ingredients and store in a covered bowl in a cool dry place 5 days in advance. The squares keep refrigerated for several weeks, individually wrapped or in 1 large sealed container.

Hot Tips

Instead of using a candy thermometer to determine the temperature of the rice syrup, boil it until it is thick and hangs in the air without dripping and pouring from a spoon or rubber scraper. It is important to slice the squares before they cool completely, as it will be difficult later, like cutting hard candy.

Meal Balance

This is a healthy whole grain snack that is low in calories, and the basic recipe is fat-free. It is ideal portable food, and great for traveling as it will not perish, and doesn't need refrigeration.

* See GLOSSARY

Now you can make healthy, natural Crispy Rice Squares, and create variations to your heart's desire.

1 - 6 ounce (170 gr.) bag Puffed Rice
2 teaspoons Cinnamon
1½ cups Rice Syrup*

1. Preheat oven to 250°F. Place the puffed rice and cinnamon, (mix together briefly) in a large stainless steel or heat proof bowl. Place the bowl in the oven to warm the bowl. (So when you add the boiling syrup, it doesn't harden when it comes in contact with a cold bowl. This ensures even mixing of the syrup with the dry ingredients.) Oil a 9" by 13" glass baking dish.
2. Bring the syrup to a boil in a small pot over medium-high heat, for 5 minutes or to 265°F on a candy thermometer. Stir the syrup and scrape the sides of the pot with a rubber scraper to prevent lumping. Pour and scrape all the syrup from the pot, and immediately mix with the dry ingredients in the bowl, to incorporate evenly. Scrape all the mixture into the baking dish. Wet your hands and press the mixture evenly into the dish. Bake for 10 minutes.
3. Cool for 10 minutes. Slice into squares with a wet knife. Cool completely to room temperature before wrapping in plastic or storing in a sealed container.

Variations:
Almond Raisin Crispy Rice Squares
Add ½-1 cup of toasted chopped Almonds, and ½-1 cup of Sultana or Thompson Raisins to the dry ingredients..

Peanut Carob Chip Crispy Rice Squares
Add ½-1 cup of toasted Peanuts, and ½-1 cup of unsweetened Carob Chips to the dry ingredients.

ALMOND COOKIES

Prep Time: 15   **Cook Time: 15**   **Makes: 2 Dozen**

Groceries

Unbleached White Flour, Soy Margarine, Ground Almonds, Whole Almonds, Maple Syrup, Rice Syrup, Almond Extract.

Do Ahead

Sift the flour after measuring. Combine the dry ingredients and store in a covered bowl in a cool dry place 5 days in advance. Mix and refrigerate the liquid ingredients in a sealed container up to 5 days in advance. Bake the cookies immediately after mixing the dough. Refrigerate the cookies for several weeks in a sealed container, or freeze for 3 months.

Hot Tips

Make wheat-free cookies by substituting barley flour for the wheat flour. Substitute various nuts for the ground almonds, and whole almonds for variety. We use rice syrup instead of barley malt or maple syrup as a glaze, because it is pale and will not darken the cookies too much.

Meal Balance

This is a very satisfying, portable snack between meals. It is ideal for traveling as it will not perish, and doesn't need refrigeration for up to 1 week or more.

This is a healthy interpretation of the popular Chinese almond cookies enjoyed in restaurants. Whole almonds are a beautiful decoration - the brown nuts against the wheat cookies.

±2½ cups Unbleached White Pastry Flour
½ cup ground blanched Almonds
¼ teaspoon Sea Salt
¾ cup Soy Margarine (dairy-free)
½ cup Maple Syrup*
1½ teaspoons Almond Extract
20-24 Whole Almonds
1 tablespoon Rice Syrup*
2 teaspoons Water

1. Preheat oven to 375°F. Combine the first three dry ingredients in a large bowl. Mix the next three wet ingredients until smooth in a separate bowl. Blend the wet into the dry, and knead briefly into a pliable dough. If it is too sticky to shape into balls with your hands, gradually add up to ½ cup of sifted flour until you have the right consistency. (Different flour, margarines, and ground almonds vary in moisture content affecting the consistency.)
2. Roll the dough into 20-24 balls, ±1" in diameter. Place the balls on an oiled or non-stick baking tray. Flatten the balls into 1/3" to ½" thick cookies with a spatula. Press the whole almonds into the center of each cookie.
3. Glaze: Mix the rice syrup and water in a small bowl and brush the mixture over each of the cookies. Bake for 12 to 15 minutes, or until golden.

Note: This is the only recipe containing margarine (it is not ideal healthy because it contains hydrogenated oils), but it contributes to the texture. You may substitute ¼-½ cup of tahini (depending on the consistency) if desired with good results.

* See GLOSSARY

PEANUT BUTTER CAROB CHIP COOKIES

Prep Time: 5   **Cook Time: 15**   **Makes: 12**

Groceries

Whole Wheat Pastry Flour, Carob Chips, Peanut Butter, Maple Syrup.

Do Ahead

Combine the dry ingredients and store in a covered bowl in a cool dry place 5 days in advance. Mix and refrigerate the liquid ingredients in a sealed container up to 5 days in advance. Bake the cookies immediately after mixing the dough. Refrigerate the cookies for several weeks in a sealed container, or freeze for 3 months.

Hot Tips

For variety, substitute almond, hazelnut or sunflower butter for the peanut butter, also because many people are allergic to peanuts. Make wheat-free cookies by substituting barley flour for the wheat flour. Use unsweetened carob chips for low fat, caffeine and dairy-free.

Meal Balance

This is a very satisfying, portable snack between meals. It is ideal for traveling as it will not perish, and doesn't need refrigeration for up to 1 week or more.

Children and adults love these rich and delicious cookies. They may not be fat-free, but they certainly are fast & fun!

4 cups Whole Wheat Pastry Flour
1¼ cups unsweetened Carob Chips
½ teaspoon Sea Salt
1½ cups Peanut Butter*
1¼ cups Maple Syrup*
½ cup Corn or Safflower Oil

1. Preheat oven to 350°F. Combine the first three dry ingredients in a large bowl. Mix the remaining three wet ingredients in a separate bowl until smooth. Add the wet ingredients to the dry, mixing until no lumps of flour remain.
2. Spoon ±2 tablespoons of dough for each cookie onto an oiled or non-stick cookie tray. Bake for 15 minutes or until golden brown. Cool on the tray for 15 minutes before removing with a spatula, as they will be too soft while hot.

Variations:
Almond Carob Chip Cookies
Substitute Almond Butter for the peanut butter.

Peanut Carob Oatmeal Power Bars
Substitute 1 cup of Rolled Oats for 1 cup of the flour. Transfer to an oiled 8" X 8" baking dish and bake for 25 minutes. Cool to room temperature for 1 hour before slicing into bars.

Sesame Carob Chip Cookies
Substitute Tahini for the peanut butter.

* See GLOSSARY

STRAWBERRY DELIGHT TOFU MOUSSE CAKE

Prep Time: 20   **Cook Time: 15**   **Makes: 1**

Groceries

Strawberries, Rolled Oats, Whole Wheat Pastry Flour, Tofu, Soymilk, Maple and Rice Syrup, Agar Flakes, Vanilla Powder, Arrowroot, Almond Extract.

Do Ahead

The crust can be baked and refrigerated, well wrapped, 1 week in advance, or frozen for 3 months. Pour the filling into the pan immediately and set. Cover the top in plastic (before adding fruit topping) and refrigerate in a sealed container for up to 4 days in advance, or freeze 1 month.

Hot Tips

The wax paper lining in the pan creates smooth sides for the tofu filling. Place the strawberries cut side down, pointing in to the center, around the periphery of the cake, and continue until the top is covered. Use any seasonal fruit instead of strawberries, or make attractive combinations.

Meal Balance

This is soy good! The crust and filling are both very healthy. Enjoy after a light balanced meal based on whole grains and vegetables.

* See GLOSSARY

This is simply beautiful. Serve each slice in a pool of Cinnful Chocolaty Sauce, if desired, turning this into a sinfully rich, low fat indulgence.

1 Oat Crust, see recipe page 204
1 pound (454 gr.) fresh Tofu* pressed**
3/4 cup Maple Syrup*
2 tablespoons Vanilla Powder
1/4 tsp. Almond Extract
1/3 cup each Agar Flakes** and Rice Syrup*
1/2 cup Soymilk*
1 pint strawberries, sliced in half lengthwise
Glaze, see recipe on page 214

1. Crust: Preheat oven to 350°F. Press Oat Crust mixture into the base of an oiled 8" spring-form pan, with the sides lined with wax paper. Poke a few holes with a fork in the crust to prevent if from puffing. Bake for 10 minutes. Cool to room temperature.
2. Filling: Purée tofu, maple syrup, vanilla and almond extract in a food processor until fairly smooth. In a small pot over medium heat, gently boil 1 cup of water and the agar 5 minutes, or until dissolved (do Fridge Test**). Stir in the rice syrup and soymilk. Purée the agar mixture in with the tofu mixture in the food processor for 1 minute or until silky smooth. (Scrape the sides of the food processor bowl to incorporate and purée completely.)
4. Pour the filling over the crust, in the spring-form pan and set at room temperature for 30 minutes. Chill for 1 hour or more.
5. Decorate with strawberries. Prepare the glaze, and brush or.pour it over, coating the fruit evenly. Serve immediately or chilled.

** See Agar in TRICKS OF THE TRADE

TANGERINE KIWI LAYER PIE

Prep Time: 20　　　　**Cook Time: 30**　　　　**Makes: One 8" pie**

Groceries

Apple and/or Orange Juice, Kiwis, Tangerines, Agar Flakes, Cinnamon Stick, Arrowroot, Oat Crust, Glaze.

Do Ahead

Make extra crusts for the Carob Cream Pie and Apple Cherry Almond Flan and freeze up to 3 months, wrapped and sealed. Prepare the pie crust and fruit filling, cover with plastic wrap and refrigerate up to 3 days before adding the sliced fruit garnish. The pie keeps refrigerated for 5 days in a sealed container (made with fresh ingredients), or 3 months frozen.

Hot Tips

For variety, use apples, apricots, bananas, blueberries, cherries, cranberries, mangos, melon, nectarines, oranges, papayas, peaches, pears, raspberries, strawberries, etc.

Meal Balance

The oat crust is quite substantial and filling. Consider this when planning the main meal. Enjoy this for dessert after a balanced meal, or between meals as a healthy grain based, fruity snack.

* See GLOSSARY
** See Agar in Tricks Of The Trade.

The colors, flavors and textures in this dessert are an adventure for your taste buds - sweet, tangy fruit, and a wholesome grain crust.

Oat Crust, see recipe page 204
1½ cups Apple Juice or Water
2 cups Tangerine or Orange Juice (or Apple)
1 Cinnamon Stick
5 tablespoons Agar Flakes*
3 tablespoons Arrowroot* or Cornstarch
3 Kiwis, peeled; dice 2, slice 1 in thin rounds
1 Tangerine, sections sliced in ½ lengthwise
Glaze, see recipe page 214

1. Prepare and pre-bake the crust as indicated. Set aside to cool. Meanwhile...
2. <u>Kiwi Layer</u>: Bring 1 cup apple juice to a boil with 2 tablespoons agar over medium heat. Simmer on low 5 minutes to dissolve agar. Do the Fridge Test**. Dissolve 1 tbsp. arrowroot in 1 tbsp. water, stir in and cook 1 minute. Purée the diced kiwi with the agar-juice mixture until smooth. Pour the purée into the pie shell. Set aside to cool 15 minutes while you prepare the...
3. <u>Tangerine Layer:</u> Bring tangerine juice to a boil with the cinnamon stick and remaining agar. Simmer 5 minutes to dissolve the agar. Do the Fridge Test**. Remove cinnamon stick. Dissolve remaining arrowroot in 2 tablespoons water, stir in and cook 1 minute. Pour on top of kiwi layer. Set aside to cool for 30 minutes, or until set. Prepare the glaze just before adding fruit slices in next step.
4. Place kiwi slices in a circle, overlapping near the edge of the crust. Place several tangerine sections cut side up in a petal pattern in the center. Brush the glaze over the fruit. Chill for 1 hour before serving.

PEACH COUSCOUS CAKE

Prep Time: 20

Cook Time: 10

Makes: 1

Groceries

Couscous, Peaches, Apple Juice, Raisins, Almonds, Cinnamon. Vanilla, Allspice, Maple Syrup, Arrowroot.

Do Ahead

You may make the couscous cake base and refrigerate well covered, (before adding the fruit topping), up to 5 days in advance. The cake, once topped with fruit and glazed, will keep refrigerated for 5 days (if made with fresh couscous).

Hot Tips

To eliminate fat, omit the almonds, but they add wonderful flavor and texture. For a simpler couscous cake, use only couscous and juice. It's a great dessert to make in hot weather as you don't need the oven. Use any berries or fruit instead of, or in combination with the peaches.

Meal Balance

This is a fabulous grain based dessert topped with fruit. Serve this after a balanced meal that is light on the grain products. You may serve the couscous cake plain, or with a fruit sauce (see Index). Garnish servings with Vanilla Tofu Cream for a treat.

This is very attractive, yet is so simple to make, and there's no baking to do. It's always a popular dessert at healthy dinner parties!

4 cups Apple Juice
3-4 ripe Peaches
2 cups raw Couscous
1 cup Raisins (Sultana or Thompson)
1 cup chopped toasted Almonds
1 tablespoon Cinnamon
1 tablespoon Pure Vanilla Extract
1 teaspoon Allspice
¼ teaspoon Sea Salt
Glaze, see recipe page 214

1. Bring apple juice to a boil and simmer the peaches in a gently boiling juice, turning them over to cook all sides for 5 minutes. Remove peaches with a slotted spoon, cool on a plate.
2. Whisk the couscous, raisins and almonds if using, cinnamon, vanilla, allspice and sea salt into the simmering juice. Remove from heat and let cool covered for 15 minutes, or until all the juice is absorbed. Meanwhile...
3. Peel and pit the peaches, slice into ¼"-½" thick wedges. Mix, then press the couscous mixture into a 10" round or 8" by 8" square dish. Decorate the cake with sliced peaches.
4. Prepare the glaze. Brush or pour it over, coating the fruit evenly. Serve immediately, or chill for 1 hour or more before serving.

Variation: **Cranberry Couscous Cake**
Substitute the peaches with 2 cups of fresh cranberries. Double the glaze ingredients. Simmer the cranberries in ¾ cup of the water for 2 minutes. Dissolve the arrowroot in the remaining ¼ cup water and maple syrup. Add to the cranberries and cook until clear and thickened. Spread evenly on the couscous cake and enjoy!

FESTIVE FRUIT KANTEN

Prep Time: 15   **Cook Time: 10**   **Serves: 8**

Groceries

Strawberries, Peaches, Kiwi, Apple Juice, Agar Flakes, Maple Syrup, Arrowroot.

Do Ahead

This sets at room temperature, although it sets quicker if chilled. Store refrigerated in a large sealed mold or individual sealed servings, for up to 5 days.

Hot Tips

Make a decorative pattern with the fruit; place the kiwi rounds as the center of a flower, with the peach wedges as petals, and create a border all around the edge of the serving dish with the strawberry halves, placed cut side down, and the points facing into the center. Substitute various fruits; green and red grapes, mangos, oranges, raspberries, etc., for variety.

Meal Balance

This is fat-free, nutritious dessert. Enjoy it after a complete balanced meal. The kanten sets just like a gelatin. It has essential minerals and vitamins from the agar, which is a sea vegetable (see H.H.I.H.), and the fresh fruit and fruit juice.

* See GLOSSARY
** See Agar in Tricks Of The Trade

This is a colorful, refreshing dessert - ideal in hot weather. Serve with Vanilla Tofu Cream for a luscious topping if desired.

3 medium Peaches
1 pint Strawberries, sliced in ½ lengthwise
1 Kiwi, peeled, sliced into 1/8" thick rounds
4 cups Apple Juice
4 heaping tablespoons Agar Flakes*
Glaze
2 teaspoons Arrowroot*
½ cup Water
2 tablespoons Maple Syrup*

1. Bring 6 cups of water (or enough to submerge the peaches) to a boil and simmer the peaches for 5 minutes. Remove with a slotted spoon and let cool on a plate. Peel and pit the peaches. Slice 1-2 of the peaches into ¼"-½" wedges for decoration (the amount will depend on the size and shape of your dish). Select a few perfectly sliced fruit for decoration. Keep fruit covered, refrigerated.
2. Bring apple juice to a gentle boil over medium-low heat with agar and simmer until agar dissolves, 5 minutes. Do Fridge Test**
3. Purée remaining peaches and strawberries (to equal 2 cups) in a food processor until smooth. Stir into juice and agar mixture. Pour into serving dish, cool to set, for 1 hour.
4. Decorate the kanten with the kiwi rounds, peach wedges and strawberry halves.
5. Glaze: Dissolve the arrowroot in water, and bring to a gentle boil with the maple syrup until clear thickened. Brush or pour over fruit topping to coat evenly, and serve. The glaze gives the fruit a clear shine and prevents them from drying out.

GINGERED PEAR COMPOTE

Prep Time: 10 **Cook Time: 5** **Serves: 4**

Groceries

Pears, Maple Syrup, Ginger, Cinnamon, Allspice, Arrowroot.

Do Ahead

This compote cooks up in a flash. Once cooled it stores refrigerated for 5 days in a sealed container. Leftovers can be served chilled, at room temperature or reheated.

Hot Tips

Extract all the flavor possible out of the grated ginger by soaking it in the 1 cup of water for 5 minutes, then strain and squeeze the fibers. Now you can cook as indicated, and you have already taken care of the ginger part.

Meal Balance

This dessert is fat free. It is delicious as is, although you may serve it garnished with Tofu Whipped Cream. Serve on Tofu French Toast and Whole Wheat Pancakes, or as a gourmet topping on breakfast porridge.

Apples, apricots, blueberries, cherries, cranberries, grapes, kiwi, mango, papaya and peaches can all be added or substituted in colorful, delicious combinations.

1 cup Water
4 ripe Pears, diced 1"
¼ cup Maple Syrup*
1 teaspoon grated fresh Ginger**, or to taste
½ teaspoon Cinnamon
¼ teaspoon Allspice
¼ teaspoon Sea salt
1½ tablespoons Arrowroot*
3 tablespoons Water

1. Bring 1 cup of water to a boil over medium high heat with the pears, syrup, ginger, spices and salt. Reduce heat to low and simmer for 2 minutes, until pears are no longer raw, yet still firm and in tact.
2. Dissolve the arrowroot in the 1½ tbsp. water, stir in and simmer for 1 minute, until clear and thickened.

Variation:
Plum Peach Compote
Substitute 2 large ripe Plums and 2 ripe Peaches for the pears.

Green & Red Grape Compote
Substitute 1½ cups of seedless Green Grapes and 1½ cups of seedless Red Grapes for the pears. Leave the grapes whole, or slice them in half or quarters.

* See GLOSSARY
** See TRICKS OF THE TRADE.

HIMALAYAN RICE PUDDING

Prep Time: 15   **Cook Time: 25**   **Serves: 6-8**

Groceries

Cooked Rice, Soymilk (optional), Apple Juice, Raisins, Apricots, Dates, Cardamom, Cinnamon, Clove.

Do Ahead

The rice pudding keeps refrigerated for 5 days in a sealed container (made with freshly cooked rice), or 3 months frozen. Nuts, such as raw or toasted almonds, cashews or pistachios may be cooked in, or added at the end as garnish.

Hot Tips

Use raw bulgur, couscous, millet, quinoa or Thai Jasmine White Rice instead for variety. Using rice syrup instead of maple syrup will make the rice pudding lose its creamy texture, and become liquid (see GLOSSARY).

Meal Balance

This is a fat-free grain based dessert, or between-meals-snack. The large proportion of rice in this recipe may be considered when planning your main meal. Serve it with a light pasta main dish, or an entrée with little or no whole grain brown rice, such as one of the breads, casseroles or pies, etc.

* See BROWN RICE in STAPLES
** See GLOSSARY

You'll feel like trekking the peaks - stimulated by the sweet spices, and energized by the natural sugars in dried fruits and whole grains. Make it fat-free by using water instead of soymilk, and leave out the nuts.

1 cup Apple Juice
1-2 teaspoons Cinnamon
1 teaspoon ground Cardamom, or to taste
¼ teaspoon ground Clove, or to taste
2 cups cooked Brown Rice* (+/or Sweet Rice)
±3 cups Soymilk or Water
¼ cup dried unsulphured Apricots, diced ½"
¼ cup Sultana or Thompson Raisins
¼ teaspoon Sea Salt, or to taste
½ cup Maple Syrup**, or to taste
¼ cup dried, pitted Dates, diced ½"
¼-½ cup chopped, toasted nuts (optional)

1. Bring the juice to a boil in an enamel coated or stainless steel pot over medium heat, with the spices.
2. Add the rice and soymilk or water, the apricots, raisins and sea salt. Return to a boil. Reduce heat to low and cook covered for 20 minutes, stirring occasionally to prevent sticking at the bottom, or until creamy and thick. Add soymilk or water as necessary.
3. Add maple syrup, dates and nuts (if using), and cook for 5 minutes. Adjust consistency and sweetness to taste and serve hot. You may cool and serve chilled it desired.

Variation: **Rice Pudding From Scratch**
To make this from *raw* rice, cook 1 cup brown rice in 2 cups water for 45 minutes. Add the juice, spices, ½ teaspoon sea salt, soymilk or water, apricots and raisins and cook 15 minutes. Add the syrup and dates (and nuts if using) and cook 5 minutes. Adjust consistency and sweetness to taste.

HOPI INDIAN APPLE PUDDING

Prep Time: 5   **Cook Time: 10**   **Serves: 4-6**

Groceries

Dried Apples, Cornmeal, Apple Juice, Maple Syrup, Cinnamon.

Do Ahead

Trim the dried apples to remove the center membranes that may have been missed by the manufacturer. The pudding keeps refrigerated for 5 days, or frozen for 3 months in a sealed container.

Hot Tips

For variety, substitute dried apricots, dates, peaches, pears, raisins, etc., for the apples. Bulgur, couscous or cream of wheat may be used instead of cornmeal.

Meal Balance

This is a grain and fruit based pudding. Consider reducing the grain proportion of the main meal and serve a light pasta dish, or a grain dish with plenty of vegetables.

Native American, or Indian puddings are made with their staple grain of corn, and locally available fruit such as apples, which were dried for storing. Maple syrup tapping was taught to the first settlers by the natives, who used it to season and sweeten many recipes.

1 cup (packed) Dried Apples; trim & chop
1 cup Cornmeal, finely ground
2 cups each Apple Juice and Water
2 teaspoons Cinnamon
¼ teaspoon Sea Salt
½-¾ cup Maple Syrup* (to taste)

1. Bring the apples and cornmeal to a boil in the juice and water, over medium heat. Stir the cornmeal with a whisk to prevent lumping and sticking on the bottom. Add the cinnamon and sea salt, reduce heat to low, and simmer covered for 5 minutes.
2. Remove pot from the heat and let rest for 10 minutes to let cool.
3. Purée the mixture in a food processor until smooth with the maple syrup to taste (½ cup will be sweet, with the apple flavor more pronounced, 2/3 to 3/4 cup of syrup will intensify the sweetness and the maple syrup flavor).

* See GLOSSARY

STRAWBERRY PUDDING

Prep Time: 5   **Cook Time: 0**   **Serves: 6**

Groceries

Strawberries, Rice, Maple Syrup, Lemon, Vanilla, Apple Juice.

Do Ahead

The pudding keeps refrigerated for 5 days in a sealed container (if you can restrain yourself and exercise such self control)!

Hot Tips

For a smooth texture, use freshly cooked rice. Left-over rice hardens, and produces a grainy pudding. White rice may be used for a smoother pudding, as it has less or no fiber compared to brown rice. White Thai Jasmine rice makes an aromatic, light pudding with a delicate, sweet taste. Substitute fresh or Silken Tofu (choose the Lite variety for less fat) for rice. Tofu has more fat, but the bonus is a richer, creamier pudding. Cooked Millet or Couscous may substitute the rice. Other fruit may substitute for strawberries.

Meal Balance

Serve this after a balanced meal, or as a snack between meals. You may lighten up on your grains in the main meal when you serve a grain based dessert.

* See STAPLES
**See GLOSSARY

This is so wonderfully healthy - whole grains and fresh fruit blended into a fat free, ready in a jiffy dessert!

1 pint Strawberries
1½ cups cooked Brown Rice
½ cup Maple Syrup**
½ Lemon, grated zest and juice
1 tablespoon Pure Vanilla Extract
±½ cup Apple Juice, Soymilk or Water

1. Pick out 6 perfect strawberries to garnish individual servings or one large one to garnish a whole dish.
2. Purée the cooked rice in a food processor with the remaining ingredients until smooth, adding enough juice to achieve a creamy texture (the pudding thickens after it has chilled for a few hours or overnight). Garnish with the strawberry/ies and serve.

Variation:
Banana Cinnamon Pudding
Use 3 very ripe peeled Bananas instead of the strawberries, and add 1-2 tsp. cinnamon (to taste).

Cappuccino Pudding
Omit the strawberries. Add ¼ cup of Grain Coffee Powder, 1 tablespoon of Carob Powder (optional), and ¼ teaspoon of Coffee Extract (optional). Adjust sweetness to taste.

Lemon Vanilla Pudding
Omit the strawberries. Add 1 tbsp. of Vanilla Extract or Powder, and 1 teaspoon of Lemon Extract, and adjust flavors and sweetness to taste.

SWEET POTATO PUDDING

Prep Time: 5   **Cook Time: 10**   **Serves: 4**

Groceries

Sweet Potato, Maple Syrup, Soymilk, Vanilla, Cinnamon.

Do Ahead

This pudding will store up to 5 days refrigerated in a sealed container.

Hot Tips

You may peel the sweet potato or butternut squash before dicing if you want an ultra smooth texture. Otherwise the skin becomes very soft once cooked, and purées very nicely.

Meal Balance

Serve this as dessert or a snack, and as a fix for sweet cravings. These naturally sweet vegetables balance blood sugar levels, helping the pancreas and spleen functions. There is an abundance of vitamin A in orange vegetables (see Beta-carotene in H.H.I.H.)

This is simple, satisfying and nourishing. Like sweet, smooth baby food for all ages.

1 Large Sweet Potato (2 cups diced)
1 cup Water
¼ teaspoon Sea Salt
1 tablespoon Pure Vanilla Extract, or to taste
1 teaspoon Cinnamon
±¼ cup Maple Syrup*
±¼ cup Soymilk* or Water

1. Wash the sweet potato and trim off the ends and blemishes. Dice into ½" cubes and bring to a boil in the water in a pot over medium-high heat. Add the sea salt, reduce heat and simmer for 10 minutes, or until the sweet potato is very tender.
2. Transfer to a food processor or a blender, and add vanilla and cinnamon. Purée until smooth, adding maple syrup and soymilk to desired sweetness and consistency.

Variation: To make this dessert lower in calories and fat free, omit the maple syrup and soymilk. You will have a less sweet and creamy result, but it is still very satisfying. For variety, Butternut Squash may substitute the sweet potato.

* See GLOSSARY

INSTANT CHOCOLATY PUDDING

Prep Time: 5 **Cook Time: 0** **Serves: 4**

Groceries

Silken Tofu, Carob Powder, Maple Syrup, Vanilla and Almond Extract.

Do Ahead

This stores refrigerated 5 days in a sealed container, and frozen for 3 months.

Hot Tips

The benefits of carob are that it is lower in fat than chocolate, and has no caffeine. You will love the taste and sensorial satisfaction. Use the silken tofu *lite,* it's a lower fat tofu product.

Meal Balance

Serve after a balanced meal of grains or pasta and vegetables.

Ladies, for a PMS fix, this pudding can be your whole meal! But seriously, this is rich and wonderful, yet light and easy on the digestion.

1 - 10.5 oz. (297 gr.) pk. Silken Tofu* Lite
1/3 cup Carob or Cocoa Powder
1/3 cup Maple Syrup*
1 tablespoon Pure Vanilla Extract
¼ teaspoon Almond Extract

1. Purée all ingredients until creamy and smooth. Serve and enjoy immediately!

<u>Variations</u>:
Black Forest Pudding
Add ½ teaspoon of Cherry Extract and purée with the above ingredients.

Mocha Pudding
Substitute Grain Coffee Powder (or instant coffee) for the carob powder.

Vanilla Pudding
Omit the carob powder and add 1 extra tablespoon of Vanilla Extract.

Cinnful Chocolaty Sauce
Increase both the carob power and maple syrup to ½ cup. Add 1 tablespoon of cinnamon, and Soymilk or Water to desired consistency.

* See GLOSSARY

BLUEBERRY PEACH PARFAIT

Prep Time: 10   **Cook Time: 5**   **Serves: 4**

Groceries

Tofu, Blueberries, Peaches, Maple Syrup, Vanilla Powder, Almond Extract.

Do Ahead

The tofu cream keeps refrigerated for 5 days, or 2 months frozen in a sealed container. The fruit purée keeps for 3-4 days refrigerated in a sealed container.

Hot Tips

Assemble the parfait and serve within a few hours, or the blueberries will begin to die the tofu a purple color—unless you want this effect. Apples, apricots, cherries, cranberries, grapes, kiwi, mango and papaya can all be added or substituted in colorful, delicious combinations. Alternate the Tofu Cream with the Instant Chocolaty Pudding, Black Forest or Mocha Pudding for a beautiful contrast of white and chocolate brown layers. **Note: Liquid vanilla extract can substitute, but the vanilla powder is white and will not darken and liquefy the tofu cream as much.

Meal Balance

This recipe provides a substantial amount of soy protein. Consider this when planning the menu, and go lightly on soy products in your main meal.

This is very visually attractive, and cooling in hot weather.

1 pound (454 gr.) Tofu* Extra Firm
3/4 cup Maple Syrup*
2 tablespoons Vanilla Powder**
¼ teaspoon Almond Extract
3 Peaches
2 tablespoons Maple Syrup*
1 pint Blueberries

1. <u>Tofu Cream Layer</u>: In a blender, purée the tofu, maple syrup, vanilla and almond extract (add a little water or soymilk if necessary) to a very smooth consistency. Scrape the sides of the food processor bowl, and purée for 1-2 minutes, until the tofu is no longer grainy. Transfer to a bowl and chill while preparing the fruit.
2. <u>Fruit Filling</u>: a) Bring water (enough to submerge the peaches) to a boil over medium-high heat. Reduce heat and simmer the peaches for 5 minutes. Peel and seed. Slice 1 peach into 12 thin wedges and set aside for garnish. Purée remaining peaches with 1 tablespoon of maple syrup until smooth, and set aside in a bowl.
b) Save 12 beautiful large blueberries for garnish. Purée remaining blueberries and maple syrup. Set aside in a bowl.
3. Layer alternately, in each parfait or wine glass; blueberry purée, then tofu whipped cream, then peach purée, then tofu whipped cream again. Repeat layers if space and ingredients allow. Garnish each serving with 3 blueberries in the center, and 3 peach slices pointing into the center. Serve immediately, or chill for 30 minutes.

* See GLOSSARY

MANGO MOUSSE SORBET

Prep Time: 5 **Cook Time: 10** **Serves: 4-6**

Groceries

Mango, Agar Flakes, Silken Tofu Lite, Lemon, Rice Syrup, Almond Extract.

Do Ahead

Make the sorbet and freeze for 3 hours, and up to 3 months. Remove from the freezer, and refrigerate or keep at room temperature to thaw, at least 1 hour before serving.

Hot Tips

For variety, substitute apples, apricots, bananas, blueberries, cherries, cranberries, kiwis, melon, nectarines, oranges, papayas, peaches, pears, raspberries, strawberries, etc.

Meal Balance

This is very cooling and refreshing in hot weather, after a balanced meal based on grains and vegetables.

This is delightful and fruity with richness from the silken tofu. Make the Kiwi Lime Mousse Sorbet variation and serve a scoop of each with Ravishing Raspberry Coulis or Cinnful Chocolaty Sauce.

1 cup Water
1 rounded tablespoon Agar Flakes*
1 - 10.5 oz. pk. Silken Tofu* Lite Extra Firm
1½ cups Mango, peeled and diced
½ cup Maple Syrup*
2 tablespoons Lemon Juice

1. Bring water to a boil in a small pot over medium heat, with the agar flakes. Reduce heat and simmer for 5 minutes or until the agar is dissolved. Do the Fridge Test**.
2. Purée the tofu and remaining ingredients in a food processor until smooth. Add and scrape all the agar liquid from the pot and blend with the tofu mixture.
3. Transfer to a metal dish, cover with plastic wrap and then foil, and freeze for 3-4 hours. Break the frozen mixture into chunks and purée into a smooth icy mousse. Scoop with an ice-cream scoop into serving dishes.

<u>Variation</u>: **Kiwi Lime Mousse Sorbet**
Substitute the mango with peeled and diced Kiwi. Substitute the lemon juice with 3-4 tablespoons Lime Juice (to taste).

* See GLOSSARY
** See Agar in TRICKS OF THE TRADE

TUTTI FRUTTI GELATI

Prep Time: 10   **Cook Time: 5**   **Serves: 6**

Groceries

Tofu, Soymilk, Agar Flakes, Maple Syrup, Green Seedless Grapes, Red Seedless Grapes, Mango, Vanilla.

Do Ahead

This will store in the freezer up to 4 months in a sealed container, or in molds. Remove from the freezer 1 hour or more before serving if you want your ice cream somewhat soft.

Hot Tips

Make sure you purée the mixture (without the fruit) until very smooth. Scrape the sides of the food processor bowl and continue to purée until the tofu is no longer grainy in texture. In step 3, freezing the gelati until partially set before adding the fruit is so the fruit doesn't settle to the bottom, like it does if it's added at the start of freezing.

Meal Balance

This is a wonderful summer soy treat. Enjoy after a balanced meal based of grains or pastas and vegetables.

* See GLOSSARY
** See Agar in TRICKS OF THE
   TRADE

This is cool and creamy with bursts of colorful fresh fruit.

1½ cups Water
1 rounded tablespoon Agar Flakes*
1 10.5 oz. pk. Silken Tofu* Lite Extra Firm
2/3-¾ cup Maple Syrup*, or to taste
2 teaspoons Vanilla Powder or Extract
¼ cup Red Seedless Grapes, diced ¼"
¼ cup Green Seedless Grapes, diced ¼"
¼ cup Peach or Mango, seeded, diced ¼"

1. Bring water to a boil in a small pot over medium heat, with the agar flakes. Reduce heat and simmer for 5 minutes or until the agar is dissolved. Do the Fridge Test**.
2. Purée the tofu, syrup and vanilla, in a blender or food processor until very smooth. Blend in the agar mixture.
3. Freeze 1-2 hours. Mix in fruit and freeze 1-2 hours more, or until set, and serve.

Variations: **Neapolitan Ice Cream**
1. Vanilla Ice Cream; omit fruits from above recipe, purée remaining ingredients until smooth. Set aside.
2. Strawberry Ice Cream; make another batch of Vanilla Ice Cream as in step 1, replacing the soymilk with 1 cup of chopped strawberries, and ¼ teaspoon of strawberry extract, and purée until partially smooth, leaving chunks. Set aside.
3. Chocolaty Ice Cream; omit the carob chips, or leave them in if desired, from the Chocolaty Chocolate Chip Ice Cream (next recipe). Set aside.
4. Freeze each flavor until fairly solid before adding another, to keep colors distinct (place the container on its side so the three colors wil be visible from the top). Note: This makes a triple volume recipe.

CHOCOLATY CHIP ICE CREAM

Prep Time: 10   **Cook Time: 5**   **Serves: 6**

Groceries

Tofu, Soymilk, Agar Flakes, Maple Syrup, Carob Powder, Vanilla, Cinnamon, Carob Chips.

Do Ahead

This will store in the freezer up to 4 months in a sealed container, or in molds. Remove from the freezer 1 hour or more before serving if you want your ice cream softer than a block of ice!

Hot Tips

Make sure you purée the mixture (without the chips) until very smooth, scrape the sides of the food processor bowl and continue to purée until the tofu is no longer grainy in texture.

Meal Balance

This is a very cooling dessert that is rich in soy protein, and the carob chips add substance. Serve after a light summer meal of grain or pasta salads and vegetables.

This is so much like chocolate ice cream. Need we mention that it is healthy, and low fat?

1 cup Water
1 rounded tablespoon Agar Flakes*
1 10.5 oz. pk. Silken Tofu* Lite Extra Firm
2/3-¾ cup Maple Syrup*
¼ cup Carob Powder
2 teaspoons Cinnamon
¼ cup unsweetened Carob Chips

1. Bring the water to a boil in a small pot over medium heat, with the agar flakes. Reduce heat and simmer for 5 minutes, or until the agar is dissolved. Do Fridge Test**.
2. Purée the remain ingredients, except for the carob, chips until smooth. Blend in the agar mixture.
3. Add and mix in the carob chips. Pour into one large or several individual molds, and freeze for 2-4 hours, or until set.

Variations:
Vanilla Pistachio Ice Cream
Omit the carob powder, cinnamon and carob chips. Add and purée 1 tablespoon of Vanilla Powder with the tofu, soymilk and syrup until smooth. Add ½ cup of shelled pistachios and purée partially.

Swiss Almond Mocha Ice Cream
Reduce the carob powder to 1 tablespoon. Omit the carob chips. Add and purée ¼ cup of Grain Coffee Powder (or instant coffee), and ¼ teaspoon Coffee Extract (optional) with the tofu, soymilk, syrup, carob powder and cinnamon. Add ¼ cup of toasted, whole or chopped Almonds.

* See GLOSSARY
** See Agar in TRICKS OF THE TRADE

RAVISHING RASPBERRY COULIS

Prep Time: 5   **Cook Time: 0**   **Makes: ±1½ cups**

Groceries

Raspberries, Maple or Rice Syrup, Almond and Vanilla Extract.

Do Ahead

Purée the coulis and refrigerate up to 2 days in advance or freeze for up to 3 months in a sealed container.

Hot Tips

For variety use apples, apricots, bananas, blueberries, cherries, cranberries, kiwis, mangos, melon, nectarines, oranges, papayas, peaches, pears, strawberries, etc. When using rice syrup, double the volume, or to taste as it is less sweet than maple syrup

Meal Balance

Serve as a sauce over cakes, flans, Tofu French Toast, ice cream, pancakes, pies, etc. Enjoy after a balanced meal based of grains or pastas and vegetables.

This bright red puree adds a sweet tangy explosion to Dark & Delicious Carob Cake, Peach Couscous Cake or Carob Cream Pie.

1 - 12 ounce package fresh Raspberries
½ cup or Water
2 tablespoons Maple* or Rice Syrup*
¼ teaspoon Almond Extract
¼ teaspoon Pure Vanilla Extract

1. Purée the raspberries and soymilk or water in a food processor or blender until smooth. Press the purée through a mesh strainer to extract the seeds.
2. Combine the seedless raspberry purée with the remaining ingredients. Adjust consistency and sweetness to taste and serve.

Variations: **Cantaloupe Orange Coulis**
Substitute 1½ cups of diced Cantaloupe, peeled and seeded, for the raspberries; and use 1 cup of Orange Juice instead of the ½ cup water. Simply purée everything together. Adjust consistency and sweetness to taste.

Peaches & Cream Coulis
Substitute 1½ cups diced Peach, peeled, seeded and diced for the raspberries. Use ½ cup of Soymilk instead of the water. Simply purée everything together. Adjust consistency and sweetness to taste.

* See GLOSSARY

FAVORITE FRUIT SAUCE

Prep Time: 10   **Cook Time: 5**   **Serves: 6**

Groceries

Apple Juice, Apple, Peach, Pear, Maple Syrup, Cinnamon, Vanilla, Allspice.

Do Ahead

Refrigerate the cooked fruit sauce in a sealed container for up to 3 days. You may soak the *dried* fruit (see variation), refrigerated in a sealed container for up to 5 days before cooking, and 5 days after cooking.

Hot Tips

This recipe is virtually fat free—calories yes—but not many. For extra flavor and crunch (and only a little extra fat and calories), add ¼ cup of toasted nuts or seeds. Substitute the pear and apple with 1 cup each of green seedless grapes and red seedless grapes for a very colorful variation. You may leave the grapes whole or slice them into halves.

Meal Balance

Serve this dessert as a compote on its own, or as a topping on the Whole Wheat Pancakes or Tofu French Toast. This is great as an alternative topping for the Couscous Cake or the Tofu Mousse Cake. Enjoy after a balanced meal based of grains or pastas and vegetables.

Tofu French Toast, Griddle Cakes and Pancakes will never be the same once you experience them with this fruit sauce.

2 cups Apple Juice and 2 cups Water
1 Apple, diced ½"-1" chunks*
1 Peach, diced (or 1 Mango or 2-3 Apricots)
1 Pear, diced ½"-1" chunks*
½ cup Maple Syrup**
1 tsp. each Cinnamon, Pure Vanilla Extract
¼ teaspoon each Allspice and Sea Salt
5 tablespoons Arrowroot** or Cornstarch

1. Bring the apple juice, and 1¾ cups of water to a gentle boil over medium heat, with the fruit, maple syrup, spices and sea salt. Reduce heat to low, simmer for 2 minutes.
2. Dilute the arrowroot in the remaining ¼ cup of water. Stir into the juice and fruit and simmer 1 minute or until clear and thickened.

<u>Variations</u>: **Lemon Maple Raisin Sauce**
Omit the fruits; apple, peach and pear. Add ¼ cup of Lemon Juice (±1 Lemon) and 1 cup of Raisins (Sultana or Thompson).

Winter Fruit Sauce
Soak one variety or a combination of dried fruits (apples, apricots, dates, peaches, pears, raisins, etc.) equaling 2 cups, in an extra 1¼ cups of apple juice for 1-2 hours. Cook as above adding the 2 cups of apple juice indicated.

* See CUTTING TO THE CHASE
** See GLOSSARY

CAF-FIEND FREE!

Stimulants give us an immediate boost, but they don't provide true energy. Our nervous system becomes over stressed and once the stimulating "fix" wears off, leaves us feeling burnt-out and more exhausted. Wean yourself from caffeine gradually. The beverages in the next chapter are alternatives that refresh and satisfy!

CHAPTER 9

QUICK QUENCHERS

Bistro Beverages
Party Drinks & Punch

CHEERS, LOVE !

SOYACCINO

Prep Time: 1 **Cook Time: 5** **Serves: 4**

Groceries

Coffee, Soymilk, Cinnamon, Carob or Cocoa Powder.

Do Ahead

Prepare the coffee up to 1 week in advance. Once simmered, simply cool to room temperature and refrigerate in a glass jar. Reheat only as much as you need. You may use fresh brewed coffee, and make it ahead as long as you take it away from the heat. Leaving coffee on the hot element results in a heavy, bitter, over brewed flavor.

Hot Tips

Grain Coffee (made from roasted barley, chicory, etc.) is caffeine free and tastes very similar to the real thing. Even decaffeinated coffee has 1-3% caffeine, yet is a healthier alternative for those in transition from regular coffee. Use *organic coffee* or grain coffee with soymilk—if you use commercial brands of coffee, the soymilk may separate and appear curdled due to a chemical reaction.

Meal Balance

You can enjoy this after a healthy balanced dinner, without any trouble falling asleep at night. Enjoy after a balanced meal based of grains or pastas and vegetables.

This is an ideal, rich creamy beverage to top off a Latin or Mediterranean flavored meal that was perhaps hot, spicy and stimulating.

3 cups Water
1/3 cup Grain Coffee*
1 cup Soymilk*
Cinnamon, Carob or Cocoa Powder

1. Mix water and soymilk in a small pot and bring to a simmer on medium heat for 1 minute. Whip the coffee and soymilk in the blender, until frothy (whip for 1 minute or so to get them very foamy).
2. Pour into cups and scrape the foam from the blender onto the coffee. Sprinkle with a dusting of cinnamon, carob or cocoa powder and serve immediately.

* See GLOSSARY

CAFE AU LAIT

Prep Time: 1   **Cook Time 1**   **Serves: 4**

This is rich and satisfying enough to dispel chocolate and sweet cravings.

Groceries

Grain Coffee Powder, Soymilk.

Do Ahead

Once cooled, store this in the refrigerator for 1 week in a glass jar or sealed pitcher.

Hot Tips

Serve chilled or hot! You may substitute regular or decaffeinated coffee (choose the organic Swiss water process). Use organic coffee or grain coffee with soymilk. If you use regular commercial brands of coffee, the soymilk may separate and appear curdled due to a chemical reaction.

Meal Balance

This is a delicious beverage to finish off a wholesome balanced meal, or at any time of day. Enjoy after a balanced meal based of grains or pastas and vegetables.

3 cups water
1/3 cup Grain Coffee Powder*, or to taste
1 cup Soymilk*, Almond or Rice Milk
Maple* or Rice Syrup* to taste if desired

1. Mix the water with the grain coffee powder and bring to a simmer over medium heat for 1 minute.
2. Add soymilk and syrup stirring constantly. Pour into bowls or mugs and serve.

* See GLOSSARY

ICED CINNAMON COFFEE

Prep Time: 5   **Cook Time: 6**   **Serves: 6**

Groceries

Coffee, Soymilk, Maple Syrup, Vanilla.

Do Ahead

This keeps refrigerated for 5 days in a glass jar or sealed pitcher.

Hot Tips

Use organic coffee or grain coffee with soymilk. If you use regular commercial brands of coffee, the soymilk may separate and appear curdled. If you serve ice cubes with this beverage, add them as you serve it. Do not refrigerate extra iced coffee with ice cubes as they will melt and dilute the flavor.

Meal Balance

This is a very satisfying, low fat substitute for chocolaty desserts, and cool and refreshing on hot days.

This is a cool and refreshing treat on hot days. The cinnamon adds zing!

3 cups water
1 cinnamon stick
1/3 cup Grain Coffee Powder*, or to taste
1 cup Soymilk* or Rice Milk, or to taste
¼ cup Maple Syrup*
1 tablespoon Pure Vanilla Extract

1. Bring water to a boil with the cinnamon stick for 5 minutes. Stir in the grain coffee powder and simmer for 1 minute.
2. Set coffee aside to cool for 30 minutes. Mix in remaining ingredients and chill for 1 hour before serving.

Note: You may substitute almond milk, or carob or vanilla flavored soymilk for regular soymilk.

* See GLOSSARY

CHOCOLATY MILK SHAKE

Prep Time: 5   **Cook Time: 0**   **Serves: 4**

Groceries

Soymilk, Silken Tofu, Maple Syrup, Almond Butter, Carob Powder, Vanilla.

Do Ahead

This stores refrigerated for 5 days in a sealed container. It may have a slightly grainy texture from the settling of the carob powder, so whip it again before serving. It also freezes well for 3 months.

Hot Tips

To reduce fat, omit the almond butter, if you don't mind giving up the nutty richness. The tofu adds body and thickness (as an ice cream does in commercial shakes), but you may omit it to further reduce fat and calories, although the milk shake will be much thinner in consistency. Use carob powder for a caffeine-free version.

Meal Balance

You may freeze this into popsicles or ice-cream for variety.

This bodacious beverage is a healthy soy treat, that is very filling and refreshing. A summer staple!

2 ½ cups Soymilk,* Almond or Rice Milk
1 - 10.5 oz (297 gr.) pk. Silken Tofu* Lite
¼ cup Maple syrup*
2 tablespoon Almond Butter
2 tablespoon Carob Powder or Cocoa
1 tablespoon pure Vanilla Extract

1. In a blender, mix the soymilk with the remaining ingredients until whipped smooth. Adjust consistency and sweetness to taste. Top with Rice Dream** if desired.

Variation:
Cola Float
Substitute the soymilk with a natural cola drink (sugar and chemical free - available in natural food stores). Top with Rice Dream**.

Vanilla Milk Shake
Omit the carob or cocoa powder, and add another tablespoon of vanilla.

* See GLOSSARY
** A brand of top quality dairy, sugar-free ice cream.

MANGO LASSI

Prep Time: 5 **Cook Time: 0** **Serves: 4-6**

Groceries

Mango, Soymilk, Mango Juice, Silken Tofu, Lemon, Garam Masala (optional).

Do Ahead

This keeps refrigerated for up to 5 days in a glass jar or sealed pitcher.

Hot Tips

To reduce fat, use water or extra fruit juice instead of soymilk. The garam masala is a traditional spice used in India, which you may omit, or substitute with cinnamon. Various fruit or berries may be used in place of the mango, and in creative combinations.

Meal Balance

This is a creamy, fruity cooler that will be a refreshing drink on hot days. Have it before, between or after a balanced meal of grains and vegetables.

New Delhi is a fascinating city that juggles time honored culinary traditions, while growing as a modern metropolitan capital. This is a popular drink in many regions, except they use dairy curd.

2 very ripe, medium Mangos
± 2 cups Soymilk*, (Almond, Rice Milk or Water)
±1 cup Mango Juice (Apple or Orange Juice)
1 - 10.5 oz. (297 gr.) pk. Silken Tofu* Lite
2 tablespoons Lemon Juice (½ Lemon)
1½ teaspoons Garam Masala (optional)
¼ teaspoon Sea Salt
4 small sprigs of fresh Mint (optional)

1. Slice the mangos into 12 wedges lengthwise. Peel 4 of the wedges (¼ of 1 mango), dice into ½" chunks and set aside.
2. Peel, seed and purée the remaining ¾ of the mango with the remaining ingredients (except the mint sprigs) in a blender or food processor until smooth. Adjust the consistency with the soymilk and juice to desired thickness.
3. Divide among serving glasses, top with diced mango and garnish each serving with a sprig of mint.

Variation:
Pineapple Lassi
Substitute the mango with 2 cups diced Pineapple.

Silky Mango Pudding
Omit the soymilk, mango and lemon juice, and the garam masala. Add ¼ cup of maple syrup and ½ teaspoon cinnamon (optional). Purée until silky smooth, and adjust sweetness to taste. Serve garnished with mint (optional).

*See GLOSSARY

STRAWBERRY BANANA SMOOTHIE

Prep Time: 5   **Cook Time: 0**   **Serves: 4**

Groceries

Bananas, Strawberries, Soymilk, Maple Syrup, Cinnamon, Vanilla.

Do Ahead

Store refrigerated for up to 3 days in a glass jar or sealed pitcher. Shake leftovers before serving as settling will occur.

Hot Tips

This beverage thickens after it sits for a while, or after being refrigerated, so the consistency may need adjusting again before serving.

Meal Balance

This is filling, not fattening. Serve it as a snack-beverage, between meals, or as a dessert after a balanced meal based of grains or pastas and vegetables.

This is fruity, refreshing and very nutritious. You may substitute various colorful fruits and berries in adventurous combinations.

½ pint very ripe Strawberries
2 very ripe Bananas
2 cups Soymilk*, Almond or Rice Milk
1-1½ cups of water
¼ cup Maple Syrup*
2 teaspoons pure Vanilla Extract
1 teaspoon Cinnamon Powder (optional)

1. In a blender, puree all the ingredients, adding water to desired consistency. Serve and enjoy immediately.

Variation:
Pear Peach Smoothie
Substitute the strawberries with 2 very ripe Pears and 2 very ripe Peaches, peeled** and seeded.

Strawberry Banana Sauce
Omit the soymilk and purée the ingredients with enough water as necessary to achieve a sauce-like consistency. Serve over the Peach Couscous Cake, Strawberry Delight Tofu Mousse Cake, Apple Cherry Almond Flan, Carob Cream Pie (see Index) for a low fat, sensorial indulgence.

* See GLOSSARY
** See Peach Couscous Cake, page 213 for peach peeling instructions.

SPICED ICED APPLE TEA

Prep Time: 5   **Cook Time: 5**   **Serves: 6**

Groceries

Bancha or Barley Tea, Cinnamon Sticks, Apple Juice, Lemon.

Do Ahead

This will store refrigerated in a glass jar or sealed pitcher for 1 week. Make and refrigerate extra bancha or barley cinnamon tea for a refreshing drink that stores refrigerated for several weeks in a glass jar or sealed pitcher.

Hot Tips

If you like to serve ice cubes with this beverage, do so as you serve it. Do not refrigerate extra tea with ice cubes as they will melt and dilute the flavor. This is delightful as a hot tea also!

Meal Balance

This is a real thirst quencher for hot and humid summer days. Serve before, between or after a complete balanced meal.

Use a high quality brand of organic apple juice. It's naturally very sweet and has a lively bouquet of flavor.

2 cups Water
1 teaspoon Bancha (Kukicha) Twig Tea* or
1 teaspoon Roasted Barley Tea*
1-2 Cinnamon Sticks (to taste)
2 cups Apple Juice
2 tablespoon Lemon Juice (½ Lemon)

1. Bring the water to a boil in a small pot over medium heat, with tea and cinnamon sticks. Simmer the tea for 1-5 minutes (or longer, depending on how strong you like it). Cool to room temperature for 30 minutes.
2. Combine the cooled tea with the remaining ingredients and chill for 1 hour or more. Serve in tall glasses, and garnish the edge of each glass with a slice of lemon, and a slice of apple.

Variation: Substitute various fruit juices for the apple juice.

* See GLOSSARY

HOLIDAY CRAN-APPLE CIDER

Prep Time: 5   **Cook Time: 10**   **Serves: 8**

Groceries

Apple Juice, Cranberry Juice, Allspice Berries, Cinnamon Sticks, Whole Cloves, Ginger.

Do Ahead

Combine ingredients and refrigerate overnight (or up to 5 days) to infuse the juices with the spices. Refrigerate the simmered spiced cider up to 2 weeks in a glass jar or sealed pitcher.

Hot Tips

To intensify the spice flavor, simmer the fruit juice with the spices for up to 1 hour. Otherwise, marinating the mixture for several hours in advance heightens the flavor.

Meal Balance

Serve as a refresher before a meal, as an afternoon or evening tea or with dessert after a balanced festive meal.

Thanksgiving, Christmas and New Year's celebrations are favorite times to enjoy apples, cranberries and sweet spices, yet this is wonderful at any time of the year.

1 quart Apple Juice
1 quart Cranberry Juice
2 cups Water
12 Allspice Berries
8 Whole Cloves
4 Cinnamon Sticks
4 slices fresh Ginger, large rounds, 1/8" thick

1. Bring all the ingredients to a gentle boil over medium-low heat. Reduce heat to low and simmer for 10 minutes, or longer for a stronger flavor.
2. Strain the cider and serve in ceramic cups or mugs garnished with a slice of apple and a few fresh cranberries if desired.

MELON GINGER PUNCH

Prep Time: 10   **Cook Time: 0**   **Serves: 6**

Groceries

Cantaloupe, Rosé Wine, Maple or Rice Syrup, Ginger.

Do Ahead

Refrigerate for 4 days in a glass jar or sealed pitcher.

Hot Tips

Use non-alcoholic wine if desired. Substitute apple or other varieties of fruit juice for the wine. Beer instead of wine makes an interesting variation. Rum, vodka or other spirits will add more Punch! Substitute honeydew, cranshaw or watermelon for the cantaloupe. This tastes better the second day after the flavors marinate and intensify.

Meal Balance

Serve before a meal to wet the appetite, between meals to tide you over, with dessert or as the dessert, after a balanced meal.

For a summer barbecue or party, this hits the spot!

1 Cantaloupe
1 Bottle Rosé Wine or 1 quart Apple Juice
±¼ cup Maple or Rice Syrup*, or to taste
1-3 tablespoons Ginger Juice**, or to taste
6 small sprigs of fresh Mint

1. Cut the melon into halves. Remove the seeds and slice the melon halves into wedges. Peel the skin and dice the inner pulp into chunks. Purée the pulp in a blender or food processor.
2. Mix all ingredients and chill for 1 hour or more in a large pitcher. Serve in shapely glasses garnished with sprigs of mint.

Variation: **Summer Melon Ginger Soup**
Omit the maple syrup. Reduce the wine to ½ cup, and purée with the melon. Blend in 1½ cups soymilk, ¼ cup white miso, or ½ teaspoon sea salt, or to taste, with the ginger juice. Serve garnished with sprigs of basil, cilantro, dill, mint or parsley.

* See GLOSSARY
** See TRICKS OF THE TRADE

GALA PUNCH

Prep Time: 20   **Cook Time: 10**   **Serves: 8**

Groceries

Clementines, Green and Red Grapes, Apple Juice, Maple or Rice Syrup, Anise Seeds, Cinnamon Stick, Ginger, Champagne or Sparkling Wine (Non-alcoholic if desired).

Do Ahead

Refrigerate the boiled juice and spices in a glass jar overnight (or up to 5 days) to infuse the juices with the spices. The punch keeps refrigerated in a glass jar or sealed pitcher for 3 days, although the champagne or wine will lose their bubbly effect.

Hot Tips

You can double up on the champagne or wine, and use the "with-alcohol" varieties if desired, for a lower proportion of fruit, and stronger champagne or wine flavor. You may substitute an equal volume of beer for the champagne or wine. To intensify the spice flavor, simmer the fruit juice with the spices for up to 1 hour.

Meal Balance

Serve as an apéritif, a party drink or with dessert after a balanced festive meal.

This is a colorful, fruity concoction for barbecues, parties and celebrations.

1 quart Apple Juice
8 slices Ginger, 1/8 thick, large rounds
1 teaspoon Anise Seeds
1 Cinnamon Stick
1 tbsp. Clementine Rind, finely julienned
¼ cup Maple* or Rice Syrup*, or to taste
1 cup Clementines, cleaned and sectioned
1 cup Green Seedless Grapes, halved
1 cup Red Seedless Grapes, halved
1 bottle chilled Champagne

1. Bring the apple juice to a gentle boil over medium-low heat with the ginger, anise, cinnamon, clementine rind and syrup. Reduce heat to low and simmer for 10 minutes. Cool to room temperature for 30 minutes and chill for 1 hour or more.
2. Slice each clementine section into half lengthwise, exposing the inner orange flesh for a more attractive presentation, if desired. Strain the apple juice and combine with the fruit and champagne.
3. Serve in a large punch bowl or pitcher.

* See GLOSSARY

Getting The Show On The Road!

MENU MAGICIAN
FAST MENU
FUN MENU

STAPLES
Brown Rice - Grains - Pasta - Pie Crusts - Porridge
COOKING WHOLE GRAINS
COOKING BEANS
SPEEDY HOMEMADE SEITAN

CUTTING TO THE CHASE
CUTTING STYLES
HOW TO CHOP

TRICKS OF THE TRADE

PANTRY PERENNIALS

FAST MENU

	SUNDAY	MONDAY	TUESDAY	WEDNESDAY	THURSDAY	FRIDAY	SATURDAY
BRUNCH / BREAKFAST	Fresh Juice Pancakes with Fruit Sauce Tofu Mish Mash Homefries Tempeh Bacon (make extra bacon and grill tofu for Monday's lunch) Café au Lait	Millet & Cornmeal with Dates Bancha Tea	Rolled Oats with Kasha & Dried Apples	Millet & Cornmeal with Dates Bancha Tea	Rolled Oats with Kasha & Dried Apples	Cream of Wheat & Teff with Peaches Barley Tea	Barley & Quinoa with Apricots Herbal Tea
LUNCH		Club Sandwich with Grilled Tofu & Tempeh Bacon Spiced Iced Apple Tea	Humus (made Sunday) on Whole Wheat Fresh Green Salad Tahini Lemon Sauce	Somen Nori Maki with Tempeh Teriyaki (made Tuesday) Watercress with Lemon Soy Dressing	Seitan Souvlaki and Pita Bread with Salad Garnish Greek Salad	Peanutty Patties (made Wednesday) Brussels Sprouts Lemony Miso Mustard Dressing	Fast & Fun Hot Pasta Salad (use extra pasta from Thursday dinner)
SNACK	Sesame Carob Chip Cookies	Almond Raisin Crispy Rice Squares	Pumpkin Seed Caramel Popcorn	Carrot Raisin Oatmeal Power Bars	Peanut Butter Carob Chip Cookies	Cranberry Apple Muffins	Carrot Raisin Oatmeal Cookies
DINNER	Garbanzo & Zucchini Bisque (make Falafel and Humus) Lasagna Fresh Green Salad Italian Dressing Tutti Fruit Gelati	Baked Falafel (made Sunday) Whole Wheat Pita Salad Garnish Tahini Lemon Sauce (extra for Tuesday) Herbal Tea Strawberry Pudding	Hot & Sour Soup Wok Around the Clock (make Somen Nori Maki for Wednesday's lunch) Chinese Tea Almond Cookies	Millet & Cauliflower (make left overs into Peanutty Patties) Mushroom Onion Gravy (make extra for Friday's dinner) Steamed Greens Chocolaty Pudding	Pasta Primavera (make extra pasta for Saturday lunch) Fresh Green Salad Italian Dressing Barley Tea Sweet Potato Pudding	Kasha & Caraway Mushroom Onion Gravy (made Wednesday) Steamed Greens Herbal Tea Gingered Pear Compote	Grains on the Go (make Nori Rolls) Vitality Stew Party Vegetable Rolls Bancha Tea Festive Fruit Kanten

FUN MENU

	SUNDAY	MONDAY	TUESDAY	WEDNESDAY	THURSDAY	FRIDAY	SATURDAY
	BRUNCH	BREAKFAST	BREAKFAST	BREAKFAST	BREAKFAST	BREAKFAST	BREAKFAST
	Tofu French Toast Lemon Maple Raisin Sauce	Barley & Quinoa with Apricots Herbal Tea	Cream of Wheat & Teff with Peaches Barley Tea	Oats & Amaranth with Raisins Bancha Tea	Creamy Rice & Currants Barley Tea	Oats & Amaranth with Raisins Bancha Tea	Creamy Rice & Currants Barley Tea
	LUNCH	LUNCH	LUNCH	LUNCH	LUNCH	LUNCH	LUNCH
	Turkish Menemen Cinnamon Sweet Potatoes Grain Coffee Strawberry Banana Smoothie	Nori Rolls with Marinated Tofu & Vegetables (made Saturday) Steamed Broccoli Japanese Dressing	Pumpkin Seed Pesto with Parsley Garlic Ribbons (use seeds from last Tuesday) Fresh Salad	Shiitake Broth with Noodles, Tofu & Watercress Sizzling Bok Choy & Bean Sprouts	Barley Soup with Mushrooms & Leeks Roasted Rutabaga Salad Steamed Greens	Three Grain Johnnycake Southern Black Eyed Peas Fresh Green Salad	Hazel Basil Barley Bread Savory Stratford Stew Steamed Greens
	SNACK	SNACK	SNACK	SNACK	SNACK	SNACK	SNACK
	Blueberry Pecan Oat Muffins	Sweet & Fruity Corn Bread	Raspberry Oatmeal Squares	Orange Date Muffins	Hopi Indian Apple Pudding	Barbados Banana Bread	Gold Metal Carrot Cake
	DINNER	DINNER	DINNER	DINNER	DINNER	DINNER	DINNER
	Borsch with Tofu Sour Cream Mushroom Vegetable Pie Herbed Kale & Cauliflower Lattice Top Apple Apricot Pie	Manali Lodge Lentil Dahl Indian Almond Pilaf Kashmir Potato Salad Gingered Cabbage Mango Lassi	Hearty Minestrone Risotto Florentine Tri-Color Antipasto Soyaccino Strawberry Delight Tofu Mousse Cake with Cinmful Chocolaty Sauce	Split Pea Soup Country Pot Pie Butternut Squash with Dijon Ginger Sauce Fresh Green Salad Poppy Seed Dressing Spiced Iced Tea Apple Peach Crisp	French Onion Soup Tomato Leek Quiche Cauliflower & Broccoli Au Gratin Café au Lait Dark & Delicious Carob Cake	Yucatan Yam Soup Paella Valencia Spaghetti Squash with Marjoram Caesar Salad Soyaccino Tangerine Kiwi Layer Pie	Cream of Carrot Pasta Alfredo with Portabella Mushrooms Beautiful Boiled Salad Bancha Tea Apple Cherry Almond Flan

STAPLES

Here are lists of Staples you'll want to keep in stock for variety and to enjoy all the wonderful international possibilities.

Grains

Amaranth,
Barley, Barley Flour
Brown Rice: Basmati
               Long Grain
               Medium Grain
               Short Grain
               Sweet
               Thai, Jasmine
Bulgur
Corn, Corn Flour, Cornmeal,
Couscous
Cracked Wheat
Kamut
Millet,
Oats: Rolled
              Steel Cut
              Whole
Popcorn Kernels
Quinoa,
Spelt
Teff,
Wehani Rice
White Rice (various)
Whole Wheat Berries
Whole Wheat Flour
Wild Rice

Pastas

Corn Macaroni, Spaghetti, etc.
Genmai (Japanese rice noodles)
Kamut, Quinoa, Spelt, Rice Pastas
Soba Noodles (Japanese Buckwheat)
Somen (Japanese style square spaghettini)
Gourmet Flavored: Angel Hair,
                             Ribbons, etc.
Whole Wheat Pasta (various shapes)
Udon (Japanese style square spaghetti)
Vegetable Colored Pasta: Bow Ties,
                  Elbows, Fettuccini, Shells,
                  Spirals, Spaghetti, etc.

Beans

Aduki/azuki
Anasazi
Black Beans, Black Turtle
Black Eyed Peas
Chickpeas
Great Northern
Kidney (Red, White)
Lentils (Brown, Green, Split Red)
Mung
Navy
Peas, Split Peas (Green, Yellow)
Pinto
Soybeans (Black, Yellow)

Establish a daily and weekly routine using the Time Saving Strategy outlined in the Introduction. This only requires a little planning, and the benefits to your health and well being are priceless. If possible, have cooked grains and/or pasta in the refrigerator at all times. It's very easy to create meals around these essential staples.

STORING

Whole grains, pasta, beans, flour, nuts and seeds are ideally stored in a cool dry place, away from direct sunlight. Flour, nuts and seeds may be refrigerated if desired, when storing for longer periods.

SORTING

Whole grains should to be sorted through to remove dirt, stones and undesirable grains. (Once while chewing brown rice I heard a loud "Crack-crunch!" sound and thought my tooth had broken on a small stone in the rice. Luckily only the stone was crushed).

WASHING

Wash whole grains in cold water and strain. Repeat if necessary until washing water is clear. Cracked and rolled grains (such as bulgur, cornmeal, rolled oats) need not be washed before cooking.
Beans should also be sorted and washed before being soaked and/or cooked.
Nuts and seeds can be sorted and washed before toasting and/or used in various recipes.

COOKING

There are many ways to cook grains, but basically you can either boil or pressure cook. (Steaming is used in some cultures, especially for rice and couscous.)

Boiling results in fluffier, more separate grains. The energy derived will be light and relaxed.

Pressure cooking is quicker due to the higher heat, which is possible because it will not overflow and boil over, the lid is sealed. With little, if any evaporation of moisture from a pressure cooker, less water is needed than for boiling. Pressure cooking increases the energy and vitality derived, due to the compact, intense cooking style.

Variation: Roast grains in a cast iron or stainless steel skillet over medium-high heat until aromatic and golden. This will add a heartier nutty flavor and increase the warming effect of your grains. This is wonderful for those colder days. When you use a cast iron skillet, the grains will absorb some iron which increases the nutritional value. Then cook grains as indicated.

Brown Rice

BOILING METHODS

(See also COOKING WHOLE GRAINS chart below for water measurements and cooking time for the various grains.)

PRE-SOAKING

For ideal results, presoak sorted and washed brown rice for a minimum of 1 hour, up to 8 hours or over-night. Your rice will be sweeter, more thoroughly cooked and easier to assimilate and digest. Soaking allows the complex carbohydrates and natural sugars to break down and release into the soaking water. Pre-soak sorted and washed rice in the measured amount of water for cooking, and cook it in this soaking water.

1. Bring rice and water to a boil over medium-high heat. Add ½ teaspoon of sea salt per cup of raw rice, cover and reduce heat to low. Simmer the rice for 45 minutes.
2. Remove from heat and allow to rest 5 minutes before removing the lid. This will allow the steam to settle so that the rice does not stick to the pot. (See REMOVING COOKED GRAINS FROM THE POT below.)

DIRECT BOIL

Sort, wash and bring to a boil gradually. The gentle simmering in the beginning replaces the soaking step.

1. Bring sorted and washed rice gradually to a boil on medium-low heat. This gives the rice a chance to slowly begin to absorb the water as it does when it is soaked.
2. Add ½ teaspoon of sea salt per cup of raw rice, cover and reduce heat to low. Simmer the rice for 55 minutes.

RUSH BOIL

1. Simply bring the sorted and washed rice quickly to a boil on high heat.
2. Add ½ teaspoon of sea salt per cup of raw rice, cover and reduce heat to low.
3. Simmer for 60 minutes. You may cook it for less time, 45 minutes minimum, but the flavor and texture is superior with the longer cooking time.

PRESSURE COOKING

(See also the COOKING WHOLE GRAINS chart below for water measurements and cooking times for the various grains.)

You may *PRE-SOAK*, *DIRECT* or *RUSH BOIL* your brown rice, as mentioned above, directly in your pressure cooker.

1. Add ½ teaspoon of sea salt per cup of raw rice, close the lid and bring up to pressure on medium-high heat.
2. Once the pressure gauge is hissing, reduce heat to low and simmer for 40 to 45 minutes. (You can pressure cook the rice for less time, 30 to 35 minutes for firmer, and more separate grains. The longer cooking time increases digestibility and sweetness, and they will be stickier).
3. Remove from heat and open the pressure gauge to let steam escape. The pressure will release quickly and result in fluffier rice. If you wait for the pressure to come down without opening the gauge, the rice will be soggier. This is especially a consideration if you are making several cups of rice as it will take a long time for the pressure to come down.
4. Let the rice sit for five minutes before opening the lid. (See REMOVING COOKED GRAINS FROM THE POT below)

REMOVING GRAINS FROM THE POT

Wooden rice paddles* are ideal for removing and serving grains. Otherwise a large serving spoon will do.

1. Remove the pot of cooked grains from the heat, remove the lid and place a bamboo mat* over the pot. The mat allows steam to escape so the grains do not become soggy. Let the grains sit for 5 minutes. This allows caramelized grains at the bottom of the pot to soften for easy removal.
2. Moisten the wooden paddle (so that the grains will not stick) and loosen the grains from all around the sides of the pot. Then divide the grains into eight pie sections.
3. Scoop down and remove a section of grains and distribute it evenly into the serving dish. Continue with the remaining sections. This ensures even distribution of the top and bottom layers that have different textures resulting from the way various grains settle naturally. This technique for removing cooked grains is especially effective when you are cooking different varieties of grains, beans, nuts and seeds together.

    * Available in Asian Grocers, kitchen supply stores and some natural food stores..

Grains

(See also the COOKING WHOLE GRAINS chart below for water measurements and cooking times for the various grains.)

RICE COMBOS

An ideal proportion is 25% of your desired grain (amaranth, barley, bulgur, kasha, millet, quinoa, wild rice, etc.) combined with 75% rice. You may combine different varieties of brown rice with white rice as well as another grain.

OTHER COMBOS

Many grains can be combined to make delicious varieties. Two, three or more grains may be cooked together. Kasha has a strong robust flavor and marries well with milder tasting grains. You may also choose to combine grains by their length of cooking time. Kasha, millet and quinoa cook in 15 to 25 minutes. Bulgur and couscous only need to be added to boiling water, then set aside to absorb the liquid.

Pasta

With so many wonderful styles of noodles and pasta available of the highest quality organic ingredients, you can create an endless variety of recipes. Make larger amounts to last two or three meals and use them in different recipes.

1. Bring 3 quarts of water to a rolling boil on high heat. Add 1 teaspoon of sea salt, and stir in dry pasta. Cover the pot while the water resumes boiling, and stir every minute or so, to prevent the pasta from sticking.

2. Reduce heat to medium and gently boil pasta until cooked through but still firm and not mushy—"al dente". This will take anywhere from 1-2 minutes for the angel hair varieties, and up to 12 minutes for the thicker style pasta. Stir occasionally until pasta is cooked.

3. Drain the pasta in a colander. (Save the cooking water to use in sauces, soups, and stews if desired. See SOUP STOCK recipe in TRICKS OF THE TRADE). Rinsing is not necessary, and it is preferred not to, as the starch on the pasta will absorb and adhere to sauces much better. Refrigerate extra pasta in a sealed container for 3-4 days. (The pasta does not need to be cooked in oil to prevent sticking as it will automatically separate when it comes in contact with any broth, dressing, liquid or sauce.)

Pie Crusts

WHOLE WHEAT CRUST (makes one 8" covered pie, or two open pie shells)

3 cups Whole Wheat Pastry Flour
½ teaspoon Sea Salt
2/3 cup Corn Oil
±½ cup Cold Water

1. Combine the flour and salt, then mix in the oil until crumbly. Add enough water to form a dough that is pliable but not sticky.

2. Roll 2/3 of the dough between two sheets of wax paper to ±1/6" thickness. Shape into a circle to fit the pie dish. Remove the top sheet of wax paper and transfer the dough to the pie dish, peeling off the wax paper.

3. Roll the remaining 1/3 of dough between the sheets of wax paper as above. Shape into a circle to fit the pie dish as a top crust. Remove the top sheet of wax paper.

4. Place 2 cups of filling in the base crust. Cover the filling with the top crust. Fold and crimp the edges of the dough together all around. Pierce steam vents in a decorative pattern on top. Bake as indicated.

Variations:
Toasted Oats & Whole Wheat Crust
Substitute 1 cup of the whole wheat flour for 1 cup of Toasted Rolled Oats. (Toast them in a 350°F oven for 10 minutes or until golden brown. Grind the oats to a coarse meal in a food processor.)

Whole Wheat & Rye Crust
Substitute 1 cup of the whole wheat flour for 1 cup of rye flour.

Porridge

Whole grains, cooked into a hot creamy porridge for breakfast gives stable enduring energy for hours. Dry cereal and bread are more processed and will not provide you with as much nutrition and vitality as natural grains.

Make several mornings' worth of porridge. Once cooled, divide it among sealable containers to store in the refrigerator, for up to 5 days.

Make delicious varieties and combinations that you really enjoy, so you look forward to having it again the next day. Be creative, and you will not repeat the same porridge until you cannot remember when you had it last. (See COOKING WHOLE GRAINS chart following.)

CHART COOK CODES

The following codes apply to the COOKING WHOLE GRAINS chart on the facing page. (See previous pages for more details about sorting, washing, boiling and pressure cooking and examples of grain combinations.)

A. **SIMPLE BOIL**: Bring water and grains to a boil on medium-high heat. Add sea salt (½ teaspoon per cup of grain, or to taste) and reduce heat to low. Simmer, boiling gently, until liquid is absorbed.

B. **PRE-SOAK**: Soak grains for one hour or more (overnight). Bring grains and soaking water to a boil over medium-high heat. Add sea salt (½ teaspoon per cup of grain, or to taste), and reduce heat to low. Simmer, boiling gently, until liquid is absorbed.

C. **PORRIDGE**: Bring water and grains to a boil over medium-high heat. Add sea salt (½-1 teaspoon per cup of grain, or to taste), and reduce heat. Simmer, boiling gently, on low until thick and creamy. You may add a cinnamon stick and raisins or other dried fruit if desired during cooking. Toasted nuts or seeds may also be added during cooking or as a garnish. Dry-roast grains before boiling if desired.

D. **INSTANT**: Bring water or vegetable stock to boil. Add sea salt (½ teaspoon per cup of grain, or to taste) and stir in grains. Cover and remove from heat. Grains will be ready once all the liquid is absorbed.

COOKING WHOLE GRAINS

GRAIN (1 CUP)	COOK CODE	WATER (BOIL)	TIME (BOIL)	WATER (PC)	TIME (PC)
Amaranth	A, B	2	25	1½	15
	C	4	25	3	15
Arborio, Risotto	A	2	20	1¾	15
Barley, Hulled	A, B	3½	55	3	45
	C	5	55	4½	45
Barley, Pearled	A, B	3	45	2½	30
	C	4½	45	4	30
Brown Basmati Rice, Brown Long Grain, Brown Thai Jasmine	A, B	1¾	30	1¼	20
	C	3	30	2½	20
Brown Medium Grain, Brown Short Grain, Brown Sweet Rice	A, B	2	45	1½	35
	C	4	45	3½	35
Bulgur	D	2	0	N/A	N/A
Cornmeal, Polenta (fine to coarsely ground)	A,	3½	10-30	2½	8-20
	C	5	10-30	4	8-20
Couscous	D	2	0	N/A	N/A
Cracked Wheat	A	2	30	1½	20
Kasha	A,	2	10	1½	8
	C	4	10	3½	8
Kamut	B	1¾	50	1¼	40
Millet	A,	2½-3	25	2-2½	15
	C	5	25	4	15
Quinoa	A,	2	20	1½	15
	C	4	20	3½	15
Oats, Rolled	C	4	30	3	20
Oats, Steel Cut	C	4½	45	3½	30
Oats, Whole (soak overnight)	C	5	60	4	45
Spelt	B	1¾	50	1¼	40
Teff	C	4	20	3½	15
Wheat Berries	B	1¾	50	1¼	40
Wehani Rice	A, B	2	50	1½	40
White Rice	A	1¾	10	1¼	8
Wild Rice	B	2½	50	2	40

PC = Pressure Cooking (see previous pages for details)
TIME = Minutes

COOKING BEANS

BEANS (1 cup dry)	WATER (in cups)	BOILING TIME	PRESSURE COOKED	YIELD (in cups ±)
Aduki	3	1-1½ hours	1 hour	3½
Anasazi	3	1-1½ hours	1 hour	3½
Black, Black Turtle	3	1-1½ hours	1 hour	3½
Black Eyed Peas	2½	1-1¼ hours	45-60 minutes	3
Black Soybeans	3	1½-2 hours	45-60 minutes	3½
Chickpeas (Garbanzo)	3½	1½-2 hours	1-1½ hours	4
Great Northern	3½	1½-2 hours	1-1¼ hours	4
Kidney beans	2½	1-1½ hours	45-60 minutes	3
Lentils, Brown, Green*	2½	25-35 minutes	15-20 minutes	3
Lentils, Split Red *	2½	20-30 minutes	10-15 minutes	3
Mung	2½	45-60 minutes	30-45 minutes	3
Navy	3	1-1½ hours	45-60 minutes	3½
Peas, Green Split*	3	1-1¼ hours	30-45 minutes	3½
Pinto	3	1½-2 hours	1-1½ hours	3½
Soybeans, Yellow	3½	2-2½ hours	1½-2 hours	4

* Not necessary to soak prior to cooking.

Gas Free Beans

People always want to know the best way to cook beans for digestibility, and to reduce gas. Here is a surefire method:

1.   Soak your beans for 8 hours or overnight unless otherwise noted (*).
2.   Discard soaking water. Add fresh water to cover and bring water and beans to a boil over high heat. Cook for 15 minutes without the lid on the pot to let gases escape. Remove the pot from the heat and let set aside for 1 hour.
3.   Discard the cooking water and add fresh water again. Bring to a boil over medium-high heat with 1 bay leaf per cup of beans, and a 1" piece of kombu (see glossary) per cup of beans. The bay leaf and kombu are optional but they do make a difference in the digestibility and flavor of beans. Reduce heat to low and boil gently.
4.   Cook the beans until *very* tender, instead of *just* tender, for 1-2 hours, as necessary. Time may vary from the COOKING BEANS chart above depending on the freshness and moisture content of the beans. Cook the beans without the lid for the first 15-30 minutes to further eliminate the gases.
5.   Add sea salt (½ teaspoon per cup of beans, or to taste) and cook the sea salt into the beans during the last 15 minutes. This also aids digestibility and flavor.

SPEEDY HOMEMADE SEITAN

INGREDIENTS: 1½ cups Whole Wheat Bread Flour
3 cups Gluten Flour
4½ cups water

MIXING: 1.   Sift the Whole Wheat Bread Flour through a wire mesh strainer to remove the bran. Measure the flour to obtain 1½ cups after sifting.
2.   Mix the two kinds of flour together in a large bowl. Add the water and mix well with a whisk and then with your hands to make sure the flour has been completely incorporated and no lumps remain.
3.   The dough should be a very thick porridge-like batter.

COOKING METHODS:

STEAMED

1.   Place the batter into a heat-proof dish.
2.   Fill a large pot with 2" of water and place a steamer basket inside. Place the dish containing the batter on top of a steamer basket, and close the lid on the pot.
3.   Bring the water to a boil and steam until the batter is set in the center and no longer gluey, approximately 1 hour.

BAKED

1   Preheat oven to 350ºF. Place the batter into a 9" by 13" glass baking dish. Cover the dish with foil.
2.   Fill a larger second baking dish with a ½" of water, and then place the first dish inside the larger dish.
3.   Bake for 1 hour, or until it is set in the center and no longer gluey. Check occasionally to make sure the water has not evaporated from the larger dish.

SLICING: Once the seitan has cooled enough to handle, remove it from either the steaming or baking dish (whichever method used). Slice it into ½" thick slabs the size of a steak. Now you have WHEAT MEAT! See the following page for the final step, boiling the seitan in a savory stock. Choose the stock that best resembles the flavor of the recipes in which it will be used.

Note: The steaming or baking time of 1 hour, and the cooking in stock time is not very "SPEEDY", granted, But you can be busy doing other things. The traditional method requires constant manual labor as well as the lengthy cooking time.

Seitan Stocks

BASIC

8 cups Water (as necessary)
2 Bay Leaves
½ cup Tamari* (or extra sea salt)
1 tablespoon Sea Salt*

CHICKEN

8 cups Water (as necessary)
¼ cup Tamari*
1½ tablespoons Sea Salt*
1 tablespoon Poultry Seasoning

BEEF

8 cups Water (as necessary)
¾ cup Tamari*
1½ teaspoons Sea Salt*
1 teaspoon ground Cumin
1 teaspoon Rosemary (crushed)
1 teaspoon Thyme
½ teaspoon Pepper

THAI PORK

8 cups Water (as necessary)
2 Bay Leaves
¼ cup Tamari*
¼ cup of fresh Ginger slices
1½ tablespoons Sea Salt*
1 tablespoon ground Coriander
½ teaspoon ground Cloves

BOILING:

1. Place seitan slices neatly in a pot, all tucked and stacked to take up as compact an area as possible. Place them according to the pattern in which they were sliced.

2. Pour enough water over the seitan to cover by 1-2" as the seitan will absorb water as it cooks. Add tamari, sea salt, and your choice of seasonings from the recipes above. Select according to the style of "cuisine" or ethnic flavor you want create. Bring to a boil over medium-high heat.

3. Reduce heat and simmer, boiling gently, for 30-45 minutes. Add enough tamari and/or sea salt to achieve a stock that is more salty than you would season a soup. Make it as salty as a brine, so it preserves the seitan while it is stored in the stock.

4. Cool the seitan to room temperature. Store refrigerated in a sealed container. It keeps well for 2-4 weeks, providing the seitan is well covered in the stock, and the stock is seasoned enough. If a whitish film shows on the top of the seitan after storing it for some time, simply slice off the white part, and use the rest, providing it does not taste sour.

Note: Diced vegetables such as carrots, celery, garlic, onions, parsley, and parsnips may be cooked in the seitan stock for extra flavor and nutrients. Once cooled, remove the seitan from the stock, and strain the stock to remove the vegetables before storing, as vegetables will turn sour after a week to 10 days.

CUTTING TO THE CHASE

Vegetables are an important part of our diet. These beautiful and delicious gifts from Mother Nature are so good for us. Their colors and flavors, shapes and textures create artistry and sensorial pleasure that is an essential aspect of our nourishment.

(See the H.H.I.H. for nutritional statistics, and the INDEX for recipes.)

CHOPPING BOARD

The debate between wood and plastic has been settled by a study that was conducted by a plastic board manufacturing company, to their dismay. The results proved that there are natural chemicals in wood that kill harmful bacteria. The plastic board samples multiplied harmful bacteria.
Oil a new board, and then occasionally again every few months, with vegetable oil to prevent it from drying out and splitting.
Wet your board with a clean moist cloth on the cutting surface before and after chopping each vegetable. This will prevent the juices from the vegetables absorbing into the wood—especially important when you are chopping chilies, garlic, onions and scallions. Beets, carrots, radishes, red cabbage and berries will stain your board unless it is wet.

STORING

To retain as much flavor, freshness and nutrients as possible, keep vegetables stored in plastic bags or sealed containers. This prevents moisture loss. Vegetables left exposed, even if kept in the "crisper- drawers", become limp and dehydrated.
Broccoli, fresh herbs, sprouts and leafy greens should be used up within a few days. Brussels sprouts, cauliflower, celery, Chinese cabbage and leeks keep 1 week or more. Head cabbage and root vegetables such as carrots, onions, potatoes and winter squash keep for months stored in a cool dry root cellar, or refrigerated.

WASHING

Wash vegetables in cold water. Organic vegetables only need to be rinsed and/or gently scrubbed with a natural bristle brush to remove soil.

Note: Peeling vegetables is not necessary, even when they are not organically grown. If chemicals are *in* the soil, they will be *in* the vegetables, through and through. Use as much of the vegetable as possible—the *WHOLE* food. The outer layers of carrots, parsnips, rutabagas and sweet potatoes, for example, contain fiber and an abundance of nutrients. This is where the vegetable was in direct contact with the soil—its source of food. *Do* peel waxed vegetables.

CUTTING STYLES

You can enhance the taste, texture and appearance of foods by the cutting style. Cooking time is also effected by whether the size is large or small.

Crispy Summer Salads

Raw salads are light and most refreshing with finely sliced colorful vegetables, such as cucumber, red cabbage, red radishes, etc. Grating vegetables, especially carrots, is appropriate for salads. Instead of grating, make carrots and other vegetables more visually appealing by slicing them into very fine julienne. Lettuce may be torn, shredded into strips or sliced into bite size pieces.

Springtime Stir Fries

Stir fries and sautés are best suited to julienne, matchstick style or thin diagonal ½ moon sliced vegetables. This cutting style allows for quick cooking, to tender-crisp in a minimal amount of time.

Warming Soups

Soups are most attractive and delicious with diced or sliced vegetables that can easily fit on your soup spoon. By cutting the vegetables into small pieces, more flavor and juices cook into the broth. (See also SOUP STOCK in TRICKS of the TRADE.)

Hearty Stews

Stews provide us with strength, vitality and warmth by the hardy ingredients, and with the long slow cooking. By cutting the vegetables such as cabbage, carrots, celery, onions, parsnips, potatoes and winter squash into large chunks, they retain their distinct shape, more flavor and energy, and are satisfying in cold weather.

Note: Use as much of the entire vegetable as possible, to retain nutrients, and receive the energy of the whole plant. Studies and research in Vibrational Medicine show that plants have life force, which we take in when we consume them. Different plants have unique energetic tendencies and characteristics, and enhance different aspects of our lives, create certain moods and behavior, and heal various organs. This will be addressed in great depth in a future book.

HOW TO CHOP

Apple

Diced: Slice a washed apple into 8 wedges from the top where the stem is, to the base, through the center core (in other words, slice in half, then each half into halves, then each quarter into halves).
Use a small paring knife to remove the seeds and center membranes from each wedge.
Chop each wedge across in half or thirds to obtain half inch pieces.

Bok Choy

Julienne: All greens that have a thicker stem part than the leafy part can be cut in this manner; beet greens, Chinese and nappa cabbage, collard, kale, Swiss chard, etc.

Lay a washed bok choy leaf on your board and slice along where the white and green parts meet, to remove the leafy part from the stem.
Stack all the stems in a pile, (three or four at a time), and slice across into thin diagonal strips approximately ¼ inch thick.
Slice all the green leafy parts along the center, and pile all the left halves and right halves together facing each other, so the direction of the veins are going the same way . Slice along the direction of the veins into long ¼ inch strips.
Chop across the pile of strips into two inch lengths.

Broccoli

Flowerettes: Cauliflower may also be cut in this way.

Remove the flower cluster from the stems where it begins to branch out.
Separate the individual cluster branches into similar sized flowerettes by running a knife from the base of the branch to the top of the flower.
Lay the stem on the chopping board and slice off the outer fiber in a flat strip, along one side. Roll the stem over on to the cut side, and make a square stem by slicing the outer fiber from the other three sides.
Half the stem lengthwise and then slice diagonally into match-sticks.
To dice it, slice the stem again lengthwise in quarters, and then across into cubes.

BRUSSELS SPROUTS,   See Red Radishes for how to quarter.

BURDOCK,   See Carrot matchsticks.

Carrot

Trim the minimum from the carrot, to use as much of the vegetable as possible. The top of the root, where the vegetable grew from a seed is the center of the plant—the balancing point between the root and the tops. This is the strongest part of the plant. (Likewise in Oriental martial arts, the abdomen, our seed of life, is known as the seat of strength.) Do not chop off this top part. Simply clean around the knob where the dirt collects, with a knife, and scrub it with a natural bristle vegetable brush.

Flowers: Choose a carrot that is straight, and symmetrical in shape, with as little contrast as possible between the thickness of the top with the thickness of the point. Slice into the length of the carrot, 1/6" deep on an angle. Slice again, ¼" away from the first slice, 1/6" deep, and angle the knife toward the first slice. Remove a thin long wedge from the length of the carrot.
Remove two to four more long wedges from the length of the carrot all around.
Slice across the carrot, making 1/8 to 1/4 inch thick flowers. Chop the remaining strips of wedges and use in recipes.

Greens: Fresh tops are colorful, delicious and extremely nutritious.
Separate the long stems from the leaves.
Slice the stems into ¼ to ½ inch diagonal sections.
Chop the tops into ½ inch sections.
Cook the stems briefly before adding the leaves.

Half Moons: Slice the carrot in half lengthwise and lay each half cut-side down on the board.
Slice across into 1/8 to 1/4 inch sections for regular ½ moons.
Slice across diagonally, into 1/8 to 1/4 inch sections for diagonal ½ moons.

Logs: Choose a carrot that is approximately seven inches long and 1-1½ inches in diameter.
Slice off a long strip from the length of the carrot to make one side flat.
Continue with the remaining three sides to make a long square carrot.
Slice the carrot lengthwise into quarters, to make four long square logs.

Matchsticks: Slice a washed carrot across diagonally into 1/8 to 1/4 inch thick rounds, making thin oval discs. Slice thinner for fine matchsticks.
Stack a few oval discs together, three or four at a time, and slice them into long strips, approximately 1/8 to 1/4 inch thick. Slice thinner for fine matchsticks.

CAULIFLOWER,   See Broccoli

CHINESE CABBAGE,   See Bok Choy

COLLARD,   See Bok Choy

Cucumber

Half Moons: For an added decorative effect, use a fork to make grooves along the length of the cucumber.
Slice in half lengthwise, and lay them cut side down on the chopping board. Slice across the cucumber halves to make thin half moons.
For a variation, leave the cucumber whole and slice it into thin rounds.

Logs: Peel the cucumber if it is waxed. Quarter it length-wise.
Remove the seeds with a spoon or knife and slice each quarter again lengthwise into ¼ inch thick logs.
English cucumbers are usually not waxed, and therefore peeling is not necessary. Their seeds are usually so fine that seeding is optional.

KALE,   See Bok Choy

Leek

Prep: The roots of the leeks may be sliced, rinsed and chopped and used in recipes. They have a wonderful flavor and are full of nutrients.
Cut across the leek where the green tops meet the stem at the white part. Remove any yellowed, damaged or fibrous thick leaves from the top green part.
Slice the tender fresh greens across diagonally into thin strips.
Slice down the length of the white part to the base and rinse well between the layers to remove any dirt.

Diced: Slice down the white part again lengthwise to make quarters.
Slice across into ½ inch sections.
Slice down the green part lengthwise to make quarters.
Slice across the green tops into ½ inch sections.

Julienne: Follow the above steps for Prep.
Slice the base where it is solid into thin match-sticks. (See Carrot matchsticks.) Slice the white parts across diagonally into thin strips, ¼ inch wide.
Slice the green parts across diagonally into thin strips, ¼ inch wide.

NAPPA CABBAGE,   See Bok Choy

Radish

Greens: Use the radish greens when they are available, and fresh, they are delicious and very nutritious.
Slice the stem where it meets the red root part and rinse the greens well. Chop the greens into ½ inch sections.

Half Moons: Slice the red radishes into halves from the top to the base.
Slice across into thin half moons.

Quarters: Use the greens as mentioned above.
Slice the red radish into halves from the top to the base.
Slice each half again into quarters.

Rutabaga

Triangles: Slice a washed rutabaga from the top to the base just as far as the center. Make another slice approximately ½-1 inch beside the first slice, again cutting into the center, to remove a wedge shape from the rutabaga. Slice across the wedge into 1/8-1/2 inch thick triangles.

Scallion

Julienne: Use the scallion roots when they are fresh and white, they are delicious and full of nutrients. These little roots give energy, they have the strength to hold the whole plant up in the ground.
Slice the roots at the base. Rinse out the dirt and chop into ¼" pieces.
Add them with the white part of the scallion in recipes.
Slice the scallion across where the greens meet the white stem.
Cut the white part in half lengthwise. Slice across diagonally into ¼ inch thick strips.
Stack the green tops together, and slice diagonally into ¼" thick strips.

Winter Squash

Diced: Remove the top stem. Cut the squash in half through the center from top to bottom. Trim the hard flesh from the center of the stem and bottom, and any crusty blemishes or bruises. Scoop out the seeds with a spoon. Slice the squash into ½"-1" wedges, and then slice across the wedges into cubes.

ZUCCHINI,   See Carrot or Cucumber logs.

TRICKS OF THE TRADE

Agar

To make sure that the agar flakes are cooked and fully dissolved in the liquid you plan to gel, do the following Fridge Test. Take a spoonful of the boiling liquid from the pot and rest it carefully (to avoid spilling) in the refrigerator for 1-2 minutes.
Once it is cooled, you can see if it is as firm as you want it, before you cool and set the whole recipe. To make it more firm, simply add more agar flakes to the liquid and cook for a few minutes until dissolved. Test another spoonful. To make it less firm, add a little more liquid.
Agar will set at room temperature and does not need to be refrigerated.
Agar will not cook and dissolve in oily liquids.
One tablespoon of flakes will set one cup of liquid. One teaspoon of powder will set one cup of liquid. (See also GLOSSARY and H.H.I.H.)

Bread Crumbs

For one cup of bread crumbs you need three to four slices of bread. Place the bread on a cookie sheet, uncovered, and toast them in a preheated 350ºF oven until brittle and golden brown. Once cooled and dried out, break the slices into pieces and grind them in your food processor to fine crumbs. For plain bread crumbs (non-toasted), just dry out the bread slices until brittle in a warm oven, break them into pieces and grind as above. Store your bread crumbs refrigerated in a sealed container for several weeks, or frozen for three to four months.

Corn Oil

Unrefined cold pressed corn oil has a deep yellow color. It adds a buttery flavor and is a healthier alternative to butter in various savory and sweet dishes, without the saturated animal fats. (See Cholesterol in H.H.I.H.)

Ginger Juice

When you want the fresh juice without the ginger fibers, first grate fresh ginger root on a fine grater. Remove all the fibers from the grater and squeeze the juice into a dish. Place the fibers in a small strainer. Rinse the grater with some liquid from the recipe, to rinse off the remaining ginger. Strain the fibers with the liquid and squeeze to extract as much ginger flavor as possible. (See also H.H.I.H.)

Jalapeno Chili

The seeds inside of chili peppers are super hot and can cause harm to eyes and sensitive skin. You may choose to wear rubber gloves when handling chilies. Slice the chili in half lengthwise and remove the seeds and white membrane. Julienne the halves lengthwise, and then finely slice across to mince. Wash your hands and rinse the cutting board well before toughing anything or anyone else. If you want a super spicy dish, please go ahead and use the seeds, but don't say I didn't warn you!

Kombu

This humble sea vegetable is used often in Asian cooking to flavor broth and various vegetable and bean dishes. Kombu contains glutamic acid. When cooked with beans and legumes, it helps to break down the cellulose fiber of the beans making them more digestible and removing the gaseous effects. The abundance of minerals also aids in digestion by alkalizing and balancing the acidity of the carbohydrates, fat and protein in beans.

Rinse the dried strip of kombu briefly to clean off the dust and excess sea salt, (use one inch of dried kombu per cup of broth, grains or beans). Soak the kombu until soft in a small amount of water and use this soaking water. Slice the kombu into thin julienne or dice into small pieces so that it evenly distributes throughout your recipe, or you may leave it whole. In bean dishes it will dissolve almost completely by the time the beans are cooked. You may reuse the kombu after flavoring a broth. Simply let it dry out again to save it for later. (See GLOSSARY, H.H.I.H.)

Miso

The fermentation process in making miso creates an age mellowed salty paste that has the deep rich tangy taste very much like strong cheese. Because its distinctive robust flavor is so delicious, miso is easy to overuse. As a guide, use about one teaspoon per cup of liquid when seasoning sauces, soups and stews. The different types of miso vary in saltiness, so adjust accordingly.

Gourmet Use: Miso is versatile and can be used as a seasoning to enhance the flavor of bean dishes, dips, dressings, sauces, grains, soups, stews and vegetable dishes. Use a miso that is medium-dark for a deep rich flavor. Use white or pale miso when you want a light and sweet taste, and it will not darken recipes such as cream sauces. (See also GLOSSARY and H.H.I.H.)

Medicinal Use: Do not boil unpasteurized miso or the beneficial digestive enzymes will be rendered inactive. Simmer gently for three to four minutes at the end of cooking, to unify its medicinal qualities with the dish it is seasoning.

Noodles

Nori Maki Filling: Bring two quarts of water to a rolling boil. Meanwhile, make bundles with the noodles (Soba, Somen or Udon styles) about the size of a large coin and secure each bundle with a small strong elastic band at one end. Place the elastic as far as possible to the end so that the length of the noodles can be cooked as far as possible.

Place the noodle bundles in the boiling water. Open up the individual noodles near the elastic with a fork or chopsticks, as they begin to soften, so they cook thoroughly near the secured end.

Once cooked, remove the bundles with tongs by the elastic and hold them up to drain and align themselves straight and untangled. Roll them up in a sushi mat (available in Asian Grocers and Natural Food Stores) to drain and keep their roll shape before rolling them into toasted nori sheets. Use a dry sushi mat when making the nori rolls or the nori sheets will become soggy.

Nori Maki

Toast the nori sheet (they are available toasted or not toasted), by simply holding it, shiny side up, over an electric element, or gas burner (some friends have successfully managed over a candle). Keep moving the nori sheet over the heat or it will burn. The nori will change from black to a greenish-black color when it is toasted. (See also GLOSSARY and H.H.I.H.)

Place a toasted nori sheet on a bamboo sushi mat or thick dish towel. Spread ±1½ cups of cooked rice evenly onto the nori, leaving a ½" border of nori showing at the base edge closest to you, and a 2" border at the top. Place the fillings horizontally across the rice, through the center from left to right. Using the mat or towel for support, roll the nori sheet, jellyroll fashion, beginning at the base. As you roll, pull the mat back so it doesn't get rolled inside. Encase the filling with the rice inside the nori. The nori will stick to itself where the base edge overlaps with the top border.

Seitan

Press seitan to extract excess liquid for optimum flavor absorption of marinades and seasonings. Wrap it in a paper towel (to protect it from lint) and then in a dish cloth. Place a small board over it and then a heavy object on top, (such as the base of a food processor or a kettle full of water) and set aside for one hour. The liquid from the seitan will be absorbed by the towel, so the seitan will soak up the juices of marinades and seasonings more efficiently. (See also GLOSSARY and H.H.I.H.)

Soup Stock

The list of YES vegetables below are naturally sweet and create a delicious savory stock to use in sauces, soups, stews and various other recipes. The NO list includes vegetables that are too bitter or strong in taste and will overpower the flavor of your stock. As you peel onions and trim your vegetables, save and store them in a sealed container in the refrigerator until you have enough to fill a large pot.

1. Add water to fully cover the vegetables, 1-2 bay leaves (depending on your volume of vegetables), 1-2 tablespoons each of sea salt, herbs and/or spices if desired. (See the various stocks in SPEEDY HOMEMADE SEITAN for ideas.)
2. Bring to a boil on high heat, covered. Reduce heat to low, and simmer for 20 minutes, or until the vegetables are very tender.

3. Remove the lid and continue to simmer the vegetables for another 20 to 30 minutes to reduce the liquid and intensify the flavor.

4. Once cooled, strain and squeeze the vegetables well to extract all their juices. Well-salted stock will store refrigerated for up to one week, or frozen for three months in a sealed container.

YES

Bell Peppers
Bok Choy
Broccoli
Buttercup Squash*
Butternut Squash*
Cabbage
Carrots
Cauliflower
Celeriac
Celery
Chinese Cabbage
Corn, Corn Cobs
Garlic
Ginger
Leeks
Mushrooms
Onions
Nappa Cabbage
Noodle Water
Parsley
Parsnips
Potatoes
Scallions
Snow Peas
Spinach

YES continued

Summer Squash
Sweet Potatoes
Tomatoes
Vegetable Cooking Water
Zucchini

NO

Arugula
Beets (unless you are making Borsch)
Broccoli Rabe (Rapini)
Brussels Sprouts (small amounts are OK)
Carrot Greens
Collard (small amounts are OK)
Cucumber Skins
Escarole
Kale (small amounts are OK)
Radiccio
Radishes (small amounts are OK)
Red Cabbage
Rutabaga (small amounts are OK)
Sprouts
Stems of Vegetables
Turnips (small amounts are OK)
Watercress

Toasted Sesame Oil

The toasting of the sesame seeds gives this oil its intense aromatic quality and wonderful flavor. Use it when you want an Asian flair in your recipe. The toasting of the seeds also gives this oil a smoked-hickory flavor and pithy taste that adds a rich, savory meatiness to recipes. (See also GLOSSARY and H.H.I.H.)

Tofu

Poached: This is optional, but recommended for those who are not in love with the flavor of tofu, or for people with weak digestion. When using fresh tofu in recipes that are not cooked, such as salads, cheese, dips, dressings, marinades, puddings, spreads and tofu ice cream, poaching the tofu will make it more digestible and subtly more palatable by eliminating the raw soybean flavor. Simply slice the tofu block into four large cubes (to reduce cooking time and cook it more evenly through to the center), and poach them in simmering water for one or two minutes, until heated through to the center. Boiling the tofu and cooking it longer than this makes it rubbery. Remove and drain the tofu, and press it to extract the liquid (see below).

Pressed: This is optional, but recommended, for optimal absorption of broth, marinades and seasonings. Extract the excess water in tofu by wrapping it in a paper towel (to protect it from lint) and then in a dish towel. Place a small board on top and then a weight such as the base of your food processor or a kettle full of water. After one hour, remove the towels and use the tofu immediately to make "cheese", in marinades, soups, stews and stir fries. Pressing is not necessary in recipes that you purée and add liquid such as dips, dressings, puddings, spreads, toppings and tofu ice cream. (See index for recipes.)

Umeboshi Paste

Use this when you want a salty-sour taste in dips, dressings, sauces, grains, soups, stews and vegetable dishes. It imparts a cheesy flavor, especially when combined with tahini. (See also GLOSSARY and H.H.I.H.)

PANTRY PERENNIALS

Here is a list of all the healthy ingredients - a variety of groceries and non-perishables to have on hand. Replenish them regularly so that you always have what it takes to create quick and exciting dishes. You may want to include other favorite items that are not listed below, such as traditional ethnic foods of your ancestral origins.

Cupboards

Agar* Flakes or Powder
Apple Juice**, Apple Cider Vinegar
Arrowroot*, Cornstarch
Baking Powder and Soda
Bancha Tea, Barley Tea (Roasted) *
Brown Rice Syrup* and Vinegar*
Carob* Chips and Powder
Dried Coconut, unsweetened (optional)
Grain Coffee*
Maple Syrup*, Rice Syrup*
Miso* (Refrigerate pasteurized varieties.)
Olive Oil
Sea Salt*
Sea Vegetables: Arame*, Dulse*, Kombu* Nori*
Silken Tofu*, Lite (in aseptic boxes)
Soymilk* (in aseptic boxes)
Tamari* (Shoyu)
Umeboshi Paste and Vinegar*

Herbs & Spices

Allspice, Anise
Basil
Caraway, Cayenne, Clove
Cinnamon, Cinnamon Sticks
Coriander, Cumin, Curry
Crushed Dried Red Chili Flakes
Fennel, Ginger
Marjoram, Mustard
Oregano
Paprika
Pepper, Black and White
Poultry Seasoning
Rosemary
Sage
Tarragon
Thyme
Turmeric
Vanilla (pure liquid extract and powder)

Fridge

Condiments and Pickles
Mustard, Natural Stone Ground*
Nayonaise*, Nuts, Nut Butters
Oils: Corn, Safflower, Sesame, etc.
Seeds, Seed Butters
STAPLES; Grains, Pasta, Seitan
Tofu, Vegetables
Whole Grain Bread Products

Freezer

Corn Tortillas
Tempeh*
Veggie Burgers and Hot Dogs, etc.
Whole Wheat Tortillas
Extra Servings of prepared dishes to reheat

* see GLOSSARY

Fridge Map

SHELVES	LEFT SIDE	RIGHT SIDE
TOP	Beverages Bread products Breakfast foods	Lunch—designated foods to be reheated as required and/or lunches ready and packaged "to go"
MIDDLE	Dinner—designated STAPLES (grains, pasta, beans) and prepared vegetables for dinner	Salad ingredients Green vegetables Cabbages
LOWER	Fresh tofu Homemade Seitan Nuts* and Nut Butters Seeds* and Seed Butters	Onions* Squash* Root vegetables* Tubers*
DOOR	Bottles and jars Condiments, Oils, Pickles, etc.	* May be stored in a cool dry place or root cellar.

Find an organization and system that suits your needs and refrigerator. You may place this map on the outside of the refrigerator door so everyone knows where to find things, and where to put them back. Every aspect of our lives is a reflection of our lives as a whole, including our inner condition; physical, mental and spiritual. Order begets order. Keep your refrigerator and all areas of the kitchen, your home, office, etc., tidy, clean and organized.

"MAN AND SOIL
ARE NOT TWO"

Since the industrial revolution and to some extent earlier, we lost the understanding of what it is to eat and live naturally, in harmony with our environment.

Now, medical and scientific research and studies are proving what traditional cultures have known instinctively all along.

An ancient proverb "Man and Soil are not Two" sums it up perfectly. What we do to nature we inevitably do to ourselves. We are nature, a mirror of our environment, and our health and well being depends on this planet, our mother earth. Let's care for her, and keep ourselves healthy.

HEALTH & HEALING
INFORMATION HIGHWAY

ANTIOXIDANT

Antioxidants are compounds that protect cells from damage caused by unstable oxygen molecules called free radicals. Free radicals are believed to be responsible for initiating many forms of cancer as well as premature aging. Whole natural foods are sources of antioxidants.

BARLEY, PEARLED - see Hippocrates and Zinc.

BEANS

Beans lower bile acid production by 30% in men with a tendency toward elevated bile acid. Bile acids are necessary for proper fat digestion but in excess have been associated with causing cancer, especially in the large intestines. Case control studies showed that pinto and navy beans were effective in lowering bile acid production in men with high risk for this condition. Also, men with high cholesterol who ate a diet including 1/2 cup daily of dried,(or approximately 1-1 1/2 cups cooked) pinto, navy, kidney and other beans had an average drop in cholesterol levels of 20% after 3 weeks.

A study led by principal researcher Dr. Dean Ornish of the Preventive Medicine Research Institute in Sausalito, CA found up to 37.8 percent improvement in blocked arteries for patients on a low fat grain, bean and vegetable based diet. In contrast, the coronary blockages in the control group who ate a standard diet increased 42.7 percent to 46.1 percent. Sources: Dean Ornish et al., "Can Lifestyle Changes Reverse Coronary Heart Disease?" Lancet 336:129-33, 1990 and *Dr. Dean Ornish's Program for Reversing Heart Disease* (New York: Random House, 1990).

DIET and REVERSAL of CORONARY HEART DISEASE		
	VEGETARIAN DIET	**STANDARD DIET***
Total Cholesterol	Down 24.3%	Down 5.4%
LDL Cholesterol	Down 37.4%	Down 5.8%
Blood Pressure	127/79	131/77
Angina Frequency	Down 91%	Up 165%
Angina Duration	Down 42%	Up 95%
Angina Severity	Down 28%	Up 39%
Clogging of Arteries	Down 2.2%	Up 3.4%
Atherosclerotic Progress	18 of 22 Subjects Improved	10 of 19 Subjects Worsened
*Controls were given the American Heart Association Diet (with Fat Allowed to 30% kcal) which was considered "prudent". Source: Lancet, 1990.		

BETA-CAROTENE & VITAMIN A

Beta Carotene and Cataracts - Blindness due to cataracts afflicts 50 million persons worldwide. Doctors at Brigham and Woman's Hospital in Boston conducted studies with 1,380 people, 450-79 years old. They found that the people who received supplements of garden vegetables high in vitamins A, B, C and E were 37% less likely to have cataracts.

Beta Carotene and Heart Disease - Vegetables and fruits high in beta-carotene can reduce the risk of heart disease by about half in people with clogged arteries. In a report to the American Heart Association, researchers followed 333 male doctors who had coronary artery disease. After six years of study, the men who took beta-carotene had ten heart attacks compared to seventeen in the placebo group. Beta-carotene is found primarily in fruits such as apricots and cantaloupes, and in dark green, orange and yellow vegetables such as carrots and tops, kale and other leafy greens, winter squash.

Beta Carotene and Immunity - Researchers at the University of Arizona reported that retinoids and carotenoids (foods and substances high in Vitamin A and beta-carotene) can stimulate some human immune responses, including some heightened anti-tumor cell activity, increased natural killer cell response and activated lymphocytes.

Beta Carotene and Lung Cancer- A Chicago study found that regular consumption of foods containing beta carotene, a precursor to Vitamin A, protects against lung cancer. Over a period of 19 years, a group of 1,954 men at a Western Electric plant were monitored and those who
regularly consumed orange and yellow vegetables such as squash, carrots, dark green lettuce, spinach, broccoli, kale, Chinese cabbage, peaches, apricots and other carotene-rich food had significantly lower lung cancer rates than controls.

BUCKWHEAT

Buckwheat, related to the rhubarb family, is one of the few plant foods abundant in lysine, an essential amino acid usually found in foods of animal origin. It also contains a bioflavonoid called "rutin" that is used to treat capillary fragility, a condition characterized by easy bruising and bleeding gums. Studies show that buckwheat may also help to keep glucose level under control more efficiently than other types of carbohydrates, which is good for people with diabetes.

CALCIUM

Researchers from Creighton University in Omaha, Nebraska and Purdue University in West Lafayette, Indiana, reported that the calcium contained in kale is readily absorbed by the body, and more efficiently than the calcium contained in milk. "We interpret our findings as evidence of good bio-availability for kale calcium, and low-oxalate vegetable greens as well." They listed collard greens, broccoli, turnip and mustard greens. Spinach, Swiss chard, beet greens and rapini are very high in calcium and iron, but they contain oxalic acid which binds with calcium, and inhibits absorption. These high oxalate vegetables are recommended for occasional, not regular consumption, for optimum health. (See also Osteoporosis)

CALCIUM CONTENT IN VARIOUS FOODS

LEAFY GREEN VEGETABLES	mg*	SEA VEGETABLES	mg*
Broccoli	246	Agar-Agar	100
Collard Greens	177	Arame	146
Daikon Greens	80	Dulse	137
Dandelion Greens	74	Hijiki	152
Kale	103	Kombu	76
Mustard Greens	97	Nori	100
Parsley	61	Wakame	130
Spinach	83	GRAINS & SEEDS	
Turnip Greens	126	Buckwheat	57
Watercress	90	Sesame Seeds	331
BEANS & PRODUCTS		Sweet Almonds	81
Azuki Beans	37	Sunflower Seeds	40
Chickpeas	75	Brazil Nuts	53
Kidney Beans	70	Hazel Nuts	60
Navy Beans	95	DAIRY FOODS	
Soybeans	131	Milk	288
Miso	40	Eggs	27
Natto	103	Goat's Milk	315
Tempeh	142	Cheese, various	100-350
Tofu	128	Yogurt	272

Figures are for average servings: Greens (1/2 cup cooked); Beans (1 cup cooked); Sea vegetables (1/4 cup cooked); Grain (1 cup cooked); Nuts and Seeds(1 tablespoon); Dairy (1 cup, 1 large egg or 1 slice cheese). US RDA varies from 800-1200 mg/daily. Source: USDA and Japan Nutritionists Association

CAULIFLOWER-CRUCIFEROUS VEGETABLES

Researchers examined 155 people in their 50's who had no signs of colon cancer. Half had polyps growing in their colon; half with no polyps ate more cruciferous vegetables. The less cruciferous vegetables consumed, the greater the risk for polyps and the larger and more abnormal the polyps.

CHINESE DIET

A Chinese research project challenged modern dietary assumptions in the early 1990's. Sponsored by the US National Cancer Institute and Chinese Institute of Nutrition and Food Hygiene, the study correlated average food and nutrient intakes with the disease mortality rates in 65 rural Chinese countries. The typical Chinese diet included a high proportion of cereals and vegetables and a low content of meat, poultry, eggs and milk. Less that 1% of deaths were caused by coronary heart disease, and breast cancer, colon cancer, lung cancer and other malignancies common in the West were comparatively rare. The following statistics are among the researcher's chief findings:

- Fat consumption should ideally be reduced to 10-15% of calories to prevent degenerative disease not 30% as usually recommended. Continued...

- The lowest risk of cancer is generated by the consumption of a variety of fresh plant products.
- Eating animal protein is linked with chronic disease. Compared to the Chinese who derive 11% of their protein from animal sources, Americans obtain 70% from animal food.
- A rich diet that promotes early menstruation may increase a woman's risk of cancer of the breasts and reproductive organs.
- Dairy food is not needed to prevent osteoporosis, the degenerative thinning of the bones that is common among older women.
- Meat consumption is not needed to prevent iron deficiency anemia. The average Chinese consumes twice the iron Americans do, primarily from plant sources and shows no sign of anemia.

Dr. Colin Campbell, a Cornell biochemist and principal American director of the project, noted "Usually the first thing a country does in the course of economic development is to introduce a lot of livestock. Our data is showing that this is not a very smart move and the Chinese are listening. They are realizing that animal based agriculture is not the way to go."

CORN

About half of all present day Pima Indians of Arizona have diabetes. This is the highest incidence of the disease in the world and has been associated with their shift to a modern diet of sugary and fatty foods. Studies show that when the Indians return to their ancestral diet of local vegetables, beans and traditional strains of corn long cultivated by the tribe, it significantly lowered insulin production and blood sugar levels after meals, compared with diets high in potatoes and white bread.
In 1971, a South African doctor observed that he had not diagnosed a single case of schizophrenia in tribal Africans living on an unrefined carbohydrate diet, whereas this disease is the most common psychosis among urbanized Africans. He attributed the development of mental illness to white sugar and refined corn flour.

DAIRY

"Parents should be alerted to the potential risks to their children from cow's milk products", declared the Physicians Committee on Responsible Medicine in a policy statement. "Milk should not be required or recommended in Government guidelines." "There is evidence accumulating that it is not good for infants", said Dr. Benjamin Spock, world renowned pediatrician. Source: "Cow's Milk and Children: A New No-No?", New York Times, September 30, 1992.

DAIRY & CRIME

Excessive milk consumption is connected with juvenile delinquency in a study by criminologists. Researchers at the University of Washington monitored the dietary intake of thirty chronic youthful offenders, and compared them to a group of behaviorally disordered children from the local school district in Tacoma, Washington. They found that the male offenders consumed an average of 64 ounces of milk a day, while the control group drank an average of 30 ounces. For girls, the figures were 35 and 17 ounces respectively. "In some situations," they concluded, "eliminating milk from the diet can result in dramatic improvements in behavior, especially in hyperactive children". They cited other studies showing that up to 90 percent of offenders had a symptom history associated with milk intolerance or allergy. Source: Alexander Schauss, Diet, Crime and Delinquency (Berkeley, Calif. Parker House, 1981), p.p. 13-14.

DIET & MENTAL HEALTH

At Massachusetts Institute of Technology, researchers have investigated the effects of food on the brain and nervous system. Studies show that brain chemistry and function can be influenced by a single meal. whole grains and other foods high in complex carbohydrates have the capacity to increase the brains' intake of tryptophan, and amino acid that aids in the relief of pain and in lowering blood pressure and has been associated with lifting depression and improving sleep. Meals high in animal protein lower levels of tryptophan reaching the brain.

A New Hampshire psychiatrist reported that a vegetarian diet (MB) had benefited many of his patients who were chronically and severely mentally ill. He described a case of a young woman with a history of severe depression who had been in state hospital for two years and treated with antidepressants and anti-psychotic medications. Tests by his department found that the woman was hypoglycemic and the diet high in complex carbohydrates, which avoided animal food and sugar, resulted in steady improvement, reduced medication and return to normal functioning. Other patients have had great success, have been weaned of medication and are fully functional.

DIETARY GOALS & ORGANIC FARMING

In 1981 a panel of the American Association for the Advancement of Science met to evaluate the impact of implementing *Dietary Goals for the United States*. Beyond an improvement in public health, the symposium found the dietary changes would have far-reaching social and economic benefits.

FERMENTED FOODS

Fermented foods such as miso, tamari or shoyu (natural soy sauce), tempeh and other soy products, as well as traditionally made pickles and sauerkraut, offer many health benefits such as better food assimilation and the establishment of a beneficial intestinal microflora. The lactobacillus in these foods can inhibit the action of pathogenic bacteria in the intestines. For example, during World War 11, prisoners of war in the Pacific who ate tempeh were observed to be less affected by dysentery, a tropical disease. By reducing harmful bacteria in the digestive tracts, fermented foods can reduce the risk of colon cancer and a variety of intestinal disorders. See also Miso, Tamari Soy Sauce.

FOOD & ENDURANCE

In 1983, A Japanese professional baseball team the Seibu Lions, climbed from last place to first place by switching to a vegetarian diet centered around brown rice, tofu, vegetables and soybean products. The team manager restricted the players' intake of meat, sugar and white rice and told the men that animal food increases an athlete's susceptibility to injuries. Conversely, natural foods protected the body from sprains and dislocations and keeps the mind clear and focused. Previously, in 1982, the Lions were ridiculed by their arch rivals, the Nippon Ham-Fighters, a team sponsored by a major meat company. However, the Lions defeated the Ham-Fighters, for the Pacific League Crown and continued to the Japan World Series and beat the Chunichi Dragons. The Lions won the championship again the following year.
Continued...

Food & Endurance continued -

In New Haven, Connecticut, Irving Fisher devised tests to measure diet and endurance of Yale athletes eating animal food, vegetarian athletes (from Battle Creek Sanitarium in Michigan), and vegetarians who were sedentary. The tests included holding the arms outstretched as long as possible, deep knee bends until exhaustion, and repeated leg raises. The vegetarians excelled in all three tests and the sedentary vegetarians generally exhibited stronger endurance than the athletic meat-eaters.
"The results of the comparisons would indicate that the users of low protein and the non-flesh dietaries have far greater endurance than those who are accustomed to the ordinary American diet.," Fisher concluded. Source: Irving Fisher, "The Influence of Flesh Eating on Endurance," Yale Medical Journal 13205-21, 1907.

DIET, EXERCISE AND ENDURANCE						
	Arm Holding		Deep Knee Bending		Leg Raising	
Type of Diet & Exercise	No	Average	No	Average	No	Average
Meat-Eating Athletes	15	10 minutes	9	383 times	6	279 times
Vegetarian Athletes	19	39 minutes	16	927 times	6	288 times
Sedentary Athletes	13	64 minutes	5	535 times	1	74 times
Source: Yale Medical Journal, 1907						

GINGER

Ginger stimulates the appetite, gets circulation moving, relieves digestive troubles and gives warm energy. Externally, ginger is used in making a compress to place over the kidneys, intestines or other areas of the body to stimulate circulation and relieve pain. In China, dried ginger is used to treat upset stomachs and to warm up the body.

Ginger root can benefit the heart and circulatory system by slowing blood clotting. In studies at Mount Pleasant Hospital Addiction Studies Foundation in Lynn, MA. ginger has been shown to inhibit thromboxane synthetase, a primary factor in platelet aggregation. Researchers noted that in contrast to drugs, ginger had minimal side effects. The scientists concluded "the indications for ginger as a therapeutic agent may be far reaching in psychiatry and medicine".

Ginger is on the list of foods being investigated by the National Cancer Institute for its potential anti-cancer properties. Studies show that ginger may inhibit the action of prostaglandin, which is responsible for triggering an inflammatory response in the body.

HIPPOCRATES

"Let food be thy medicine and thy medicine food."

Continued...

Hippocrates continued - For thousands of years, the human family has been living free from degenerative disease in harmony with nature. Today, about 90% of people in modern society die from heart disease, cancer, diabetes, Alzheimer's disease, AIDS and other chronic illnesses. These diseases are primarily the result of our imbalanced modern way of life, especially the modern way of eating which is high in fat and sugar, low in fiber and laden with chemicals. Nearly 2500 years ago in ancient Greece, Hippocrates, the Father of Medicine, taught that proper food was the foundation of human health and happiness. This is enshrined in the original Hippocratic Oath:

"I will apply dietetic measures for the benefit of the sick according to my ability and judgment; I will keep them from harm and injustice."

Hippocrates recommended a way of eating based principally on barley, wheat and other whole cereal grains that grew in the Hellenistic world. Traditional physicians in the Far East, the Middle East, India, Africa, the Americas and other cultures also passed along dietary wisdom based on the grains, vegetables and other predominantly plant-quality foods native to their environment. For many generations, the relation between food and disease has been neglected in modern society. In medical schools, the Hippocratic Oath was rewritten. The word "dietetic" was taken out—we might say, surgically removed! Upon graduation, medical students today pledge to apply unspecified *"measures for the benefit of the sick"*.

Now after several centuries in which drugs and surgery have dominated medical treatment, modern science and medicine are rediscovering the power of food to maintain optimal health and happiness to prevent and relieve illness. They are also beginning to recognize that the way we eat has a profound impact on mental and psychological health, as well as on the health of society and the environment.

Hippocrates taught a natural healing method emphasizing environmental and dietary factors. He especially recommended whole barley, the staple in ancient Greece and the Mediterranean, supplemented with wheat and other grains and their products, along with simple, safe compresses made of grains, vegetables, and plants that could be prepared at home. In his lectures and essays, Hippocrates focuses on the energetics of food. In *Tradition of Medicine*, he explained:

"I know too that the body is affected differently by bread according to the manner in which it is prepared. It differs accordingly as it is made from pure flour or meal with bran, whether it is prepared from winnowed or unwinnowed wheat, whether it is mixed with much water or little, whether well mixed or poorly mixed, overbaked or underbaked, and countless other points besides. The same is true of the preparation of barley meal. The influence of each process is considerable and each has a totally different effect from another. How can anyone who has not considered such matters and come to understand them, possibly know anything of the diseases that afflict mankind? Each one of the substances of a man's diet acts upon his body and changes it in some way and, upon these changes his whole life depends..."

Source: Hippocratic Writings, G.E.R. Lloyd, editor, J. Chadwick and W.N. Mann, translators New York.

IDEAL PROPORTIONS

The leading health authorities all concur that a diet based on whole grains, beans, vegetables and fruits is ideal. This low fat vegetable quality diet has been the staple of advanced cultures around the world. From the Incas and Mayans in South America, and the Native American Indians, to the Hunzas in the Himalayas and the peasants in rural China, whole grains and vegetables have sustained these peoples disease free and in vigorous health. Study after study reveal that diet and disease are linked. Natural foods are proven to prevent illness as well as cure or heal serious diseases. Too often, people go through the full gamut of conventional medicine's invasive procedures; drugs with serious side effects, operations to remove parts of the body, chemotherapy, etc. More often than not, this is totally avoidable, unnecessary and very harmful. Statistics show that those following the conventional medical route to deal with disease are 5 time more likely to die than those who choose the natural way of healing. (Please consult a macrobiotic counselor, like myself, or someone in your area for guidance. Michio Kushi's *Cancer Prevention Diet*, and many other publications are available through the Kushi Institute, and there is an international directory of macrobiotic centers, counselors and practitioners, see page 283.)

50% to 60% Whole Grains
Complex carbohydrates (see GLOSSARY) derived from whole grains and grain products should constitute 50% to 60% of our daily food intake. Porridge, whole grain breads, pastas, and the full spectrum of whole grains from around the world offer enjoyment and variety while reaping healthful benefits and abundant energy. It is important to acknowledge that simple carbohydrates, such as those found in fruits and fruit derived sweeteners, honey, potatoes, sugar and sugar products, etc., are not ideal and can lead to health complications. As well, the energy they provide burns very quickly and leaves us for craving more, unsatisfied and not properly nourished.

30% to 35% Vegetables (& Small Amounts of Sea Vegetables)
Vegetables are approximately 30% to 35% of our daily consumption, choosing a balance between the leafy green vegetables and the orange and yellow squashes and root varieties (see Beta-Carotene, Cruciferous Vegetables and Fiber in GLOSSARY). Macrobiotic understanding goes beyond what we see under a microscope; calcium, carbohydrates, protein, vitamins, etc. The macroscopic view considers the seasons and climatic conditions when selecting appropriate foods. In the summer we eat more fruit and salads, because they are in season, and also because they have a high water content and a cooling effect on the body. In the winter we prefer hot meals and more soups and stews for their heartiness and warming qualities. Sea vegetables are delicious in bean dishes, salads, sautés, soups, stews, etc., a few times per week.

5% to 10% Beans & Legumes
Beans, legumes, soybean products; tempeh, tofu, etc., are to be enjoyed daily or every other day as a side dish, in soups, stews or cooked with grains and pasta. The proportion varies from person to person, depending on their lifestyle. Men and physically active people in general prefer to eat hearty servings daily. Those who are involved in mentally oriented activities tend to eat small volumes. (Some individuals may occasionally enjoy high quality (naturally raised, organic) low fat animal products; dairy, fish, poultry, wild game, etc., as a supplement.)

5% to 15% Fruit, Nuts, Seeds
These foods can be included as desserts, condiments, or combined with other foods. Keep the nuts and seeds to a minimum as they are high in fat, but essential.

ISOFLAVONES

Isoflavones are compounds similar to natural estrogen but with one important difference: these plant estrogens may help prevent hormone-dependent cancers and even prevent hot flashes in menopausal women. Sources: especially soybean products such as miso, soymilk and tofu.

IRON

Whole oats are an excellent source of iron: 4.6 mg per 100 grams of oats. Other whole grains high in iron are millet which has 6.89 mg, buckwheat 3.1 mg and whole wheat 3.1 per 100 grams.

IRON CONTENT IN VARIOUS FOODS

WHOLE GRAINS	mg*	SEA VEGETABLES	mg*
Buckwheat	3.1	Arame	1.5
Millet	6.8	Dulse	1.6
Oats	6.8	Hijiki	3.2
Soba	5.0	Kombu	1.9
Whole Wheat	3.1	Nori	5.6
BEANS		Wakame	1.3
Azuki Beans	4.8	SEEDS	
Chickpeas	6.9	Pumpkin Seeds	3.2
Lentils	6.8	Sesame Seeds	3.0
Soybeans	7.0	Sunflower Seeds	2.4
Tempeh	5.0	ANIMAL FOODS	
LEAFY GREENS		Milk	0.1
Beet Greens	3.3	Beef	3.6
Dandelion Greens	3.1	Chicken	1.6
Mustard Greens	3.0	Egg Yolk	6.3
Parsley	6.2	Beef Liver	6.5
Spinach	3.1	Oyster	5.5

Figures are per 100 grams (3.5 oz) except seeds (1 tablespoon) and sea vegetables (1/4 cup cooked). US RDA varies from 10-18 mg/daily. Source: USDA and Japan Nutritionist Association.

KIDNEY STONES

In a study designed to measure the effect of a low animal protein diet on the risk of urinary stone disease, researchers in Britain reported that a nation-wide survey of vegetarians in the UK showed that the prevalence of kidney stone formation was 40 to 60 percent (or half) of the general population. The scientists concluded that "the findings support the hypothesis that a diet low in animal protein reduces the risk of urinary stone formation". Increase of fiber and reduction of sugar, refined carbohydrates and animal protein significantly reduced the excretion of calcium, oxalate and uric acid in the urine.

LEAFY GREEN VEGETABLES

Green is the color of peace, and leafy green vegetables contribute to a more peaceful mind, family and home. Upward growing green vegetables balance the downward energy of root vegetables. In warmer weather, have a larger proportion of greens and seasonal vegetables. In colder weather use more hardy roots. They are flexible, soft and tender and enhance these qualities in our physical, mental and spiritual condition. As well as containing beta-carotene, calcium, iron and many other nutrients, they are high in fiber and important for digestion. Have one to two cups of lightly cooked dark green vegetables daily for optimum health.

LENTILS

Lentils provide a slow, steady source of energy, midway between the quick growth of vegetables and the calm, peaceful strength of whole grains. They are a good source of protein and are very low in fat.
A study in the Caspian of Iran—a region where Esophageal cancer is high and a modern fast food diet has been adopted—has led researchers to conclude that the disease is associated with a lower intake of lentils and other pulses, cooked green vegetables and other whole foods. (See also Zinc.) H. Hormodozian et al. "Dietary Factors and Esophageal Cancer in the Caspian Littoral of Iran", Cancer Research 35:3493-98, 1975.

MANGANESE

Manganese activates the enzymes that are necessary for the utilization of biotin, vitamin B and vitamin C. It is needed to form strong bones and may play a role in preventing osteoporosis. It is also essential for the proper function of the nervous system and production of sex hormones. Manganese is an antioxidant. Sources: leafy green vegetables, nuts, peas and whole grains.

MILLET

Millet grows in colder climates, Canada, Korea, Japan, northern regions of China, USA, and some parts of Europe and Africa. It is warming to the body and most beneficial consumed in the autumn and winter. Millet is especially good for the stomach, spleen and pancreas. An epidemiological study found that populations with a low risk of esophageal cancer in Africa and Asia consume more millet, cassava, yams, peanuts and other foods high in fiber or starch than high risk groups. S.J. Van Rensburg, "Epidemiology and Dietary Evidence for a Specific Nutritional Predisposition to Oesophageal Cancer), Journal of the National Cancer Institute, 67:243-51, 1981.

MISO

Miso is strengthening to the blood and immune system, stomach and intestines. It gives warm energy, is packed with protein and isoflavones, and is low in fat and high in sodium. It should be used sparingly by those who are sodium sensitive or who have high blood pressure, until the condition is regulated.

MISO & BREAST CANCER

Researchers at the Departments of Nutrition Sciences and Biostatistics/ Biomathematics, University of Alabama at Birmingham, ran tests to discover why the incidence of breast cancer is 60% lower in first generation Japanese immigrants to Hawaii, compared to subsequent generations of Japanese born in Hawaii. They found that feeding rats miso delayed the appearance of induced breast cancer, showed a trend toward lower numbers of cancers per animal, a trend toward higher numbers of benign tumors (rather than malignant) and a trend toward a lower growth rate of cancers compared with controls. "Data suggests that miso consumption may be a factor producing a lower breast cancer incidence in Japanese women", the researchers concluded. "Organic compounds found in fermented soybean based foods may exert a chemoprotective effect" (See also Fermented Foods, Tamari Soy Sauce.) J.E. Baggot et al. "Effects of Miso and NaCl on DMBA - Induced Rat Mammary Tumors", Nutrition and Cancer 14:103-09, 1990.

MISO & RADIATION

In August 1945, at the time of the atomic bombing of Japan, Dr. Akizuki was director of the Department of Internal Medicine at Saint Francis Hospital in Nagasaki, one mile from the center of the blast. He fed his staff and patients a strict diet of brown rice, miso and tamari soy sauce soups, wakame and other sea vegetables, Hokkaido pumpkin and sea salt, and prohibited the consumption of sugar and sweets. As a result, he saved everyone in his hospital, while many other survivors in the city perished from radiation sickness. "People who eat miso are up to five times more resistant to radiation than people not eating miso", is the conclusion of scientific studies conducted by Kazumitsu Watanabe, Professor of Cancer and Radiation at Hiroshima University's Atomic Bomb Radiation Research Center. This study indicates that miso is a preventive measure against radiation. "Miso Protects Against Radiation", Ymuri Shinbun, July 16, 1990.
"Miso is helping some of our patients with terminal cancer to survive" reported Lidia Yamchuk, MD and Hanif Schaimandarov, MD, doctors in Cheljabinsk. Personal communication to Alex Jack, April 1991.

MISO SOUP & CANCER

A diet rich in soy foods, especially miso soup, produces genistein, a natural substance that blocked the growth of new blood vessels that feed a tumor. Researchers from Children's University Hospital in Germany reported that genistein also deterred cancer cells from multiplying, and could have significant implications for the prevention and treatment of solid malignancies including those of the brain, breast and prostate. "Chemists Learn Why Vegetables Are Good For You", NY Times, April 13, 1993.

ONIONS

Naturally sweet cooked onions are recommended for people with diabetes, along with other naturally sweet vegetables such as carrots, parsnips and winter squash. Cooked onions have a calming, peaceful energy which is good for infants and young children. Medicinally, onions are good for the stomach, spleen and pancreas. An old folk remedy for a variety of ailments, onions are being investigated by the National Cancer Institute for their potential cancer fighting properties. In addition, studies show that onions can help reduce blood cholesterol levels, lower blood pressure and prevent dangerous blood clots. Continued...

ONIONS continued -

A 1989 Chinese study described in the Journal of National Cancer Institute showed that people who ate the highest amounts of onions had the lowest rate of stomach cancer. People who eat onions can raise their HDL, the "good" cholesterol.

OSTEOPOROSIS

Osteoporosis is characterized by thinning of the bones and susceptibility to fracture. It commonly affects elderly people in modern society. (See also Calcium and Vegetarian VS Non-Vegetarian.)

POTASSIUM

Potassium helps to regulate the body's water balance and normalizes heart rhythm. A recent study showed that an increase in dietary potassium can significantly reduce blood pressure in hypertensive people. Potassium is also essential for the normal functioning of nerves and muscles. Good food sources of potassium include; beans, dried apricots and dates, garlic, kelp, parsley, nuts, seeds, potatoes and most fruit and vegetables.

REFINING WHEAT

The loss of nutrients in refining wheat is very high as you can see in the chart below. It is best to use whole wheat pasta, breads and flour, preferably organically grown.

NUTRIENTS LOST in REFINING WHOLE WHEAT			
NUTRIENT	LOST (%)	NUTRIENT	LOST (%)
Thiamin (B1)	77.1	Sodium	78.3
Riboflavin (B2)	80.0	Chromium	40.0
Niacin	80.8	Manganese	85.8
Vitamin B6	71.8	Iron	75.6
Pantothenic acid	50.0	Cobalt	88.5
Vitamin E	86.3	Copper	67.9
Calcium	60.0	Zinc	77.7
Phosphorous	70.9	Selenium	15.9
Magnesium	84.7	Molybdenum	48.0
Potassium	77.0		
Source: American Journal of Clinical Nutrition, 1971			

SEA VEGETABLES

Scientists at the Gastro-Intestinal Research Laboratory at McGill University in Montreal reported that a substance derived from the sea vegetable kelp could reduce by 50-80 percent the amount of radioactive strontium absorbed through the intestine. The experiments were designed to devise a method to counteract the effects of nuclear fallout and radiation.

SELENIUM

This mineral helps prevent cancer and strokes. It works with glutathione, a tripeptide in the body and is also synergistic with Vitamin E, meaning that the combination is far more potent than either of them alone.
Selenium is an antioxidant; it protects cells against unstable molecules that can damage DNA and trigger cancerous growths. People who live in areas where soil is rich in selenium (and therefore is present in the locally grown food and water) have significantly lower incidences of strokes than do people who live in selenium-poor areas. Good food sources are; broccoli, garlic, onions, red grapes and whole wheat.

SESAME SEEDS

Sesame seeds are an excellent source of oil. They are very high in calcium and other nutrients. Studies suggest that sesame seeds protect against both cancer and heart disease.

SESAME OIL

In one Japanese study published in the Japanese Journal of Cancer Research, sesame oil reduced the amount of bile acids in rats. Bile acids are believed to produce cancerous changes in the cells of the intestinal wall which may cause colon cancer. Thus, by reducing the amount of bile, sesame protects against colon cancer. In another study, researchers injected various spice extracts into mice with tumors. Although all the spices increased the life span of the mice, only the sesame extract produced any significant reduction in tumor growth. In a study that appeared in The Journal of Lipid Research, sesamin, a lignin from sesame oil, was fed to rats to investigate its effect on cholesterol. Based on this study, researchers speculate that sesamin may be a useful cholesterol lowering agent.

SHIITAKE MUSHROOMS

Medicinally, shiitake has many uses, from lowering body temperature to purifying the blood and protecting against hardening of the arteries and tumors. Shiitake contains a compound called lentinen, which can stimulate the immune system to ward off infections and viruses. In Japan, lentinen is used as a treatment for cancer. Japanese scientists at the National Cancer Center Research Institute reported that shiitake mushrooms have a strong anti-tumor effect. In experiments with mice, polysaccharide preparations from various natural sources, including shiitake mushrooms, markedly inhibited the growth of induced sarcomas resulting in "almost complete regression of tumors...with no sign of toxicity". G. Chilhara et al. "Fractionation and Purification of the Polysaccharides with Marked Anti-tumor Activity, Especially Lentinen, from Lentinus Edodes", Cancer Research, 30:277-81, 1970.

SOYMILK

Soymilk is cholesterol and lactose free, and is safe for people who are lactose intolerant or allergic to cow's milk. Soymilk is packed with protein, B vitamins and minerals, and is a good source of isoflavones. Naturally processed soymilk may be given to babies as a supplement to cereal grain milk, but is not recommended as a substitute for mother's milk.

SQUASH

Medicinally, squash is very calming and nourishes the stomach, spleen and pancreas, helping to stabilize blood sugar levels. Winter squash is warming and strengthening, ideal for autumn and winter soups and stews. High in fiber, it relieves constipation. Do not peel the skin as it is edible and contains much of the fiber, and becomes soft once cooked. The orange inner flesh is rich in Vitamin A and C, potassium calcium, and other nutrients. Varieties; acorn, buttercup, butternut, chestnut, delicatta, hubbard, pumpkin, sweet dumpling, sweet mamma.

SUGAR

The widespread availability and consumption of refined sugar is a primary cause of degenerative disease and mental and emotional disorders. (During the Middle Ages, refined sugar was locked away in apothecary shops as a dangerous drug.)

A survey found that women with anxiety symptoms associated with PMS, including nervous tension, mood swings, irritability, insomnia, ate 2½ times as much sugar as women without PMS, or with mild cases. G.E. Abraham, "Magnesium Deficiency in Premenstrual Tension", 1:68-73, 1982.

Whether processed naturally or artificially, all highly refined sweeteners should be strictly avoided. The following sweeteners are not considered "better" than sugar; sucrose, glucose, fructose, corn syrup, brown sugar, honey, molasses. Sugar substitutes (those little pink and blue packets that are found in restaurants' sugar bowls with the sugar packets) are *extremely* refined chemicals and are worse than refined white sugar for health. (See also: Corn, Diet & Mental Health, Food & Endurance and Kidney Stones.)

EFFECT of SUGAR on AGGRESSION and ANTISOCIAL BEHAVIOR in an INCARCERATED JUVENILE POPULATION		
Frequency of Infractions by Groups	Standard Diet	Sugarless
Low (O to 1.0 infractions per 10 days)	9 (26%)	11 (46%)
Average (1.1 to 3.0 infractions per 10 days)	13 (38%)	11 (46%)
High (3.1 or more infractions per 10 days)	12 (35%)	2 (8%)
Source: International Journal of Biosocial Research, 1982.		

SULFORAPHANE

Sulforaphane is a compound found in cruciferous vegetables such as broccoli, Brussels sprouts cabbage and kale. It stimulates animal and human cells to produce cancer fighting enzymes.

SWEET POTATOES - See Beta-carotene and Potassium.

TAMARI SOY SAUCE

The high rate of stomach cancer in Japan caused some Japanese scientists to speculate that a diet high in soy sauce might be a factor. However, researchers at the University of Wisconsin observed just the opposite. In laboratory tests, mice given fermented soy sauce experienced 26 % less cancer that mice on a regular diet. Also soy-supplemented mice averaged about one quarter the number of tumors per mouse as the control group. The researchers concluded that soy sauce "exhibited a pronounced anticarcinogenic effect. See also Fermented Foods, Miso.

TEMPEH

Tempeh is recommended for restoring energy and vitality. Tempeh is easy to digest and is appropriate for any age, even just-weaned babies. Tempeh is rich in protein, fiber, minerals, vitamins and isoflavones. It is a natural source of Vitamin B_{12}. Nursing mothers are especially susceptible to low levels of Vitamin B_{12} because of the demands of their growing baby. In 1977, researchers found that the Vitamin B_{12} content of typical samples of traditionally made tempeh sold commercially in North America ranged from 1.5 to 6.3 micrograms per average 3.5 ounce serving. The adult RDA for B_{12} is 3 micrograms, to the tempeh contained 50-210%. "Production of Vitamin B_{12} in Tempeh, A Fermented Soybean Product", Applied and Environmental Microbiology 34:773-76, 1977.

TOFU

In 1983, the USDA approved the use of soy products and other vegetable protein products. In a review of the health benefits of soy, researchers from the Department of Food Science at the University of Illinois noted:

- Soy products were comparable with milk in protein quality for preschool and older children.
- Except for premature infants, soy protein can serve as a sole protein source in the human diet. Soy foods are high in protease inhibitors that inhibit the action of various enzymes that have been associated with causing cancer.
- Soy formulas are lactose free and may benefit infants and small children who are sensitive to cow's milk protein which can cause diarrhea, emesis, vomiting and weight loss.
- Soy products can reduce cholesterol and triglycerides in subjects with high lipid levels and protect against heart disease.
- Soy foods are useful in decreasing blood glucose responses compared with other high fiber foods and may prevent diabetes. Source H.L. Ashraf et al. "Use of Tofu in Preschool Meals", Journal of the American Dietetic Association 90:114-16, 1990.

Tofu is a good source of calcium. One cup cooked has 128 mg of calcium.

SOY FOODS & CANCER

At a workshop sponsored by the National Cancer Institute on the role of soy products in cancer prevention, medical researchers presented evidence that soybeans and soy products such as tofu, miso and tempeh can help prevent the onset of induced cancer in laboratory animals. Mark Messina and Stephen Barnes, "The Role of Soy Products in Reducing Risk of Cancer", Journal of the National Cancer Institute, 83-541, 1991.

Soy Foods continued...

SOY FOODS & CANCER continued -

British researchers reported in 1993 that natural phytoestrogens found in whole grains and soybean products, such as tofu, may protect against breast cancer. Professor Nick Day, Director of the Institute for Public Health at Cambridge, explained that components found in these foods appeared to work in the same way as tamoxifen, a drug that has been used in conventional therapy. "Certainly 50 grams of soy protein daily has a major effect on hormonal activity in pre-menopausal women" says Dr. Day. Tamoxifen has been associated with harmful side effects, while a diet high in tofu and whole grain products may prove as effective, he concluded. Source: "Tofu May be a Weapon Against Cancer", London Times, October 24, 1993.

In one study done at the University of Tokyo, Japanese cancer researchers found that people who regularly ate tofu were less at risk for stomach cancer than those who did not.

UMEBOSHI

In the far east, medicinal *foods* have been traditionally used to help relieve coughs, colds, flu, fatigue, headaches, migraines and other symptoms. Umeboshi plums have citric acid which neutralizes and eliminates lactic acid in the body and picric acid which stimulates the liver and kidneys to cleanse the blood.

VEGETARIAN VS NONVEGETARIAN

A Michigan State study found that the average women who ate meat had lost one-third of her skeletal structure by age 65. Meanwhile, vegetarian women of comparable age had less that half of the bone loss and were more active, less likely to break bones, maintained erect postures and healed bones more quickly.

VEGETARIAN and NONVEGETARIAN NUTRITIVE VALUE of FOOD INTAKE
(as a PERCENTAGE of the 1980 RDA*)

DIET	NUMBER	FOOD ENERGY	PROTEIN	CALCIUM	IRON
Vegetarian	464	83%	150%	104%	103%
Nonvegetarian	35,671	84%	165%	87%	102%
	MAGNESIUM	PHOSPHOROUS	VITAMIN A	THIAMIN	RIBOFLAVIN
Vegetarian	95%	146%	163%	117%	136%
Nonvegetarian	83%	136%	132%	113%	124%
	PERFORMED NIACIN	VITAMIN B_6	VITAMIN B_{12}	VITAMIN C	
Vegetarian	114%	76%	156%	176%	
Nonvegetarian	124%	75%	176%	147%	

*Average per individual per day (1977-78) measured as daily intake, % of RDA, for all sexes and ages except breast-fed infants, based on 3 consecutive days of dietary intake.

VITAMIN A - See Beta-carotene.

VITAMIN B$_{12}$

Animal foods commonly believed to be high in B$_{12}$ may actually be low or deficient. In lab tests commissioned by an independent research in 1989 and 1990, no identifiable B$_{12}$ was found in beef liver, Swiss cheese and chicken breast. In contrast, sea vegetables measured up to 9 mcg, tempeh 4 mcg and miso .7 mcg. The researchers attributed the decline in B$_{12}$ levels to environmental pollution and modern chemical agriculture, especially the depletion of cobalt in soils which promotes B$_{12}$ synthesis. (See also Tempeh.)

VITAMIN K

This vitamin is essential for proper blood clotting. Recent studies suggest that it is also import for calcium absorption which means that it may play an indirect role in helping prevent osteoporosis. Good sources of Vitamin K include: soybean oil, green leafy vegetables, broccoli and alfalfa.

ZINC

Zinc deficiencies are increasingly common in pregnant mothers, teenagers and in the elderly. It has been associated with learning disabilities, infertility, immuno-depression, sickle-cell anemia, slower healing of wounds and other disorders. Whole sources of zinc include brown rice, barley, whole wheat, rye, oats, other whole cereal grains, nuts, sunflower and pumpkin seeds, sea vegetables, lentils and peas, watercress and parsley. National Academy of Sciences, Diet and Health and Michio Kushi.

Information Source:

Let Food be Thy Medicine, by Alex Jack
Published by One Peaceful World Press
PO Box 10, Becket, MA 01223 USA
Tel: (413) 623-2322 Fax: (413) 623-8827

For more information on health and healing, including; books, educational programs and seminars, contact:

The KUSHI INSTITUTE
PO Box 7,
Becket, MA
01223 USA
Tel. (413) 623-5741
Fax. (413) 623-8827

Their activities include; One Peaceful World Press, Global Communications Network, Macrobiotic Food Relief, Educational & Cultural Tours, Summer Conference and Children's Memorial & Shrine.

GLOSSARY

A

Agar - is a clear sea vegetable that comes in bar form, flakes or powdered and is used like gelatin in making kantens or aspics, by boiling and simmering it in liquid for approximately 10 minutes until dissolved. (Also see TRICKS OF THE TRADE and H.H.I.H.)

Arame - is a black sea vegetable that resembles thick hair. It originates as a leaf and is shredded and dried. Use it (after soaking in water for 15 minutes) raw in salads or cooked in soups, stir fries and sautés. (See H.H.I.H.)

Arrowroot - is a powdered starch used for thickening liquids, sauces, gravies, glazes, etc. by dissolving it in a small amount of liquid: 1 tablespoon of arrowroot dissolved in 2 tablespoons of water or liquid will thicken one cup of liquid. It is similar to cornstarch in appearance but once cooked it is clear and shiny rather than cloudy and translucent like cornstarch.

B

Bancha Tea - or Kukicha tea consists of the leaves and stems from Japanese tea bushes that are at least three years old. This tea is high in calcium, aids digestion, and has no chemicals, dyes or caffeine. It is ideal for regular consumption at any time of the day, and is wonderful either hot or cold.

Barley Flour - can be substituted for wheat flour in bread, cakes, cookies, pies and muffins. It has a delicate moist quality that is light and satisfying, and gives a cake-like consistency to bread and muffins. The flour may be dry-roasted in a skillet until pale golden and fragrant for a nuttier taste, before adding into recipes.

Barley, Pearled or Pot - has been polished to remove the outer fiber in varying degrees, depending on the brand. It requires less cooking time than whole (hulled) barley. Barley flakes, rolled barley is available (similar to rolled oats) and can be used in porridge, soups and stews. (See Hippocrates in H.H.I.H.)

Beta-Carotene - is a precursor to Vitamin A that is associated with reduced risk of cancer, heart disease and other sicknesses. Foods naturally high in beta-carotene are the orange and yellow vegetables such as carrots, squash, dark green vegetables such as kale, broccoli and Chinese cabbage, and orange fruit such as apricots, peaches and cantaloupes. Recent studies prove that beta carotene, taken as a supplement is a health risk. The conclusion of the research states that the pills cause cancer, and result in higher mortality rates. "Beta-carotene is no magic bullet", and supplements are no substitute for a healthy diet. (See H.H.I.H.)

Basmati Rice - is an aromatic rice that is a long grain variety native to India. Wonderful in soups, salads, stir fries, as a simple grain or mixed with other varieties of rice, grains or beans.

Brown Rice - is the most balanced of all the cereal grains. The size, shape, color, texture and proportion of carbohydrates, fat, protein and minerals falls in the middle of the spectrum of the seven principal grains: millet, barley, buckwheat, corn, oats, rye, whole wheat berries. Brown rice is particularly beneficial to the brain and nervous system, our species' most developed organs. Unpolished whole natural brown rice is higher in minerals, protein and flavor than white rice, which is mostly starch.

Brown Rice, Sweet - is a more glutinous or sticky variety that has a sweeter flavor, and is more opaque white than regular brown rice. It is often used in sushi or dessert, such as amasake, a Japanese favorite made by fermenting sweet rice with koji until it is very sweet. Unpolished whole natural sweet brown rice is higher in minerals, protein and flavor than white rice, which is mostly starch.

C

Capers - are available in most stores, gourmet shops in jars in the condiment\pickle section. They are small buds from a plant native to the Mediterranean, pickled in brine, and add a spicy sour burst of flavor to salads, sauces, vegetable dishes, etc.

Carob - is obtained from an evergreen tree of the locust family, native to the Mediterranean region. The carob bean is about the size of a large lima bean. When it dries on the trees, it falls to the ground and is harvested. Carob powder is used as cocoa powder, yet it has no cocoa butter or caffeine, and is lower in fat.

Cholesterol - is a waxy constituent of all animal fats and oil, which can contribute to heart disease, cancer and other illnesses. Vegetable-quality foods do not contain cholesterol. The liver naturally produces all the serum cholesterol needed by the body. (See H.H.I.H.)

Cilantro - is also known as Chinese parsley and fresh coriander. This herb is common traditionally in Asian, Mexican and South American cuisine and adds a pungent freshness to recipes.

Complex Carbohydrates - are starches or sugars in whole grains, vegetables, seaweed and fruits that are gradually metabolized and supply a slow, steady source of energy and nutrients. Simple carbohydrates, such as those provided by sugar and potatoes, release into the blood stream quickly, and are burned off quickly.

Cruciferous Vegetables - are dark green leafy vegetables of the mustard family, including broccoli, cabbages, Brussels sprouts, kohlrabi, kale, cauliflower, mustard greens, rutabaga and turnips. They are associated with reduced risk of cancer.

D

Dulse - is a purplish red sea vegetable native to the North Atlantic coastal regions and enjoyed as a snack in the Maritimes, New England and Western Europe. It can be eaten raw, soaked and chopped into salads, simmered into soups and other dishes at the end of cooking or made into a condiment.)See H.H. I.H.)

F

Fiber - is the part of whole grain, vegetables and fruits that is not broken down in digestion and gives bulk to wastes. It is essential for healthy intestines and bowel movements. Colon cancer is primarily caused by low-fiber, high animal protein diets.

G

Ginger, pickled - is available packaged in sealed plastic pouches from Natural Food Stores, Gourmet and Asian shops. It is a salty sour spicy addition to Nori Rolls, salads or as a condiment on grains, pasta and vegetables. (See H.H.I.H.)

Grain Coffee - is a powder made from roasted barley, chicory, dandelion, and some brands include acorns and figs. It has a coffee-like flavor and no caffeine and can be used as you would instant coffee powder in beverages, puddings and cakes, etc.

K

Ketchup, natural - contains natural (preferably organic) ingredients without the addition of sugar, white vinegar, color, preservatives or other refined products. The Chili Style has extra spices added. Make your own by adding cayenne pepper to taste.

Kombu - is a flat wide ribbon shaped sea vegetable that is dark green in color. It is dried into strips approximately six inches long and one inch wide. Available in Natural Food Stores and Asian Grocers, usually in packages of 50 grams. It is traditionally used in cooking beans and to flavor soup stocks and other broths. (See also H.H.I. H. and TRICKS of the TRADE.)

M

Maple Syrup, pure - is available in cans and bottled. This sweetener is an ideal replacement for cane sugar or honey in desserts and various other recipes. It has a more balanced reaction on the functions of the pancreas and our blood sugar levels than cane sugar or honey. Find out if the maple syrup manufacturer uses lard or pork bones in the process. They do this to stabilize the liquid while they reduce it. Vegetable oil is preferred.

Miso - There are as many varieties of miso as there are fine wines. Barley Miso is made with barley, soybeans and sea salt. Rice Miso is made with rice, soybeans and sea salt, etc. Among the many varieties, Chickpea, Millet and Natto miso are fairly common. Black Soybean, Dandelion and Leek miso are a few of the more gourmet varieties. The paste is a result of fermentation for several months for the lighter the colored or white varieties, and up to 2-3 years for the dark colored varieties. Choose a miso brand that has not been pasteurized, with active beneficial enzymes. Boiling destroys the enzymes, so it is preferable to gently *simmer* pasteurized miso for three to four minutes, for its medicinal properties. (See H.H.I.H. and TRICKS of the TRADE.)

Mustard, stone ground - There are several brands available in Natural Food Stores, Gourmet Shops and Markets that have a high quality cider vinegar and contain no sugar, color, or other unwanted additives. The flavor of these brands is superior.

N

Natural foods - are whole foods that are unrefined and untreated with artificial additives or preservatives.

Nayonaise - is a brand made by Nasoya and is a high quality dairy and egg-free mayonnaise that has an excellent flavor and texture. There are other brands, but read the labels to ensure you are buying the best quality ingredients with no additives.

Nori - is a sea vegetable sold in plastic packages in the form of rectangle sheets. They are available pre-toasted or regular (which will need to be toasted when using for nori maki, as a wrapper for sushi rolls). It can also be eaten as is, like chips. (See Iron in H.H.I.H., and also TRICKS of the TRADE.)

O

Oats, rolled - preferably organically grown. Rolled oats (old fashioned) take less time to cook than whole unprocessed oats. They take more time than the oat flakes or quick cooking varieties, but are much creamier, better tasting and more nutritious. (See Iron and Zinc in H.H.I.H.)

P

Peanut Butter, natural - Buy freshly ground for the best flavor and freshness at your local natural food store, or buy the jar brands that are pure and natural. Commercial brands are hydrogenated, contain sugar and other unwanted additives.

R

Rice Syrup, Brown - is made from brown rice, cereal enzymes (Koji) and water in a natural process that breaks down the complex carbohydrates into a sweet syrup. It has half the sweetness of cane sugar, maple syrup or honey, so increase the volume when substituting in certain recipes. Rice Syrup has a very delicate, balanced reaction on the pancreas and blood sugar levels, and is more suitable for diabetics than other sweeteners. Some brands of rice syrup are not suitable for baking (which is one reason we use maple syrup in desserts) as the enzymes break down the flour and disrupt the chemistry of the recipe. It is impossible to thicken these brands of rice syrup with arrowroot, cornstarch or kuzu/kudzu.

Roasted Barley Tea - is made of whole barley grains that are roasted to a dark brown color, like roasted coffee. Boil in water and steep for 2-5 minutes, to create a tea that is richly sweet and bitter, similar to coffee but not as sharp. It is caffeine free and delicate enough to serve plain. Roasted barley tea helps to relieve tiredness, improves mental clarity, aids digestion and can be served at any time, hot or cold.

S

Saturated Fats - are fats found primarily in meats, poultry, eggs, dairy food and a few vegetable oils such as coconut and palm tree oil, which raise serum cholesterol and contributes to atherosclerosis.

Sea Salt - is salt obtained from the ocean as opposed to land salt (which requires mining and upsets the environment). It is either sun baked or kiln baked. High in essential trace minerals, the same minerals that some believe can be derived from pill supplements. Include high quality sea salt, and salty seasoning such as tamari and miso, and for all the natural trace minerals our blood needs to maintain a healthy alkaline pH balance. Sea salt contains no chemicals, sugar or other additives.

Seitan - is a remarkable, versatile ingredient suitable in a wide variety of dishes. It resembles cooked meat in color and texture. Made from whole wheat flour in a process that removes most of the starch and bran, the result is a high gluten content, concentrated vegetable protein (wheat) which has no saturated fat or cholesterol. Loosely translated, "seitan" means "the right protein substitute". It has been used in China for millennia, and was created by the monks who abstained from meat for spiritual development. It contains 60%-80% carbohydrates, 8%-15% protein, 1.5%-2% minerals and vitamins such as B-Complex and E. Seitan is absolutely fat-free, and creates strength and vitality. (See STAPLES, TRICKS of the TRADE and H.H.I.H.)

Shiitake Mushrooms - are very popular and native to the Orient. Shii means oak, and these large, golden fungi traditionally grow wild from fallen oak trees. Black or brown topped Chinese mushrooms, they are available fresh in some vegetable stores or dried in Asian shops, Natural Food Stores and some Supermarkets. They have an intense and aromatic flavor that is wonderful in soups, broth, stir fries and in grain and noodle dishes. (See H.H.I.H.)

Shoyu - is a dark brown fermented liquid seasoning made from soybeans, wheat, salt and water. It is a natural, unprocessed and additive free product similar in appearance to commercial soy sauce, but the flavor and health promoting qualities of the traditionally made shoyu, are superior. (See Tamari in H.H.I.H)

Soba - noodles are a major ingredient in Japanese cooking, and have a delicious, robust flavor. They are made from buckwheat flour, and wheat flour in some varieties. Forty percent soba includes 40% buckwheat and 60% wheat. One hundred percent soba is the strongest and most expensive variety, and a superior food for very cold weather or strenuous activity.

Soymilk - is a milky beverage made primarily from soybeans and water, that can be used as you would use milk on cereal, desserts, in coffee or tea, in creamy soups or sauces, etc. The aseptic packages do not need refrigeration, but once opened should be used up within one week. EdenSoy is one of the highest quality brands, containing no added oil. Vita Soy makes a very rich and creamy soymilk that is wonderful in coffee. Carob, chocolate, strawberry and vanilla flavors are available. The Lite varieties are watery, like skim milk. (See H.H.I.H.)

Sunflower Butter - is a paste made from ground sunflower seeds that resembles smooth peanut butter in texture, but has a darker color. (See H.H.I.H.)

T

Tahini - is a versatile product made from ground sesame seeds that resembles a more liquid version of smooth peanut butter, and has a more light, beige color. Use in dips, sauces, spreads, etc. (See also H.H.I.H.)

Tamari - is the liquid brine that rises to the top of miso during the fermentation process is a very thick, dark liquid (and is not readily available). Although the word Tamari is used frequently on labels (and in most recipe books, including this one) for natural soy sauce, the correct term is Shoyu. (See also Shoyu and H.H.I.H.)

Tempeh - is a soybean product that is available (usually frozen) in Natural Food Stores. It has a slightly nutty, mildly smoky flavor and a chewy meat-like texture and can substitute for meat and poultry in main dishes and stews. Traditionally a product from Indonesia, it is made by fermenting whole soybeans with a culture (Koji) that binds it into a dense cake. It can be diced, sliced or crumbled into various recipes. Black spots and white mold are a healthy result of the fermentation process. A pink color is a sign that the tempeh has gone bad and should be discarded. (See H.H.I.H.)

Toasted Sesame Oil - is a dark colored oil made from pressing sesame seeds that have been toasted, resulting in a fragrant, intensely flavored oil that is common in Asian cooking. Use sparingly as its flavor goes further than other oils. (See also Tricks of the Trade and H.H.I.H..)

Tofu, Silken - is available fresh or in aseptic boxes that do not need refrigeration before opening. This tofu is softer and silkier than regular fresh tofu and is used pureed in recipes like dips, puddings, dressing, sauces or cubed and gently simmered into a soup at the end of cooking. In stir fried dishes, it will fall apart. Its smooth texture makes it a great substitute for sour cream or yogurt in various recipes.

Tofu - is made from the liquid extracted from soybeans that is curdled with an agent such a nigari, much like making cheese with cow's milk. Available in most grocery stores in soft, firm or extra firm. It is a very versatile product. Once the fresh tofu package has been opened, store the tofu in a container covered with water, refrigerated approximately one week. Change the water every 2 to 3 days.

U

Umeboshi Paste - is made from puréed umeboshi plums, that are sour plums pickled with sea salt and shiso leaves (beefsteak plant) which give it a pink color.

Umeboshi Vinegar - is the brine liquid that results in the pickling of the umeboshi plums that has a pinkish red color and a salty-sour taste (See also H.H.I.H. and TRICKS)

V

Vinegar, Brown Rice - is less acidic than apple cider vinegar and so it has a less sharp, more delicate sour taste. Naturally fermented brown rice vinegar, and apple cider vinegar have more nutritional value, and less chemicals, than the highly processed white vinegar products.

INDEX

D

Notes

Notes

Notes

Notes

Notes

Notes

Notes

Notes

Notes

NETWORK OF FELLOW FOOD LOVERS

We hope you are enjoying **FAST & FUN FOOD *For People on the Go!*** as much as we did creating it. To absolutely ensure your delight and fulfillment we selected esteemed individuals, females and males, to participate in *Project Feedback*. They consulted on various aspects and/or worked with a rough draft of the book, recording their advice and constructive criticism, as well as their praise. Their feedback is especially valuable because of their diversity and range of experience, in random order:

Non-vegetarians:
A chef at a Five Star Hotel.
A TV show host of a TSN aerobic workout and fitness professional.
A publisher of University medical research and psychotherapist.
An amateur chef of traditional Greek cuisine and polarity therapist.
Inexperienced meat and potatoes style home cooks.

Vegetarians:
The wife of a Mr. Universe, Weider spokesman and college faculty.
A top reporter for a TV news station.
Licensed nutritionists.
World renown macrobiotic-natural health care teachers and authors.
A registered nurse, homemaker, mother.
A publisher of a journal on alternative lifestyles and spiritual issues.
An ex-caterer experienced in polish and gourmet natural cuisine.
Owners of natural food stores, with many years experience.
Homemakers and mothers with varying degrees of cooking experience.

Here's what they're saying about **FAST & FUN FOOD** *For People on the Go!*

"On a scale from 1 to 10, all the recipes we've tried are a 10. My choosy kids are loving it too!"

"Your book really helps me get organized and be time efficient. I learn a lot of helpful tips."

"Inspiring...I love the creative chapter themes...the recipes are perfect for my busy lifestyle."

"I've been looking for a book like this for years. It is sure to be a great success!"

We invite you to join our Network of Fellow Food Lovers and participate in Project Feedback. All your comments (fill in facing page) are greatly appreciated, and will be recorded for future revised editions. You'll be on our mailing list and receive our newsletter, including information of all our exciting activities. Together we are creating the foundation for global great health through a truly enjoyable, environment and user-friendly series of cookbooks.

Warmest regards, Karen Claffey.

Please fill in facing page and send to: **KAREN'S KITCHEN**
12473 Fleming, Pierrefonds, Quebec H8Z 1E4 Canada
Tel: (514) 684-9559 / Fax: (514) 685-9996

Great  *Gifts!*

"Cooking for the Love of Life"

FAST & FUN FOOD *For People on the Go!*

Give a cookbook to a family member, friend, spouse or lover. Ideal for all occasions!

KAREN'S KITCHEN APRONS
(with pink and green logo and slogan)
Available in *Berry Hot Pink* or *Stainless Teal Green*, one size fits all.

KAREN'S KITCHEN T-SHIRTS
(with pink and green logo and slogan)
Available in white cotton, Large And Extra Large.

QTY	DESCRIPTION	SUB TOTAL	TOTAL
	FAST & FUN FOOD *For People on the Go!*	CAN $19.95 USA $14.95	
	7% GST (Canada only): 6.5% sales tax (for Quebec addresses):	CAN $21.35 QUE $22.73	
	Shipping: Surface mail @ Can. $4.95/US $3.95 (Please allow 3-4 weeks for delivery.)	CAN $26.30 QUE $27.68 USA $18.90	
	KK APRONS @ CAN $14.99/US $8.99 each. Including shipping:	CAN $19.99 USA $14.99	
	KK T-SHIRTS @ CAN $14.99/US $8.99 each. Including shipping:	CAN $19.99 USA $14.99	

Payment Enclosed: ❑ Check (payable to **Karen Claffey**) ❑ Money Order

ORDER NOW!

Please send this to: **KAREN'S KITCHEN** 12473 Fleming, Pierrefonds, Quebec H8Z 1E4 Canada Tel: (514) 684-9559 / Fax: (514) 685-9996

Project Feedback

1. Where did you buy your copy of **FAST & FUN FOOD** *For People on the Go!?*

   _____

2. What dietary practice do you follow?
   ❑ Meat based ❑ Fish, Poultry ❑ Lacto-Ovo Vegetarian ❑ Vegan ❑ Macrobiotic
   Comments:_____   _____

   _____

3. How has **FAST & FUN FOOD** *For People on the Go!* made a difference in your
   dietary habits and lifestyle, and enjoyment of natural foods?

   _____

   _____

4. Has the TIME SAVING STRATEGY helped you to eat healthy more consistently?
   Do you plan ahead? Are you bringing portable foods with you when needed?

   _____

   _____

5. Which recipes appeal to you most, and why?

   _____

   _____

6. What is more important to you? ❑ Nutrition   ❑ Time   ❑ Taste   ❑ Visual appeal
   Comments:

   _____

   _____

7. Suggestions: (please feel free to include additional pages)

   _____

   _____

   _____

   _____

The following four companies supply highest quality natural foods, and are reknown pioneers in the industry. You'll find these products in your local natural food stores, and as demand and popularity is increasing, they are becoming available in all groceries stores and supermarkets internationally!

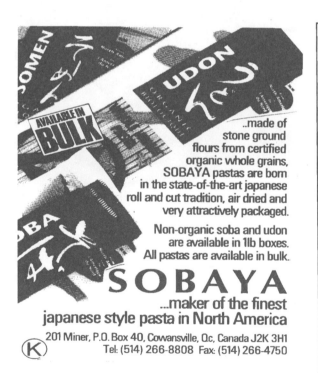

Food For A New Generation

Burger Burgers

Made entirely from vegetable sources, this juicy, tender burger is ideal for those who want to cut down on fat without compromising on great taste.

Try our Garden Vegetable Patties

Made from garden fresh vegetables (onions, carrots, peas, corn, green beans, red pepper, squash, water chestnuts) and a blend of fine herbs & spices.

ABOUT THE AUTHOR

Fourth generation of gourmet chefs and pastry chefs, **Karen Claffey** is host-creator of **KAREN'S KITCHEN**, Montreal's popular **CF Cable TV** cooking show.

Studies in natural foods began in 1984, as a means to heal life threatening illnesses. This led to living in Boston and Becket, MA to train at the **Kushi Institute** where she became head chef and assistant kitchen manager to Wendy Esko. Karen also assisted in the counseling department, entered Michio Kushi's book; Nine Star Ki on the computer for them, and launched the Kushi Institute Extension Program with Charles Millman.

Karen's inherent talent—the fusion of gourmet cooking with natural vegetarian ingredients—had patrons praising and lining up for her specialties, at **Ecos Café** in **Toronto** where she was head chef-manager. This led to an exciting top position cooking for the 'Stars' at **Real Food Daily** in **Santa Monica**.

As president of **KAREN'S KITCHEN** Cooking School in Montreal, she teaches a full range of classes; from the most creative international vegan cuisine to the most powerful, balanced eating for optimum health and healing.

Karen gives dietary-lifestyle consultations for everything; from achieving ideal weight to healing specific illnesses. In addition, she is a highly reputed shiatsu massage therapist.

Karen can be heard regularly on Montreal's radio air waves talking about health and healing, and the benefits and importance of eating delicious, natural vegetarian foods.